"Ron Riggio and Sherylle Tan's new book, *Leader Interpersonal and Influence Skills: The Soft Skills of Leadership*, offers cutting-edge research and conceptual frameworks that greatly advance the field of leadership studies and practice. Riggio and Tan's collection of top experts create a more nuanced and evidence-based foundation for the emerging science of personal and interpersonal skills in leadership. Those seeking hard data on soft skills will find it here, making this cutting-edge volume both a reference for scholars and a handbook for those seeking to build further strengths in leaders."

—**Daniel Goleman**, author of *Emotional Intelligence*

"Those of us who study leadership and have also served in leadership positions know that the biggest challenges are the 'soft skills.' Riggio and Tan have put together a much-needed look at these critical skills and have included works from the known experts in the field. A must-read for both academics and practitioners."

—**Leanne Atwater**, PhD, Editor of *Leadership Quarterly*

"Riggio and Tan have assembled an absolute cornucopia of wisdom and practical knowledge about the 'soft skills' that all leaders absolutely must develop if they intend to be successful. Every chapter is a gem. Don't miss a word of it!"

—**Jean Lipman-Blumen**, PhD, Claremont Graduate University

LEADER INTERPERSONAL AND INFLUENCE SKILLS

Nontechnical interpersonal and influence skills make up more than half of effective leadership, yet there has been a gaping hole in the research literature on the "soft skills" of leaders/managers. This volume, with contributions from experts in leadership and interpersonal skills, showcases how important soft skills like communication, persuasion, political savvy, and emotional abilities are to leaders who inspire, motivate, and move followers toward the accomplishment of goals.

Ronald E. Riggio, PhD, is the Henry R. Kravis Professor of Leadership and Organizational Psychology and the former Director of the Kravis Leadership Institute at Claremont McKenna College. His research focuses on leadership, organizational psychology, and emotional and nonverbal communication, and he is the author/editor of more than a dozen books and more than 150 articles and book chapters. His leadership interests include charismatic and transformational leadership, the role of communication and social skills in leader effectiveness, and the early development of leadership in children, adolescents, and young adults. He has received awards for teaching and research, and is committed to "giving away" research on leadership and psychology through popular writings and his *Psychology Today* blog, "Cutting Edge Leadership."

Sherylle J. Tan, PhD, is the Director of Internships and KLI Research at the Kravis Leadership Institute at Claremont McKenna College. Her current research focuses on undergraduate leadership education and program evaluation of leadership development programs. Specifically, the research on undergraduate leadership education seeks to establish an ongoing assessment of the long-term impact of leadership development and training in higher education. Much of Dr. Tan's research and publications focus on applying developmental theory and methods to understanding the issues of leadership development, women and leadership, work and family, and child development.

Leadership: Research and Practice Series
A James MacGregor Burns Academy of Leadership Collaboration

Series Editors
Georgia Sorenson, Ph.D., Research Professor in Leadership Studies, University of Maryland and Founder of the James MacGregor Academy of Leadership and the International Leadership Association.

Ronald E. Riggio, Ph.D., is the Henry R. Kravis Professor of Leadership and Organizational Psychology and former Director of the Kravis Leadership Institute at Claremont McKenna College.

Scott T. Allison and George R. Goethals
Heroic Leadership: An Influence Taxonomy of 100 Exceptional Individuals

Michelle C. Bligh and Ronald E. Riggio (Eds.)
Exploring Distance in Leader-Follower Relationships: When Near is Far and Far is Near

Michael A. Genovese and Janie Steckenrider (Eds.)
Women as Political Leaders: Studies in Gender and Governing

Jon P. Howell
Snapshots of Great Leadership

Aneil Mishra and Karen E. Mishra
Becoming a Trustworthy Leader: Psychology and Practice

Dinesh Sharma and Uwe P. Gielen (Eds.)
The Global Obama: Crossroads of Leadership in the 21st Century

Ronald E. Riggio and Sherylle J. Tan (Eds.)
Leader Interpersonal and Influence Skills: The Soft Skills of Leadership

Thanks for everything. Keep up the excellent leadership and keep this terrific program going. Ron Riggio

LEADER INTERPERSONAL AND INFLUENCE SKILLS

THE SOFT SKILLS OF LEADERSHIP

EDITED BY

Ronald E. Riggio

and

Sherylle J. Tan

Routledge
Taylor & Francis Group

NEW YORK AND LONDON

First published 2014
by Routledge
711 Third Avenue, New York, NY 10017

and by Routledge
27 Church Road, Hove, East Sussex BN3 2FA

Routledge is an imprint of the Taylor & Francis Group, an informa business

Library of Congress Cataloging-in-Publication Data

Leader interpersonal and influence skills : the soft skills of leadership / [edited by]
    Ronald E. Riggio, Sherylle J. Tan. — 1 Edition.
        pages cm. — (Leadership: research and practice)
    1. Leadership—Psychological aspects.   I. Riggio, Ronald E., editor of
compilation.   II. Tan, Sherylle J., editor of compilation.
    HD57.7.L4113 2014
    658.4′092—dc23
    2013022934

ISBN: 978-0-415-84231-0 (hbk)
ISBN: 978-0-415-84232-7 (pbk)
ISBN: 978-0-203-76053-6 (ebk)

Typeset in Minion
by Apex CoVantage, LLC

Printed and bound in the United States of America by Sheridan Books, Inc. (a Sheridan Group Company).

Contents

About the Editors

Ronald E. Riggio, PhD, is the Henry R. Kravis Professor of Leadership and Organizational Psychology at Claremont McKenna College. Dr. Riggio's research interests center on charismatic and transformational leadership, the role of communication skills in leader effectiveness, and the development of leadership potential across the lifespan. He has published nearly two dozen authored or edited books and more than 150 articles and book chapters. He has also served as a consultant to dozens of organizations, large and small, across the business, education, and nonprofit sectors. He is the co-editor, along with Georgia Sorenson, of the Routledge/Taylor & Francis book series *Leadership: Research and Practice*.

Sherylle J. Tan, PhD, is the Director of Internships and KLI Research at the Kravis Leadership Institute at Claremont McKenna College. Dr. Tan's current research focuses on undergraduate leadership education and program evaluation of leadership development programs. Specifically, the research on undergraduate leadership education seeks to establish an ongoing assessment of the long-term impact of leadership development and training in higher education. Much of Dr. Tan's research and publications focus on applying developmental theory and methods to understanding the issues of leadership development, women and leadership, work and family, and child development. Dr. Tan co-edited a book with Amy Marcus-Newhall and Diane Halpern, *The Changing Realties of Work and Family: A Multidisciplinary Approach* (2008). Additionally, Dr. Tan has more than 10 years of experience as an evaluation consultant for nonprofit agencies providing services for children and families in Southern California. Dr. Tan has a BA in psychology from the University of California, Irvine and an MA and a PhD in psychology with an emphasis in applied developmental psychology from Claremont Graduate University.

About the Contributors

Adrianna Andrews-Brown is a graduate of the University of the Pacific; she has a master's degree in educational administration and leadership with an emphasis in student affairs. Her undergraduate degree is in psychology from the University of Alberta. She is currently the coordinator of student services at Royal Roads University. Her research interests are in leadership development for undergraduate students.

Gerard Beenen is an assistant professor of management at the Mihaylo College of Business & Economics, California State University–Fullerton, where he teaches courses in organizational behavior, organizational change, and team leadership. His research interests include workplace motivation and learning and managerial interpersonal skills. His research has been published in *Human Resource Management, Academy of Management Learning and Education,* and the *Journal of Computer Mediated Communication.* His research has been funded by the Graduate Management Admissions Council and the National Science Foundation. He completed his PhD in organizational behavior and theory at Carnegie Mellon University. He also has an MBA from the Kellogg School of Management at Northwestern University and an MA from Fuller Seminary in Pasadena. Prior to his academic career, he was CEO of a cancer care center, cofounder of an Internet software firm, and a management consultant with Bain & Company.

Richard E. Boyatzis is Distinguished University Professor and a professor in the Departments of Organizational Behavior, Psychology, and Cognitive Science at Case Western Reserve University and Human Resources at ESADE. Using his Intentional Change Theory (ICT) and complexity theory, he continues to research sustained, desired change at all levels of human endeavor from individuals, teams, organizations, communities, countries, and global change. He was ranked #9 Most Influential International Thinkers by an 11,000 HR Director Survey in *HR Magazine.* He is the author of more than 150 articles on leadership, competencies, emotional intelligence, competency development, coaching, and management education. His articles on coaching, since 2000, have included longitudinal studies and now fMRI studies of coaching effectiveness. His books include *The Competent Manager*; the international best seller *Primal Leadership* with Daniel Goleman and Annie McKee; *Resonant Leadership* with Annie McKee; and *Becoming a Resonant Leader* with Annie McKee and Fran Johnston. Professor Boyatzis has a BS in aeronautics and astronautics from MIT and an MS and a PhD in social psychology from Harvard University.

Cary Cherniss is a professor of applied psychology at Rutgers University. He received his PhD in psychology from Yale University and specializes in the areas of emotional intelligence, work stress, leadership development, and planned organizational change. He has published more than 60 scholarly articles and book chapters and seven books, including *The Emotionally Intelligent Workplace* with Daniel Goleman and *Promoting Emotional Intelligence in the Workplace: Guidelines for Practitioners* with Mitchel Adler. His research has been funded by such resources as the National Institute of Mental Health and the U.S. Office of Population Affairs. Furthermore, he has consulted with many organizations in both the public and private sectors, including American Express, Johnson & Johnson, the U.S. Coast Guard, AT&T, and the U.S. Office of Personnel Management. He currently is the director and cochair of the Consortium for Research on Emotional Intelligence in Organizations, a fellow of the American Psychological Association, and a member of both the Academy of Management and the Society for Industrial and Organizational Psychology.

Jay A. Conger is the Henry Kravis Research Chair Professor of Leadership at the Kravis Institute at Claremont McKenna College. His research interests include executive leadership, charismatic leadership, influence approaches, and leading organizational change. He has authored 14 books and more than 100 articles and book chapters. Widely acclaimed as an educator, Professor Conger has been named among *Business Week*'s "Top Ten Worldwide Management Gurus" and the *Financial Times*' "World's Top Educators."

Shane Connelly is an associate professor in the Department of Psychology at the University of Oklahoma. She earned her PhD from George Mason University and has more than 15 years of experience working with private industry and government organizations on applied research projects.

Her research interests focus on leadership, emotions in the workplace, and ethical decision making. She is also interested in ethical decision making in organizations, particularly how to assess and train research ethics in various scientific domains. She has published numerous articles on leadership, emotions, and integrity and serves on the editorial boards of *The Leadership Quarterly* and *Human Performance*. She is a member of the American Psychological Association (Divisions 5 and 14), the American Psychological Society, the Academy of Management, and the Society for Industrial and Organizational Psychology. She is also a founding faculty member and serves on the governing board and executive committee of the Center for Applied Social Research.

Annick Darioly received her PhD in work and organizational psychology from the University of Neuchatel, Switzerland, in 2011. She served as a postdoctoral fellow at the Kravis Leadership Institute at Claremont McKenna College in 2012. There, she collaborated with Professor Ronald E. Riggio on a project entitled "Nepotism in Leadership." Annick Darioly is currently a lecturer in leadership at the Department of Work and Organizational Psychology at the University of Neuchatel. Her research interests include the leadership and its dark side, the leader's competence and incompetence, the leader's nonverbal behavior, and the perceptions of nepotism in leadership. Her work has been published in *European Journal of Work and Organizational Psychology, Ergonomics,* and *Journal of Applied Social Psychology,* and has been presented at various national and international conferences. During her PhD, Annick Darioly was editorial assistant of the *Swiss Journal of Psychology.*

Eric A. Day is an associate professor of psychology at the University of Oklahoma, where he is part of the doctoral program in industrial and organizational (I-O) psychology. He earned his PhD in I-O psychology from Texas A&M University, an MS in I-O psychology from the University of Central Florida, and a BS in psychology from James Madison University. He is a member of the American Psychological Association (APA), Association for Psychological Science, Academy of Management, the Society for I-O Psychology, and APA's Exercise and Sport Psychology Division 47. His research interests span both personnel psychology and organizational behavior, including topics in personnel assessment, selection, training and development, and group dynamics. Much of his research involves the study of human performance and complex skill acquisition with emphases on individual differences in ability and motivation, cognitive and social processes, expert-novice differences, decay and adaptability, and team-based training. He currently serves on the editorial board for the *Journal of Applied Psychology*.

Ceasar Douglas is the chair and Jim Moran Associated Professor of Management. He teaches courses in organizational behavior and strategic management, and his research interests are in the areas of work team development, leadership, and leader political skill. He received his PhD in management from the University of Mississippi. Prior to his academic career, Dr. Douglas worked for 15 years as a manufacturing manager for Clorox Company, Sun Chemical, Hexcel Chemical, and Herman Miller. He serves on the board of directors of Southern Management Association (SMA) and on the editorial boards of the *Journal of Management, The Leadership Quarterly,* and *The Journal of Leadership and Organization Studies.*

B. Parker Ellen III is an organizational behavior and human resources doctoral student in the Florida State University College of Business. His research focuses on leadership and social influence and has been featured in *The Leadership Quarterly.* He has presented work on leadership at national and international conferences and received the 2013 John C. Flanagan Award for best student contribution at the Society for Industrial and Organizational Psychology Annual Conference. Parker holds a bachelor's degree in civil engineering from Auburn University, and a master of science degree in managerial sciences from Georgia State University, where he received the Carl A. Bramlette, Jr. Scholastic Achievement Award. Prior to returning for his PhD, Parker spent nine years in the consulting engineering industry in project management and executive capacities. He is a registered professional engineer, is on the editorial board of the *Journal of Leadership & Organizational Studies,* and has served as a director for several nonprofit organizations.

Gerald R. Ferris is the Francis Eppes Professor of Management and professor of psychology at Florida State University. He received a PhD in business administration from the University of Illinois at Urbana-Champaign. He has research interests in the areas of social influence processes in human resources systems. Ferris is the author of numerous articles published in such journals as the *Journal of Applied Psychology, Organizational Behavior and Human Decision Processes, Personnel Psychology, Academy of Management Journal,* and *Academy of Management Review.* He served as editor of the annual series *Research in Personnel and Human Resources Management* from 1981 to 2003. Ferris has received a number of distinctions and honors. In 2001 he was the recipient of the Heneman Career Achievement Award, and in 2010 he received the Thomas A. Mahoney Mentoring Award, both from the Human Resources Division of the Academy of Management.

Tamara Friedrich is an assistant professor of management at Savannah State University, where she teaches courses on leadership, organizational behavior, creativity and entrepreneurship, and general management. She received her PhD in industrial and organizational psychology from the University of Oklahoma in 2010 and has been a faculty member at Savannah State since then. Her primary research interests fall into the broad categories of innovation and leadership, however much of her recent research falls into the intersection of these two areas. She has also conducted research on leadership in a collective context and how leadership is influenced by the social environment. Her work has appeared in several books and journals, including *The Leadership Quarterly, Creativity Research Journal,* and *Human Resource Management Review.* Finally, Dr. Friedrich is the cofounder and director of the Center for the Advancement of Creativity and Entrepreneurship (The ACE Center) at Savannah State, which focuses on developing student entrepreneurs, sponsoring faculty and student research, planning events to promote creativity and entrepreneurship, and developing a curriculum that supports these efforts.

Sean T. Hannah is the Tylee Wilson Chair of Business Ethics at Wake Forest University. He focuses on the study of exemplary leadership and the development of competence and character in leaders. He received his PhD in management from the University of Nebraska–Lincoln, an MBA and an MPA from Syracuse University, and a master's in national security studies from the Marine Corps University. He has published more than 50 papers on leadership with articles in the top journals including the *Academy of Management Journal, Academy of Management Review, Personnel Psychology, Journal of Applied Psychology, Organizational Behavior and Human Decision Processes, Journal of Organizational Behavior, The Leadership*

Quarterly, Business Ethics Quarterly, and many others. He is a retired U.S. Army colonel with 26 years of service including numerous command and staff positions in Europe, Cuba, Panama, Southwest Asia, and the United States. He served in combat during Desert Storm and Operation Sea Signal, and at the Pentagon on 9/11. He has served from the lowest tactical levels to the highest strategic levels, and has served on the staff of two chiefs of staff of the army and an assistant secretary of the army.

Peter L. Jennings is the research director for the Center for the Army Profession and Ethic (CAPE) located at the U.S. Military Academy at West Point. He completed his doctoral studies at the W.P. Carey School of Business at Arizona State University. Dr. Jennings's research focus is the psychology of character and its significance to the practice of leadership. His current research explores the role of character in small unit combat leadership. Dr. Jennings's prior professional experience includes executive management positions at IBM as well as military service as an infantry officer in the U.S. Marine Corps. Dr. Jennings holds a BS in economics from Miami University and an MBA from Michigan State University.

Stefanie K. Johnson received her PhD in industrial-organizational psychology from Rice University in 2004 and is currently an assistant professor of management at the University of Colorado–Denver. Her research interest is leadership, including the role of emotions in leadership, gender in leadership, charismatic/transformational leadership, and leadership development. Her other work has focused on selection, teams, and work-family balance.

Amanda Klabzuba is a consultant for the global assessment team at Kenexa and has been involved in a wide range of projects, including job analysis, competency modeling, test development, and ROI follow-up on selection tools. Dr. Klabzuba has worked with customers designing and validating assessments across a variety of industries, such as hospitality, retail, sales, and health care. She has published and presented work on a variety of topics, including leadership assessment and development, emotional intelligence and regulation, creativity and innovation in organizations, and content analysis. Dr. Klabzuba's primary areas of interest are high-stakes assessment, change management and implementation planning, and simulated assessment research. She earned a bachelor's degree in psychology and a master's degree and a PhD in industrial-organizational psychology from the University of Oklahoma.

Krystal Miguel is a graduate student in higher education and organizational behavior at Claremont Graduate University. She holds an MA in educational administration and leadership from the University of the Pacific and a BA in rhetoric and American studies from the University of California–Berkeley. Her current research focus is on the development of coaching and mentoring interventions for social and emotional competence and social skill development in nontraditional and underrepresented college students.

Susan Elaine Murphy is director of the School of Strategic Leadership Studies and associate professor of leadership studies at James Madison University. Dr. Murphy earned her PhD and MS in organizational psychology from the University of Washington, where she also earned an MBA at the Michael G. Foster School of Business concentrating in organizational behavior and human resources. She has published numerous articles and book chapters on leadership, leadership development, and mentoring. Her current edited volume with Rebecca Reichard is *Early Development and Leadership: Building the Next Generation of Leaders*. Her other works include the book *Power Mentoring: How Successful Mentors and Protégés Make the Most of Their Relationships* (with Ellen Ensher) and four edited books. Her research examines leadership effectiveness across the developmental span. She also serves on the editorial board of *The Leadership Quarterly*. Before working in academia she worked as a research scientist at Battelle-Seattle consulting in the areas of leadership and management education, as well as organizational change for clients in the United States and Japan in for-profit, nonprofit, and public sector organizations. Dr. Murphy continues designing, delivering, and evaluating leadership development programs today, as well as other organizational development initiatives and has consulted with close to 50 organizations.

Angela Passarelli is a master coach, instructor, and doctoral candidate in organizational behavior at the Weatherhead School of Management, Case Western Reserve University. Her research focuses on how developmental relationships support behavior change, particularly in the context of leader development. She draws on neuroscience and psychophysiology to explore the implicit dynamics of these relationships. Her work has been published in various journals including *The Leadership Quarterly, Consulting Psychology Journal: Practice and Research,* and the *Journal of Experiential Education.* Angela holds an MS in educational administration from Texas A&M University and a BS in psychology and general business from James Madison University.

Shaun Pichler, PhD, is an associate professor of management at the Mihaylo College of Business & Economics, California State University–Fullerton, where he teaches courses in organizational behavior and human resource management. He received his PhD in human resource management from Michigan State University. His research program is centered around fairness and support in organizations and involves research on discrimination and diversity, work-family issues, performance management and appraisal, and international HRM. He has published in outlets such as *Behavior Research Methods, Human Resource Management, International Journal of Human Resource Management, Journal of Occupational & Organizational Psychology, Journal of Vocational Behavior,* and *Personnel Psychology,* among others. His work has been cited by the U.S. Congress among a variety of professional and other outlets.

Stefanie Putter is a doctoral candidate in industrial-organizational psychology at Colorado State University. Stefanie is also a leadership consultant, working with several consulting firms in Colorado. With a solid background in leadership development and training, Stefanie has presented at national and international conferences, coauthored several book chapters, and facilitated leadership workshops for front-line leaders and executives throughout the United States and Canada. Overall, Stefanie has extensive research and consulting experience applying psychological principles to help organizations identify and develop their talent.

Joanna Royce-Davis is the dean of students at the University of the Pacific. In addition, Joanna has the honor of serving on the faculty of the Benerd School of Education and collaborating with faculty and student life colleagues to support the development of future higher education leaders in her role as the director of Pacific's graduate program in student affairs. Joanna's scholarship focuses on leadership and identity development, spirituality and student learning, and influences on student persistence. The winner of the Region VI NASPA Scott Goodnight award for Outstanding Performance as a Dean, she earned her BS from Indiana University, her MA from San Jose State University, and her PhD from Syracuse University.

Gregory Ruark is a senior research psychologist at the Fort Leavenworth Research Unit, a field unit for the U.S. Army Research Institute for the Behavioral and Social Sciences. He earned his PhD from the University of Oklahoma and has more than six years of experience working for the Department of Defense. His research interests include leadership, emotion management, nonverbal communication, and cross-cultural competencies. His current research focuses on collective leadership, cultural adaptability, and task switching. His research on decoding nonverbal behaviors received the 2011 Department of the Army Research & Development Achievement Award for Technical Excellence. He is a member of the American Psychological Association (Divisions 14 and 19) and the Society for Industrial and Organizational Psychology.

Marianne Schmid Mast received her PhD in psychology from the University of Zurich, Switzerland, in 2000. She has been a postdoctoral fellow at the Department of Psychology at Northeastern University, USA, and an assistant professor at the University of Fribourg, Switzerland. Since 2006, she has been a full professor of psychology at the Department of Work and Organizational Psychology at the University of Neuchatel, Switzerland. Her research focuses on the study of interpersonal interactions, verbal and nonverbal behavior, and social perception in the realm of dominance hierarchies. She has a particular research interest in how interpersonal power affects the accuracy of social perception and social judgments and in how power affects interpersonal behavior. She uses virtual environment technology for the study of interpersonal behavior as well as automatic computer sensing for the analysis of verbal and nonverbal behavior. Her work was published in *Journal of Nonverbal Behavior, Journal of Personality and Social Psychology, Personality and Social Psychology Bulletin, Journal of Applied Social Psychology,* and *Journal of Personality Assessment.* Professor Schmid Mast is a member of the editorial board of the *Journal of Nonverbal Behavior.*

Craig R. Seal is an assistant professor of management at California State University–San Bernardino. He was the founding director of the Center for Social Emotional Competence at Pacific. His scholarship is on the practical application of emotional intelligence research, including coaching competence. He received his PhD from George Washington University, MA from Boston College, and BS from Santa Clara University. Before returning to academia, he was an accomplished manager and executive with experience in the nonprofit, real estate, and staffing industries, working for the Santa Clara Community Action Program, Goodwill Industries, Coldwell Banker, and Aquent, Inc.

Viviane Seyranian is a postdoctoral research associate at the Rossier School of Education and a lecturer at the Department of Psychology at the University of Southern California. She earned her PhD and MA in applied social psychology from Claremont Graduate University and holds a bachelor's degree *cum laude* in psychology and government from Claremont McKenna College. Her research focuses on leadership, social influence, social identity framing, communication, and education.

James K. Summers is an assistant professor of management at Iowa State University. He earned his PhD at Florida State University in organizational behavior and human resource management. He has taught courses on contemporary leadership, negotiation, organizational behavior, and human resource management. His research interests include team structure and change, social influence processes including political skill, the nature of work relationships, and executive work design. Jim has published his work in the *Academy of Management Journal, Journal of Management, Journal of Organizational Behavior, Journal of Vocational Behavior, Human Resource Management Review,* and the *Journal of Occupational and Health Psychology.* He is on the editorial board of *Business Horizons* and is a member of the Academy of Management and the Society of Industrial and Organizational Psychology.

Darren C. Treadway is an associate professor of organization and human resources at the University of Buffalo. His research interests include social influence processes in organizations with particular reference to organizational politics, political skill, leadership, bullying, and stigmatization. His research has been published in leading journals such as the *Journal of*

Applied Psychology, Journal of Management, The Leadership Quarterly, Journal of Organizational Behavior, and *Human Relations.* Most recently, he coedited the forthcoming Society for Industrial and Organizational Psychology Frontier Series book *Politics in Organizations: Theory and Research Considerations* with Gerald R. Ferris. His research has twice been awarded the Emerald Publishing Citation of Excellence as one of the top 50 business publications and has been awarded the *Journal of Management* Best Paper Award. Prior to his employment with SUNY, he was on faculty at the University of Mississippi where he was twice named Researcher of the Year. His cumulative contributions earned him the 2009 SUNY at Buffalo Exceptional Scholar—Young Investigator Award.

William B. Vessey is currently the senior scientist managing the team risk research portfolio within the NASA Behavioral Health and Performance Research Element at the Johnson Space Center. He received his PhD in industrial and organizational psychology from the University of Oklahoma in 2012 with a minor in quantitative psychology. His primary research interests fall into the broad categories of teams, leadership, and creativity with specific focus on teamwork over long durations, team leadership, and collective leadership. He is a member of the American Psychological Association, the Academy of Management, and the Society for Industrial and Organizational Psychology. His work has appeared in several books and journals, including *The Leadership Quarterly, Creativity Research Journal, Creativity and Innovation Management, The Encyclopedia of Creativity,* and *Leadership 101.*

Hongguo Wei is a second year doctoral student in the Organizational Behavior Department at Case Western Reserve University. Her interests focus on emotion, emotional intelligence, and leadership. Also, she is interested in looking at the differences of emotional and social competencies between effective Chinese and Western executive leaders.

The **Kravis-de Roulet Leadership conferences**, which began in 1990, are annual leadership conferences funded jointly by an endowment from Henry R. Kravis and the de Roulet family. This perpetual funding, along with additional support from the Kravis Leadership Institute and Claremont McKenna College, attracts the finest leadership scholars and practitioners as conference presenters and participants. The 21st annual

Kravis-de Roulet Leadership Conference, "Understanding and Assessing Soft Leader Skills," was held in Claremont, California on February 24–25, 2012.

The **Kravis Leadership Institute** at Claremont McKenna College (CMC) is a premier academic center for the promotion and understanding of responsible, innovative leadership. KLI provides unique opportunities for CMC students to develop as outstanding real-world leaders in the public, private, and social sectors.

Series Foreword

Years ago I took a long walk in an Arizona garden with John W. Gardner, former cabinet secretary, founder of Common Cause, and Stanford-based leadership scholar. Then in his eighties and in a philosophical frame of mind, he lamented that higher education did not educate people to lead, but rather to advise leaders. In particular, he felt, schools of public administration produced competent bureaucrats and technocrats, but failed in their responsibility to produce leaders.

Universities have long offered courses on the technical aspects of leadership: cognitive and critical thinking skills, decision making, setting direction, goal setting, zero-based budgeting, branding, strategy, and even visioning and human resource management, but something has been missing and we even know what it is, we just don't know what to do about it.

People. The subtle but mysterious art of softly and sometimes invisibly managing a meandering herd of irascible, free-thinking, unconscious, acting out, quotidian dum-dums.

We've known this was the territory for a long time, beginning with the Ohio and Michigan studies of the 1940s where leadership was framed by the classic two-factor model, Initiation (Task Performance) and Consideration (People Skills). Somehow the latter was thought to either be a mother's domain or a recessive gene, in any event, largely unavailable and unknowable. You had it or you didn't, and good luck to you.

Now we're finding how absolutely central those people skills are to a healthy and productive work environment, especially as the business sector grows more service oriented and diverse. According to a widely cited study from *Harvard Business Review* discussed in this book, most of us would prefer to work for a "lovable fool" than a "competent jerk." And our dirty little secret is that high-performing organizations are desperately seeking "lovable stars" and desperately transitioning or furtively coaching "competent and incompetent jerks." The takeaway on organizations is that people skills trump task performance any day, any way.

To end at the beginning, this sagacious and rich book puts an end to the bifurcation of Task and Consideration and brings us the "hard science" of "soft skills." It is the work of Ron Riggio and other leading scholars in the field, produced for the 21st Kravis-de Roulet Leadership Conference

"Understanding and Assessing Soft Leader Skills" at Claremont McKenna College. It is a real treasure for educators, scholars, trainers, consultants, and all of us who are interested in addressing John Gardner's concern.

Georgia Sorenson

1

The "Hard" Science of Studying and Developing Leader "Soft" Skills

Ronald E. Riggio

The serious study of leadership and management has had a glaring omission for more than a century. Leadership/management experts will assert that there are two sides to leading: the "hard" side of analyzing, planning, making decisions, and strategizing, and the "soft" side of leadership that involves inspiring, motivating, and persuading followers, building good working relationships, networking, rallying, and cajoling. The problem is that the vast majority of scholarship on the skills needed for effective leadership has focused on the hard skills. In fact, MBA programs focus almost entirely on developing the hard skills, and only give lip service (and a very small part of the curriculum) to the soft skills of leadership. Indeed, a classic critique by Porter and McKibbin (1988) found just that. They concluded that few of the practical elements of managing/leading people were actually taught in business schools. More than two decades later, things have not changed much. There is still not enough research and education dedicated to the interpersonal, "soft" side of management and leadership.

The title of this chapter suggests that studying and developing the soft side skills of leadership is hard . . . difficult. Researchers have developed no accepted, guiding models for categorizing leader soft skills (nor understanding where the hard skills leave off and the soft skills begin). Instead, there are odd collections of competencies, abilities, and behaviors that constitute the soft side of leadership. Moreover, there are no comprehensive, guiding frameworks for skill development. A wide variety of practices and techniques are used to develop leader interpersonal and influence skills, and scholars have little knowledge as to the effectiveness of these techniques, nor of the impact of training programs. This book, and the conference it emanated from, seeks to pull together some of the more important research on leader interpersonal and influence skills, to examine frameworks, to look at leadership development practices in the area of soft skills; in short, to try to move things forward.

THE KRAVIS-DE ROULET CONFERENCE ON "SOFT LEADER SKILLS"

On February 24–25, 2012, we held the 21st Kravis-de Roulet Leadership Conference at Claremont McKenna College, entitled "Understanding and Assessing Soft Leader Skills." We invited a number of noted leadership experts whose research has focused on leader interpersonal and/or influence skills, as well as experts in emotional and nonverbal communication. We also published a call for papers and received a number of submissions, and we invited some of those authors to also present their research at the conference. One thing that did surprise us was the rather small number of submissions—far fewer than we had received for other leadership conference calls for papers. It seemed that few scholars were researching the soft skills, which our call suggested consisted of the "interpersonal skills, communication skills, persuasion skills, political savvy, and emotional abilities used by leaders."

In the response to our call for papers, we were a bit surprised by both the low number and the broad scope of the submitted papers. Some of the topics seemed far afield from the domain of interpersonal and soft leader skills, such as research on virtual teams and communication technology, work on leader self-definition and identity, and research on leader character/ethics. The last topic was included and is represented in this book by Jennings and Hannah, in chapter 7. We began to realize that the soft side of leadership cut quite a wide swath.

The first day of the conference was a closed session with the conference presenters and invited scholars and guests. This day was designed to discuss issues related to the conceptualization and understanding of leader soft skills. We hoped to get our arms around the domain and to provide definitions, make connections among topics, and perhaps gain new insights. Another goal was for the presenters to preview their next day's presentations in order to better integrate the topics and to discuss this book. Through this exchange, our eventual chapter authors had a good understanding of what would eventually become the book's chapters, so that they could cross-reference each other's work and come to some common understanding of the nature and scope of the topic.

One thing was clear from the outset. People did not like the term *soft skills*. So the discussion turned to labeling and defining the domain. We considered a number of terms: *conceptual skills, interpersonal skills, communication skills,* and so forth. In the end, we settled on the title of this book: *interpersonal and influence skills,* but the subtitle still uses the term *soft skills* for clarity's sake. This issue of what to call the domain of leader "soft skills" will likely continue into the future.

It was clear to many of the participants that we lacked an agreed-upon framework for conceptualizing leader interpersonal and soft skills. Several of our presentations, and several of the chapters in this book, suggest specific frameworks for leader skills—although none of them is comprehensive enough to represent the broad domain of leader skills discussed throughout the day.

A third concern that emerged from our first day discussion was that of measurement. A number of techniques were discussed, but some participants expressed concern that reliance on ratings—either self-ratings or ratings by others—was deficient. Many of the studies presented in this book rely on ratings of leader interpersonal or influence skills, including self-report ratings and ratings by others (including 360-degree ratings from supervisors, subordinates, and others). Socially desirable responding (for self-report assessments), halo effects, and other biases are a problem with ratings. Clearly, observational methods or performance-based measures (e.g., assessment center exercises) could more accurately assess some of these skills, but these are expensive and time consuming to obtain, particularly in work organizations.

Another issue concerned whether there was a hierarchy of leader interpersonal skills, such that simpler, more basic skills lay at the foundation, with more complex skills building from the basic skills. Along the same line, are the skills of higher-level leaders more complex or different from, or the same as, the skills needed for the success of lower-level leaders? Another possible way that soft skills could be arranged concerned the locus of the skills, with skills of self-management/leadership at the core, interpersonal dyadic skills at the next level (think, perhaps, concentric circles), and group-level skills at the outermost level.

The final portion of the discussion on the first day of the conference focused on developing soft skills. Nearly all of the scholars in attendance had conducted some sort of leadership soft skills training at their universities with students, with managers in organizations, or with community groups. Moreover, everyone acknowledged that there are a great many leadership development efforts taking place worldwide as part of what Barbara Kellerman (2012) refers to as the "leadership industry"—leadership trainers, executive education programs, consultants, and the like. There was general agreement, however, that there is a dearth of sound studies of the impact of interpersonal skill training programs. Avolio, Reichard, Hannah, Walumbwa, and Chan (2009) conducted a meta-analysis of leadership development programs, both experimental and real world, and determined that on the whole these efforts led to modest positive outcomes. However, they made no distinction between programs that focused on hard versus soft leadership skills, and many, such as research on Pygmalion leadership training (e.g., leaders holding and conveying positive expectations for follower performance), likely blend hard and soft skills. One thing is certain, however: Leadership development takes a significant investment of time, and soft skills may take longer to develop than the more analytical/cognitive skills of leadership. Some participants likened leadership development to psychotherapy or long-term executive coaching, but insisted that it is important to continually assess growth and change.

THE BOOK

The book begins with three chapters that represent very different models for capturing the soft skills of leadership. In chapter 2, Shaun Pichler and Gerard Beenen describe a project to derive a framework for classifying and measuring managerial interpersonal skills. They begin with the literature and with qualitative interviews of managers in order to develop broad categories of managerial/leadership interpersonal skills. They then empirically derive general interpersonal skill factors, and come up with three: *supporting, motivating others,* and *managing conflict.* In chapter 3, Ronald Riggio presents his model of basic social skills, which represents the most fundamental building block of interpersonal communication—the ability to send, receive, and regulate the interpersonal communication of information and feelings. The Social Skill Model emphasizes the importance of emotional skills, as well as more complex and sophisticated social-verbal skills. While Pichler and Beenen try to map the domain of leader soft skills from the macro perspective, Riggio begins at the most micro level, and provides a foundation for more complex leader interpersonal and influence skills. While these two models are certainly viable ways of depicting the domain of the soft skills of leadership, much more work remains in mapping the wide range of skills that make leaders effective at the interpersonal level.

In chapter 4, Cary Cherniss and Richard E. Boyatzis discuss the popular construct of emotional intelligence and the related concepts of emotional and social competences and present these as a framework for understanding the domain of leader interpersonal soft skills, and for guiding leader skill development. Although grounded in the basics of emotion, emotional understanding, and the communication and management of emotions, Cherniss and Boyatzis go beyond this and bring in elements of personality and social competence. The chapter provides guidelines and examples of interpersonal and emotional skill development programs for leaders.

The next section of the book focuses on the role of emotions in leader interpersonal skills. In recent years, there has been a surge in research on the role that emotions play in leadership, and these three chapters review much of this work. In chapter 5, Annick Darioly and Marianne Schmid Mast begin to lay the groundwork by reviewing research on nonverbal communication and leadership. Much of nonverbal communication is grounded in emotions, and this far-ranging chapter discusses how leaders use nonverbal cues to express themselves, to gain leadership positions, and to build good leader-follower relationships. Moreover, skill in nonverbal communication is linked to emotional intelligence, so this chapter builds on the previous chapter.

In chapter 6, Shane Connelly and colleagues discuss the critical role of leader emotion management in the development of more complex leadership skills, such as conflict resolution, negotiation, risk management, and the building of leader-follower relationships. In addition to providing a detailed review of research on emotions and emotion management in leadership, the authors give directions for leader development. Both chapters in this section offer a wealth of important references for the further exploration of leadership and emotions.

The third section of the book focuses on leader influence and political skills. When we first envisioned this book, we did not consider character a part of a leader's soft skills, but colleagues convinced us otherwise. Drawing on classic philosophy from the ancient Greeks, Peter L. Jennings and

Sean T. Hannah suggest that character is a critical, foundational element for leader social influence, and that is the focus of chapter 7. They argue that character is key in establishing trust with followers, and that this is the foundation of leader influence.

In chapter 8, Darren C. Treadway and colleagues provide an overview of the leader's use of political skills and suggest this perspective as a lens for viewing the interpersonal influence that a leader wields in groups, teams, and organizations. They argue that political skill is the foundation for effective leader behavior that helps mobilize teams to achieve collective goals. Their perspective is quite consistent with notions of social intelligence and social skills introduced earlier in the book.

In chapter 9, Viviane Seyranian suggests that leaders construct a shared vision with followers in an effort to achieve goals and social change. Drawing heavily on Social Identity Theory, she argues that leaders use this social identity framing to influence group members, near and distant, to achieve collective goals.

The final section of the book focuses on the development of leader interpersonal and influence skills. In chapter 10, Jay A. Conger begins by discussing how leaders can best use psychological principles—particularly drawing on research from memory researchers—to persuade and influence followers. Conger suggests that by leveraging memory science and adhering to basic principles that aid memory and retention, a leader can better influence his or her followers. The chapter provides very specific and straightforward guidelines for leaders to use when communicating to followers and other constituents.

Increasingly, leader development is taking place in curricular and co-curricular programs in universities (and even earlier in high schools), and in chapter 11, Craig R. Seal and colleagues present a model for one such program. Labeled "Responsible Leadership Development," this program rests on a foundation of ethics and focuses on both self-development (intrapersonal) and the development of social and emotional skills. Going beyond simply focusing on leadership, the authors examine the soft skills needed for successful adult development. As the chapter states, "leadership development is for everyone," and Seal and colleagues focus on the social and emotional competences necessary for successful development as adults and leaders. This chapter is quite broad and can be a good starting point for exploring one of the many paths for early leader development.

In chapter 12, Susan Elaine Murphy, Stefanie Putter, and Stefanie K. Johnson review a wide range of leadership development efforts taking place in industry, in professional graduate programs, and at all levels in higher education. They show that these programs, substantially focused on developing the soft skills of leaders, are both curricular and cocurricular and use a number of theoretical and practical approaches. This comprehensive chapter is a terrific starting point for understanding how leadership development efforts are proceeding, in the area of the soft skills of leadership. Their survey includes the top companies for leader development, top schools of engineering, medicine, and business, and undergraduate programs.

Finally, in chapter 13 Richard E. Boyatzis, Angela Passarelli, and Hongguo Wei present an overview of one of the most focused and longest-lasting efforts in graduate-level business education, the Weatherhead School of Management's program at Case Western Reserve University, and an evaluation of the success of this program. It offers a model that should be emulated in trying to understand how leadership development efforts are paying off.

CONCLUSIONS

What lessons have we learned from the conference and this edited collection? First and foremost, the domain of leader interpersonal and influence skills is enormous—ranging from character to intrapersonal development processes to skills and competencies to higher-level political and persuasion skills. Second, although there is no agreed-upon model for conceptualizing this vast range of skills, researchers have made good attempts to capture large parts of the range, and some of these foundational models are useful starting points for scholars and practitioners. Finally, it is clear that when it comes to the soft skills of leadership, practice is way out in front of research, and that may not be a good thing. All one needs to do is go online to find hundreds of leadership development programs that focus on the soft skills of leadership—programs on soft skills, emotional intelligence, interpersonal skills, influence skills, and communication skills. These development programs are offered by the most esteemed business schools, major training and development organizations, university extended education programs, for-profit universities, and independent trainers and consultants. The programs range in length from a few hours to a few days (and in some cases longer, multiweek programs). Yet, there is little in the way of uniform frameworks guiding these development programs, and there is little, if any, sound evaluation of the programs' effectiveness.

We hope that this book will serve two major purposes: First, it presents some of the cutting-edge research and theory on the interpersonal and influence skills of leaders, ranging from long-standing models and findings to more recent work. We hope that this will be both a reference for scholars and a motivator to increase scholarly research on this important topic. Second, we hope that programs designed to develop leaders' interpersonal and influence skills will take heed of the research and models that exist and will use them to guide training efforts, and that they will conduct sound evaluation of program outcomes.

REFERENCES

Avolio, B.J., Reichard, R.J., Hannah, S.T., Walumbwa, F.O., & Chan, A. (2009). A meta-analytic review of leadership impact research: Experimental and quasi-experimental studies. *Leadership Quarterly, 20*(5), 764–784.

Kellerman, B. (2012). *The end of leadership.* New York: HarperCollins.

Porter, L.W., & McKibbin, L.E. (1988). *Management education and development: Drift or thrust into the 21st century.* New York: McGraw-Hill.

Section I

Foundational Models for Leader Interpersonal Skills and Competencies

2

Toward the Development of a Model and a Measure of Managerial Interpersonal Skills

Shaun Pichler and Gerard Beenen

Interpersonal skills are an important part of effectively working with and leading others. Although organizations, educational institutions, accrediting bodies of collegiate schools of business, and scholars are increasingly interested in managerial interpersonal skills, there is little agreement as to what exactly these skills are, what these skills predict, or how we should measure them. This chapter describes a research program that aims to develop a new, multidimensional measure of managerial interpersonal skills (MIPS) that can serve as a useful tool for both scholars and management development professionals. We explain the need for such a measure, examine the connections between managerial interpersonal skills and other types of leadership behaviors discussed in this book, and present some of our preliminary findings in developing an MIPS measure.

Interpersonal skills are a critical, if not essential, part of effectively managing and leading others. Interpersonally skilled managers are more successful (Dierdorff, Rubin, & Morgeson, 2009; Van Velsor & Leslie, 1995) and interpersonally skilled leaders are more effective (Mumford, Campion, & Morgeson, 2007). Given that interpersonal skills are one of several sets of core skills necessary for managers (Mintzberg, 1980), it comes as no surprise that business schools are increasingly interested in training and education to improve these skills (GMAC, 2005). In fact, managers spend most of their time interacting and communicating with subordinates, peers, and superiors (e.g., Hinds & Kiesler, 1995; Rubin & Dierdorff, 2009). This is perhaps increasingly important in the sense that work organizations are increasingly diverse (Kossek & Pichler, 2006). Management practitioners know that employees leave organizations because managers or leaders fail to treat them with dignity and respect. This is why most would prefer to work for a "lovable fool" than a "competent jerk" (Casciaro & Lobo, 2005). There is little doubt that managerial interpersonal skills are critical to getting things done in organizations.

While scholars, educators, and practitioners concur that managerial interpersonal skills are important, experts have reached no clear agreement as to what exactly these skills are or what they comprise. Despite the increasing scholarly and practical interest in managerial interpersonal skills, no agreed-upon model or taxonomy of these skills exists to guide research and practice. Rather, a variety of different models of managerial interpersonal skills offer a range of perspectives as to what exactly managerial interpersonal skills are (e.g., Kantrowitz, 2005; Klein, DeRouin, & Salas, 2006). With no overarching model guiding the field, a variety of disparate measures exist for a host of skills that might be classified as interpersonal in nature such as social skills (Riggio, 1986), communication (Rubin & Martin, 1994), conflict management (Van de Vliert & Kabanoff, 1990), political skills (Ferris et al., 2005), and others. There is, however, no well-validated measure of managerial interpersonal skills. Without a clear understanding of the nature of managerial interpersonal skills and how to measure them, assessing them is difficult at best. Furthermore, we are unable to have a clear understanding of how these skills relate to other important managerial skills (i.e., how they fit into the nomological net of managerial competencies).

The goal of this chapter is to describe a research program focused on developing a model and measure of managerial interpersonal skills. We first explain our approach to understanding the domain of managerial interpersonal skills, and our approach to developing the Managerial Interpersonal Skills (MIPS) Scale. We also briefly describe some preliminary findings related to the factor structure and measurement features of the survey. Our intention is to define the nature of MIPS (i.e., what these skills are and are not), their factor structure, and their relationships with other important work-related skills and constructs. By describing our research program, we aim to provide a process guide to other researchers and management development professionals interested in assessing skills in this domain.

RELATED RESEARCH AND RESEARCH PROGRAM FOCUS

A variety of models help us understand what managers "do." Some models are based on managerial functions (e.g., planning, controlling, coordinating), others on roles (i.e., expectations about appropriate behaviors), and still others on management skills (e.g., communication skills, technical skills, decision-making skills). Across these models there is some agreement that managers occupy three main interrelated roles: interpersonal, informational, and decisional (e.g., Mintzberg, 1980). The interpersonal role involves motivating employees and generating and maintaining a web of relationships with internal and external stakeholders. From a skill-based perspective, managers need technical, conceptual, and interpersonal skills to be effective (e.g., Dierdorff et al., 2009; Katz, 1974; Pavett & Lau, 1983). Technical skills pertain to specialized (e.g., functional) knowledge acquired through formal education and training, such as the ability to interpret a balance sheet (technical accounting skills) or to develop a new product launch plan (technical marketing skills). Conceptual skills allow managers to understand and solve complex problems, such as imagining how a particular marketing strategy might play out based on various assumptions about demand, customer preference, competition, and so forth. Interpersonal skills help managers work with, communicate with, and effectively lead individuals and groups.

Lines of research have attempted to conceptualize general interpersonal skills in adults (e.g., Riggio, 1986). Other informative literatures related to interpersonal skills have taken more of a trait-based approach, such as social intelligence (Thorndike, 1936) and emotional intelligence (Mayer & Salovey, 1997). Still others have focused on more specific skills such as communication (Rubin & Martin, 1994) and political skills (Ferris et al., 2005).

Though these literatures are important in their own right and inform our understanding and perspective of managerial interpersonal skills, none has attempted to identify, define, and measure those skills that are inherently interpersonal with a specific focus on the managerial domain. Furthermore, to our knowledge, researchers have created no general model to represent the key skill clusters that focus on a mid-level understanding of managerial interpersonal skills. Klein and colleagues (2006) comprehensively reviewed more than 58 theoretical frameworks that included 400 component skills that we might classify as interpersonal in nature. Based on this, they argued that interpersonal skills can be classified into two higher-order dimensions: communication and relationship development. These in turn consist of 12 subdimensions—five for communication (active listening, oral, written, assertive, and nonverbal communication) and seven for relationship development (cooperation and coordination, trust, intercultural sensitivity, service orientation, self-presentation, social influence, and conflict resolution and negotiation).

Though we believe their review is a step in the right direction, our goal is to identify a more parsimonious cluster of skills (e.g., three to five) that can serve as a basis for assessment and training. We acknowledge that more granular assessments of microskills are important, particularly as managers advance toward increasing levels of interpersonal expertise. However, we also contend it is critical to start with a smaller set of mid-level skills that balance comprehensiveness and specificity. Furthermore, it is not clear whether some of Klein and colleagues' (2006) numerous skill clusters (e.g., written communication, coordination) are distinctly interpersonal or are potentially more technical or conceptual in nature. It also is not clear whether skills such as written or verbal *outbound* communication are qualitatively similar to *inbound* communication skills such as active listening or attentiveness to nonverbal cues. Certainly, the conceptual, technical, and interpersonal skill domains (Dierdorff et al., 2009) do overlap in some areas. This should not detract us from attempts at clearly distinguishing the boundaries of each with an exclusive focus on the interpersonal domain.

The focus of our research therefore departs from prior research in that we are interested exclusively in *managerial interpersonal* skills. We also are attempting to identify the relevant skills at the appropriate level of specificity so that practicing managers and management development professionals can easily grasp both the definition and application of these skills. As our own starting point, *we define managerial interpersonal skills as competencies that help managers understand, communicate with, motivate and influence others, and resolve conflicts in goal-directed organizational settings.* Our focus is on higher-order interpersonal skills that managers use daily. We are not attempting to define a comprehensive set of all possible micro-level interpersonal skills that managers exercise. Instead, we are interested in those essential skills that managers need to be effective in their supervisory roles.

We also acknowledge that managers use interpersonal skills that are situation specific. For instance, assertively communicating expectations in one organization or cultural context may be considered overstepping one's bounds in another organization or cultural context. Our primary interest is those skills that are generalizable across a variety of situations and cultural settings that may predict more situation-specific types of skills. Research on specific negotiation skills in Nadler, Thompson, and Van Boven (2003), for instance, is certainly relevant to managerial interpersonal skills. We expect that the interpersonal skills we are attempting to measure are relevant to and will likely be predictive of success in more situation-specific or context-specific interpersonal situations.

We are also less interested in the more granular or basic types of skills that arc related to and may comprise the higher-order types of skills we are attempting to model. Related research has focused on, for instance, a micro skills approach to training managerial interpersonal skills (Maellero, 2011). In this approach, the intent is to train managers in highly specific, hierarchically configured skills. For instance, one might be interested in probing as a subdimension of active listening, which in turn is a subdimension of communication skills, which may be considered a rudimentary interpersonal skill. Other researchers have focused specifically on skills that may be more problem based, such as dealing with uniquely difficult interpersonal situations like a problem employee (Lopes, 2011). In such situations, an array of specific skills such as persuasion, demonstrating empathy, active listening, communicating effectively, negotiation skills, and others may be relevant. The focus of this and other related literatures is more granular than our research, and the attempt is to predict much more specific types of behavior.

RESEARCH PROGRAM OVERVIEW

Our research program involves three phases: preliminary research and model development (Phase I), model testing (Phase II), and model validation (Phase III). Given that there is no widely accepted model or taxonomy of managerial interpersonal skills, the first phase of our research involved a review of the literature, qualitative structured interviews with practicing managers and executives, and analysis of existing qualitative survey data collected by the Graduate Management Admissions Council (GMAC) of MBA program admissions officers. The purpose of this first phase was to consider and build upon previously completed research and to develop a model of managerial interpersonal skills with the focus described earlier based, in part, on the knowledge and experience of practicing experts (managers and admissions officers). Although we had our own conceptions of the types of interpersonal skills that are important for managerial success, we wanted to triangulate sources to develop a fully informed preliminary model.

Phase I: Identifying the Dimensions of Managerial Interpersonal Skills: Research Review and Qualitative Data Collection

In this first phase of research, concepts from existing research and practicing experts became the basis for preliminary scale items that were to comprise our measure. Before consulting practicing managers, we carefully reviewed the academic and business press to develop a preliminary model of managerial interpersonal skills. This was our starting point and first attempt to synthesize the literature, though we realized this model would potentially change in later stages of our research.

Our original model of managerial interpersonal skills included four categories or potential factors: self-management, communication, social acumen, and influence. Self-management included initiative, emotional control, and self-awareness; communication included oral and nonverbal communication; social acumen included interpreting emotions, relationship building, and managing conflict; influence included motivating others, development and coaching, and political skills.

Self-management is an interpersonal competency based on the emotional intelligence literature. *Emotional intelligence* (EI) is the "ability to monitor one's own and other's feelings and emotions, to discriminate among them, and to use this information to guide one's thinking and action" (Salovey & Mayer, 1990, p. 189). Research shows EI is positively related to the quality of social interactions at work (Lopes et al., 2004; Lopes, Salovey, Côté, & Beers, 2005), leader emergence, and task performance (Lopes, Côté, & Salovey, 2006). The most widely validated model (Mayer & Salovey, 1997) posits EI is comprised of four interrelated abilities: (1) perceiving emotions, (2) using emotions for information processing and (3) for understanding emotional language, and (4) managing emotions in one's self and others. The four-dimensional model is supported empirically (e.g., Mayer, Salovey, Caruso, & Sitarenios, 2003). The managing emotions (or emotion regulation) dimension "is probably the most important for social interaction because it influences emotional expression and behavior directly" (Lopes et al., 2005, p. 113).

Since Mintzberg (1973) revealed that managers spend a majority of their time communicating, *communication skills* have been viewed as critical to managerial success (Brownell, 2003) and thus as a key dimension of interpersonal skills. Several studies highlight how poorly most college graduates communicate (Pfeffer & Fong, 2002). Guo defines communication as "the exchange of thoughts, ideas, and emotions, between sender(s) and receiver(s)" (2009, p. 9). Most organizational behavior textbooks identify key dimensions of communication as including written, verbal/oral, nonverbal, and active listening (e.g., Robbins & Hunsaker, 2003; Robbins & Judge, 2013; Whetten & Cameron, 2011).

Social acumen describes social skills, which have been associated with entrepreneurial success (Baron & Tang, 2009), contextual and task performance (Morgeson, Reider, & Campion, 2005), and higher compensation (Ferris, Witt, & Hochwarter, 2001). Our original model suggested social acumen is the dimension of managerial interpersonal skills that conveys expertise in both surmising and responding to social dynamics in organizational settings. Social acumen can be thought of here as competencies that allow managers to understand the emotions, motivations, and thoughts of others in work settings and to form and execute appropriate responses.

Influence skills concentrate on persuading and motivating others to accomplish individual or organizational goals, and have been viewed as a social skills dimension of leadership skills (e.g., Morgeson et al., 2005; Mumford et al., 2007) or an aspect of political skills (e.g., Ahearn, Ferris, Hochwarter, Douglas, & Ammeter, 2004). We conceptualized influence skills as the ability to understand and assess the motivational level of others in regards to organizational goals, and to develop and execute strategies for sustaining others' motivation to pursue those goals.

Our interviews with practicing managers allowed us to further consider our original model—and to refine it with our aforementioned goals in mind. We conducted structured in-depth interviews with 27 practicing managers and executives. Using unaided recall so as not to bias their responses, we simply asked them to list, describe, define, and provide specific examples of interpersonal skills they viewed as critical to be an effective manager. We then iteratively reviewed interview transcriptions to identify specific skill categories and more general themes. This resulted in 78 specific skill categories that cohered under five key themes or skill clusters: managing self, communicating, supporting, motivating others, and managing conflict.

> *Managing self.* Our interviews suggested that interpersonal skills start with self skills. Consistent with the literature (Whetten & Cameron, 2011), this skill cluster involves being in tune with and

being able to effectively control one's emotions. A new theme of interpersonal ethics also emerged as part of this skill cluster. Interviewees described behavioral virtues such as honesty, trust, and integrity as essential to managing others, consistent with work on authentic leadership (e.g., Zhu, Riggio, & Sosik, 2010).

Communicating. This was the most frequently mentioned skill. The interpersonal components of communication expressed in the interviews included communicating supportively, active listening, and accurately interpreting nonverbal cues. Another facet of this skill cluster included setting clear expectations with colleagues and subordinates.

Supporting. Managers identified proactive interpersonal support and relationship development as a skill paramount to managerial success. The phrase "treating others as human beings" emerged repeatedly, capturing the essence of this skill (cf. Amabile & Kramer, 2007). Creating a work environment where employees feel comfortable relating to and communicating with supervisors and peers, such as stating an unpopular opinion, seemed to be an important aspect of managerial interpersonal skills. The importance of support in an interpersonal context is consistent with research in the work-family and broader psychology literatures (e.g., Kossek, Pichler, Bodner, & Hammer 2011).

Motivating others. While motivation is a topic in all organizational behavior textbooks, it has not been traditionally classified as interpersonal. Typically in organizational textbooks, motivational skills are scattered across a variety of other skills such as leading others, clarifying expectations, persuading, and providing effective feedback (e.g., Robbins & Hunsaker, 2003, p. 4). Our interviewees viewed this skill as inherently interpersonal. At its core, this skill involves customizing interactions to match people's preferences and styles. Some participants described it as a "continuous tailoring of rewards, recognition and interactions with employees."

Managing conflict. Many interviewees viewed interpersonal conflicts as inevitable aspects of managing that require attention. This skill focused on "de-escalating difficult emotional situations," with empathy as an integral part of effectively managing conflict.

Several features distinguished our revised five MIPS dimensions (managing self, communicating, supporting, motivating others, managing conflict) from our initial four dimensions (self-management, communication, social acumen, influence). First, each cluster seemed to logically precede the next in a sort of hierarchical manner. Layers of an onion provides a suitable metaphor to describe the different layers of interpersonal skills, with self-management at the core and other more complex skills following or developing out from the center and serving as outer layers of the "onion." For instance, consistent with pedagogical literature and research on leadership (e.g., Whetten & Cameron, 2011), managing self and accurate self-awareness are a starting point for effective interpersonal interactions. Communicating effectively is a necessary condition for building supportive relationships, which in turn is a foundation for effectively motivating others. Competently managing interpersonal conflict requires proficiency in each of the other four interpersonal skill clusters. Thus, our preliminary model of managerial interpersonal skills suggested a sequence exists in terms of the ordering of skills conceptually, which also suggests a sequence in how these skills might be trained most effectively.

Second, communication was the most pervasive dimension in that it was mentioned most frequently, and it was somewhat intertwined with supporting, motivating others, and managing conflict. For instance, a number of interviewees viewed active listening as a critical element of developing supportive relationships. Many also noted that communicating clear expectations and goals was an important part of motivating others effectively. Competence in conflict resolution also requires one to exercise effective communication skills.

Third, consistent with theory on social skills (Riggio, 1986; Riggio & Reichard, 2008), a common theme that emerged was the perceptual and behavioral components seen as pertinent to the latter four skill clusters. The perceptual component involved assessing and understanding subordinates' different individual preferences and motivational profiles. The behavioral component involved tailoring one's interactions with a particular subordinate in a way that accounts for these differences. We called this perceptual-behavioral repertoire "interpersonal assessment." By interpersonal assessment we mean understanding how individuals differ from one another and tailoring the way in which one interacts with different individuals. This mirrors the social acumen construct. For instance, it is important for managers to understand how different individuals are motivated, given individual differences in sources of motivation (e.g., intrinsic versus extrinsic). The notion that effective managers understand the psychological composition of their individual employees is not necessarily new, and is consistent with research on leadership (e.g., individualized consideration;

Judge, Piccolo, & Ilies, 2004) and idiosyncratic deals (Rousseau, 2005). We contend, however, that this notion of interpersonal assessment has been largely overlooked in the literature on managerial interpersonal skills, despite being an integral part of these competencies.

What was clear from our first phase of research was our measure should be multidimensional, which is a change from previous approaches (e.g., Ferris et al., 2001). Survey data from MBA program admissions officers in the United States and abroad, collected by the GMAC, further informed our model development and were highly consistent with data from our qualitative interviews. One hundred eighty-five MBA admissions officers from 22 countries responded to a survey that asked them to define "soft skills." Though not all soft skills are interpersonal (see Chapter 3 of this volume), those skills mentioned that were interpersonal could be classified as motivating, supporting, political skills, communicating, and managing self—in order of frequency (highest to lowest). We view political skills (see Chapter 8 of this volume) under the rubrics of managing self (e.g., controlling one's emotions under stress), motivating others (e.g., persuasion), and managing conflict (e.g., bringing divergent factions together). The fact that these admissions officers represented 22 countries provided at least some indication that the skill clusters identified through our literature review and qualitative research were somewhat generalizable across cultural contexts.

Phase II: Pilot Testing a Preliminary Managerial Interpersonal Skills (MIPS) Scale

While our Phase I model had the benefit of being informed by a variety of sources, it was nevertheless preliminary. In fact, the model changed once again when we were able to develop and test some preliminary scale items with pilot data. This was the second phase of our research: pilot testing our items with two different types of samples—further refining both our items and our overall measure.

First, we developed a large pool of just more than 100 items, based on our structured interviews with practicing managers and executives. We used specific behaviors mentioned most frequently by our interviewees as the basis for many of the item stems we developed. We also developed items based on common experience in organizations and the types of skills and behaviors identified in leading scholarly sources, textbooks, book chapters, and popular articles. In other words, we wanted to select behaviors that interviewees seemed to consistently mention that converged with other sources that supported the face validity of our scale items.

Once we developed an initial pool of items that we felt fully represented each of our five factors, we pilot tested these items extensively. The original pool of items was pilot tested with both graduate and undergraduate business students who were evaluating their current or most recent supervisor. A variety of criteria were considered in order to evaluate the effectiveness of each individual item, including both conceptual (e.g., clarity of meaning) and statistical (e.g., inter-item correlations and item discrepancies) criteria. Based on this process, an initial set of about 50 items seemed to do the best job of potentially assessing our five dimensions.

Exploratory factor analysis, however, indicated a three-factor model consistently emerged as best explaining the underlying structure of the data. These three factors were clearly interpretable as three of our original dimensions—supporting, motivating others, and managing conflict, with a number of items not loading on a clear factor. This surprised us at first, and led us to make a couple of observations. First, the managing self items did not seem to work well with the rest of the item pool in general, though a small number, primarily focused on emotional control, were part of a managing conflict factor. We interpreted this to mean that aspects of managing self, such as being aware of one's own emotions, are inherently more *intrapersonal* than *interpersonal* and are perhaps misrepresented when conceptualized as an aspect of managerial interpersonal skills.

Second, our communication items did not create a clear, discrete factor. Rather, items intended to assess communication loaded on each of these three factors. That is, communication seemed to be more of a meta-skill and key aspect of the three empirically derived dimensions: supporting, motivating others, and managing conflict. Upon further consideration, this made sense conceptually and was consistent with the pervasive nature of communication skills that came out of our qualitative interviews. Consequently, we were open to the possibility that communication items may be best incorporated as components of these three dimensions. When we reran this model with the best-performing items, a clear three-factor structure emerged, each factor with an eigenvalue above one, with 71% of the variance in the data explained.

We then conducted a second pilot study with a larger organizational sample of subordinates in an educational institution who evaluated their direct supervisors. This time, we did a confirmatory factor analysis based on our revised a priori, three-factor model (supporting, motivating others, managing conflict). The three-factor structure fit the data well and seemed to offer the best representation of interpersonal skills using our revised items. The same three factors were then supported from an additional graduate business student sample, with participants evaluating their current or most recent direct supervisor.

To summarize, our initial literature review and qualitative research led us to five clusters of managerial skills that we deemed distinctly interpersonal. Pilot testing our MIPS scale, however, indicated a three-factor model—supporting, motivating others, managing conflict—was a more robust representation of MIPS, and this was supported by both exploratory and confirmatory factor analysis with separate pilot samples. For an illustration of our model, see Figure 2.1. Communication seemed to be an important aspect of supporting, motivating, and managing conflict, with at least one communication-oriented item loading on its respective topical factor. For instance, an initial item "actively listens to my cares and concerns" loaded on the "supporting" dimension of MIPS, while "communicates clear goals and expectations" loaded on our "motivating others" dimension. Interpersonal

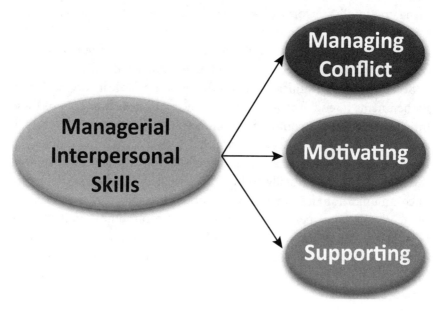

FIGURE 2.1
MIPS three-factor model

assessment also seemed to be an important aspect to each of these skills. Similarly, interpersonal assessment items loaded on their relevant factor, not on a single interpersonal assessment factor. For instance, the item "understands how different personalities contribute to conflicts" loaded on the conflict management factor.

Phase III: Further Research and Validation of Our Three-Factor MIPS Scale

Our current and ongoing phase of research involves more robust validation and testing of our three-factor model using our revised and pilot tested item pool. Our goal is to test the convergent, discriminant, and predictive validity of the three factors in our revised model using paired data from managers and their employees from multiple organizations across different industries. We also plan to measure contextual features of these organizations, such as climate and perceptions of organizational support, to understand how differences at the organizational and work unit levels are related to managerial interpersonal skills and their correlates.

We expect that each of the three MIPS dimensions will be most strongly related to other logically related constructs in ways that support both the convergent and discriminant validity of each factor. That is, though we would expect all three factors to be correlated with general supervisor support, the individualized consideration dimension of transformational leadership, and political skill, we also would expect each dimension to have a stronger relationship with only one of each. For instance, we expect that our supporting factor should correlate more strongly than the other two factors with general supervisor support. Our motivating others factor should have the strongest correlation with the individualized consideration dimension of transformational leadership. Managing conflict, on the other hand, should have the strongest correlation with political skills.

We also expect that each of the three factors will explain unique variance in relevant criteria, with some factors having stronger associations than others. For example, supporting should contribute to more effective relationships between supervisors and subordinates, and lower work stress. Consequently, supporting should be the best predictor of work-family conflict. Motivating others should contribute to heightened subordinate work effort and engagement. As a result, motivating others should be the best predictor of motivation to perform, performance, and performance improvement. Managing conflict should contribute to effective resolution of difficult and challenging interpersonal situations. We therefore expect managing conflict to be negatively related to a conflict avoid style of conflict management at work.

MANAGERIAL INTERPERSONAL SKILLS AND OTHER IMPORTANT LEADERSHIP COMPETENCIES AND ABILITIES

We have described a research program aimed at defining managerial interpersonal skills in a way that balances their breadth and specificity. Our understanding of prior research, along with extensive qualitative research, resulted in three facets of managerial interpersonal skills we believe to be most critical—developing supportive relationships with others (supporting), effectively motivating others to learn and perform their roles and responsibilities (motivating), and constructively getting divergent parties to pursue common goals (managing conflict). This volume addresses a number of other competencies and abilities that are part and parcel with effective leadership, including social skills, communication skills (Chapters 3, 5), emotional intelligence (Chapters 4, 6), ethical character and virtue (Chapter 7), and political skills (Chapter 8). It is important to understand several ways in which our conception of managerial interpersonal skills both relates to and is distinct from these other critically important competencies and abilities. We do this in regards to our focus on skills versus abilities or traits, our attempt to define a mid-level set of skills, and our interest in formulating an elegant framework for training and developing these skills.

First, our focus is on behavioral skills or competencies that can be trained. We are not trying to identify interpersonal abilities or characteristics, though we acknowledge some traits may predict such skills. For instance, emotional intelligence as a trait should contribute to effective relationship development skills (i.e., supporting), as well as skillful handling of challenging, emotionally charged situations that may require an ability to self-regulate (i.e., managing conflict). We also concur ethical character is an important part of effective leadership. In fact, our own qualitative research uncovered what we called "interpersonal ethics" as a potential component of our model. In defining boundaries between skills and character, however, we would argue that character is closer to a trait than a skill, while at the same time acknowledging that ethical character can be developed. We further acknowledge that some facets of the skills we have identified spill over from the behavioral to the conceptual or perceptual realms. For instance, the skills with which managers customize their interactions with others so as to take into account individual differences and preferences—what we called interpersonal assessment—implies the exercise of perceptual qualities that may be contingent on one's emotional intelligence. Nonetheless, our goal is to assess the behavioral exchanges of managers and subordinates that are indicative of the exercise of such skills.

Second, our goal was to define a mid-range cluster of interpersonal skills, rather than a more granular, highly specific set of skills. For instance, Klein and colleagues (2006) identified 12 interpersonal skills in their taxonomy. One can take a deep dive into communication skills, social skills, or political skills. For instance, a focus on communication and social skills might include nonverbal communication, active listening, clearly communicating expectations, understanding the social motivations of others, and so on. Our intention was to identify a comprehensive set of skills that managers also can get their arms around. It is our view that the higher-order skills that we have identified should be correlated with these more granular skills.

Finally, our goal here was to provide a starting point versus a more advanced or complex model to facilitate training and skill development. While training designed around highly specific micro skills is certainly needed, we also believe managers would be more able to allocate effort and attention to a focused set of three skill dimensions, than, say, 12, or worse yet, more than 400 (Klein et al., 2006). Our findings also at least imply a logical ordering of skill development. Managers are more likely to be effective at motivating subordinates if they have been successful at developing supportive relationships with them. They also should be better at managing conflict and bridging faultiness between individuals when they understand how to motivate those individuals. As competence is built in these three foundational areas, managers then have an opportunity to deepen their competencies in each area.

DISCUSSION

Managerial interpersonal skills (MIPS) are important if not essential to effective management and leadership. The interpersonal role is one of three major roles that managers occupy, and research suggests that this is the role in which managers spend most of their time. To the extent that managers are effective in this role, they are not only more likely to be perceived as effective by those around them; they also enjoy more career success than their less interpersonally effective peers. Perhaps it comes as no surprise that business schools and managers themselves are increasingly interested in training and education to improve managerial interpersonal skills.

We assert that managerial skills are increasingly important, in part because organizations are rapidly becoming more diverse. More women have entered the workforce and are continuing to do so, especially in the professional-managerial classes, at rates greater than men. The labor force in the United States and other industrialized societies is also increasingly diverse with respect to racioethnicity, for instance. It is thus more important than ever before for mangers to be sensitive to and supportive of these and other interpersonal differences, which is an important aspect of interpersonal skillfulness generally, and supportive behavior more specifically.

Likewise, increased interest in work-life balance among academics, practitioners, and employees themselves is another important reason for managers to be interpersonally savvy. Our research identified interpersonal assessment as an important aspect of managerial interpersonal skills. Managers are effective when they notice, understand, and behave in a way that is consistent with the unique circumstances and motivations of individual employees. We suggest that managers who are effective at interpersonal assessment will more effectively support their employees in a variety of ways, including, more specifically, their unique work-life challenges and needs.

We are attempting to understand managerial interpersonal skills and their importance in work organizations. We are not aware of other research programs or research teams attempting to understand managerial interpersonal skills in a similarly multiphasic way. Previous conceptual attempts at understanding the nature of managerial interpersonal skills, such as that demonstrated by Klein and colleagues (2006), as well as other more empirical attempts, such as that by Dierdorf and colleagues (2009), have advanced our understanding considerably. Our aim is to build on their contributions to formulate a parsimonious yet sufficiently comprehensive model of managerial interpersonal skills.

Our model, as described earlier, is a three-factor model that includes supporting, motivating, and managing conflict. Intuitively, we believe that these skills follow a logical order or sequence. That is, effectiveness at supporting others may be an important predictor of effectiveness with motivating others, which may be predictive of one's effectiveness at managing conflict. This should be tested empirically with longitudinal data. We hope that other researchers will consider this possibility. We also urge human resources professionals and other groups interested in training related to managerial interpersonal skills, such as business schools and professional development organizations, to think carefully about how different interpersonal skills might build upon one another.

We hope that one of the ways in which we have contributed to research on managerial interpersonal skills is by revealing the importance of a multiphasic, mixed method approach to understanding a relatively understudied topic or construct. Our model of managerial interpersonal skills went through two major changes. The first change was informed by qualitative interviews with practicing managers and executives. The second change was informed by empirically testing potential scale items with employed students, working professionals, and managers through two different series of pilot testing. These changes from our original model, which was based more exclusively on our own assessment of the literature and experiences as related to managerial interpersonal skills, document the importance of collecting multiple and varied types of data from different sources—in our case, qualitative data, data from program administrators, and working professionals and managers.

Through these changes, skills that we thought were important as a single factor, namely communication skills, were found to be related in important ways and actually indicative of other skills. This is a new and perhaps important way for various interested groups to think about communication skills in organizations. We were originally surprised that communication did not seem to represent its own dimension or factor in a multidimensional model of managerial interpersonal skills. In retrospect, however, it makes sense that communication is such a pervasive skill that it is an essential ingredient in other interpersonal skills, such as being supportive and motivating others.

We also discovered that self-management skills, which we originally conceived of as an aspect of interpersonal effectiveness, are more intrapersonal in nature. Certainly, textbooks and research reports have suggested, sometimes strongly, that self-management is key to interpersonal effectiveness. This may be true. In other words, self-management skills may be related to and perhaps even predictive of the three types or dimensions of managerial interpersonal skills in our model. In other words, managers who are more self-aware and able to manage their emotions, for instance, might be more effective at supporting others and managing conflict in organizations. This is an important direction for future research, one that we hope to pursue in our own research. What is important to note based on our current research findings is that self-management does not seem to be part of managerial interpersonal skills—at least, not empirically.

CONCLUSION

We have proposed interpersonal skills can be conceptualized as a higher-order managerial skill set consisting of the capacity to develop productive and supportive relationships, to motivate others, and to resolve interpersonal conflicts, all while making effective use of communication (e.g., actively listening to build supportive relationships, communicating clear expectations to motivate others). Our understanding is based on a review of prior research, qualitative data collected from practicing managers, and empirical pilot testing of a preliminary survey instrument. We believe that focusing on these three dimensions provides an optimal mid-level understanding of these skills that researchers, managers, trainers, and educators can use.

ACKNOWLEDGMENTS

This research was supported by a generous Management Education and Research Institute grant from the Graduate Management Admissions Council. The coauthors would like to thank Lori Muse, Stephanie Lee, and David Borchardt for their contribution to this research.

REFERENCES

Ahearn, K. K., Ferris, G. R., Hochwarter, W. A., Douglas, C., & Ammeter, A. P. (2004). Leader political skill and team performance. *Journal of Management, 30,* 309–327.
Amabile, T. M., & Kramer, J. S. (2007, May). Inner work life: Understanding the subtext of business performance. *Harvard Business Review,* 72–83.
Baron, R. A., & Tang, J. (2009). Entrepreneurs' social skills and new venture performance: Mediating mechanisms and cultural generality. *Journal of Management, 35,* 282–306.
Brownell, J. (2003). Applied research in managerial communication: The critical link between knowledge and practice. *Cornell Hotel and Restaurant Administration Quarterly, 44*(2), 39–49.

Casciaro, T., & Lobo, M. S. (2005). Competent jerks, lovable fools, and formation of social networks. *Harvard Business Review,* June 1.

Dierdorff, E. C., Rubin, R. S., & Morgeson, F. P. (2009). The milieu of managerial work: An integrative framework linking work context to role requirements. *Journal of Applied Psychology, 94,* 972–988.

Ferris, G. R., Treadway, D. C., Kolodinsky, R. W., et al. (2005). Development and validation of the political skill inventory. *Journal of Management, 31,* 126–152.

Ferris, G. R., Witt, L. A., & Hochwarter, W. A. (2001). Interaction of social skill and general mental ability on job performance and salary. *Journal of Applied Psychology, 86,* 1075–1082.

Graduate Management Admissions Council (GMAC). (2005). *Corporate Recruiters Survey: General report.*

Guo, K. L. (2009). Effective communication in health care: Strategies to improve communications skills for managers. *The Business Review, 12*(2), 8–17.

Hinds, P., & Kiesler, S. (1995). Communication across boundaries: Work, structure, and use of communication technologies in a large organization. *Organization Science, 6,* 373–393.

Judge, T. A., Piccolo, R. F., & Ilies, R. (2004). The forgotten ones? The validity of consideration and initiating structure in leadership research. *Journal of Applied Psychology, 89,* 36–51.

Kantrowitz, T. M. (2005). *Development and construct validation of a measure of soft skills performance* (Unpublished dissertation). Georgia Institute of Technology, Atlanta, GA.

Katz, R. L. (1974). Skills of an effective administrator. *Harvard Business Review, 52,* 90–102.

Klein, C., DeRouin, R. E., & Salas, E. (2006). Uncovering workplace interpersonal skills: A review, framework, and research agenda. In G. P. Hodgkinson & J. K. Ford (Eds.), *International review of industrial and organizational psychology* (vol. 21, pp. 80–126). New York: Wiley & Sons, Ltd.

Kossek, E. E., & Pichler, S. (2006). EEO and the management of diversity. In P. Boxell, J. Purcell, & P. Wright (Eds.), *Handbook of Human Resource Management* (pp. 251–272). Oxford: Oxford University Press.

Kossek, E. E., Pichler, S., Bodner, T., & Hammer, L. (2011). Workplace social support and work-family conflict: A meta-analysis clarifying the influence of general and work-family specific supervisor and organizational support. *Personnel Psychology, 64*(2), 289–313.

Lopes, P. N. (2011). Managing challenging interpersonal situations at work: Socio-emotional judgment and response flexibility. In S. Pichler, L. Muse, & B. Beenen (Cochairs), *Managerial interpersonal skills: The state of the science.* Academy of Management meeting.

Lopes, P. N., Brackett, M. A., Nezlek, J. B., Schütz, A., Sellin, I., & Salovey, P. (2004). Emotional intelligence and social interaction. *Personality and Social Psychology Bulletin, 30,* 1018–1034.

Lopes, P. N., Côté, S., & Salovey, P. (2006). An ability model of emotional intelligence: Implications for assessment and training. In V. U. Druskat, F. Sala, & G. Mount (Eds.), *Linking emotional intelligence and performance at work: Current research evidence with individuals and groups* (pp. 53–80). Mahwah, NJ: Lawrence Erlbaum Associates.

Lopes, P. N., Salovey, P., Côté, S., & Beers, M. (2005). Emotion regulation ability and the quality of social interaction. *Emotion, 5*(1), 113–118.

Maellero, R. (2011). The effective leader course. In S. Pichler, L. Muse, & B. Beenen (Cochairs), *Managerial interpersonal skills: The state of the science.* Academy of Management meeting.

Mayer, J. D., & Salovey, P. (1997). What is emotional intelligence? In P. Salovey & D. Sluyter (Eds.), *Emotional development and emotional intelligence: Implications for educators* (pp. 3–31). New York: Basic Books.

Mayer, J.D., Salovey, P., Caruso, D., & Sitarenios, G. (2003). Measuring emotional intelligence with the MSCEIT V2.0. *Emotion, 3,* 97–105.

Mintzberg, H. (1973). *The nature of managerial work.* New York: Harper & Row.

Mintzberg, H. (1980). *The nature of managerial work.* Englewood Cliffs, NJ: Prentice-Hall.

Morgeson, F.P., Reider, M.H., & Campion, M.A. (2005). Selecting individuals in team settings: The importance of social skills, personality characteristics, and teamwork knowledge. *Personnel Psychology, 58,* 583–611.

Mumford, T.V., Campion, M.A., & Morgeson, F.P. (2007). The leadership skills strataplex: Leadership skill requirements across organizational levels. *Leadership Quarterly, 18,* 154–166.

Nadler, J., Thompson, L., & Van Boven, L. (2003). Learning negotiation skills: Four models of knowledge creation and transfer. *Management Science, 49*(4), 529–540.

Pavett, C. M., & Lau, A. W. (1983). Managerial work: The influence of hierarchical level and functional specialty. *Academy of Management Journal, 26,* 170–177.

Pfeffer, J., & Fong, C.T. (2002). The end of business schools? Less success than meets the eye. *Academy of Management Learning & Education, 1*(1), 78–95.

Riggio, R.E. (1986). Assessment of basic social skills. *Journal of Personality and Social Psychology, 51,* 649–660.

Riggio, R.E., & Reichard, R.J. (2008). The emotional and social intelligences of effective leadership: An emotional and social skill approach. *Journal of Managerial Psychology, 23,* 169–185.

Robbins, S.P., & Hunsaker, P.L. (2003). *Training in interpersonal skills: Tips for managing people at work.* Upper Saddle River, NJ: Prentice Hall.

Robbins, S. P., & Judge, T. A. (2013). *Organizational behavior.* Upper Saddle River, NJ: Prentice Hall.

Rousseau, D.M. (2005). *I-deals: Idiosyncratic deals workers bargain for themselves.* New York: M.E. Sharpe.

Rubin, R. B., & Dierdorff, E. C. (2009). How relevant is the MBA? Assessing the alignment of required MBA curricula and required managerial competencies, *Academy of Management Learning & Education, 11,* 208–224.

Rubin, R.B., & Martin, M.M. (1994). Development of a measure of interpersonal communication competence. *Communication Research Reports, 11,* 33–44.

Salovey, P., & Mayer, J. D. (1990). Emotional intelligence. *Imagination, Cognition and Personality, 9,* 185–211.

Thorndike, R.L. (1936). Factor analysis of social and abstract intelligence. *Journal of Educational Psychology, 27,* 231–233.

Van de Vliert, E., & Kabanoff, B. (1990). Toward theory based measures of conflict management. *Academy of Management Journal, 33*(1), 199–209.

Van Velsor, E., & Leslie, J.B. (1995). Why executives derail: Perspectives across time and cultures. *Academy of Management Executive, 9*(4), 62–72.

Whetten, D.A., & Cameron, K.S. (2011). *Developing management skills.* Upper Saddle River, NJ: Prentice Hall.

Zhu, W., Riggio, R.E., & Sosik, J.J. (2010). *The effect of authentic transformational leadership on follower and group ethics.* Paper presented at 2010 Academy of Management in Montreal.

3

A Social Skills Model for Understanding the Foundations of Leader Communication

Ronald E. Riggio

In his seminal work, Mintzberg (1973) observed managers and leaders and concluded that much of the managerial job consisted of communication—face to face, on the telephone, or in written memos and correspondence. Effective and skilled communication is arguably the most basic foundation of leadership. This chapter reports on a nearly 30-year-old model of basic communication skills, and explores how this model can be used as a framework for understanding the most basic components of leader communication. These basic communication skills can be seen as the building blocks for more sophisticated interpersonal and influence skills. In addition to presenting the model, this chapter discusses relevant research as well as potential applications to leader development.

A MODEL FOR BASIC SOCIAL/COMMUNICATION SKILLS

Beginning in the late 1970s, I was working with Howard S. Friedman and other colleagues on exploring measures of individual differences in nonverbal communication skill. Specifically, we were attempting to identify and assess people's abilities to successfully communicate nonverbally. An edited collection by Robert Rosenthal (1979) reviewed much of this research at the time.

The greatest focus in nonverbal communication skill has historically been on the ability to accurately decode nonverbal messages, such as facial cues of emotion. The performance-based measure, the Profile of Nonverbal Sensitivity (PONS; Rosenthal, Hall, DiMatteo, Rogers, & Archer,

1979), is a noteworthy (albeit dated) example of this line of research. The PONS is a film/video test of nonverbal decoding skill that presents an actress displaying nonverbal cues in various channels (facial, body, vocal cues). An individual's decoding accuracy is assessed by the percentage of correctly decoded video segments. Researchers also made early attempts to measure ability to accurately encode or send nonverbal/emotional messages through both performance-based and self-report measures (e.g., Buck, 1978; Friedman, Prince, Riggio, & DiMatteo, 1980; Zuckerman & Larrance, 1979).

For the most part, researchers were interested only in particular nonverbal communication skills, such as encoding and decoding ability, ability to detect nonverbal cues of deception (De Paulo & Rosenthal, 1979a, 1979b), and ability to monitor and control nonverbal displays (Snyder, 1974). A comprehensive model was not available, so a program of research was launched to attempt to define and assess, not only the broad domain of nonverbal skills, but to also include skills in verbal/social communication. The latter was stimulated by the early, but long-abandoned, research on social intelligence (Thorndike, 1920; Thorndike & Stein, 1937). The result of this program of research is the Social Skills Model, which will be described shortly.

It is interesting to note that much of the research on nonverbal skill was used as a foundation for the now popular construct of emotional intelligence (EI; Goleman, 1995; Salovey & Mayer, 1990), particularly what is known as the "abilities model" of emotional intelligence (Mayer & Salovey, 1997; Mayer, Salovey, & Caruso, 2000). For example, one component of the abilities model of EI is "accurately perceiving emotions in self and others." This is directly related to nonverbal/emotional decoding skill. Another EI component is "managing emotions," which is similar to the notion of controlling the display and experience of one's emotions, which is considered a key nonverbal/emotional skill. More recent, and also discussed in this volume, is the notion of emotional and social competences as a way of understanding the foundation of interpersonal skills (see Cherniss, 2000; Cherniss & Boyatzis, this volume).

The Social Skills Model is relatively straightforward and based on the model for dyadic communication typically illustrated in basic communication courses. According to the model, there are three basic communication skills: encoding or *expressiveness*, decoding or *sensitivity*, and regulation or *control*. Each of these skills operates in both the nonverbal or *emotional*

TABLE 3.1

The Basic Social/Communication Skill Dimensions

Emotional/Nonverbal Skills	
Emotional Expressiveness:	Skill in sending (encoding) nonverbal and emotional messages. Persons high in EE are spontaneously expressive, animated, and often referred to as charismatic.
Emotional Sensitivity:	Skill in receiving (decoding) emotional and nonverbal messages. Persons high in ES are emotionally empathic, observant, and responsive to others' feelings, but may be susceptible to "emotional contagion."
Emotional Control:	Skill in regulating and controlling the expression of emotional messages. Persons high in EC seem emotionally distant, but are able to mask felt emotional states with a different emotional expression.
Social/Verbal Skills	
Social Expressiveness:	Verbal speaking skill and the ability to engage others in conversation. SE is related to, but distinct from, being outgoing and extraverted.
Social Sensitivity:	Verbal decoding skill (listening ability), but also involves one's knowledge of social rules and conventions. In extremes, SS can lead to social anxiety and withdrawal.
Social Control:	Sophisticated social role-playing skill. SC is related to being tactful and socially competent.

and the verbal or *social* domains. The result is the six basic communication skills presented in Table 3.1.

Although the model seems simplistic, the specific skill dimensions are actually quite complex and most are multifaceted. These six basic skills are assessed via the Social Skills Inventory (SSI) self-report, which is a 90-item measure, with 15 items assessing each of the six skills. The SSI was first introduced in a validity study (Riggio, 1986), and was published in a revised version by Consulting Psychologists Press (Riggio, 1989), and more recently by Mind Garden (Riggio & Carney, 2003). Since their initial validation, the Social Skills Model and the SSI have been used for assessing and developing the basic communication skills that are so essential for effective leadership. We review some of that research later.

What follows is a more detailed definition of each of the basic social skill dimensions.

EMOTIONAL/NONVERBAL SKILLS

In the Social Skills Model, the terms *emotional* and *nonverbal* are used more or less interchangeably because communication of emotion is primarily nonverbal in nature. We can verbally label emotions, but to truly communicate happiness, anger, or sadness, the nonverbal cues of these emotions—facial expression, tone of voice, gestures, and posture—need to be appropriate and clearly displayed. Therefore, one half of the Social Skills Model is represented by skill in emotional/nonverbal communication.

Emotional Expressiveness

Emotional expressiveness is the ability to accurately convey nonverbal cues of emotions to others. It is linked to temperament in that some individuals are naturally more emotionally expressive. Emotionally expressive persons are typically animated, with facial expressions and body movements that convey emotions—both positive and negative. As the saying goes, emotionally expressive persons "wear their hearts on their sleeves," so it is easy for others to know their emotions and feelings.

Research on emotional expressiveness has suggested that it is a key element of "personal charisma" (Friedman et al., 1980; Riggio, 1986, 1987), and that connection has important implications for charismatic leadership, as we shall see. Persons possessing high levels of emotional expressiveness are well liked in initial encounters, have wider and deeper social support networks, and seem to connect well and easily with others (Friedman, Riggio, & Casella, 1988; Riggio, 1986).

Emotional Sensitivity

The construct of emotional sensitivity is the ability to accurately decode the emotions and feelings of others. As scholars have noted, skill in emotional decoding/sensitivity has received the most research attention (see Hall & Bernieri, 2001). Persons possessing emotional sensitivity are attentive to others' emotions and nonverbal cues, and because of their ability to read emotions, they are often described as "empathic." Indeed, research has demonstrated a connection between the personality trait of empathy and nonverbal decoding skill (Riggio, Tucker, & Coffaro, 1989).

In extremes, emotional sensitivity can become problematic. Extreme emotional sensitivity can lead one to become prone to "emotional contagion" effects—vicariously feeling the emotions of others. I later argue that balance among the various emotional and social skill dimensions is needed for effective communication/social skills.

Emotional Control

Ability to regulate and control nonverbal and emotional displays is labeled "emotional control." In recent years, the regulation of emotions has received a great deal of research attention (Gross, 2007, 2008). Emotion regulation has to do with both intrapersonal and interpersonal emotional regulation, while emotional control from the Social Skills Model is primarily about interpersonal regulation of the display of emotional messages and cues.

Persons possessing emotional control can stifle and control their display of emotions and present a different emotional display to cover up a felt emotion (i.e., putting on a happy face to cover sadness or anger). In extremes, emotional control, particularly if the individual lacks emotional expressiveness, can lead to the impression that the individual is emotionally cold and distant, but combined with emotional expressiveness, individuals possessing emotional control are good emotional actors.

SOCIAL/VERBAL SKILLS

While the second half of the Social Skills Model consists of the more social-cognitive communication skill counterparts of the emotional skills—expressiveness, sensitivity, and control—they are more complex. These skills include verbal communication in the sending, receiving, and regulation of verbal messages, but they also include complex abilities to read social situations, understand subtle social norms, respond to social cues, adhere to social scripts, and regulate one's own social behavior. Collectively, these skills are best represented by the terms *social competence* or *social intelligence*.

Social Expressiveness

The ability to speak spontaneously and to engage others in social inter-action is termed *social expressiveness*. Although social expressiveness is correlated with extraversion, it represents the skill that extraverted (and emotionally expressive) individuals use to engage others. Socially expres-sive persons are good public speakers and skilled in making small talk. They are comfortable and confident in social encounters, and this leads to greater participation in social interaction and more positive first impres-sions (Riggio, 1986).

Social Sensitivity

Social sensitivity is the most complex of the basic social skill dimensions. It includes verbal decoding skill and sensitivity to the nuances of verbal communication, ability to read social situations, and knowledge of social norms and scripts (i.e., understanding appropriate and inappropriate behavior in typical social situations). Social sensitivity allows an individual to monitor his or her actions in social situations and determine what is appropriate and tactful.

In extremes, however, social sensitivity can be quite problematic. Too much social sensitivity can lead to self-consciousness and a tendency to overanalyze social situations and over critique one's own social behavior. As a result, there is a slight to moderate correlation with social anxiety.

Social Control

The final dimension is *social control,* which is a sophisticated social role-playing skill. Persons scoring high on social control are poised, tactful, and confident in all types of social situations and are able to regulate social interactions (and their own social behavior). Social control is a core ele-ment of what makes people appear socially competent. It is very consistent with notions of social intelligence.

The SSI and the model look at both the amount of each skill dimen-sion, but also the balance or equilibrium among the various social skills. An equilibrium index operates as a warning indicator that some com-bination of low and high social skill dimensions can be problematic. For example, high levels of emotional expressiveness and low levels of emotional control suggests a person who is hyper-animated and emotionally unrestrained. The opposite pattern—low expressiveness and high emotional control—suggests a person who appears emotionally withdrawn and distant. Looking at the entire profile—the amount of each social skill dimension and the balance or imbalance among the various dimensions—provides insight into communication patterns that may be either beneficial or detrimental to the establishment and maintenance of key social relationships, and has obvious relevance to the leader-follower relationship.

The total score on the SSI provides a general indication of an individual's possession of emotional and social competences, and has been used in a number of research studies. In general, total score on the SSI has predicted several social outcomes. For example, total SSI score is positively correlated with effectiveness in initial interactions (Riggio, 1986), measures of psychosocial adjustment, and the depth and quality of social support networks (Riggio & Zimmerman, 1991), and is negatively correlated with loneliness, shyness, and social maladjustment (Riggio, Watring, & Throckmorton, 1993; Segrin & Flora, 2000). The equilibrium index of the SSI has also been associated with psychopathology, with imbalance in the various social skill dimensions associated with greater pathological symptoms in outpatients from mental hospitals (Perez & Riggio, 2003; Perez, Riggio, & Kopelowicz, 2007). In summary, possession of basic communication skills and a well-balanced profile of these skills are predictive of positive social outcomes and have important implications for leader emergence and leadership effectiveness.

EMOTIONAL/NONVERBAL SKILLS AND LEADERSHIP

The surge in interest in emotional intelligence has led to the belief that a great deal of leadership involves the intellectual processing and communication of emotions (e.g., Caruso & Salovey, 2004; Goleman, 1998). This is in direct contrast to traditional and historical models of effective leadership, which focused primarily on leader cognitive skills: decision making (e.g., Vroom & Yetton, 1973), setting direction (e.g., Conger, Spreitzer, & Lawler, 1999), goal setting (e.g., Locke & Latham, 1984), and strategy (Adair, 2010; Cannella, Finkelstein, & Hambrick, 2009). Although effective leadership does involve a focus on the leadership task and the decisions a leader must make, research dating back to the Ohio State and University of Michigan studies (e.g., Bass & Bass, 2008; Riggio, 2006) noted that task focus was only half of the successful leadership equation. A concern with people—the "people skills" of a leader—was just as important. So bringing emotions into leadership was a logical progression, because emotions, and emotional communication in particular, should be critical to the development of strong leader-follower relationships.

The past dozen or so years has seen great interest in leader emotions, so it makes sense that skill in emotional communication would be implicated in leader effectiveness. The Social Skills Model allows us to examine in some detail how basic emotional skills may relate to leadership. Beginning with emotional expressiveness, the most obvious connection is between ability to express emotions and ability to arouse or inspire followers. Emotional expressiveness has long been thought a key element of inspirational and charismatic leadership (Bass, 1990; Riggio, 1987). A growing body of research demonstrates that emotional expressiveness is an important part of what causes people to label a leader as charismatic. For instance, research by Awamleh and Gardner (1999) showed that speakers who exhibited more emotionally expressive nonverbal behaviors were considered charismatic, and studies that manipulate charisma in leaders require them to exhibit the nonverbal cues associated with emotional expressiveness, including animated facial expressions, tone of voice, and gestures (e.g., Cherulnik, Donley, Wiewel, & Miller, 2001; Shea & Howell, 1999; see also Darioly and Schmid Mast, this volume). Groves's (2006) research suggests that emotionally expressive leaders are actually more effective than are nonexpressive leaders, and the expression of positive emotions is believed to be associated with effective leadership beyond charismatic/transformational leaders (Connelly & Ruark, 2010). It is, in fact, the ability to express emotions, and create an emotional contagion process, whereby followers become infected with the charismatic leader's emotions, that is believed to be at the heart of the charismatic leader's ability to inspire and influence followers (Bono & Ilies, 2006; Cherulnik et al., 2001; Riggio, 1987).

Emotional sensitivity is also implicated in successful leadership by virtue of the need for leaders to establish strong relationships and emotional bonds with followers. As a foundation, leaders need to be able to decode followers' emotions in order to address their concerns, understand what followers are feeling, and to recognize and manage followers' negative emotions (Thiel, Connelly, & Griffith, 2012). Studies have found that emotional decoding skill is related to leader emergence and transformational leadership behavior (Rubin, Munz, & Bommer, 2005; Walter, Cole, der Vegt, Rubin, & Bommer, 2012). As mentioned, there is a connection between emotional sensitivity and empathy, and research suggests that empathic leaders are more successful (Kellett, Humphrey, & Sleeth, 2002, 2006).

Emotional control is also theoretically important for effective leadership. In many circumstances, leaders must control their display of emotions— particularly negative emotions associated with anger, stress, or fear. It is easy to imagine that a leader must appear calm, cool, and collected in a crisis to lead effectively. However, too much emotional control, on a day-to-day basis, can lead followers to believe that the leader is cold and emotionally unresponsive. Again, the notion of balance between emotional skills/ competencies is critical. Research on emotion management and the implications for leadership (and leader development) are discussed in great depth by Shane Connelly and colleagues in chapter 6 of this book.

An obvious concern that relates to leader emotional control is the notion of "emotional labor," which is regulating and managing the display of emotions in line with the normative requirements of the organization or the position (Ashforth & Humphrey, 1993; Hochschild, 1983). The emotional labor required by leaders may, over time, take a toll in terms of the well-being of the leader, although this has been largely unexplored.

In summary, emotional skills contribute to effective leadership in many ways, ranging from the expressive skills required to motivate and inspire followers, to the emotional sensitivity necessary to develop close interpersonal relationships, to the ability to control and regulate emotions in order to effectively play the role of leader. Gooty, Connelly, Griffith, and Gupta (2010) provide an excellent and detailed review of research on leadership and emotions, which includes sections on emotional competencies/skills.

SOCIAL/VERBAL SKILLS AND LEADERSHIP

While emotional skills and competencies are important for effective leadership, our research has suggested that social skills/competencies may be even more important. This makes sense because social skills involve sophisticated understanding of social norms, roles, and scripts, and leadership itself is a complex social role. While emotions clearly play a part in effective leadership, the leadership relationship may be less of an emotional one than other interpersonal relationships (e.g., spouses/lovers, friends, family members). Indeed, emotions are more restrained in the workplace than in the home because of display rules that limit the expression of emotions at work. For example, emotional outbursts—both positive and negative—are likely more pronounced with friends and loved ones than with coworkers.

Particularly important in enacting the leadership role are the skills of social expressiveness and social control. Social expressiveness is verbal speaking skill and ability to engage others in social interactions. This skill is important in formal and informal communication and relationship building, but also relates to the impression a leader makes. High-level leaders are often called upon to represent the group through formal speeches and presentations. Social control is a sophisticated role-playing skill, and relates to both leader impression management and sociability. The combination of these two skills—social expressiveness and social control—has been labeled "savoir-faire," which translates to "knowing how to do" in social situations (Riggio, Eaton, & Funder, 2010). In fact, a recent study found that this combination of social skills completely mediated the relationship between extraversion and leadership potential in a general population of adults (Guerin et al., 2011). The social skills associated with savoir-faire appear to account for the relationship often found between extraversion and leadership (e.g., Bono & Judge, 2004). In other words, it is not extraversion itself that relates to leadership effectiveness, but the extravert's ability to channel extraversion through skilled social performance.

The theoretical relationship between the skill of social sensitivity and leadership is likely more complex. Social sensitivity involves attentiveness to social cues and situations, and an awareness of how one's own behavior affects others. As a result, it is likely important in building good interpersonal relationships, so there is an expected positive relationship with good leadership. However, social sensitivity has not been shown to be related to leadership emergence or effectiveness, likely because socially sensitive individuals tend to be cautious and analytical in social relationships and emerging as a leader requires a sort of bold, "devil-may-care" attitude that is incompatible with social sensitivity. Theoretically, social sensitivity plays a part in the leader's ability to be attentive to others, to monitor and govern his or her own behavior, and may be related somewhat to leader humility. More research is needed.

Our research is just beginning to explore the relationships among the various social skill dimensions and aspects of leadership. Early studies used the total score on the SSI as a general measure of social competence and found relationships between total SSI score and various measures of social effectiveness, including effectiveness in social relationships (Funder, Furr, & Colvin, 2000); the depth and breadth of social support networks (Riggio & Zimmerman, 1991); appearing truthful and honest (Riggio, Tucker, & Throckmorton, 1987); and psychological constructs such as empathy, self-confidence/efficacy, and a reversed relationship with measures of shyness and social anxiety (see Riggio & Carney, 2003 for an overview).

Related more to leader emergence and leadership potential/effectiveness, the total score on the SSI was found to be predictive of success in mock hiring interviews (Riggio & Throckmorton, 1988) and to performance in a managerial/leadership assessment center (Riggio, Aguirre, Mayes, Belloli, & Kubiak, 1997). In experimental studies, Riggio, Riggio, Salinas, and Cole (2003) found that social skills (total SSI score) predicted who was selected as a leader in student teams, and leaders high on social skills were more effective leaders, particularly on tasks that involved team interaction. Research and informal observation has also suggested that social skills scores increase with managerial level in organizations. For example, in a study of fire service officers, higher-level officers (chiefs) tended to be more socially skilled than captains (Riggio et al., 2003).

In summary, we have used the Social Skills Model to examine social behavior in a variety of settings, but most recently in an effort to directly study the role that possession of basic communication and social skills play in leader emergence and effectiveness. The next section sets out an agenda for future research on social communication skills and leadership, and also discusses our efforts to develop these social skills and the implications for leader development.

SOCIAL SKILLS AND LEADERSHIP: IMPLICATIONS FOR RESEARCH, PRACTICE, AND LEADER DEVELOPMENT

One reason that it is difficult to study the interpersonal skills necessary for effective leadership is the lack of frameworks for operationalizing interpersonal skills, and a lack of measurement tools. Pichler and Beenen lay out in chapter 2 an empirically derived framework for leader/managerial interpersonal skills, and other chapters talk about other means and frameworks. The approach discussed here—the Social Skills

Model—takes leader interpersonal skills to their barest essentials, the core elements of interpersonal communication—sending, receiving, and regulation of messages, verbal and nonverbal.

Although leader interpersonal skills are nearly always mentioned as important to leadership success, scholars have conducted remarkably little empirical research on the topic. Given this scarcity of research, research on leader interpersonal skills can take innumerable directions. A major goal of this chapter is to introduce the Social Skills Model as one avenue for investigation of the individual characteristics that are the building blocks of leaders and leadership. Here are some of the possible research directions hinted at by the research discussed earlier:

First, there has been renewed interest in the role of individual differences as predictors of leadership, as suggested by a recent special issue of *The Leadership Quarterly* on "Leadership and Individual Differences." This is partially driven by a revival of interest in leader personality traits, but also by the introduction of new individual differences such as emotional and social intelligence and leader character, as well as interest in the genetic determinants of leadership. These individual differences are seen as the precursors of leader behaviors (Antonakis, Day, & Schyns, 2012). Yet, long ago, scholars argued that interpersonal skills, such as nonverbal expressiveness and sensitivity, are the "manifestations" of personality traits, and that such skills are more proximal to behaviors than traits (Friedman, 1979). Our research that suggested that trait extraversion was mediated by possession of social skills argues that a skill-based approach may be a more productive approach than a trait-based approach for research precision, but also in terms of leader selection and (especially) development (i.e., researchers see traits as difficult to alter, but see skills as more malleable).

Second, analyzing leadership using an interpersonal skills framework will allow us to shed light on the process of leadership. For example, the very popular theory of Transformational Leadership states that it is made up of four components: Inspirational Motivation, Idealized Influence, Individualized Consideration, and Intellectual Stimulation (Bass & Riggio, 2006). Research using the basic social skills could shed light on how transformational leaders enact these components. For example, we assume that expressive skills, both nonverbal/emotional expression and verbal fluency, are critical in the transformational leader's ability to inspire and motivate. Skills in expression and control would be important in the ability of the transformational leader to enact Idealized Influence—in particular

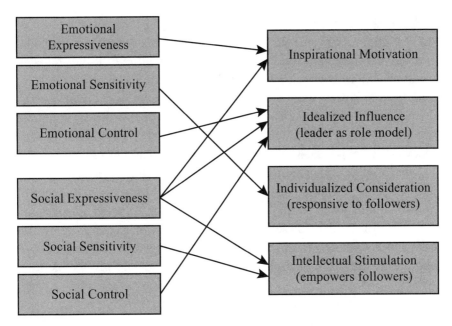

FIGURE 3.1
Social skills and transformational leadership

Idealized Influence would be related to the savoir-faire elements of social expressiveness and social control. Figure 3.1 illustrates the hypothesized relationships that should exist between the various skills in the Social Skill Model and the four components of transformational leadership.

As noted in Figure 3.1, emotional sensitivity is theoretically linked to a transformational leader's Individualized Consideration (being empathic and responsive to followers). Ability to decode emotional expressions in others is a well-researched skill, and many means exist to measure possession of emotional decoding skill/sensitivity (Hall & Bernieri, 2001). This skill approach may prove more precise in understanding the dynamics of Individualized Consideration than research focusing on trait empathy.

Interesting, research on emotional sensitivity and interpersonal sensitivity suggests that women may have an advantage over men in this skill (Hall, 1990). This may explain why women have more transformational leadership qualities than do men (Eagly, Johannesen-Schmidt, & Van Engen, 2003). In other words, women have a social skill advantage that enhances certain components of transformational leadership behavior (i.e., Individualized Consideration).

Again, this is only the tip of the research iceberg. Many other aspects of leadership may be investigated through a social skills lens. For example, an entire line of research could look at the dyadic nature of leader-follower communication, focusing on the shared social communication skills between leaders and followers, and noticing systematic disconnects or breakdowns in the communication process. This approach might be consistent with, and enhance our understanding of, other leadership theories, such as Leader-Member Exchange (LMX) Theory (Graen & Uhl-Bien, 1995).

What are the implications of the Social Skill Model for leader development? Over the past 25 years, we have focused on the development of nonverbal and social skills. The SSI has been used as a diagnostic starting point for many of these development efforts. Managers, leaders, and others have completed the self-report SSI and received detailed feedback to guide communication and social skill improvement. This is sometimes accompanied by subordinate or peer ratings of the managers' communication strengths and weaknesses. [We are currently working on validating an other-rated, 360-degree feedback version of the SSI.] For example, in many instances, managers have been surprised to find out that they have relatively low scores on the sensitivity scales of the SSI, and coupled with low ratings from followers on "effective listening," this revelation is often the trigger needed for the managers to participate in a listening skill development program.

Over the years, we have embarked on experimental programs to enhance basic communication and social skills, and have developed methodologies and exercises for skill development. We recently published a manual for professional trainers to guide the development of social skills, which is available from Mind Garden (www.mindgarden.com), the publisher of the SSI. This manual (Riggio & Merlin, 2011) contains a variety of exercises as well as instructions on how to use the SSI and other assessment methods to provide baseline measurements of trainees' possession of social skills.

Evidence suggests that efforts to improve nonverbal and social skills are successful; however, these are abstract and complex skills and require a great deal of time and effort to develop. Two notable examples of experimental skill training programs are dissertations by Taylor (2002) and Nodarse (2009), which both used social skill training, based on the Social Skills Model, to guide the development of communication and leader charisma. Both studies found increases in social skills (in particular, they found enhancements in how "leader-like" participants looked after training), but such gains depend on the length of the development program and the participants' motivation to develop.

SUMMARY AND CONCLUSIONS

This chapter presented the Social Skills Model as a framework to guide research and development on leader interpersonal ("soft") skills. The Social Skills Model was intended to focus on general communication skills, not leader skills per se. However, it has obvious applications to leadership and fits well with existing and popular leadership theories, particularly those that focus on leader communication and interpersonal relationship development as core components of effective leadership. Other frameworks can be used to guide leader interpersonal skill development, but these reside in the communication literature, particularly in the realm of clinical psychology. For decades interpersonal and communication skills have been targeted for development in married couples (e.g., Gottman, 1999, 2011), in shy individuals (e.g., Carducci, 1999; Zimbardo, 1977), and in a variety of clinical/psychopathological populations (e.g., Bellack, Mueser, Gingerich, & Agresta, 2004). Some of these frameworks and methodologies might be adapted for leadership development.

Research has demonstrated the validity and efficacy of the Social Skills Model for communication and social skill assessment and development, and we are continuing to conduct research on the social skills–leadership relationship, as well as evaluating the effectiveness of social skills training for leaders/managers. We believe that this is a promising area for research and leadership development.

REFERENCES

Adair, J. (2010). *Strategic leadership: How to think and plan strategically and provide direction.* London: Kogan Page.

Antonakis, J., Day, D. V., & Schyns, B. (2012). Leadership and individual differences: At the cusp of a renaissance. *Leadership Quarterly, 23,* 643–650.

Ashforth, B. E., & Humphrey, R. H. (1993). Emotional labor in service roles: The influence of identity. *Academy of Management Review, 18,* 88–115.

Awamleh, R. A., & Gardner, W. L. (1999). Perceptions of leader effectiveness and charisma: The effects of vision content, delivery, and organizational performance. *Leadership Quarterly, 10,* 345–373.

Bass, B.M. (1990). *Bass & Stogdill's handbook of leadership* (3rd ed.). New York: Free Press.

Bass, B.M., & Bass, R. (2008). *The Bass handbook of leadership* (4th ed.). New York: Free Press.

Bass, B.M., & Riggio, R.E. (2006). *Transformational leadership* (2nd ed.). Mahwah, NJ: Lawrence Erlbaum.

Bellack, A.S., Mueser, K.T., Gingerich, S., & Agresta, J. (2004). *Social skills training for schizophrenia.* New York: Guilford.

Bono, J.E., & Ilies, R. (2006). Charisma, positive emotions, and mood contagion. *Leadership Quarterly, 17,* 317–334.

Bono, J.E., & Judge, T.A. (2004). Personality and transformational and transactional leadership: A meta-analysis. *Journal of Applied Psychology, 89,* 901–910.

Buck, R. (1978). The slide-viewing technique for measuring nonverbal sending accuracy: A guide for replication. *JSAS Catalog of Selected Documents in Psychology, 63.*

Cannella, B., Finkelstein, S., & Hambrick, D.C. (2009). *Strategic leadership: Theory and research on executives, top management, teams, and boards.* New York: Oxford University Press.

Carducci, B.J. (1999). *Shyness: A bold new approach.* New York: HarperCollins.

Caruso, D.R., & Salovey, P. (2004). *The emotionally intelligent manager: How to develop and use the four key emotional skills of leadership.* San Francisco, CA: Jossey-Bass.

Cherniss, C. (2000). Social and emotional competence in the workplace. In R. Bar-On & J.D.A. Parker (Eds.), *Handbook of emotional intelligence* (pp. 433–458). San Francisco, CA: Jossey-Bass.

Cherulnik, P.D., Donley, K.A., Wiewel, T.S.R., & Miller, S.R. (2001). Charisma is contagious: The effect of leaders' charisma on observers' affect. *Journal of Applied Social Psychology, 31,* 2149–2159.

Conger, J.A., Spreitzer, G.M., & Lawler, E.E. (Eds.) (1999). *The leader's change handbook: An essential guide to setting direction and taking action.* San Francisco, CA: Jossey-Bass.

Connelly, S., & Ruark, G. (2010). Leadership style and activating potential moderators of the relationships among leader emotional displays and outcomes. *Leadership Quarterly, 21,* 745–764.

DePaulo, B.M., & Rosenthal, R. (1979a). Ambivalence, discrepancy, and deception in nonverbal communication. In R. Rosenthal (Ed.), *Skill in nonverbal communication: Individual differences* (pp. 204–248). Cambridge, MA: Oelgeschlager, Gunn & Hain.

DePaulo, B.M., & Rosenthal, R. (1979b). Telling lies. *Journal of Personality and Social Psychology, 37,* 1713–1722.

Eagly, A.H., Johannesen-Schmidt, M.C., & Van Engen, M.L. (2003). Transformational, transactional, and laissez-faire leadership styles: A meta-analysis comparing men and women. *Psychological Bulletin, 129,* 569–591.

Friedman, H.S. (1979). The concept of skill in nonverbal communication: Implications for understanding social interaction. In R. Rosenthal (Ed.), *Skill in nonverbal communication: Individual differences* (pp. 2–27). Cambridge, MA: Oelgeschlager, Gunn, & Hain.

Friedman, H.S., Prince, L.M., Riggio, R.E., & DiMatteo, M.R. (1980). Understanding and assessing nonverbal expressiveness: The Affective Communication Test. *Journal of Personality and Social Psychology, 39,* 333–351.

Friedman, H.S., Riggio, R.E., & Casella, D. (1988). Nonverbal skill, personal charisma, and initial attraction. *Personality and Social Psychology Bulletin, 14,* 203–211.

Funder, D.C., Furr, R.M., & Colvin, C.R. (2000). The Riverside Behavioral Q-sort: A tool for the description of social behavior. *Journal of Personality, 68,* 451–489.

Goleman, D. (1995). *Emotional intelligence.* New York: Bantam.

Goleman, D. (1998). *Working with emotional intelligence.* New York: Bantam.

Gooty, J., Connelly, S., Griffith, J., & Gupta, A. (2010). Leadership, affect and emotions: A state of the science review. *Leadership Quarterly, 21,* 979–1004.

Gottman, J.M. (1999). *The marriage clinic: A scientifically based marital therapy.* New York: Norton.

Gottman, J.M. (2011). *The science of trust: Emotional attunement for couples.* New York: Norton.

Graen, G.B., & Uhl-Bien, M. (1995). Relationship-based approach to leadership: Development of leader-member exchange (LMX) theory of leadership over 25 years: Applying a multi-level, multi-domain perspective. *Leadership Quarterly, 6,* 219–247.

Gross, J.J. (Ed.). (2007). *Handbook of emotion regulation.* New York: Guilford.

Gross, J.J. (2008). Emotion regulation. In M. Lewis, J.M. Haviland-Jones, & L.F. Barrett (Eds.), *Handbook of emotions* (3rd ed., pp. 497–512). New York: Guilford.

Groves, K.S. (2006). Leader emotional expressivity, visionary leadership, and organizational change. *Leadership and Organization Development Journal, 27,* 566–583.

Guerin, D.W., Oliver, P.H., Gottfried, A.W., Gottfried, A.E., Reichard, R.J., & Riggio, R.E. (2011). Childhood and adolescent antecedents of social skills and leadership potential in adulthood: Temperamental approach/withdrawal and extraversion. *Leadership Quarterly, 22*(3), 482–494.

Hall, J.A. (1990). *Nonverbal sex differences: Accuracy of communication and expressive style.* Baltimore, MD: Johns Hopkins University Press.

Hall, J.A., & Bernieri, F.J. (Eds.) (2001). *Interpersonal sensitivity: Theory and measurement.* Mahwah, NJ: Lawrence Erlbaum.

Hochschild, A.R. (1983). *The managed heart.* Berkeley: University of California Press.

Kellett, J.B., Humphrey, R.H., & Sleeth, R.G. (2002). Empathy and complex task performance: Two routes to leadership. *Leadership Quarterly, 13,* 523–544.

Kellett, J.B., Humphrey, R.H., & Sleeth, R.G. (2006). Empathy and the emergence of task and relations leaders. *Leadership Quarterly, 17,* 146–162.

Locke, E.A., & Latham, G.P. (1984). *Goal setting: A motivational technique that works.* Englewood Cliffs, NJ: Prentice-Hall.

Mayer, J.D., & Salovey, P. (1997). What is emotional intelligence? In P. Salovey & D.J. Sluyter (Eds.), *Emotional development and emotional intelligence* (pp. 3–34). New York: Basic Books.

Mayer, J.D., Salovey, P., & Caruso, D.R. (2000). Models of emotional intelligence. In R.J. Sternberg (Ed.), *Handbook of intelligence* (2nd ed., pp. 396–420). New York: Cambridge University Press.

Mintzberg, H. (1973). *The nature of managerial work.* New York: Harper & Row.

Nodarse, B.C. (2009). A nonverbal approach to charismatic leadership training. *Dissertation abstracts international: Section B. Sciences and engineering, 70*(11-B), 7269.

Perez, J.E., & Riggio, R.E. (2003). Nonverbal social skills and pathology. In P. Philippot, R.S. Feldman, & E.J. Coats (Eds.), *Nonverbal behavior in clinical settings* (pp. 17–44). New York: Oxford University Press.

Perez, J.E., Riggio, R.E., & Kopelowicz, A. (2007). Social skill imbalances in mood disorders and schizophrenia. *Personality and Individual Differences, 42,* 27–36.

Riggio, R.E. (1986). Assessment of basic social skills. *Journal of Personality and Social Psychology, 51,* 649–660.

Riggio, R. E. (1987). *The charisma quotient.* New York: Dodd-Mead.

Riggio, R. E. (1989). *Manual for the social skills inventory.* Palo Alto, CA: Consulting Psychologists Press.

Riggio, R. E. (2006). Behavioral approach to leadership. In S. Rogelberg (Ed.), *Encyclopedia of industrial/organizational psychology* (pp. 48–50). Thousand Oaks, CA: Sage.

Riggio, R. E., Aguirre, M., Mayes, B. T., Belloli, C., & Kubiak, C. (1997). The use of assessment center methods for student outcome assessment. *Journal of Social Behavior and Personality, 12,* 273–288.

Riggio, R. E., & Carney, D. C. (2003). *Manual for the social skills inventory* (2nd ed.). Redwood City, CA: Mind Garden.

Riggio, R. E., Eaton, L., & Funder, D. (2010, July). Sophisticated social role-playing skills: The essence of savoir-faire. Paper presented at the meeting of the European Association for Personality Psychology, Brno, Czech Republic.

Riggio, R. E., & Merlin, R. K. (2011). *Social skills training guide: A resource guide for social skill training and development.* Redwood City, CA: Mind Garden.

Riggio, R. E., Riggio, H. R., Salinas, C., & Cole, E. J. (2003). The role of social and emotional communication skills in leader emergence and effectiveness. *Group dynamics: Theory, research, and practice, 7,* 83–103.

Riggio, R. E., & Throckmorton, B. (1988). The relative effects of verbal and nonverbal behavior, appearance, and social skills on evaluations made in hiring interviews. *Journal of Applied Social Psychology, 18,* 331–348.

Riggio, R. E., Tucker, J. S., & Coffaro, D. (1989). Social skills and empathy. *Personality and individual differences, 10,* 93–99.

Riggio, R. E., Tucker, J., & Throckmorton, B. (1987). Social skills and deception ability. *Personality and Social Psychology Bulletin, 13,* 568–577.

Riggio, R. E., Watring, K., & Throckmorton, B. (1993). Social skills, social support, and psychosocial adjustment. *Personality and individual differences, 15,* 275–280.

Riggio, R. E., & Zimmerman, J. A. (1991). Social skills and interpersonal relationships: Influences on social support and support seeking. In W. H. Jones & D. Perlman (Eds.), *Advances in personal relationships* (vol. 2, pp. 133–155). London: Jessica Kingsley Press.

Rosenthal, R. (Ed.). (1979). *Skill in nonverbal communication: Individual differences.* Cambridge, MA: Oelgeschlager, Gunn, & Hain.

Rosenthal, R., Hall, J. A., DiMatteo, M. R., Rogers, P. L., & Archer, D. (1979). *Sensitivity to nonverbal communications: The PONS test.* Baltimore, MD: Johns Hopkins University Press.

Rubin, R. S., Munz, D. C., & Bommer, W. H. (2005). Leading from within: The effects of emotion recognition and personality on transformational leadership behavior. *Academy of Management Journal, 48,* 845–858.

Salovey, P., & Mayer, J. D. (1990). Emotional intelligence. *Imagination, Cognition, & Personality, 9,* 185–211.

Segrin, C., & Flora, J. (2000). Poor social skills are a vulnerability factor in the development of psychosocial problems. *Human Communication Research, 26,* 489–514.

Shea, C. M., & Howell, J. M. (1999). Charismatic leadership and task feedback: A laboratory study of their effects on self-efficacy and performance. *Leadership Quarterly, 10,* 375–396.

Snyder, M. (1974). The self-monitoring of expressive behavior. *Journal of Personality and Social Psychology, 30,* 526–537.

Taylor, S. J. (2002). *Effects of a nonverbal skills training program on perceptions of personal charisma. Dissertation abstracts international: Section B. Sciences and engineering, 63*(2-B), 1091.

Thiel, C. E., Connelly, S., & Griffith, J. A. (2012). Leadership and emotion management for complex tasks: Different emotions, different strategies. *Leadership Quarterly, 23,* 517–533.

Thorndike, E. L. (1920). Intelligence and its uses. *Harper's Magazine, 140,* 227–235.

Thorndike, R. L., & Stein, S. (1937). An evaluation of the attempts to measure social intelligence. *Psychological Bulletin, 34,* 275–285.

Vroom, V. H., & Yetton, P. W. (1973). *Leadership and decision-making.* Pittsburgh, PA: University of Pittsburgh Press.

Walter, F., Cole, M. S., der Vegt, G. S., Rubin, R. S., & Bommer, W. H. (2012). Emotion recognition and emergent leadership: Unraveling mediating mechanisms and boundary conditions. *Leadership Quarterly, 23*(5), 977–991.

Zimbardo, P. G. (1977). *Shyness: What it is. What to do about it.* New York: Jove.

Zuckerman, M., & Larrance, D. (1979). Individual differences in perceived encoding and decoding abilities. In R. Rosenthal (Ed.), *Skill in nonverbal communication: Individual differences* (pp. 171–203). Cambridge, MA: Oelgeschlager, Gunn, & Hain.

Section II

Leader Emotional Competencies

4

Using a Multilevel Theory of Performance Based on Emotional Intelligence to Conceptualize and Develop "Soft" Leader Skills

Cary Cherniss and Richard E. Boyatzis

Leadership research and theory has long emphasized the importance of so-called soft skills for leader effectiveness. These include specific interpersonal and communication skills such as active listening, providing feedback effectively, and dealing with conflict. Soft skills also could involve more general abilities such as empathy, assertiveness, and resilience. One of the earliest and most respected leadership development programs, the "Human Relations Training Program," which was developed at Pennsylvania State University in the 1950s, taught many of these skills (Hand, Richards, & Slocum, 1973). More recent leader development programs have continued to emphasize training in skills such as "motivating, coaching, giving direction, and providing positive and negative feedback" (Hunt & Baruch, 2003).

Much of the research on leadership effectiveness also points to the importance of emotional and interpersonal abilities. From the classic distinction between task-oriented and relationship-oriented behaviors (Fleishman, 1955; Likert, 1961; Stogdill & Coons, 1957) to the more recent work on leader-member exchange (Graen & Uhl-Bien, 1995) and transformational leadership (Bass & Riggio, 2006), research has pointed to the importance of social and emotional competencies for effective leadership.

Thus, for decades we have known that many personal and interpersonal skills are important for effective leadership, but what has been missing is a "theory of performance" for thinking about how these different abilities are related to each other as well as to performance. Also, while both researchers and practitioners have recognized the existence of a common thread connecting these abilities, the labels they have developed for it, such as soft skills, have not been very satisfying.

In this chapter, we introduce a theory of performance based on *emotional intelligence* (EI) and *emotional and social competence* (ESC) and suggest how it provides a promising way of organizing many of the abilities that are so important for effective leadership. In the first part of the chapter we clarify what is meant by EI and briefly summarize a few studies suggesting a link to leader effectiveness. Next we describe four major models of EI and note the assessment methods associated with each. Then we present a theory of performance based on a broader multilevel theory of personality, and we show how it can help clarify the relationship between the various EI models. We also show how other ways of conceptualizing interpersonal leader skills can be integrated using the theory. In the last part of the chapter we suggest implications for leadership development efforts and describe two programs that illustrate those implications. We also note implications for future research and theory on leadership.

THE CONCEPT OF EMOTIONAL INTELLIGENCE AND ITS ROLE IN EFFECTIVE LEADERSHIP

A rising young executive in a large steel company, who had just been assigned to a new group the week before, joined his management team when it met with one of the company's biggest customers, a major car company. The meeting did not go well. He found himself sitting in a room with more than 20 engineers from the car company who told him that his company was near the bottom on their list of suppliers. "We were lousy in everything—quality, on-time delivery, invoicing—everything," he later said.

When asked about his personal reactions during that meeting, he said, "I had a 'holy shit' moment! I had been in the job literally a week. So part of it was, 'Oh my God, what the hell am I going to do?' Also I thought about how my new team had been in the business for awhile, and I thought, 'What the hell have you guys been doing here?'" As his anxiety rose and his anger simmered, this leader's initial response was to think to himself, "I'm going to clean house!"

But then he realized that "you just can't react viscerally every time something comes up because it scares people away." He also realized that it would be counterproductive to express any of his negative emotions when he was in the room with the customer. So he calmed down and, as he left the meeting with his battered group, he said, "We're going to meet in my office at 8 tomorrow morning. Until then, think about how we got here and what we should do to fix it."

The next day this leader started the meeting by calmly asking his management team, "What's going on?" Rather than assigning blame or trying to motivate the group with fiery exhortations, he wanted first to find out what was contributing to the problems that the customer had identified. As the team members responded with their own concerns, explanations, and justifications, the leader just listened and occasionally responded with a head nod or a paraphrase to make sure he understood them correctly. He did not react judgmentally or defensively. "I didn't think about it at the time," he later said, "but that first couple of hours was very cathartic for them."

After that meeting the whole team pulled together and worked hard to fix the problems. The result was impressive. "That car company will tell you they never saw any business turn around that quickly in one year. And as a result they began giving us more business."

This incident illustrates the importance of *emotional intelligence* (EI) for leadership. By EI we mean "*The ability to perceive and express emotion, assimilate emotion in thought, understand and reason with emotion, and regulate emotion in the self and others*" (Mayer, Salovey, & Caruso, 2000, p. 396). In this example, the new team leader demonstrated EI in several ways. He initially reacted to the client company's harsh criticism with anxiety and anger; however, he was aware of these reactions and the negative impact they could have. Rather than become overwhelmed with those feelings, he managed to calm himself down. So he demonstrated EI first by *perceiving* what was happening to him on an emotional level, and he *understood* that reacting "viscerally" would be counterproductive because it "just scares people away." Then he *used* that awareness and insight to *manage* his emotions. This resulted in his acting differently and, hopefully, in a more effective manner.

Although the leader calmed himself in a way that allowed his anger and anxiety to subside, he did not completely suppress all emotion. He *used* that emotional arousal to mobilize his team when it met the next day. But during that meeting, he again displayed EI when he started off by listening to his team members rather than blaming them or exhorting them to do better. This was the first major behavioral change he showed. Then, he again showed skill in *managing their* emotions when he inspired them to take on the challenge of fixing the problems that the client had identified. This was the second major behavioral change (from his earlier patterns and initial feelings in the situation). Thus, in a number of ways, this leader perceived, understood, used, and managed his emotions and those of others in dealing with this major crisis.

This example also illustrates how EI is related to other emotional and social abilities that those interested in leadership have studied. For instance, the leader's ability to perceive and understand his own emotions and those of others helped him to *empathize* with his team and to *listen* to them more effectively. His ability to manage and express his own emotions enabled him to maintain a *positive outlook* and to *motivate* and *inspire* his team. It is not difficult to see how the basic emotional abilities that comprise EI provide a foundation for other emotional and social competencies, including the kinds of soft skills often taught in leadership development programs.

A growing body of research supports a link between EI and leadership success. For instance, one study found that EI was correlated with ratings of achieved business outcomes ($r = .26$) and effective personal behavior ($r = .50$) in a group of executives employed by a large public service company (Rosete & Ciarrochi, 2005). EI predicted leadership performance in this study over and above what personality and cognitive intelligence predicted. Analogous findings with sales leaders showed that effectiveness was a function of the behavior of EI and SI (social intelligence), and it was greater than the impact of personality and cognitive intelligence (Boyatzis, Good, & Massa, 2012). Côté, Lopes, Salovey, and Miners (2010), in two studies of leadership emergence in groups, also found that EI predicted outcomes over and above personality and cognitive intelligence.

Another study, using a multi-rater measure of EI (the Swinburne University Emotional Intelligence Test), found that EI scores correlated with annual performance appraisals ($r = .25$) for a group of leaders working in a division of a global manufacturing company (Semadar, Robins, & Ferris, 2006). Several other studies also have found evidence supporting the link between EI and leadership effectiveness (Carmeli, 2003; Langhorn, 2004; Sy, Tram, & O'Hara, 2006; Wong & Law, 2002).

DIFFERENT MODELS AND MEASURES OF EI

Although most EI theorists seem to agree with this basic definition of EI (Cherniss, 2010), controversy has arisen over which personal qualities should be included. Theorists also disagree over the best way to measure these skills and abilities. As a result, several different models of EI have emerged during the past two decades.

Mayer, Salovey, and Caruso's (2008) four-branch ability model focuses on a few basic mental abilities that involve the processing of emotional information but are distinct from cognitive intelligence as well as most personality traits. The abilities are perceiving, using, understanding, and managing emotion. These abilities are usually measured with the Mayer-Salovey-Caruso Emotional Intelligence Test (MSCEIT), which, like a traditional intelligence test, consists of a series of puzzle-like tasks. An example is an emotion-perception subtest that asks the test taker to identify what emotions are expressed in pictures of faces.

Other models reflect a more expansive view of EI that is not so closely tied to the traditional notion of intelligence. These models are sometimes referred to as "mixed models" because they include elements of personality, motivation, and social skills as well as emotional abilities. Bar-On's (2006) model of emotional and social intelligence and Petrides's "trait" model of EI (Petrides, Pita, & Kokkinaki, 2007) include traits such as self-confidence, assertiveness, and empathy. These approaches utilize self-report measures, such as Bar-On's original version of the EQ-i and Petrides's Trait Emotional Intelligence Questionnaire (TEIQue), that closely resemble traditional personality tests. One other model, now referred to as the *behavioral approach*, also includes a wide range of personal traits, motives, and abilities (Boyatzis, 2009). However, this approach uses a multi-rater assessment, the Emotional and Social Competence Inventory (ESCI), to measure how these personal qualities are manifested in the work setting.

USING A MULTILEVEL THEORY OF PERSONALITY TO INTEGRATE THE DIFFERENT MODELS INTO AN EI-BASED THEORY OF PERFORMANCE

Although some researchers see these different models as competitors for the right to be considered the "true EI" model (Ashkanasy & Daus, 2005), others have proposed that we view them as complementary. In an earlier paper, Cherniss (2010) suggested that the four core abilities comprising the Mayer-Salovey-Caruso model seem to represent a specific kind of *intelligence*, which provides the *foundation* for the different emotional

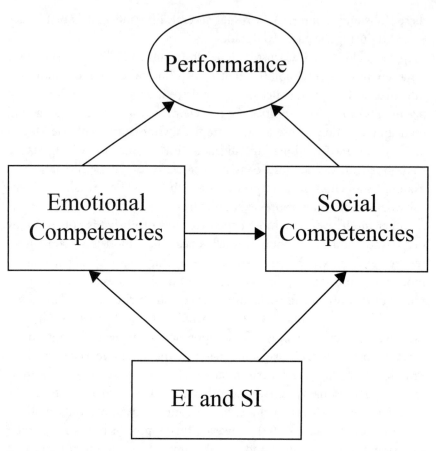

FIGURE 4.1
The relationship between EI, ESCs, and performance

and social *competencies* included in the other models. In other words, the basic EI abilities determine one's aptitude for learning and using the ESCs that are most important for effective performance, as shown in Figure 4.1. For instance, a basic EI ability such as emotion perception provides the potential for developing an EI competency such as conflict management—a person who scores high in the perception of emotion has the potential to be adept at managing conflict. However, conflict management is a competency that still must be learned (Cherniss, 2010).

The concept of an emotional or social competency in this view has a special meaning. Boyatzis (1982) defined a competency as: "Any characteristic of the person that leads to or causes effective or superior performance."

Building on this definition, Goleman defined an "emotional competence" as a "learned capability based on emotional intelligence which results in outstanding performance at work" (2001, p. 27). A social competence is a learned capability based on social intelligence (Goleman, 2006).

Building on this initial formulation, we believe that EI and ESC can be viewed as different *levels* of EI within a holistic theory of personality (Boyatzis, 2009). This theory also can provide a framework for thinking about other soft skills necessary for effective leadership and for integrating findings from various measures that may be assessing different levels of a phenomenon rather than different characteristics.

In this view, five distinct levels of personality represent what goes on within the person. The first is the physiological level consisting of neural and endocrine systems. The second level includes unconscious dispositions, such as motives, aptitudes, traits, and abilities. The third and fourth levels are made up of self-schema, which include a person's values and self-image. The fifth level consists of behavioral patterns that are observable in a particular context, such as the work setting. The five levels are interrelated; each level affects and is affected by the adjoining level. People's unconscious motives, traits, and abilities affect what they value and how they view themselves and others. Those values and beliefs, in turn, affect people's observable behavior patterns, as shown in Figure 4.2.

The ordering of the levels is based on three factors. The first is *emergence*: the higher-level competencies emerge from the lower-level core EI abilities. This aspect is consistent with our earlier notion that EI provides the foundation or aptitude for ESCs. The second factor is degree of *conscious awareness*. Levels 1 and 2 involve unconscious processes and traits. We normally are not aware of the neural mechanisms underlying our self-perceptions and behavior. Similarly, we are unaware of our EI (and sometimes are poor judges of it) unless we take a test like the MSCEIT and see our scores. The level 3 traits are somewhat more accessible to our awareness. Most of us can readily report accurately on what we most value. However, we usually need some help in identifying our underlying philosophical orientations. Level 4 competencies are by definition those that we recognize in ourselves.

The ordering of the levels also is based to some extent on degrees of *stability*. Lower-level aspects of the personality tend to be more stable and difficult to change, particularly after childhood. Our values and philosophical orientations are somewhat more malleable, but change at this level still is rare. The competencies at levels 4 and 5 are relatively easier to modify.

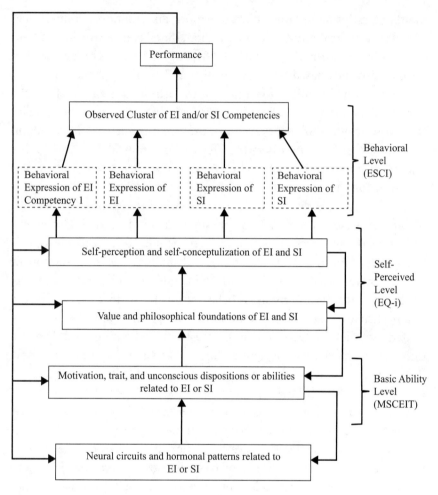

FIGURE 4.2
Emotional intelligence (EI), social intelligence (SI), and emotional and social competencies as multiple levels within the personality structure (adapted from Boyatzis, 2009; Boyatzis, Goleman, & Rhee, 2000)

These distinctions between the different levels may not hold up in every case. Some aspects of the self-image (level 4), for instance, may prove as stable as some values (level 3). But in general the higher-level characteristics are more accessible to consciousness and less stable than deeper-level traits and abilities. Also, they seem to build on those deeper-level characteristics.

The idea of a multilevel theory of personality is not new. The Boyatzis theory, which builds on an earlier formulation by McClelland (1951), also is similar to two more recent personality theories. McAdams (1996) proposed that there are three "tiers": traits and dispositions, goals and motives, and sense of self. These tiers closely resemble levels 2, 3, and 4 in the Boyatzis theory. Sheldon's multilevel theory of personality also has a level labeled "goals and motives," with another level called "self/narratives" right above it (Sheldon, Cheng, & Hilpert, 2011). Like Boyatzis, Sheldon and McAdams believe that higher-level personality characteristics emerge from lower levels.

However, all of these theorists recognize that while lower-level factors influence higher-level ones, many other factors shape the personality profile at higher levels. The theory predicts that a leader who scores high in emotion perception, a level 2 characteristic, is more likely to be viewed as empathic by those who work with him, but many other factors will influence how empathic the leader is perceived to be in a particular role and setting.

Boyatzis's theory is a general theory of personality. Figure 4.2 shows how we have used it to develop a more specific *theory of performance based on EI*. It shows more clearly than our earlier formulation (Cherniss, 2010) how the ESCs included in various models of EI are linked to the core EI abilities that make up the Mayer-Salovey-Caruso model, and how both EI and the EI (or SI) based competencies are related to performance. It is meant to include only ESCs that emerge from EI or SI. This is why we often refer to these ESCs as EI or SI competencies.

We have placed the core EI abilities at level 2 because, like other kinds of intelligence, they are highly stable dispositions that are outside of conscious awareness and based on specific neurological structures and processes (Goleman, 2001). The theory also suggests that ESCs such as values and philosophical orientations found at level 3 will be more strongly predictive of performance than the core EI abilities, but not as predictive as the self-perceptions found in EI models utilizing self-report measures, which belong at level 4. The EI and SI competencies in the behavioral model belong at level 5, closest to actual performance, because they are based on behaviors in context as observed by those who work closely with the individual. Also, the EI and SI competencies in the behavioral model were developed inductively, based on numerous studies comparing superior performers to average ones (Boyatzis, 1982; Spencer & Spencer, 1993).

This multilevel theory of personality also suggests that different measures of EI and SI tend to be linked to different levels of the personality. For instance, Mayer and colleagues' ability model, as measured by the MSCEIT, seems to tap into the core emotional abilities that are not directly observable or easily inferred to either the individual or others. Models that rely on self-report measures of traits such as empathy or positive outlook (e.g., Bar-On's model as measured by the EQ-i) seem to focus on the self-perception level. Boyatzis's behavioral approach, utilizing the ESCI, a multi-rater instrument, seems to be linked to the level of observed competencies, as is the use of behavioral coding of audiotaped critical incidents from work (Ryan, Emmerling, & Spencer, 2009; Spencer & Spencer, 1993) or videotapes of simulations or group projects (Boyatzis, Stubbs, & Taylor, 2002).

For a better understanding of the multilevel theory of performance based on EI, consider a characteristic such as empathy. Decety (2011) has discovered a particular circuit in the brain that seems to be part of the neurological foundation of empathy (level 1). When one perceives someone else in distress, this circuit is activated, which leads to an aversive response. This circuit also provides information that may inhibit aggression and trigger motivation to help. If this finding is confirmed, differences in the functioning of this circuit could be associated with differences in the ability to empathize with others.

We also can see aspects of empathy at the second level. The Faces subtest on the MSCEIT, as well as similar measures of a person's ability to perceive nonverbal behavior accurately (e.g., the DANVA or PONS), assess underlying aptitudes and abilities that facilitate empathic behavior. At the third level, that of operating philosophy, Boyatzis, Murphy, and Wheeler (2000) showed a humanistic operating philosophy to be predictive of two social competencies—understanding and relating to others—as observed in work samples through critical incident interviews and videotaped group simulations. At the fourth level, self-report EI measures such as the EQ-i assess empathy with items such as, "I'm good at understanding the way other people feel" (Bar-On, 2004). Finally, a multi-rater instrument such as the ESCI assesses empathy at the behavioral level by asking a number of people who know the target person to indicate through a set of descriptors like "Understands others by listening attentively" how often the person displays empathy.

This multilevel theory of performance suggests that EI and its vicissitudes exist at many different levels within the human organism and that some of the controversy and confusion about the different models may reflect a difference in levels. The multilevel theory of personality also suggests why there is a relatively small correlation between the measures based on the different models of EI (Mayer, Salovey, & Caruso, 2008). It is not that they are measuring unrelated constructs. Rather, they are measuring different levels of the same construct.

The EI abilities and ESCs in the various models are not particularly new; most have been studied for decades. But the theory suggests that the different constructs and measures are interrelated in a particular way, and this insight can be quite useful. It suggests, for instance, that if we are interested in teaching leaders how to manage relationships better, we should focus initially on the most relevant observed competencies and self-perceptions (levels 5 and 4), for these are more malleable and more strongly linked to performance than deeper-level values, traits, and aptitudes. But we also might need to address these deeper-level characteristics because they provide the foundation for the others. We explore this idea further in the section on leadership development.

Empirical Evidence Relating to the Theory

If this multilevel theory of performance is valid, then ESCs should be more strongly correlated with performance than the core abilities of EI as measured by the MSCEIT and similar tests because they are closer to the enactment of the behavior that produces job or life outcomes and performance. Although scholars have performed no direct tests of this prediction, two recent meta-analyses do provide relevant data. In the first, Joseph and Newman (2010) found that the overall correlation between measures of EI (e.g., the MSCEIT) and performance was .18, while the correlation between performance and measures of ESC (e.g., the EQ-i, ESCI, or TEIQue) was .47. This finding seems to support the theory. However, the results of the other meta-analysis were not as supportive. O'Boyle, Humphrey, Pollack, Hawver, & Story (2011) found that the overall correlation between EI and performance was .24, while the correlation for ESC was .28. Thus the first study supported the theory while the second one did not. Which one is more valid?

A closer examination of the two meta-analyses suggests that they used different standards for selecting studies based on the criterion measure. In the one supporting the theory, the researchers only used studies in which performance was based on supervisory ratings. The other meta-analysis included several studies based on self-report ratings. While this increased the overall N, it probably distorted the criterion score; a substantial body of research shows that self-report ratings of performance tend to be inflated, and they are only weakly correlated with supervisory, peer, or subordinate ratings (Atkins & Wood, 2002). Including studies based on self-report measures thus may have weakened the observed correlation between ESCs and performance in the second meta-analysis.

Applying the Multilevel Theory of EI to Other Constructs and Models

This multilevel theory of EI also provides a way of conceptualizing the relationship between EI and other personal and interpersonal leadership skills linked to leadership effectiveness. Skills such as active listening, deciphering who is telling the truth, or delivering tough messages can be thought of as built on the core EI abilities. More basic emotional abilities also can be incorporated into the EI-based theory of performance.

For instance, the Diagnostic Analysis of Nonverbal Accuracy (DANVA) (Nowicki & Duke, 1994) and the Japanese and Caucasian Brief Affect Recognition Test (JACBART) (Matsumoto et al., 2000) measure *accuracy of emotion perception* by presenting pictures of faces, gestures, and postures or recordings of voice tone to participants whose task is to identify correctly the emotion expressed. Although based on communication theory, these abilities closely resemble one of the core EI abilities, emotion perception, and thus could be thought of as another measure of that EI ability (Mayer, Roberts, & Barsade, 2008). Similarly, a skill such as "social control" in Riggio's (1986) Social Skills Model involves a person's ability to *influence* others and thus is similar to one of the social competencies measured by the ESCI. And like influence, social control should be related to EI, but it should be a stronger predictor of performance than any of the core EI abilities.

Many of the other skills and abilities described in this volume similarly could be integrated conceptually through this multilevel EI theory. For instance, consider Beenen, Pichler, and Muse's "Big Five Managerial Interpersonal Skills" or Treadway and Douglas's "political skill." One could use a self-report instrument to measure these skills or a multi-rater approach. The self-report measure would tap self-perceptions that might well be linked to measures of values and philosophical orientation. The multi-rater measure should be more strongly linked to performance. However, the self-perception measures should be better predictors of performance than a measure of EI abilities such as the MSCEIT. It is expected that a self-assessment method would incorporate an internal review and synthesis of feedback from others, as well as one's memory and evaluation of performance over recent history. Meanwhile, a direct ability or performance ability measure would lack the integration of information from these other sources of feedback. If a person recalls others' feedback with some degree of accuracy, then the composite self-view would incorporate information from sources who have observed a person's performance, and therefore, should be a closer reflection of actual performance. Similarly, these interpersonal leadership skills should be more strongly related to SI competencies, such as influence, conflict management, or team work than to the underlying EI abilities. Thus, the multilevel theory of EI seems to provide a way of unifying and integrating much of the previous and current work on soft leadership skills.

IMPLICATIONS OF THE MULTILEVEL THEORY OF EI FOR LEADERSHIP DEVELOPMENT

The multilevel theory of EI also can be used to address some of the most important questions relating to leadership development. For instance, it provides a strategic perspective on which skills and abilities should be taught. Specifically, the theory suggests that we should focus initially on those EI and SI competencies at levels 4 and 5 because they are most strongly linked to leadership effectiveness. It also makes sense to target level 5 competencies because that is where the most meaningful change occurs; and when people are engaged in change efforts, they are working predominantly at the behavioral level, as Cherniss and Adler (2000) showed in their review of published evidence of training impact on EI. Their review highlighted "model programs" that showed rigorous results in improvement of EI-related competencies as a result of a training or development effort *and* were published in a peer-reviewed journal. The review scanned all published literature over the prior 50 years. Although not the intent in the search, it was a curious observation that these programs tended to focus on the behavioral levels of EI or SI, and not changes in traits, values, self-image, or physiological levels of EI.

However, we also should assess the participants at more basic levels, such as self-perceptions, values, and the more basic EI abilities, which provide the foundation for these EI and SI competencies, because it might not be practical to try teaching the competencies to individuals who lack the necessary foundation at more basic levels. For instance, trying to teach a leader to act more empathically probably will be very difficult and time consuming if it goes against the individual's basic values. Greater empathy also might prove elusive if the individual is weak in basic EI abilities such as emotion perception and understanding. For those individuals, it might be more effective to help them develop compensatory strategies that could enable them to function better if they find themselves in leadership positions, rather than have them participate in frustrating and embarrassing development efforts that focus on their weaknesses.

It makes good sense to focus development efforts initially on observable ESCs because considerable evidence shows that many ESCs can be developed (Burke & Day, 1986; Cherniss & Adler, 2000); however it is not clear whether the core EI abilities can be improved much after childhood. There appears to be only one unpublished study suggesting that the core EI abilities as measured by the MSCEIT can be developed in adults. It was a doctoral dissertation involving 79 college students enrolled in a psychology of adjustment course with a similar number of students in a comparison group. Evaluation data suggested that a semester-long EI development program associated with the course did bring about an improvement in MSCEIT scores (Chang, 2006). One flaw with the study, however, is that the comparison group was not equivalent to the group receiving the intervention. While the students in the intervention group were in psychology of adjustment courses, the students in the comparison group were enrolled in a survey of psychology course. Also, most of the students in the intervention group were from the University of Hawaii, while the comparison group came from community colleges. Furthermore, the intervention group scored significantly higher in EI at pretest than did the comparison group. In addition to the lack of comparability in the two groups, there was no long-term follow-up; the students' post intervention EI was only measured at the end of the courses, so it is not clear whether the observed changes in EI were sustained once the class ended. Thus, until there is stronger evidence suggesting that the core abilities of EI can be improved, it probably makes more sense to target ESCs that are easier to improve and also more directly tied to leadership effectiveness.

A well-known example of a leadership development approach that targets the most critical competencies are the MBA programs at the Weatherhead School of Management (Boyatzis & Saatcioglu, 2008). A core part of these programs has been a first-year course in which students undergo in-depth assessment activities and then receive extensive feedback and guidance in formulating personal development plans. Both the assessment and development efforts focus on about two dozen competencies that have been studied for more than 30 years and found to be linked to effective organizational leadership (Boyatzis, 1982; Spencer & Spencer, 1993).

Students who have participated in the competency-based program have been compared with groups of students who went through more traditional programs. Boyatzis and Saatcioglu (2008) reviewed 17 longitudinal studies of the program's impact on developing EI competencies such as initiative, flexibility, empathy, persuasiveness, and self-control. Results showed improvements of 60% to 70% during the two years of the full-time MBA program, and 55% to 65% improvement during the three to five years of the part-time MBA program. And these improvements persisted up to seven years. In contrast, students from two other highly ranked business schools showed an improvement of only 2% in EI competencies (Boyatzis and Saatcioglu, 2008). And students from four other high-ranking MBA programs showed a gain of only 4% in the self-awareness and self-management competencies while declining 3% in the social awareness and relationship management competencies (Boyatzis et al., 2002). Prior to 2000, only a few MBA programs (e.g., the University of Michigan or Boston University) addressed these soft skills. With the requirement of outcome assessment by accrediting agencies and increased competitive pressure among programs, most MBA programs now have some form of workshops or courses addressing these interpersonal or actionable skills or competencies. However, the amount of attention devoted to the development of these competencies, and the quality of that attention, still varies greatly.

Another example of leadership development designed to focus on the competencies most important for performance was a study by Spencer (2001). He began by comparing two groups of managers in a large industrial controls firm. One group consisted of outstanding performers while the other was made up of more typical leaders. This initial study yielded four ESCs that were especially important for effective performance. Spencer then developed a training program in which he: (1) showed the participants what the competencies looked like; (2) assessed them on the competencies;

(3) fed back the results of the assessment; and (4) helped the participants set goals for developing one of the competencies. An evaluation study involving a matched comparison group found that the managers who participated in the competency-based training program posted $3.1 million in revenue during the following year on average, compared to $1.7 million posted by the untrained group (Spencer, 2001).

A distinctive aspect of Spencer's approach is that it took into account the context when determining which emotional and interpersonal abilities to target. As Jordan, Dasborough, Daus, & Ashkanasy (2010) pointed out, the significance of any EI-related ability for performance depends on the context. In Spencer's approach, the development effort began with a study that identified the most important competencies in the trainees' own context. Information gathered during that study also enabled the program developers to come up with clear and concrete descriptions of the competencies as they were used in context.

IMPLICATIONS FOR FUTURE RESEARCH

The multilevel theory of performance based on EI points to a number of implications for future research. To start, we need to explore further how valid the theory is. Two meta-analyses that indirectly tested part of the theory came up with conflicting findings. Future research needs to go beyond meta-analysis and test the theory more directly. Specifically, we need research that compares the predictive validity of core EI abilities as measured by the MSCEIT and ESCs as measured by self-report measures and multi-rater assessments. The theory predicts that certain ESCs will be stronger predictors of effective leadership than the core EI abilities. However, it also predicts a modest association between EI and ESC. Future research testing the theory also should include measures of values and philosophical orientations that seem important for leadership effectiveness as well as any underlying neural or hormonal variables. Multivariate research using structural equation modeling and other techniques might be especially useful in exploring the validity of the multilevel theory of EI.

Another area for future research is to explore the interrelationships of the different ESCs that have been identified and expand the scope to include other models of personal and interpersonal skills or abilities. How, for instance, do the specific skills and abilities covered in Riggio's (1986) communications-oriented model relate to EI, other ESCs, and leadership performance? The theory points to a nomological network for these different concepts that can be further explored in future research.

Ultimately the most interesting and important area for future research involves leadership development applications. One question requiring further study relates to the relative malleability of the different levels of EI (Riggio & Lee, 2007). Are ESCs measured at the behavioral and self-perception levels easier to develop than the core EI abilities? Can changes in core EI abilities be sustained? A related question involves which ESCs to target for development. The answer probably will depend on the context: One might want to focus on different ESCs depending on the kinds of challenges that leaders are facing and expect to face in the next few months. The self-directed learning approach as used by Spencer and Boyatzis provides a relatively efficient way of making leadership development context specific (Boyatzis, 2001). Future research should compare development programs based on self-directed learning with those utilizing other approaches.

The multilevel theory also suggests that we might use more comprehensive assessment methods, such as those used in assessment centers, to determine how information from the multiple levels helps a person develop in different ways. Also, organizations should offer a broad assortment of development alternatives.

Ultimately, we need to conduct research on various populations, with various methods, attempting to improve EI at various levels to help us understand which developmental approach will lead to the most positive and sustained change in leadership effectiveness.

CONCLUSION

For decades we have known that many personal and interpersonal skills are important for effective leadership, and numerous leadership development programs have tried to develop them. What has been missing is a comprehensive framework for thinking about how these different abilities are related to each other and to performance. Both researchers and practitioners have recognized that a common thread connects these abilities, but the labels they have developed for it, such as soft skills, have not been very satisfying. The recent work on emotional intelligence suggests a way of unifying this disparate body of work. More specifically, a theory of performance based on EI and derived from a broader multilevel theory of personality provides a single nomological network for these skills and abilities as well as a strategic blueprint for leadership development efforts.

REFERENCES

Ashkanasy, N.M., & Daus, C.S. (2005). Rumors of the death of emotional intelligence in organizational behavior are vastly exaggerated. *Journal of Organizational Behavior, 26*, 441–452.

Atkins, P.W.B., & Wood, R.E. (2002). Self- versus others' ratings as predictors of assessment center ratings: Validation evidence for 360-degree feedback programs. *Personnel Psychology, 55*, 871–904.

Bar-On, R. (2004). The Bar-On Emotional Quotient Inventory (EQ-i): Rationale, description, and summary of psychometric properties. In G. Geher (Ed.), *The measurement of emotional intelligence: Common ground and controversy* (pp. 115–145). Hauppage, NY: Nova Science.

Bar-On, R. (2006). The Bar-On model of emotional-social intelligence (ESI). *Psicothema, 18*(supl.), 13–25.

Bass, B.M., & Riggio, R.E. (2006). *Transformational leadership* (2nd ed.). Mahwah, NJ: Lawrence Erlbaum.

Boyatzis, R.E. (1982). *The competent manager: A model for effective performance.* New York: John Wiley and Sons.

Boyatzis, R.E. (2001). How and why individuals are able to develop emotional intelligence. In C. Cherniss & D. Goleman (Eds.), *The emotionally intelligent workplace: How to select for, measure, and improve emotional intelligence in individuals, groups, and organizations* (pp. 234–253). San Francisco, CA: Jossey-Bass.

Boyatzis, R.E. (2009). Competencies as a behavioral approach to emotional intelligence. *Journal of Management Development, 28*(9), 749–770.

Boyatzis, R. E., Goleman, D., & Rhee, K. S. (2000). Clustering competence in emotional intelligence: Insights from the Emotional Competence Inventory. In R. Bar-On & J.D.A. Parker (Eds.), *The handbook of emotional intelligence: Theory, development, assessment, and application at home, school, and in the workplace* (pp. 343–362). San Francisco, CA: Jossey-Bass.

Boyatzis, R. E., Good, D., & Massa, R. (2012). Emotional, social, and cognitive intelligence and personality as predictors of sales leadership performance. *Journal of Leadership & Organizational Studies, 19*(2), 191–201.

Boyatzis, R.E., Murphy, A., & Wheeler, J. (2000). Philosophy as the missing link between values and behavior. *Psychological Reports, 86*, 47–64.

Boyatzis, R.E., & Saatcioglu, A. (2008). A twenty-year view of trying to develop emotional, social and cognitive intelligence competencies in graduate management education. *Journal of Management Development, 27*, 92–108.

Boyatzis, R.E., Stubbs, E.C., & Taylor, S.N. (2002). Learning cognitive and emotional intelligence competencies through graduate management education. *Academy of Management Journal on Learning and Education, 1*, 150–162.

Burke, M., & Day, R. (1986). A cumulative study of the effectiveness of managerial training. *Journal of Applied Psychology, 71*, 232–245.

Carmeli, A. (2003). The relationship between emotional intelligence and work attitudes, behavior and outcomes: An examination among senior managers. *Journal of Managerial Psychology, 18*(8), 788–813.

Chang, K.B.T. (2006). *Can we teach emotional intelligence?* (Unpublished doctoral dissertation). University of Hawai'i.

Cherniss, C. (2010). Emotional intelligence: Towards clarification of a concept. *Industrial and Organizational Psychology: Perspectives on Science and Practice, 3*, 110–126.

Cherniss, C., & Adler, M. (2000). *Promoting emotional intelligence in organizations.* Alexandria, VA: ASTD.

Côté, S., Lopes, P.N., Salovey, P., & Miners, C.T.H. (2010). Emotional intelligence and leadership emergence in small groups. *Leadership Quarterly, 21*, 496–508.

Decety, J. (2011). The neuroevolution of empathy. *Annals of the New York Academy of Sciences, 1231*, 35–45.

Fleishman, E.A. (1955). Leadership climate, human relations training, and supervisory behavior. *Personnel Psychology, 6*, 205–222.

Goleman, D. (2001). An EI-based theory of performance. In C. Cherniss & D. Goleman (Eds.), *The emotionally intelligent workplace: How to select for, measure, and improve emotional intelligence in individuals, groups, and organizations* (pp. 27–44). San Francisco, CA: Jossey-Bass.

Goleman, D. (2006). *Social intelligence.* New York: Bantam.

Graen, G.B., & Uhl-Bien, M. (1995). Relationship-based approach to leadership: Development of leader-member exchange (LMX) theory of leadership over 25 years: Applying a multi-level multi-domain perspective. *Leadership Quarterly, 6*, 219–247.

Hand, H.H., Richards, M.D., & Slocum, J.W. (1973). Organizational climate and the effectiveness of a human relations training program. *Academy of Management Journal, 16*(2), 185–195.

Hunt, J.W., & Baruch, Y. (2003). Developing top managers: The impact of interpersonal skills training. *Journal of Management Development, 22*, 729–752.

Jordan, P.J., Dasborough, M.T., Daus, C.S., & Ashkanasy, N.M. (2010). A call to context. *Industrial and Organizational Psychology: Perspectives on Science and Practice, 3*.

Joseph, D.L., & Newman, D.A. (2010). Emotional intelligence: An integrative meta-analysis and cascading model. *Journal of Applied Psychology, 95*, 54–78.

Langhorn, S. (2004). How emotional intelligence can improve management performance. *International Journal of Contemporary Hospitality Management, 16*, 220–230.

Likert, R. (1961). *New patterns of management.* New York: McGraw-Hill.

Matsumoto, D., LeRoux, J.A., Wilson-Cohn, C., Raroque, J., Kooken, K., Ekman, P., et al. (2000). A new test to measure emotion recognition ability: Matsumoto and Ekman's Japanese and Caucasian Brief Affect Recognition Test (JACBART). *Journal of Nonverbal Behavior, 24*, 179–209.

Mayer, J.D., Roberts, R.D., & Barsade, S.G. (2008). Human abilities: Emotional intelligence. *Annual Review of Psychology, 59*, 507–536.

Mayer, J.D., Salovey, P., & Caruso, D.R. (2000). Models of emotional intelligence. In R.J. Sternberg (Ed.), *Handbook of intelligence* (2nd ed., pp. 396–420). New York: Cambridge University Press.

Mayer, J.D., Salovey, P., & Caruso, D.R. (2008). Emotional intelligence: New ability or eclectic traits? *American Psychologist, 63*(6), 503–517.

McAdams, D. P. (1996). Personality, modernity, and the storied self: A contemporary framework for studying persons. *Psychological Inquiry, 7,* 295–321.

McClelland, D. C. (1951). *Personality.* New York: William Sloane.

Nowicki, S. J., & Duke, M. P. (1994). Individual differences in the nonverbal communication of affect: The Diagnostic Analysis of Nonverbal Accuracy Scale. *Journal of Nonverbal Behavior, 19,* 9–35.

O'Boyle, E. H., Jr., Humphrey, R. H., Pollack, J. M., Hawver, T. H., & Story, P. A. (2011). The relation between emotional intelligence and job performance: A meta-analysis. *Journal of Organizational Behavior, 32,* 788–818.

Petrides, K. V., Pita, R., & Kokkinaki, F. (2007). The location of trait emotional intelligence in personality factor space. *British Journal of Psychology, 98,* 273–289.

Riggio, R. E. (1986). Assessment of basic social skills. *Journal of Personality and Social Psychology, 51,* 649–660.

Riggio, R. E., & Lee, J. (2007). Emotional and interpersonal competencies and leader development. *Human Resource Management Review, 17,* 418–426.

Rosete, D., & Ciarrochi, J. (2005). Emotional intelligence and its relationship to workplace performance outcomes of leadership effectiveness. *Leadership and Organization Development Journal, 26,* 388–399.

Ryan, G., Emmerling, R. J., & Spencer, L. M. (2009). Distinguishing high performing European executives: The role of emotional, social and cognitive competencies. *Journal of Management Development, 28*(9), 859–875.

Semadar, A., Robins, G., & Ferris, G. R. (2006). Comparing the validity of multiple social effectiveness constructs in the prediction of managerial job performance. *Journal of Organizational Behavior, 27,* 443–461.

Sheldon, K. M., Cheng, C., & Hilpert, J. (2011). Understanding well-being and optimal functioning: Applying the Multilevel Personality in Context (MPIC) model. *Psychological Inquiry, 22*(1), 1–16.

Spencer, L. M. (2001). The economic value of emotional intelligence competencies and EIC-based HR programs. In C. Cherniss & D. Goleman (Eds.), *The emotionally intelligent workplace: How to select for, measure, and improve emotional intelligence in individuals, groups, and organizations* (pp. 45–82). San Francisco, CA: Jossey-Bass.

Spencer, L. M., & Spencer, S. (1993). *Competence at work: Models for superior performance.* New York: John Wiley and Sons.

Stogdill, R. M., & Coons, A. E. (Eds.) (1957). *Leader behavior: Its description and measurement.* Columbus: Ohio State University, Bureau of Business Research.

Sy, T., Tram, S., & O'Hara, L. A. (2006). Relation of employee and manager emotional intelligence to job satisfaction and performance. *Journal of Vocational Behavior, 68,* 461–473.

Wong, C. S., & Law, K. S. (2002). The effect of leader and follower emotional intelligence on performance and attitude: An exploratory study. *Leadership Quarterly, 13,* 243–274.

5

The Role of Nonverbal Behavior in Leadership

An Integrative Review

Annick Darioly and Marianne Schmid Mast

One of the main activities of leaders is interacting with others (e.g., Yukl, 2010). Their interactions with followers, colleagues, or business partners happen through verbal and nonverbal behavior. In this chapter, we focus on leader nonverbal behavior (NVB). NVB plays an important role in interpersonal communication in general and accounts for a majority (about 65%–90%) of the meaning conveyed in social interactions (e.g., Crane & Crane, 2010).

NVB refers to any behavior other than speech content. However, the distinction between verbal and nonverbal behavior is not always clear. For example, "emblems," such as nonverbal gestures like the "okay" made with the thumb and forefinger or the "thumbs up" gesture, have a distinct verbal meaning. But most nonverbal cues are subject to interpretation. A distinction between speech-related NVB and speech-unrelated NVB can be helpful (Knapp & Hall, 2010). Speech-related NVB encompasses, for instance, tone of voice, speech modulation, and speech duration. Examples of speech-unrelated NVB include eye gaze, facial expressions, body movements, posture, touch, smell, mode of dress, and walking style (Knapp & Hall, 2010). Whether verbal or nonverbal behavior matters more as a source of information depends on the situation. In an equivocal situation, NVB is often referred to as a source of information. The more a situation is equivocal, the more important NVB is. People often turn to NVB for information when the NVB contradicts the verbal communication or when individuals doubt the honesty of a verbal communication (e.g., Mehrabian, 1972).

NVB is important for successful social interactions. Its functions include revealing personality characteristics, signaling interpersonal orientations (dominance, friendliness), or expressing emotions (Knapp & Hall, 2010).

When strangers meet for the first time, the impression they form about each other is mostly based on verbal and nonverbal cues (e.g., Ambady, Hallahan, & Rosenthal, 1995; Costanzo & Archer, 1989; Hyde, 2005). Regardless of whether the formed impressions are correct, they affect what one thinks about social interaction partners and how one behaves toward them. In sum, interaction partners express their states and traits—not only but also—through NVB, consciously or unconsciously, and they use NVB to form impressions about others (Mehrabian & Wiener, 1967). This process can be illustrated with the Brunswikian lens model (Brunswik, 1956) (Figure 5.1). Two perspectives are present in the model. On one hand, the model depicts the perceiver who observes the target's NVB and interprets it. The perceiver forms an impression about the target, for example, regarding the target's personality, based on the target's NVB. On the other hand, the model depicts the target and how he or she expresses himself or herself in NVB. Scholars have extensively used the Brunswikian lens model (Brunswik, 1956) to explain accuracy in social perception in different situations, including the leadership context. To illustrate, in a business meeting, on one hand a new employee typically observes the NVB of the individuals present in the meeting and infers who might be the leader through their NVB. This refers to the relationship between the perception of leadership and the observed NVB. On the other hand, the actual leader might speak more and approach more closely than the followers. This describes the relation between an individual's actual leadership and his or her NVB. If the perception of leadership and the actual leadership correspond with each other, this is accuracy. *Accuracy* as we describe it here is one aspect of a person's nonverbal communication abilities (Riggio, 2006). *Nonverbal communication abilities* are understood as individual differences in people's skills to convey nonverbal messages to others, to read others' NVB, and to regulate and control their nonverbal displays (Riggio, 2006). They are part of the domain of interpersonal skills, which are the skills a person uses to properly interact with others (Riggio, Riggio, Salinas, & Cole, 2003).

Nonverbal communication abilities and NVB play an important role in leadership (Stein, 1975). *Leadership* is the process of influencing or controlling the behavior of others in order to reach a shared goal (Northouse, 2007; Stogdill, 1950). It has even been suggested that in the leadership context, nonverbal communication is more important than verbal communication. When the leader's verbal and nonverbal cues are in contradiction, the followers are more likely to trust the leader's nonverbal cues (Remland,

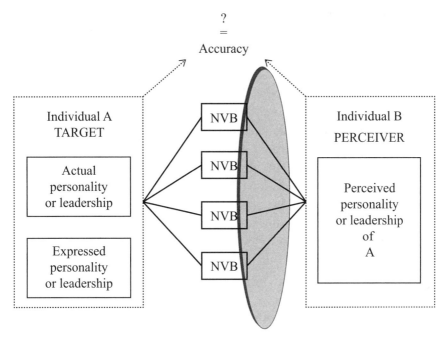

FIGURE 5.1
Leadership and NVB based on the Brunswikian lens model (Brunswik, 1956)

1981). Individuals in leadership positions express their power and authority not only verbally but also nonverbally to get followers' attention and exert influence over them, for example, by being nonverbally persuasive (using greater facial expressiveness and greater fluency and pitch variety; Burgoon, Birk, & Pfau, 1990). A number of studies have documented the effects of leader NVB on leadership effectiveness (i.e., the evaluations of leaders' competence, supportiveness, or success and leaders' effects on followers' satisfaction, motivation, and performance; Kaiser, Hogan, & Craig, 2008). For example, leaders establish a high level of mutual trust, cohesion, and sensitivity to followers' needs by demonstrating abilities to communicate nonverbally (Yukl, 2010). According to Riggio and colleagues, leaders who are able to correctly read and interpret nonverbal cues and act upon this understanding are more likely to exhibit behaviors that meet the needs of their followers (Reichard & Riggio, 2008; Riggio, 1986, 2006; Riggio & Carney, 2003), ultimately resulting in more positive perceptions of the leaders' effectiveness (Riggio et al., 2003). Uhl-Bien (2004) suggests that leaders' nonverbal interpersonal skills are part of the key features needed to build effective leader-follower relationships. Thus NVB is a crucial means through which interpersonal skills lead to effective leadership.

In this chapter, we present an integrative review regarding the role of NVB in leadership. We organize the chapter around the following central questions: Based on which NVB do individuals perceive or infer leadership in emergent hierarchies? Based on which leader NVB do followers perceive effective leadership in actual hierarchies? Which NVB do leaders exhibit? How does leader NVB impact leadership effectiveness? Consequently, the goals of this chapter are (1) to provide an overview of the empirical findings pertaining to NVB in a leadership context; (2) to show how individual differences affect the relation between NVB and leadership; (3) to discuss implications of the reported findings for leaders; and (4) to draw conclusions and make suggestions on how to advance research in this field.

NONVERBAL BEHAVIOR AND THE PERCEPTION OF LEADERSHIP

Nonverbal behavior plays an important part in the perception of leadership. Research on NVB and perceived leadership has focused on two distinct aspects: the role of NVB for *emergent leadership,* and the *perception of leadership* based on NVB. In this section, both aspects are presented and discussed.

NVB and Emergent Leadership

An *emergent leader* is defined as the person who is not assigned a leadership position but arises as a leader within a group (Guastello, 2002; Stein & Heller, 1979). The emergent leader is typically the one who has the most influence in the group (Stein & Heller, 1979). An individual emerges as a leader based on other individuals' perceptions of him or her (e.g., Gray & Densten, 2007; Schyns, Felfe, & Blank, 2007). This mechanism is explained by the Expectation States Theory (EST; Berger, Conner, & Fisek, 1974; Berger, Fisek, Norman, & Zelditch, 1977; Ridgeway & Berger, 1986). According to EST, group members form performance expectations about each other. A *performance expectation* is a "generalized anticipation of one's own or another's capacity to make useful contributions to the task"

(Ridgeway & Berger, 1986, p. 604). To the extent that all group members share these expectations, they become self-fulfilling prophecies. Expectations are affected, especially in relatively homogenous peer groups, by the NVB exhibited by the group members (Ridgeway & Berger, 1986). To illustrate, an individual who talks a lot in a group discussion might be perceived as an expert on the discussion topic, so the performance expectations for this individual are high. As a consequence, this individual is provided with more opportunities to contribute, thus gaining more influence in the group and emerging as the group's leader.

The typical research design to assess emergent leadership is to videotape group interactions, to code the NVB of each group member, and then to compare it with the group members' ratings of each other in terms of leadership (e.g., Baird, 1977; Riggio et al., 2003). Some studies have, however, used external (nongroup members) for assessing the leadership of each group member. To illustrate, in some studies (Moore & Porter, 1988; Schmid Mast, Hall, Murphy, & Colvin, 2003; Stang, 1973), external observers watched different targets and then rated their leadership or dominance (i.e., any behavior aiming at gaining influence over others; Schmid Mast, 2010). The observations yield information about which of the targets' NVB observers use to infer leadership, thus emergent leadership. People use a number of NVBs to infer leadership. For example, gazing more, especially at the end of a statement (Kalma & Van Rooij, 1982) in order to invite others to speak up, is a behavior that emergent leaders exhibit. Also, body movements such as more or fewer arm and shoulder movements contribute to perceptions of emergent leadership (Baird, 1977). The choice of seating can also affect the emergence of a leader (e.g., Heckel, 1973; Porter & Geis, 1981; Ward, 1968). In developed countries at least, leaders are often expected to sit at the head of the table. Speaking time has also been shown to relate to emergent leadership as demonstrated in a meta-analysis by Schmid Mast (2002). *Visual dominance,* defined as the ratio of the percentage of looking while speaking divided by the percentage of looking while listening (Exline, Ellyson, & Long, 1975), also shows a positive link to emergent leadership (Dovidio & Ellyson, 1982).

The most comprehensive meta-analysis on the link between NVB and emergent leadership or perceived dominance stems from Hall, Coast, and Smith LeBeau (2005).[1] Results suggest that many different cues can mark emergent leadership. Individuals are perceived as emergent leaders when they show more gazing, more nodding, and lowered eyebrows.

They are perceived as emergent leaders when they demonstrate less self-touching but more touching others. They are perceived as emergent leaders when they have a more variable tone of voice, a faster speech rate, and a lower voice pitch, as well as when they show more vocal relaxation. Additionally, they are perceived as emergent leaders when they show more erect or tense postures, have more hand and arm gestures, and more body or leg shifts, as well as more body openness. Also, they are perceived as emergent leaders when they interrupt others more often.

NVB and Perceptions of Leadership

The perception of leadership by group members is also important in established hierarchies. The power leaders have depends on how followers perceive them (Hollander & Julian, 1969; Maurer & Lord, 1991; Pfeffer, 1977).

The perception of leadership in an established hierarchy can be understood by using implicit leadership theory (ILT; e.g., Lord, de Vader, & Alliger, 1986; Lord, Foti, & Phillips, 1982). This theory holds that individuals develop a set of beliefs about the characteristics and behaviors of effective and ineffective leaders (e.g., strength, charisma, sensitivity, tyranny) based on previous experiences (Schyns & Schilling, 2010). These beliefs are outside of conscious awareness—they are implicit. Thus, followers use their beliefs to explain and evaluate their leaders' behaviors. Research suggests that the degree of matching that occurs between followers' beliefs and their leaders' behavior partially determines whether followers categorize their leaders as effective or ineffective leaders (Nye, 2002; Nye & Forsyth, 1991; Schyns & Schilling, 2010).

NVB plays a role in leadership perception. For example, Savvas and Schyns (2012) used ILT and pictures of facial expression to investigate how leadership was perceived. Participants reported their beliefs about the characteristics and behaviors of leaders. Then each participant examined a photo of a man in which the facial expression differed (neutral versus raising/lowering and pulling together the eyebrows). Raising and pulling together the eyebrows typically expresses sadness or fear, whereas lowering and pulling together the eyebrows typically expresses anger (Ekman, Friesen, & Hager, 2002). The participants then were asked to evaluate the man in the picture with respect to leadership perception using the same questionnaire in which they reported their beliefs about the characteristics and behaviors of leaders. Results showed that when the participants' beliefs matched how they perceived the man based on his facial expression, the depicted man was evaluated as more leader-like.

In sum, the implicit theories about leader characteristics that followers harbor influence how a leader is perceived. For all of these judgments, perceptions and evaluations of leadership are based on the leader's NVB. In order to complete this overview, it is important not only to understand how leadership is perceived but also how it is expressed through NVB.

NONVERBAL BEHAVIOR AND THE EXPRESSION OF LEADERSHIP

A leader's role is to provide information, to instruct, direct, coordinate, and to give feedback (Mintzberg, 1973). Obviously, encoding or sending nonverbal messages to followers, coworkers, or business partners is part of the leader role. The leader's NVB differs according to the leadership style adopted by the leader (constructive versus destructive). In this section, we review studies in which researchers examined NVB of actual leaders to identify the NVB relevant to constructive and destructive leadership theories.

One of the most effective or constructive leadership styles is the charismatic or transformational leadership style (Bass & Bass, 2008).[2] It results in increased follower satisfaction and more organizational effectiveness (Lowe, Kroeck, & Sivasubramaniam, 1996). This style typically includes NVB such as animated facial expressions, faster rate of speech, and erect posture or expansive body movements (Friedman, Prince, Riggio, & DiMatteo, 1980; Friedman & Riggio, 1981). Charismatic leaders use these nonverbal cues "to move, inspire, or captivate others" (Friedman et al., 1980, p. 133), to express a strong and confident presence, and to stimulate desired responses from followers (Gardner & Avolio, 1998). Even in an experimental setting, it has been shown that the expression of certain NVB makes people judge somebody as charismatic (e.g., Awamleh, 1997; Awamleh & Gardner, 1999; Howell & Frost, 1989; Shea & Howell, 1999). For example, Awamleh and his colleague (Awamleh, 1997; Awamleh & Gardner, 1999) presented videotaped charismatic speeches to participants. The actor was trained to use animated facial expressions and dynamic hand and body gestures, to show vocal fluency, and to maintain eye contact. Results demonstrated that leaders were perceived as charismatic when they exhibited the aforementioned NVB more than when they did not. In a laboratory experiment, Shea and Howell (1999) trained actors to be charismatic or noncharismatic leaders. Charismatic leaders were trained to maintain direct eye contact, to have an animated facial expression, to use a captivating voice tone, to lean forward toward the participants, and to alternate between pacing and sitting on the edge of the desk. Contrastingly, noncharismatic leaders were trained to maintain sporadic eye contact, a neutral tone of voice, and a neutral facial expression. The study showed that charismatic leaders interacting with the participants were perceived as charismatic when they exhibited the corresponding NVB. Consistent with the experimental studies, Groves (2006) examined actual organizational leaders and found that leader nonverbal expressivity was positively related to follower ratings of leader charisma.

In contrast, one of the less effective leadership styles is labeled "destructive leadership" (Schyns & Schilling, 2012). Destructive leaders intentionally or unintentionally affect the activities and relationships within the team or the organization (e.g., attempting to reach higher performance or to bully a follower into leaving) (Schyns & Schilling, 2012). It results in undermining the followers' satisfaction and the organization's effectiveness (Einarsen, Aasland, & Skogstad, 2007). Researchers and scholars have used many concepts to describe destructive leadership, such as "toxic leadership" (Lipman-Blumen, 2005) or "abusive supervision" (Tepper, 2000). Contrary to charismatic leadership research, NVB related to this style has almost never been investigated. In his definition of abusive supervision, Tepper (2000) included the display of NVB excluding physical contact; however, he did not mention specific NVB related to destructive leadership.

Although to date no empirical research has identified the specific NVB relevant to the expressions of destructive leadership, it is of great importance to expand this research area. For instance, researchers might want to clarify which NVB refers to destructive leadership and how destructive NVB impacts leadership effectiveness. At this point a table of the results regarding the role of NVB in leadership is provided (Table 5.1).

NONVERBAL BEHAVIOR AND EFFECTIVE LEADERSHIP

Obviously, the expression of leadership through NVB can be beneficial for leaders in order to be effective. In this section we review some of the

TABLE 5.1

Overview of Results Regarding the Role of NVB in Leadership

NVB Categories	Emergent Leadership/ Perception of Leadership	Expression of Leadership		Effective Leadership					
			Leader's supportiveness	Leader's professional success	Attraction toward the leader	Follower's performance	Satisfaction with leader	Motivation to work with leader	Meeting the leader socially
Smiling			+			+	+	+	+
Gazing/eye contact	+	+	+	+		+[a]	+	+	+
Visual dominance	+								
Lowered eyebrows	+								
Facial expressiveness/ intensity	+	+	+	+			+	+	+
Nodding	+		+						
Self-touch	-								
Other touch		+	+	+					
Hand/arm gestures	+	+			+				
Postural openness	+	+							
Postural relaxation									
Erect posture	+	+							
Forward lean									
Body/leg shifting	+								

(*Continued*)

TABLE 5.1

(Continued)

NVB Categories	Emergent Leadership/Perception of Leadership	Expression of Leadership	Leader's supportiveness	Leader's professional success	Effective Leadership				
					Attraction toward the leader	Follower's performance	Satisfaction with leader	Motivation to work with leader	Meeting the leader socially
Interpersonal distance	-				-	-	-		
Facing orientation		+							
Vocal variability	+	+	+[b]				+[b]	+[b]	+[b]
Interruptions	+		-						
Speaking time[c]	+								
Speech errors	+	-							
Faster rate of speech	+	+							
Lower voice pitch	+			+					
Vocal relaxation	+					+			
Seating position[c]									
Head of table	+								
Edge of the desk							+	+	+

Notes: The categories related to leadership are based on Hall, Coats, and Smith LeBeau's meta-analysis (2005, p. 903).

+ = positive and significant relationship (e.g., more vocal variation, more gesture); − = negative and significant relationship (e.g., less speech errors, less interruption). a. Enlarged pupil size; b. Soft voice; c. three additional NVB categories besides Hall and colleagues' meta-analysis. Blank cells = relations were not tested.

research that demonstrates the role of NVB in leadership effectiveness, integrating both aspects of leadership effectiveness: (1) the evaluations of leaders' competence, supportiveness, or success; and (2) followers' outcomes such as satisfaction, motivation, or follower/team performance (Kaiser et al., 2008).

With respect to NVB and leader evaluation, research shows that leader NVB can convey supportiveness (Remland, Jacobson, & Jones, 1983) and professional success (DePaulo & Friedman, 1998; Shamir, House, & Arthur, 1993). In an experimental study (Remland et al., 1983), Remland and colleagues asked undergraduate students to read a scenario in which different aspects of leader NVB were described and then to evaluate the leaders' supportiveness. Results showed that participants perceived leaders as supportive when they touched their followers, were oriented toward their followers, spoke with a soft voice, smiled with compassion, gazed, and nodded. In contrast, leaders who kept their distance, were leaning back, spoke in a firm voice, interrupted, did not look or smile, and turned away from their followers were perceived as nonsupportive. Moreover, DePaulo and Friedman's review (1998) demonstrated that the display of more eye contact, more gesturing, more smiling, animated facial expressions, and more pitch variation were related to professional success. Research on charismatic leadership shows that more expressive NVB is linked to more leader success (Bass, 1990; Riggio, 1998).

Leader NVB not only impacts the evaluations of leaders, but also follower outcomes. In a work context, according to the Pygmalion theory (Eden, 1990), leaders might adapt their behavior toward their followers in accordance with the leaders' expectations about followers' performance. This behavior, in turn, influences the followers' self-efficacy (Bandura, 1977) and performance (Sutton & Woodman, 1989). This influence can be beneficial as well as detrimental. For instance, if the leader expects increased performance from his or her followers, then the followers indeed show that increase; and if the leader expects decreased performance from them, then the followers show that decrease. Research demonstrated that leaders' NVB is different when interacting with followers of whom they have higher performance expectations than those of whom they have lower performance expectations. However, the difference is undetectable by followers (King, 1971). King (1971) demonstrated the Pygmalion effect in a training program for disadvantaged people using an experimental approach. He randomly selected different individuals as high aptitude personnel (HAP), leading the leaders to expect higher performance from these followers. Results showed that the HAP showed significantly higher performance than the other followers (control group). Post experimental interviews were conducted with the followers to better understand the effect. Two pictures of their leader were shown to the followers: They were identical except that one was modified to make the pupil size of the leader's eyes larger than in the other. Enlarged pupil size is indicative of favorable attitudes toward others (Janisse, 1973). Both the HAP and the control group were asked to choose the picture closest to the way their leader looked at them. The HAP picked pictures with enlarged pupils significantly more often than the control group. However, they did not notice the pupil size difference between pictures. Thus, the way a leader looks at and to his or her followers subconsciously influences the followers' performance.

Also, leaders' NVB can affect followers' satisfaction, motivation, and performance (Tjosvold, 1984). In a laboratory study (Tjosvold, 1984), participants interacted with a leader to complete a task. The leader was either directive or nondirective and behaved in a nonverbally cold or warm manner. Cold NVB consisted of a tough voice, smiling avoidance, stiff facial expression, greater interpersonal distance, and eye contact avoidance, whereas warm NVB included soft and audible tone of voice, smiling, friendly facial expression, closer interpersonal distance, and direct eye contact. Results showed that participants who interacted with a warm leader were satisfied with the leader, perceived the leader as helpful, wanted to work again with the leader, and wanted to meet the leader socially. Moreover, leaders' warm NVB coupled with directive instructions increased followers' productivity, whereas leaders' warm NVB coupled with nondirective instructions decreased followers' productivity. In the same vein, Gaddis, Connelly, and Mumford (2004) demonstrated that after a failure feedback situation in which leaders delivered the feedback in a positive and supportive way (i.e., calm voice and smile), teams performed better on the task than did teams whose leaders displayed negative affect (i.e., tense voice, negative tone of voice). In a recent experimental study, Talley (2012) demonstrated that attraction or repulsion toward a leader can be determined by the leader's hand gestures displayed during a speech. Participants watched a video of a leader using different hand gestures: positive (humility, community, and steepling hands), defensive (hands behind back or in pocket, or crossed arms), and no hand gestures. Results showed that participants perceived positive and defensive hand gestures as more immediate than no hand gestures, which were perceived as distancing. Moreover, leaders with positive hand gestures were perceived as more attractive than leaders with defensive and no hand gestures.

The way leaders use NVB to influence and guide their followers can be explained by the emotional contagion process (see Hatfield, Cacioppo, & Rapson, 1994). This process refers to followers' tendency to automatically imitate and synchronize with the facial expression, postures, tone of voice, or body movements of leaders, mostly unconsciously. This results in emotional convergence between leaders and followers, whereby followers actually feel the mimicked expressions. Empirical evidence supports this. Sullivan and Masters (1988) showed videotaped excerpts of political candidates to participants. The candidates displayed either happy/reassuring (e.g., raised eyebrows, smiles) or neutral facial expressions. Results indicated that changes in participants' attitudes of political support (i.e., measure of warmth toward the candidate) were more likely to be influenced by emotional responses to happy displays than by party identification or assessment of leadership skills. More recently, Cherulnik and colleagues (Cherulnik, Donley, Wiewel, & Miller, 2001) found that followers imitated the nonverbal cues (e.g., smiles) emanated by charismatic leaders during their talks, whereas followers did not imitate the cues of noncharismatic leaders.

We can conclude that leader NVB affects leadership effectiveness most likely through an interactive process between leader expressive NVB and followers' perception of and imitation thereof. Although there is no simple and easy recipe for leadership effectiveness (Eden et al., 2000; White & Locke, 2000), we suggest in the next section that leaders study nonverbal communication to maximize their impact on followers.

IMPORTANCE OF LEADER NVB FOR LEADERSHIP OUTCOMES

As mentioned in the introduction, effective leaders need specific interpersonal skills, and NVB is an important part of the interpersonal skills that lead to effective leadership. In this section, we provide tips on how leaders can learn to improve their nonverbal encoding and decoding skills in order to be effective.

Evidence suggests that leaders can improve their nonverbal expression of leadership through training (e.g., Frese, Beimel, & Schoenborn, 2003; Taylor, 2002; Towler, 2003; Vrij & Mann, 2005). Training of charismatic nonverbal communication (e.g., facial expressions, body gestures, eye contact, and animated voice tone) and of visionary or inspirational verbal content communication (e.g., articulating a vision, using metaphors) both showed an increase in leadership effectiveness. For example, in a study by Towler (2003), participants who received charismatic leadership training exhibited more charismatic behaviors and influenced followers to perform better on a task. In the same vein, such training successfully developed a range of NVB—using gestures, variation of speech, increased speech speed and loudness—that lead to charismatic leadership behavior (Frese et al., 2003). Using a similar approach to the two aforementioned studies, Antonakis, Fenley, and Liechti (2011) also demonstrated in two studies that charismatic leadership training positively influenced evaluations of leader charisma. The results from these studies suggest that charismatic NVB is an acquirable skill.

The skill to accurately decode subtle nonverbal cues is also important for leaders to possess, not only to understand the messages sent by followers, but also for building rapport and for responding to the needs of followers. Evidence shows that leaders might be more skilled in correctly assessing others' states and traits based on observing others' NVB than are followers (Schmid Mast, Jonas, & Hall, 2009). Moreover, accurate assessment of others by leaders is related to positive leadership outcomes, such as increases in follower satisfaction (Byron, 2007; Schmid Mast, Jonas, Klöckner Cronauer, & Darioly, 2012). Although not much is known about the possibility of training leaders' nonverbal decoding skills, Costanzo's (1992) findings suggest that leaders' NVB decoding skills can be improved. The author conducted a study in which participants received either an informational lecture on verbal and nonverbal cues, or training in detecting relevant cues in filmed interactions. In the latter condition, participants watched videotaped excerpts of social interactions and were asked to judge, for instance, the type of relationship among the social interaction partners. Then, the correct answer and the specific nonverbal cues indicative of the correct answer for each scene were pointed out to the participants. Results indicated that only participants who received the detection training significantly improved their skills to correctly interpret NVB.

It seems that it is possible to train leaders and that NVB training for leaders is beneficial for leadership effectiveness. Riggio and colleagues (Riggio, 1989; Riggio & Carney, 2003; Riggio & Reichard, 2008; Riggio et al., 2003) highlight that feedback is important to improve skills in nonverbal decoding and encoding. Leaders can become more aware of their own NVB as well as that of their followers.

LEADERSHIP, NONVERBAL BEHAVIOR, AND INDIVIDUAL DIFFERENCES

Considering leadership as an interactive dynamic between a leader and a follower, it is relevant to take into account the individual characteristics that might impact this dynamic. In this section, we discuss gender, cultural background, and other individual differences that can affect the leadership-NVB link.

Gender and Leadership

Research shows that the gender of the leader plays a significant role in the leadership context. The perception of leadership through NVB might vary according to the gender of the leader. On one hand, leadership is inferred from different NVB for female and male leaders. Perceivers rely more on downward head tilt and lowered eyebrows when assessing the leadership position of women than when assessing leadership in men (Schmid Mast & Hall, 2004b). On the other hand, the same behavior exhibited by a female or male leader results in different perceptions. Women using more eye contact, gesturing, smiling, animated facial expressions, and variations in pitch are seen as more charismatic than men showing the same NVB (Bass & Avolio, 1989).

On the other hand, women and men exhibit different NVB in leadership positions. In a leadership position, men use more expansive body positions, speak more, use a louder voice, and interrupt others more frequently than do women (Hall, 2006). However, female leaders have more expressive faces and maintain closer interpersonal distance than do male leaders (Hall, 2006).

Finally, the same NVB exhibited by female leaders and by male leaders affects followers differently. Assertive and directive behaviors (e.g., speaking first or responding quickly in conversation) are perceived more favorably in male than in female leaders (Eagly & Karau, 2002). This suggests that gender-congruent NVB affects leader perception positively and gender-incongruent NVB hurts the leader.

Although we focus on leader gender, follower gender can also be a moderator of how male or female leaders behave nonverbally and how they are perceived based on their exhibited NVB. Research in leadership emergence suggests that the interaction between the perceiver's gender and the target's gender influences how people infer leadership. For example, the cue of sitting at the end of the table held for leadership emergence (e.g., Heckel, 1973; Porter & Geis, 1981; Ward, 1968), but when individuals had the choice between a man and woman seated at each end of the table, they tended to choose a person of their own sex as leader (Jackson, Engstrom, & Emmers-Sommer, 2007). In regard to leadership position, when female leaders exhibit upright posture, high speech rate, moderate eye contact while speaking, few vocal hesitations, and calm restrained hand gestures, they influence male followers less than a male leader exhibiting similar NVB (Carli, LaFleur, & Loeber, 1995). Female leaders who exhibit the aforementioned NVB were also perceived as less likable by male followers in comparison to men exhibiting similar NVB. However, female leaders who exhibited the aforementioned NVB did not have a differential effect on female followers. For women followers, the woman leader's nonverbal cues did not affect how much followers were influenced or their liking for the leader (Carli et al., 1995).

To conclude, the relationship between leadership, NVB, and gender is complex and multifaceted. Depending on the interaction between gender and leadership position, men or women express different kinds of NVB, which affect the way others perceive the NVB they convey.

Cultural Background and Leadership

The relationship between NVB and the cultural background of the followers or leaders is also relevant to leadership. Cultural background affects how leadership is perceived and expressed. NVB takes on shared meaning in a specific cultural setting (Knapp & Hall, 2010). For example, a Japanese leader may interact at a more pronounced interpersonal distance compared to an American leader, and so cultural differences in NVB between leaders and followers might result in misunderstandings. Some authors (Matsumoto, 1990, 1991) suggest that persons from individualistic cultures (e.g., the United States) express feelings more openly and tend to be more nonverbally demonstrative than individuals of collectivistic cultures (e.g., China). Moreover, people of individualistic cultures tend to be more accurate in decoding subtle nonverbal cues (e.g., Beck, Bröske, Koster, Menzel, & Mohr, 2003; Hofstede, 2001; Matsumoto et al., 2002), and there is a cultural ingroup advantage at correctly assessing others' emotions (Elfenbein, Beaupré, Lévesque, & Hess, 2007), despite emotion recognition being universal (Ekman, 1994). The Global Leadership and Organizational Behavior Effectiveness study (GLOBE; House, Hanges, Javidan, Dorfman, & Gupta, 2004), a project that included 62 cultures, demonstrated that there are both universal characteristics and significant cultural differences concerning leadership. While charismatic leadership is preferred in many cultures, the overall behaviors associated with leadership and the expected behaviors from leaders may be dissimilar. For example, in her study, Gaal (2007) examined the relationship between charismatic/transformational leadership, NVB, and culture. Two cultures were observed: the United States (low on power distance) and Hungary (high on power distance). A male actor was asked to recite a charismatic speech in three different ways: reserved, orchestrated, and aggressive. In the *reserved* scenario, the actor had a monotone voice and did not look at the camera or move his arms. In the *orchestrated* scenario, the actor was dynamic, with an animated voice, a natural eye contact with the camera, and his palms open. In the *aggressive* scenario, the actor yelled and showed intense emotions during his speech, maintained direct eye contact with the camera, and used his arms or hands to point or knock on the podium. Participants randomly watched one of the three scenarios. The NVB displayed by the leader was perceived differently by observers in the United States than by observers in Hungary. For both countries, there was a positive relationship between the orchestrated NVB and charismatic leadership characteristics (i.e., vision, inspiration, and trustworthiness) and a negative relationship between the reserved NVB and charismatic leadership characteristics. However, the aggressive scenario was perceived as more detrimental for the perception of charismatic leadership characteristics in the United States than in Hungary compared to the two other scenarios. In the same vein, Matsumoto (1990) studied displayed emotions in Americans and Japanese. Participants saw faces portraying emotions and assessed the suitability of each in different social situations such as interactions between a leader and a follower. Results showed that on one hand, the Japanese found it suitable to express negative emotions (e.g., anger) toward followers because the expression of such behavior serves to maintain the existing culturally grounded power distance. On the other hand, the Americans discouraged leader displays of negative emotions to followers because these emphasize status differences, which is contradictory to the American culture of equality.

Although the impact of cultural difference in NVB expressed by leaders has not been covered in great detail, the research demonstrates that leaders may be perceived differently in one culture than another, and acceptable leader NVB may be culturally dependent.

Other Characteristics and Leadership

There is an almost endless list of other characteristics that do or potentially could affect the NVB-leadership relationship. For example, expressions and perceptions of leadership may differ in important ways depending on the individual's social motives (e.g., goals, desires) or on his or her emotional state (e.g., happiness, anger). A leader who argues with a follower about respecting a deadline might behave differently than a leader who wants to fire an ineffective follower. Moreover, smiling in a situation of crisis may be regarded as sarcastic rather than supportive. This idea is supported by Bucy (2000), who showed that leaders were assessed more favorably when the NVB they demonstrated was considered compatible with the message they conveyed.

The nature of the relationship the individual has with others (e.g., new or well-known followers, colleagues, leaders, or clients) might also affect the NVB-leadership relationship. Cashdan (1998) demonstrated that, in discussions, female and male leaders showed differences in NVB depending on whether they were with acquaintances or strangers. Female and male leaders spoke more in discussions with strangers than in discussions with acquaintances. Female leaders had more open body postures; in particular, their legs were more open in discussions with strangers than in discussions with acquaintances. Male leaders smiled less in discussions with strangers than in discussions with acquaintances.

Personality is certainly another important factor. For example, extraversion and dominance affect emergent leadership. *Extraversion* refers to a predisposition to be outgoing, active, or assertive (Judge & Bono, 2000), and the personality trait of *dominance* refers to a predisposition to try to influence others (Ellyson & Dovidio, 1985). Evidence indicates that personality influences sitting positions. Extraverts tend to choose seating positions that put them in the focus of the others (Cook, 1970), which then, as we discussed earlier, increases the chances for those people to emerge as leaders. In the same vein, Hare and Bales (1963) noted that people at the head, foot, or center of the table were likely to have dominant personalities. Kalma, Visser, and Peeters (1993) demonstrated that in an emergent leadership situation, individuals who scored higher on sociable dominance (i.e., high self-esteem, positive attitudes toward others, a central position in groups, a strong need to influence others, and an independent and active attitude) or aggressive dominance (negative attitudes toward others and a strong motivation to realize one's goals, even at the detriment of personal relationships) emerge as leaders, with sociably dominant individuals chosen more frequently as group leaders than aggressively dominant individuals. Moreover, sociably dominant individuals behaved differently from aggressive dominant individuals in that they looked at others more while speaking, made more eye contact, and used more gestures. Aggressively dominant individuals looked at others less while listening and interrupted more.

Some of the discussed characteristics can interact with each other and affect the NVB-leadership relationship. Not much research has looked at such complex patterns. One example is a study showing that leader gender interacted with dominance and leadership position in predicting NVB. In non leadership positions, women who were high in dominance smiled less than women who were low in dominance, while no such effect emerged for men (Schmid Mast & Hall, 2004a). There is clearly more research needed to address such complex interplays.

CONCLUSION AND OUTLOOK

The aim of this chapter is to better understand the role of NVB in leadership by showing that leader NVB is an important means for framing the relationship between leaders and followers, and for effective leadership. Differences in NVB among group members are part of the basis on which leaders emerge in groups. Moreover, followers use different leader NVB to judge and evaluate their leaders. The NVB that leaders exhibit is linked to their leadership styles, and leader NVB impacts (most of the time unconsciously) leadership effectiveness. Knowing which leader NVB is related to better or worse leadership outcomes is beneficial because it allows for the training of leaders. Leader interpersonal skill training can make leaders aware of their own NVB and provide them the tools to adapt to others' NVB. This awareness and adaptability is necessary to be effective.

Organizations that want to improve should be interested in NVB training for their leaders because it potentially increases leadership effectiveness. Moreover, knowing that NVB plays a primary role when dissonance occurs between verbal and nonverbal behavior may help in understanding the demands of leadership in organizations. Leaders are often required to show different emotions than those they actually feel. For example, during times of crisis, leaders might more easily find the right words rather than the right NVB to support their followers. However, they need to display NVB indicative of confidence and optimism even if they are as worried and anxious as their followers. Thus it is important that leaders be trained in the context of "emotional labor" (i.e., leaders are expected to display certain emotions as part of their leadership position; Humphrey, Pollack, & Hawver, 2008).

Research in nonverbal communication and leadership remains scarce. It might be relevant to know which NVB are more or less related to interpersonal skills in order to achieve a better focus in leader NVB training. For example, is touching more related to emotional or social skills according to Riggio's Social Skills Inventory (Riggio, this volume, Chapter 3; Riggio & Carney, 2003)? Moreover, much of the research focuses on the NVB of effective leaders, but we need to identify the NVB related to destructive and toxic leaders to know their effects and avoid them.

Regarding the methods used, research has tested a range of diverse NVB in relation to constructive leadership, but these typically remain on a correlational and descriptive level. We need to better understand the effects of the interactions and combinations of different NVB (e.g., touching and smiling) in order to know their effects and see whether they are perceived as effective (i.e., similar effects as incongruent verbal and nonverbal behavior). Additionally, analyzing mediators of the expression or perception of leadership (e.g., perceived competence or perceived self-confidence) are needed to better understand why NVB is used to convey or to infer leadership. Finally, methodological innovations in the study of NVB and leadership are needed. For example, computer-mediated automatic coding of NVB related to emergent leadership is being developed and might facilitate the work of researchers (Sanchez-Cortes, Aran, Schmid Mast, & Gatica-Perez, 2011).

Another important area that deserves the attention of researchers is how leaders and followers cope with the absence of some NVB in virtual teams. These specific teams use computer-mediated communication (CMC). CMC includes a variety of electronic message systems that can be supplemented by audio and video links. Examples of CMC are email, chat, or video conference. It is well established that there is little or no NVB in most of CMC (e.g., Kiesler, Siegel, & McGuire, 1984; Walther, 1996), except for video conferencing, but even in this situation NVB is limited to some extent. Because one of the functions of NVB is to reduce the ambiguity of a message, there is a high probability for misinterpretation in CMC (Sanderson, 1993). Interesting, individuals create a number of strategies to compensate for the lack of NVB in CMC. Most notable is the use of "emoticons"—smiley-faced characters used to express emotions (Walther & D'Addario, 2001). Additionally, researchers have suggested that individuals may become more precise in their use of words to more clearly communicate emotions in CMC (Newlands, Anderson, & Mullin, 2003). Research on emergent leadership in virtual teams demonstrated that emergent leaders sent more and longer email messages than their team members did (Yoo & Alavi, 2004), suggesting that they act similarly to emergent leaders in face-to-face teams who speak more (Schmid Mast, 2002).

In conclusion, additional research is needed and leader NVB training is important to reach individual, leadership, and organizational effectiveness. Thus, the future for NVB research in the leadership context and for leader development seems encouraging. This integrative review on the role of NVB in leadership provides organizations with evidence that NVB greatly influences the attribution of leadership characteristics and may be trained in order to improve interpersonal skills.

AUTHOR NOTE

Annick Darioly, Kravis Leadership Institute, Claremont McKenna College, Claremont, California, United States; Marianne Schmid Mast, Department of Work and Organizational Psychology, University of Neuchatel,

Neuchatel, Switzerland. Annick Darioly is currently at the Department of Work and Organizational Psychology, University of Neuchatel, Neuchatel, Switzerland.

We thank Claudia Raigoza and Petra Schmid for comments on previous drafts of the chapter.

NOTES

1. Hall and colleagues' meta-analysis also includes studies with personality dominance (single target). In this chapter, we only took the results on emergent leadership and perceived dominance (group interaction).
2. Whereas originally, *charisma* referred to attributes of leaders (Weber, 1980, original 1921), modern research focuses on the behavioral side of charisma, which is represented in the notion of transformational leadership (Bass, 1985). *Charismatic* and *transformational leadership* both refer to the same phenomenon (cf. Schyns, 2001) and can be used interchangeably.

REFERENCES

Ambady, N., Hallahan, M., & Rosenthal, R. (1995). On judging and being judged accurately in zero-acquaintance situations. *Journal of Personality and Social Psychology, 69*(3), 518–529.

Antonakis, J., Fenley, M., & Liechti, S. (2011). Can charisma be taught? Tests of two interventions. *Academy of Management Learning and Education, 10*(3), 374–396.

Awamleh, R.A. (1997). *Charismatic leadership: The effects of vision content, vision delivery, organizational performance, and the romance of leadership on perceptions of charisma and effectiveness.* Dissertation, University of Mississippi.

Awamleh, R.A., & Gardner, W.L. (1999). Perceptions of leader charisma and effectiveness: The effects of vision content, delivery, and organizational performance. *Leadership Quarterly, 10*(3), 345–373.

Baird, J.E. (1977). Some non-verbal elements of leadership emergence. *Southern Speech Communication Journal, 42*(4), 352–361.

Bandura, A. (1977). Self-efficacy: Toward a unifying theory of behavioral change. *Psychological Review, 84*, 191–215.

Bass, B.M. (1985). *Leadership and performance beyond expectations.* New York: Free Press.

Bass, B.M. (1990). *Bass and Stogdill's handbook of leadership: Theory, research, and managerial applications.* New York: Free Press.

Bass, B.M., & Avolio, B.J. (1989). Potential biases in leadership measures: How prototypes, leniency, and general satisfaction relate to ratings and rankings of transformational and transactional leadership constructs. *Educational and Psychological Measurement, 49*(3), 509–527. doi: 10.1177/001316448904900302.

Bass, B.M., & Bass, R.B. (2008). *The Bass handbook of leadership: Theory, research, and managerial applications* (4th ed.). New York: Free Press.

Beck, J., Bröske, A., Koster, I., Menzel, A., & Mohr, G. (2003). *Die Bedeutung kultureller Orientierung und Persönlichkeit für die Dekodierungsfähigkeit im Rahmen interpersonaler Wahrnehmung [The importance of cultural orientation and personality for decoding abilities in the context of interpersonal perception].* Unpublished manuscript. Department of Work and Organizational Psychology, University of Leipzig.

Berger, J., Conner, T. L., & Fisek, H. (1974). *Expectation states theory: A theoretical research program.* New York: Elsevier.

Berger, J., Fisek, M. H., Norman, R. Z., & Zelditch, M., Jr. (1977). *Status characteristics in social interaction: An expectation states approach.* New York: Elsevier.

Brunswik, E. (1956). *Perception and the representative: Design of psychological experiments.* Berkeley: University of California Press.

Bucy, E. P. (2000). Emotional and evaluative consequences of inappropriate leader displays. *Communication Research, 27,* 194–229.

Burgoon, J. K., Birk, T., & Pfau, M. (1990). Nonverbal behaviors, persuasion, and credibility. *Human Communication Research, 17*(1), 140–169. doi: 10.1111/j.1468-2958.1990.tb00229.x.

Byron, K. (2007). Male and female managers' ability to read emotions: Relationships with supervisor's performance ratings and subordinates' satisfaction ratings. *Journal of Occupational and Organizational Psychology, 80*(4), 713–733. doi: 10.1348/096317907x174349.

Carli, L. L., LaFleur, S. J., & Loeber, C. C. (1995). Nonverbal behavior, gender, and influence. *Journal of Personality & Social Psychology, 68*(6), 1030–1041.

Cashdan, E. (1998). Smiles, speech, and body posture: How women and men display sociometric status and power. *Journal of Nonverbal Behavior, 22*(4), 209–228. doi: 10.1023/a:1022967721884.

Cherulnik, P. D., Donley, K. A., Wiewel, T. S. R., & Miller, S. R. (2001). Charisma is contagious: The effect of leaders' charisma on observers' affect. *Journal of Applied Social Psychology, 31*(10), 2149–2159. doi: 10.1111/j.1559-1816.2001.tb00167.x.

Cook, M. (1970). Experiments on orientation and proxemics. *Human Relations, 23*(1), 61–76. doi: 10.1177/001872677002300107.

Costanzo, M. (1992). Training students to decode verbal and nonverbal cues: Effects on confidence and performance. *Journal of Educational Psychology, 84*(3), 308–313.

Costanzo, M., & Archer, D. (1989). Interpreting the expressive behavior of others: The Interpersonal Perception Task. *Journal of Nonverbal Behavior, 13*(4), 225–245.

Crane, J., & Crane, F. G. (2010). Optimal nonverbal communications strategies physicians should engage in to promote positive clinical outcomes. *Health Marketing Quarterly, 27*(3), 262–274. doi: 10.1080/07359683.2010.495300.

DePaulo, B. M., & Friedman, H. S. (1998). Nonverbal communication. In D. Gilbert, S. Fiske, & G. Lindzey (Eds.), *Handbook of social psychology* (4th ed., pp. 3–40). Boston, MA: McGraw Hill.

Dovidio, J. F., & Ellyson, S. L. (1982). Decoding visual dominance: Attributions of power based on relative percentages of looking while speaking and looking while listening. *Social Psychology Quarterly, 45*(2), 106–113.

Eagly, A. H., & Karau, S. J. (2002). Role congruity theory of prejudice toward female leaders. *Psychological Review, 109*(3), 573–598.

Eden, D. (1990). *Pygmalion in management.* Lexington, MA: Lexington Books.

Eden, D., Geller, D., Gewirtz, A., Gordon-Terner, R., Inbar, I., Liberman, M., . . . Shalit, M. (2000). Implanting Pygmalion leadership style through workshop training: Seven field experiments. *Leadership Quarterly, 11*(2), 171–210.

Einarsen, S., Aasland, M. S., & Skogstad, A. (2007). Destructive leadership behaviour: A definition and conceptual model. *Leadership Quarterly, 18,* 207–216.

Ekman, P. (1994). Strong evidence for universals in facial expressions: A reply to Russell's mistaken critique. *Psychological Bulletin, 115*(2), 268–287.

Ekman, P., Friesen, W.V., & Hager, J.C. (2002). *Facial action coding system: The manual.* USA: Research Nexus division of Network Information Research Corporation Salt lake City, UT.

Elfenbein, H.A., Beaupré, M., Lévesque, M., & Hess, U. (2007). Toward a dialect theory: Cultural differences in the expression and recognition of posed facial expressions. *Emotion, 7*(1), 131–146.

Ellyson, S.L., & Dovidio, J.F. (1985). Power, dominance, and nonverbal behavior: Basic concepts and issues. In S.L. Ellyson & J.F. Dovidio (Eds.), *Power, dominance, and nonverbal behavior* (pp. 1–27). New York: Springer.

Exline, R.V., Ellyson, S.L., & Long, B.D. (1975). Visual behavior as an aspect of power role relationships. In P. Pliner, L. Krames, & T. Alloway (Eds.), *Advances in the study of communication and affect* (pp. 21–52). New York: Plenum.

Frese, M., Beimel, S., & Schoenborn, S. (2003). Action training for charismatic leadership: Two evaluations of studies of a commercial training module on inspirational communication of a vision. *Personnel Psychology, 56*(3), 671–698.

Friedman, H.S., Prince, L.M., Riggio, R.E., & DiMatteo, M.R. (1980). Understanding and assessing nonverbal expressiveness: The Affective Communication Test. *Journal of Personality and Social Psychology, 39*(2), 333–351. doi: 10.1037/0022–3514.39.2.333.

Friedman, H.S., & Riggio, R.E. (1981). Effect of individual differences in nonverbal expressiveness on transmission of emotion. *Journal of Nonverbal Behavior, 6*(2), 96–104.

Gaal, M.A. (2007). *Cross-cultural comparison of nonverbal communication, culture, and the attribution of charismatic leadership among Hungarian and American university student* (PhD dissertation). Available from ProQuest Dissertations and Theses database. (304768522)

Gaddis, B., Connelly, S., & Mumford, M.D. (2004). Failure feedback as an affective event: Influences of leader affect on subordinate attitudes and performance. *Leadership Quarterly, 15*(5), 663–686. doi: http://dx.doi.org/10.1016/j.leaqua.2004.05.011.

Gardner, W.L., & Avolio, B.J. (1998). The charismatic relationship: A dramaturgical perspective. *Academy of Management Review, 23*(1), 32–58.

Gray, J.H., & Densten, I.L. (2007). How leaders woo followers in the romance of leadership. *Applied Psychology: An International Review, 56*(4), 558–581.

Groves, K.S. (2006). Leader emotional expressivity, visionary leadership, and organizational change. *Leadership and Organization Development Journal, 27*(7), 566–583. doi: 10.1108/01437730610692425.

Guastello, S.J. (2002). *Managing emergent phenomena.* Mahwah, NJ: Lawrence Erlbaum.

Hall, J.A. (2006). Nonverbal behavior, status, and gender: How do we understand their relations? *Psychology of Women Quarterly, 30*(4), 384–391. doi: 10.1111/j.1471–6402 .2006.00313.x.

Hall, J.A., Coats, E.J., & Smith LeBeau, L. (2005). Nonverbal behavior and the vertical dimension of social relations: A meta-analysis. *Psychological Bulletin, 131*(6), 898–924. doi: 10.1037/0033–2909.131.6.898.

Hare, A.P., & Bales, R.F. (1963). Seating position and small group interaction. *Sociometry, 26*, 480–486.

Hatfield, E., Cacioppo, J.T., & Rapson, R.L. (1994). *Emotional contagion.* Cambridge: Cambridge University Press.

Heckel, R.V. (1973). Leadership and voluntary seating choice. *Psychological Reports, 32*, 141–142.

Hofstede, G. (Ed.). (2001). *Culture's consequences.* Thousands Oaks, CA: Sage.

Hollander, E.P., & Julian, J.W. (1969). Contemporary trends in the analysis of leadership processes. *Psychological Bulletin, 71*(5), 387–397.

House, R.J., Hanges, P.J., Javidan, M., Dorfman, P.W., & Gupta, V. (2004). *Culture, leadership, and organizations: The GLOBE study of 62 societies.* London: Sage.

Howell, J.M., & Frost, P.J. (1989). A laboratory study of charismatic leadership. *Organizational Behavior and Human Decision Processes, 43*(2), 243–269. doi: 10.1016/0749-5978(89)90052-6.

Humphrey, R., Pollack, J.M., & Hawver, T.H. (2008). Leading with emotional labor. *Journal of Managerial Psychology, 23,* 151–168.

Hyde, J.S. (2005). The gender similarities hypothesis. *American Psychologist, 60*(6), 581–592. doi: 10.1037/0003–066X.60.6.581.

Jackson, D., Engstrom, E., & Emmers-Sommer, T. (2007). Think leader, think male and female: Sex vs. seating arrangement as leadership cues. *Sex Roles, 57*(9), 713–723. doi: 10.1007/s11199–007–9289-y.

Janisse, M.P. (1973). Pupil size and affect: A critical review of the literature since 1960. *Canadian Psychologist/Psychologie canadienne, 14*(4), 311–329. doi: 10.1037/h0082230.

Judge, T.A., & Bono, J.E. (2000). Five-factor model of personality and transformational leadership. *Journal of Applied Psychology, 85*(5), 751–765. doi: 10.1037/0021–9010.85.5.751.

Kaiser, R.B., Hogan, R., & Craig, S.B. (2008). Leadership and the fate of organizations. *American Psychologist, 63*(2), 96–110.

Kalma, A.P., & Van Rooij, J. (1982). Dominantie en interactieregulering: het kijkgedrag van invloedrijke personen [Dominance and regulation of interaction: Looking behaviour of influential persons]. *Nederlandse Tijdschrift voor de Psychologie en haar Grensgebieden, 37,* 431–443.

Kalma, A.P., Visser, L., & Peeters, A. (1993). Sociable and aggressive dominance: Personality differences in leadership style? *Leadership Quarterly, 4*(1), 45–64. doi: 10.1016/1048–9843(93)90003-C.

Kiesler, S., Siegel, J., & McGuire, T.W. (1984). Social psychological aspects of computer-mediated communication. *American Psychologist, 39*(10), 1123–1134.

King, A.S. (1971). Self-fulfilling prophecies in training the hard-core: Supervisor's expectations and the underprivileged worker's performance. *Social Science Quarterly, 52,* 369–378.

Knapp, M.L., & Hall, J.A. (Eds.). (2010). *Nonverbal communication in human interaction* (7th ed.). Boston, MA: Wadsworth, Cengage Learning.

Lipman-Blumen, J. (2005). *The allure of toxic leaders: Why we follow destructive bosses and corrupt politicians and how we can survive them.* New York: Oxford University Press.

Lord, R.G., de Vader, C.L., & Alliger, G.M. (1986). A meta-analysis of the relation between personality traits and leadership perceptions: An application of validity generalization procedures. *Journal of Applied Psychology, 71*(3), 402–410. doi: 10.1037/0021–9010.71.3.402.

Lord, R.G., Foti, R.J., & Phillips, J.S. (1982). A theory of leadership categorization. In J.G. Hunt, U. Sekaran, & C.A. Schriesheim (Eds.), *Leadership: Beyond establishment views.* Carbondale: Southern Illinois University Press.

Lowe, K.B., Kroeck, K.G., & Sivasubramaniam, N. (1996). Effectiveness correlates of transformational and transactional leadership: A meta analytic review. *Leadership Quarterly, 7*(3), 385.

Matsumoto, D. (1990). Cultural similarities and differences in display rules. *Motivation and Emotion, 14,* 195–214.

Matsumoto, D. (1991). Cultural influences on facial expression of emotion. *Southern Communication Journal, 56,* 128–137.

Matsumoto, D., Consolacion, T., Yamada, H., Suzuki, R., Franklin, B., Paul, S., . . . Uchida, H. (2002). American-Japanese cultural differences in judgement of emotional expressions of different intensities. *Cognition and Emotion, 16*(6), 721–747.

Maurer, T.J., & Lord, R.G. (1991). An exploration of cognitive demands in group interaction as a moderator of information processing variables in perceptions of leadership. *Journal of Applied Social Psychology, 21*(10), 821–839. doi: 10.1111/j.1559–1816.1991.tb00445.x.

Mehrabian, A. (1972). *Nonverbal communication.* Chicago, IL: Aldine-Atherton.

Mehrabian, A., & Wiener, M. (1967). Decoding of inconsistent communications. *Journal of Personality and Social Psychology, 6*(1), 109–114. doi: 10.1037/h0024532.

Mintzberg, H. (1973). *The nature of managerial work.* New York: Harper & Row.

Moore, H.A., & Porter, N.K. (1988). Leadership and nonverbal behaviors of Hispanic females across school equity environments. *Psychology of Women Quarterly, 12*(2), 147.

Newlands, A., Anderson, A.H., & Mullin, J. (2003). Adapting communicative strategies to computer-mediated communication: An analysis of task performance and dialogue structure. *Applied Cognitive Psychology, 17*(3), 325–348.

Northouse, G. (2007). *Leadership theory and practice* (4th ed.). Thousand Oaks, CA: Sage Publications.

Nye, J.L. (2002). The eye of the follower-information processing effects on attribution regarding leaders of small groups. *Small Group Research, 33*(3), 337–360.

Nye, J.L., & Forsyth, D.R. (1991). The effects of prototype-based biases on leadership appraisals. *Small Group Research, 22*(3), 360–379. doi: 10.1177/1046496491223005.

Pfeffer, J. (1977). The ambiguity of leadership. *Academy of Management Review, 2*(1), 104–112.

Porter, N., & Geis, F.L. (1981). Women and nonverbal leadership cues: When seeing is not believing. In C. Mayo & N. Henley (Eds.), *Gender and nonverbal behavior* (pp. 39–61). New York: Springer Verlag.

Reichard, R.J., & Riggio, R.E. (2008). An interactive process model of emotions and leadership. In C.L. Cooper & N. Ashkanasy (Eds.), *Research companion to emotions in organizations.* Cheltenham, UK: Edward Elgar.

Remland, M. (1981). Developing leadership skills in nonverbal communication: A situational perspective. *Journal of Business Communication, 18*(3), 17–29.

Remland, M., Jacobson, C., & Jones, T. (1983). Effects of psychological gender and sex-incongruent behavior on evaluations of leadership. *Perceptual and Motor Skills, 57*(3), 783–789.

Ridgeway, C.L., & Berger, J. (1986). Expectations, legitimation, and dominance behavior in task groups. *American Sociological Review, 51*(5), 603–617.

Riggio, R.E. (1986). Assessment of basic social skills. *Journal of Personality and Social Psychology, 51*(3), 649–660.

Riggio, R.E. (1989). *Manual of the Social Skills Inventory.* Palo Alto, CA: Consulting Psychologists Press.

Riggio, R.E. (1998). Charisma. In H.S. Friedman (Ed.), *Encyclopedia of mental health* (pp. 387–396). San Diego, CA: Academic Press.

Riggio, R.E. (2006). Nonverbal skills and abilities. In V. Manusov & M.L. Patterson (Eds.), *The SAGE handbook of nonverbal communication* (pp. 79–95). Thousand Oaks, CA: SAGE.

Riggio, R.E., & Carney, D.C. (2003). *Manual for the Social Skills Inventory* (2nd ed.). Mountain View, CA: Mind Garden.

Riggio, R.E., & Reichard, R.J. (2008). The emotional and social intelligences of effective leadership: An emotional and social skill approach. *Journal of Managerial Psychology, 23*(2), 169–185.

Riggio, R. E., Riggio, H. R., Salinas, C., & Cole, E. J. (2003). The role of social and emotional communication skills in leader emergence and effectiveness. *Group Dynamics: Theory, Research, & Practice, 7*(2), 83–103.

Sanchez-Cortes, D., Aran, O., Schmid Mast, M., & Gatica-Perez, D. (2011). A nonverbal behavior approach to identify emergent leaders in small groups. *IEEE transactions on multimedia.* doi: 10.1109/TMM.2011.2181941.

Sanderson, D. W. (1993). *Smileys.* Sebastopol, CA: O'Reilly.

Savvas, T., & Schyns, B. (2012). The face of leadership: Perceiving leaders from facial expression. *Leadership Quarterly, 23*(3), 545–566. doi: 10.1016/j.leaqua.2011.12.007.

Schmid Mast, M. (2002). Dominance as expressed and inferred through speaking time: A meta-analysis. *Human Communication Research, 28*(3), 420–450.

Schmid Mast, M. (2010). Interpersonal behavior and social perception in a hierarchy: The Interpersonal Power and Behavior Model. *European Review of Social Psychology, 21*(1), 1–33.

Schmid Mast, M., & Hall, J. A. (2004a). When is dominance related to smiling? Assigned dominance, dominance preference, trait dominance, and gender as moderators. *Sex Roles, 50*(5/6), 387–399.

Schmid Mast, M., & Hall, J. A. (2004b). Who is the boss and who is not? Accuracy of judging status. *Journal of Nonverbal Behavior, 28*(3), 145–165. doi: 10.1023/b: jonb.0000039647.94190.21.

Schmid Mast, M., Hall, J. A., Murphy, N. A., & Colvin, C. R. (2003). Judging assertiveness. *Facta Universitatis, 2*(10), 731–744.

Schmid Mast, M., Jonas, K., & Hall, J. A. (2009). Give a person power and he or she will show interpersonal sensitivity: The phenomenon and its why and when. *Journal of Personality and Social Psychology, 97*(5), 851–865. doi: 10.1037/a0016234.

Schmid Mast, M., Jonas, K., Klöckner Cronauer, C., & Darioly, A. (2012). On the importance of the superior's interpersonal sensitivity for good leadership. *Journal of Applied Social Psychology, 42*(5), 1043–1068. doi: 10.1111/j.1559–1816.2011.00852.x.

Schyns, B. (2001). The relationship between employees' self-monitoring and occupational self-efficacy and transformational leadership. *Current Research in Social Psychology, 7*(3), 30–42.

Schyns, B., Felfe, J., & Blank, H. (2007). Is charisma hyper-romanticism? Empirical evidence from new data and a meta-analysis. *Applied Psychology: An International Review, 56*(4), 505–527.

Schyns, B., & Schilling, J. (2010). Implicit leadership theories: Think leader, think effective? *Journal of Management, 20,* 141–150. doi: 10.1177/1056492610375989.

Schyns, B., & Schilling, J. (2012). How bad are the effects of bad leaders? A meta-analysis of destructive leadership and its outcomes. *Leadership Quarterly.* Retrieved from http://www.sciencedirect.com/science/article/pii/S1048984312000872doi:10.1016/j.leaqua.2012.09.001.

Shamir, B., House, R. J., & Arthur, M. B. (1993). The motivational effects of charismatic leadership: A self-concept based theory. *Organization Science, 4*(4), 577–594.

Shea, C. M., & Howell, J. M. (1999). Charismatic leadership and task feedback: A laboratory study of their effects on self-efficacy and performance. *Leadership Quarterly, 10*(3), 375–396.

Stang, D. J. (1973). Effect of interaction rate on ratings of leadership and liking. *Journal of Personality and Social Psychology, 27*(3), 405–408. doi: 10.1037/h0034940.

Stein, R. T. (1975). Identifying emergent leaders from verbal and nonverbal communications. *Journal of Personality and Social Psychology, 32*(1), 125–135. doi: 10.1037/h0076842.

Stein, R.T., & Heller, T. (1979). An empirical analysis of the correlations between leadership status and participation rates reported in the literature. *Journal of Personality and Social Psychology, 37*(11), 1993–2002. doi: 10.1037/0022–3514.37.11.1993.

Stogdill, R.M. (1950). Leadership, membership and organization. *Psychological Bulletin, 47*(1), 1–14. doi: 10.1037/h0053857.

Sullivan, D.G., & Masters, R.D. (1988). "Happy warriors": Leaders' facial displays, viewers' emotions, and political support. *American Journal of Political Science, 32*(2), 345–368.

Sutton, C.D., & Woodman, R.W. (1989). Pygmalion goes to work: The effects of supervisor expectations in a retail setting. *Journal of Applied Psychology, 74*(6), 943–950. doi: 10.1037/0021–9010.74.6.943.

Talley, L.L. (2012). Influence of leader hand gestures on the perception of nonverbal immediacy. (Order No. 3527702, Walden University). ProQuest Dissertations and Theses, 164. Retrieved from http://search.proquest.com/docview/1095122526?accountid=10141. (1095122526).

Taylor, S.J. (2002). *Effects of a nonverbal skill training program on perceptions of personal charisma* (Unpublished PhD dissertation). University of California–Riverside.

Tepper, B.J. (2000). Consequences of abusive supervision. *Academy of Management Journal, 43*(2), 178–190.

Tjosvold, D. (1984). Effects of leader warmth and directiveness on subordinate performance on a subsequent task. *Journal of Applied Psychology, 69*(3), 422–427. doi: 10.1037/0021–9010.69.3.422.

Towler, A. (2003). Effects of charismatic influence training on attitudes, behavior, and performance. *Personnel Psychology, 56*(2), 363–381. doi: 10.1111/j.1744–6570.2003 .tb00154.x.

Uhl-Bien, M. (2004). Relationship development as a key ingredient for leadership development. In S.E. Murphy & R.E. Riggio (Eds.), *The future of leadership development* (pp. 129–147). Mahwah, NJ: Lawrence Erlbaum.

Vrij, A., & Mann, S. (2005). Police use of nonverbal behavior as indicators of deception. In R.E. Riggio & R.S. Feldman (Eds.), *Applications of nonverbal communication.* Mahwah, NJ: Lawrence Erlbaum.

Walther, J.B. (1996). Computer-mediated communication: Impersonal, interpersonal, and hyperpersonal interaction. *Communication Research, 23*(1), 3–43.

Walther, J.B., & D'Addario, K.P. (2001). The impact of emoticons on message interpretation in computer-mediated communication. *Social Science Computer Review, 19*, 324–347.

Ward, C.D. (1968). Seating arrangement and leadership emergence in small discussion groups. *Journal of Social Psychology, 74*(1), 83–90.

Weber, M. (1921/1980). *Wirtschaft und Gesellschaft [Economy and society].* Tuebingen, Germany: Mohr.

White, S.S., & Locke, E.A. (2000). Problems with the Pygmalion effect and some proposed solutions. *Leadership Quarterly, 11*(3), 389–415.

Yoo, Y., & Alavi, M. (2004). Emergent leadership in virtual teams: What do emergent leaders do? *Information and Organization, 14*(1), 27–58. doi: 10.1016/j.infoandorg.2003.11.001.

Yukl, G.A. (2010). *Leadership in organizations* (7th ed.). Upper Saddle River, NJ: Pearson Education.

6

A Conceptual Framework of Emotion Management in Leadership Contexts

Shane Connelly, Tamara Friedrich, William B. Vessey, Amanda Klabzuba, Eric A. Day, and Gregory Ruark

The experience and display of emotions in organizations can be adaptive or maladaptive, depending on how individuals interpret and manage such experiences (Ashkanasy & Humphrey, 2011; Barsade & Gibson, 2007). This is particularly true in leadership domains where research suggests the use and appropriate management of emotions is a key part of effective leadership (Ashkanasy & Daus, 2002; Erez, Misangyi, Johnson, & LePine, 2008; George, 2000; Gooty, Connelly, Griffith, & Gupta, 2010; Sy, Côté, & Saavedra, 2005). The potential for a range of emotions to increase positive organizational outcomes and minimize negative ones perpetuates interest in understanding the relationship of emotion management capabilities to leader performance and how these capabilities can be developed.

We offer a model of emotion management and leadership that integrates constructs across a broad array of emotion literature and considers what leadership performance domains are likely to be most influenced by emotion capacities. Several types of emotion knowledge, skills, and abilities are specified in this model that could potentially be enhanced through training interventions. Individual differences and situational factors are considered as potential moderators of the relationship of emotion capacities to leader performance. These may influence the extent to which emotion management is needed, the effectiveness of training and development interventions, or both. Implications of this model for advancing research on emotion management and for facilitating leader development efforts are discussed.

While the conceptual and empirical research on leadership and emotion management is compelling, the current literature is open to a number of criticisms. First, problems regarding the adequacy of emotional intelligence conceptualizations, measures, and unique contributions to leadership have been the subject of recent debate (see Antonakis, Ashkanasy, & Dasborough, 2009; Harms & Credé, 2010a; Kaplan, Cortina, & Ruark, 2010). The well-known ability model of emotional intelligence (EI) includes a relatively coherent set of abilities related to the perception, use, and regulation of emotions in self and others (Mayer, Salovey, & Caruso, 2000; Salovey & Mayer, 1990). However, the main performance-based measure for these abilities has failed to show unique contributions to leadership beyond general intelligence and personality (Akerjordet & Severinsson, 2010; Harms & Credé, 2010a, 2010b). Other definitions and models of EI (emotional and social competencies—ESC) are more diffuse and lack conceptual clarity, incorporating interpersonal skills, motives, values, and self-constructs related to handling feelings, getting along with others (Boyatzis & Sala, 2004; Goleman, 1995), and facilitating intelligent behavior (Bar-On, 1997, 2006). Relationships of the self-report measures associated with these EI mixed-models and leadership outcomes have either not controlled for personality and intelligence or are a function of same source method bias (Harms & Credé, 2010a). While the emotion-specific constructs from these models may have utility, future work on emotion management and leadership will benefit from the development of new models and measures.

A second criticism of this literature relates to the nature of the criteria used in studies of leadership and emotion management. Overwhelmingly, these studies have focused on transformational leadership behavior as the outcome, or on global assessments of leader effectiveness and leader emergence. While research on emotions in the workplace has examined relationships of emotion-related constructs to specific types of outcomes, such as interpersonal effectiveness, negotiation, and risk assessment, this specificity has not translated well to the leadership literature. Little attention has been given to theorizing and measuring specific aspects of leader performance for which emotion management capabilities are likely to result in desirable outcomes (e.g., conflict resolution and providing feedback). The weak relationships of EI with global leader effectiveness and overall transformational leadership are not surprising given the wide range of leadership behavior reflected in these criteria. A large portion of the variance in these types of criteria may be driven by leadership behavior for which emotional skills and abilities are less necessary, such as intellectual stimulation, resource acquisition and management, goal setting, coordinating work activities, task-based problem solving, and organizing and planning efforts. Identifying leadership performance domains where emotion management capabilities are likely to exert significant influence is important for future research (Antonakis et al., 2009; Kaplan et al., 2010).

Related to this criterion problem is a curious lack of construct specificity on the predictor side, as well as little consideration of construct interrelationships and moderators. This is due in part to availability of a limited set of measures tapping emotion management (or EI) and to our acceptance of existing models of emotional intelligence. Research in the areas of emotion perception, the structure of emotion, emotion regulation, emotional labor, and emotional expression has the potential to improve theories, measures, and evaluation of alternative models of emotion management and leadership. Even when emotionally relevant leader performance criteria are used, emotion management capacities may show different patterns or strength of relationships with different outcomes. Additionally, individual differences and situational variables have been treated as nuisance variables or covariates rather than considered as important moderators in and of themselves. A recent exchange of papers on emotional intelligence in the *Industrial and Organizational Psychology: Perspectives on Science and Practice* journal highlighted a similar concern with the lack of consideration of context in the general literature on emotional intelligence in organizations (e.g., Cherniss, 2010; Kaplan et al., 2010). Consideration of specific emotion management knowledge, skills, and abilities (KSA), moderating variables, and alternative criteria will encourage the emergence of new models rather than relying on a one-size-fits-all approach.

Taken together, these issues have constrained considerations of whether and how emotion knowledge, skills, and abilities can be developed or trained. Emotion regulation capacities develop throughout the lifespan, beginning at a very early age. As humans develop physically, neurologically, and socially, they learn how to regulate and control emotions through various types of cues. These include external things such as parental control, discipline, and societal norms and values, and internal cues such as physiological and emotional arousal and self-regulation processes (Eisenberg, 1998). However, while most adults have some level of experience and competence in recognizing and regulating emotions, a variety of factors (e.g., individual differences, situational exposure, and developmental experiences) influence the level of competence reached. Thus, adults still display much variation in their knowledge, understanding, and skill in recognizing, regulating, and displaying emotions. Development of these skills might be influenced by aptitudes and traits as well as the quality and variety of learning/training approaches to which learners are exposed.

We present a conceptual framework of emotion management and leadership as a starting point for developing alternative models. This framework integrates literature from a number of different areas to identify emotion KSAs likely to contribute to performance in emotion-relevant leader performance domains. Individual differences and situational moderators are considered with respect to how they might influence the development and application of emotion management KSAs in leadership contexts. Finally, we discuss issues regarding the trainability of emotion KSAs. This framework may be useful for conceptualizing and testing relationships among emotion management capabilities, training interventions, and leader performance. We turn now to a consideration of leader performance domains where emotion management capacities may be particularly important.

EMOTION-RELEVANT DOMAINS OF LEADER PERFORMANCE

Effective leaders must perform well across a multitude of domains. Leaders regularly try to influence others toward accomplishing common goals (Yukl, 2006). This manifests in a wide variety of day-to-day activities, ranging from managing conflicts to making judgments and decisions. Given the interpersonal nature, high stakes, and complexity of many leader responsibilities, the management of emotions can play a critical part in how leaders perform in these situations. Figure 6.1 includes seven leader performance domains in which emotion management KSAs are likely to be critical. These include providing inspirational motivation, resolving conflict, negotiating, providing feedback, assessing risk, making ethical decisions, and thinking creatively to solve problems.

Inspirational Motivation

This aspect of transformational leadership involves articulating a compelling vision and inspiring followers to achieve that vision. A number of studies have examined the effects of leader emotional displays on follower perceptions of a leader's inspirational motivation and charisma (Bono & Ilies, 2006; Connelly & Ruark, 2010; Erez et al., 2008; Johnson, 2008; Waples &

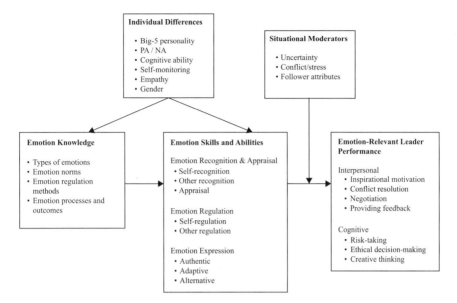

FIGURE 6.1
Emotion management in leadership contexts

Connelly, 2008). Positive leader emotional displays are contagious, result-ing in increased positive affect in followers. Followers experiencing positive mood states are more likely to perceive a clearer connection between their performance and outcomes and to appraise potential outcomes of their behavior as more desirable (Erez & Isen, 2002). However, some studies have shown that both positive and negative leader emotional displays influence follower perceptions of the leader and willingness to engage in performance-relevant behavior that supports the vision. Waples and Connelly (2008) note that outwardly directed negative leader emotions have positive effects on fol-lower behavior, but that these effects might not be realized when negative affect is directed toward followers. It seems, therefore, that leaders, knowl-edge of emotions, emotion processes, and the effects of various emotional displays could increase follower motivation through eliciting positive or negative emotions and connecting those to behavioral outcomes.

Conflict Resolution

Another area of leader performance in which emotion management KSAs are likely to exert influence is conflict resolution. Conflict is certainly an emotion-evoking experience (Bodtker & Jameson, 2001), and leaders must not only manage their own emotional experiences but also the experiences of their subordinates and others involved in the conflict. Preventing and de-escalating conflict relies in part on the organizational or group climate as well as emotion management KSAs. Schroth, Bain-Chekal, and Caldwell (2005) evaluated triggers that elicit emotion responses during a conflict, showing that effective leaders steered conversations away from certain triggers. Effective leaders can accomplish this through the use of humor, distraction, or other emotion regulation strategies. Ayoko, Callan, and Härtel (2008) showed that team emotional climate influenced how team members reacted to conflict. Because leaders are instrumental in developing and influencing team climate when affective events occur (Pirola-Merlo, Härtel, Mann, & Hirst, 2002), those with emotion management KSAs will be able to establish norms, rules, and expectations for how members of the group should deal with conflict. Leaders can emphasize the importance of recognizing emotions, regulating them, and expressing them appropriately to prevent or de-escalate conflicts.

Negotiation

Emotions are also important in negotiation processes (Barry, 2008; Druckman & Olekalns, 2008) and can influence the effectiveness of different negotiation techniques (Van Kleef, de Dreu, & Manstead, 2006). Leaders must often engage in joint decision making with parties that have different interests (real or perceived). Because negotiation requires both cooperation and competition, a natural tension occurs between the kinds of emotional experiences and displays that might emerge during negotiations. Van Kleef's emotions as social information (EASI) model suggests that displaying different emotions communicates different kinds of strategic and social information, thereby influencing the behavior of others involved in the negotiation. For example, the use of anger in negotiations has been shown to result in greater concessions due to the other side's perception of the negotiator as tough and expecting a lot out of the negotiation (Sinaceur & Tiedens, 2006; Van Kleef, de Dreu, & Manstead, 2004). Alternatively, Van Kleef (2008) points out a number of positive effects of happiness displays during negotiations, such as increased likelihood of closing a deal and desire of the other party to engage in future negotiations. Leaders' knowledge about the effects of different emotions on negotiation outcomes and their ability to display the appropriate emotions based on desired outcomes may result in greater negotiation success for leaders.

Providing Feedback

When developing subordinates, effective leaders must convey both positive and negative feedback in a way that will improve subsequent subordinate performance and maintain a good working relationship. When followers are not performing well, leaders may understandably experience negative emotions such as anger or frustration. When leaders convey negative emotions while providing feedback, they risk increasing follower levels of negative affectivity and sense of injustice, thereby reducing the effectiveness of the feedback (Baron, 1990; Gaddis, Connelly, & Mumford, 2004; Kluger & DeNisi, 1996). In essence, there appears to be some merit to breaking bad news gently, at least in a performance feedback context. However, there are some important caveats to this statement. First, while positive emotions may make followers feel interpersonally safe, they also communicate a sense that the status quo is acceptable. Thus, providing negative feedback using positive emotions has the potential to send mixed messages to followers. Additionally, there may also be a place for negative emotions in the feedback process. When leaders evoke emotions such as guilt, they may see positive results. Guilt involves a negative evaluation of some specific behavior rather than one's self in general (as is the case with shame) and triggers empathic responding (Tangney & Dearing, 2003). Studies have shown that guilt is associated with reparative behaviors like apologizing, making amends, and correcting the behavior (Tangney, Stuewig, Mashek, & Hastings, 2011; Westen, 1994). Thus, followers' guilt about instances of poor performance may be an impetus for positive future behavior such as exerting greater effort, obtaining additional training or knowledge, or seeking help from others (Tangney et al., 2011).

Risk Assessment

Leaders face many situations where they must weigh costs, benefits, and risks associated with alternative courses of action. Research on the influences of emotion on risk assessment suggests this may be of particular interest in leadership contexts. Perceptions of risk are influenced by emotions as well as cognitive evaluations of the situation. The risk-as-feelings hypothesis proposed by Loewenstein and colleagues (Loewenstein, Weber, Hsee, & Welch, 2001) suggests that because emotional reactions and cognitive evaluations are determined by different things, people experience conflict in emotional risk assessments and cognitive risk assessments. Cognitive evaluations are driven by probability estimations of outcomes and how negative or positive the outcomes are expected to be. This kind of rational thought process can occur with emotion processing, but doesn't have to. Emotion-based assessments of risk are influenced by a variety of factors. The vividness and immediacy of the situation may make risk more pronounced. Wang (2006) found that emotion-based choices were more risk seeking and more susceptible to the hedonic tone of the options presented than cognitive-based choices. Additionally, evaluations of risk in interpersonal situations were more emotionally based, while those involving money tended to be more cognitively based.

Other research on emotions and risk assessment has shown that different affective states have different effects on risk assessment. For example, positive moods result in more optimistic, risky judgments and choices, while bad moods result in pessimistic, risk-averse judgments and choices (Bower, 1981; Johnson & Tversky, 1983; Mayer & Hanson, 1995; Schwarz & Clore, 1983; Wright & Bower, 1992). Discrete emotions also have differential effects on perceptions of risk. For example, Raghunathan and Pham (1999) found that anxiety increased preference for low-risk, low-reward options, whereas sadness increased preference for high-risk, high-reward options. Lerner and Keltner (2000) found that fearful individuals make relatively pessimistic risk assessments and relatively risk-averse choices, but that angry individuals made more optimistic, risky choices.

Ethical Decision Making

Ethical leadership involves being principled, caring, setting standards, and making fair and balanced decisions (Brown & Trevino, 2006). Making such decisions involves sense-making processes that help individuals consider key causes of an ethical problem, forecast possible outcomes of decisions and actions, consider personal biases, and understand how their own and others' emotions may impact decisions (Mumford et al., 2008; Sonenshein, 2007). Emotions can serve as signals for leaders that they are facing an ethical dilemma and can influence sense-making processes such as considering other perspectives and considering consequences of one's actions (Kligyte,

Connelly, Thiel, & Devenport, in press). While scholars have conducted virtually no empirical research on emotion management and ethical decision making in leadership contexts, a number of studies have looked at the effects of discrete emotions on ethical decision making. Some research has postulated that general affect and discrete emotions such as guilt, anger, and disgust influence ethical decisions in both conscious and subconscious ways (Gaudine & Thorne, 2001; Haidt, 2001). Kligyte and colleagues (in press) found that people induced to feel anger made fewer ethical decisions on an unrelated decision-making task, while those experiencing fear made more ethical decisions than both the anger and control groups. Regulating anger using cognitive reappraisal or relaxation strategies mitigated its negative effects, resulting in ethical decisions comparable to the control group. Another study by Thiel, Connelly, and Griffith (2011) showed that certainty appraisals associated with anger hindered ethical decisions and resulted in the application of sense-making strategies associated with retaliation and less helping of others. Finally, Connelly, Helton-Fauth, and Mumford (2004) showed that certain positive and negative emotions facilitated ethical decisions in a management context, while other positive and negative emotions hindered such decisions.

Creative Thinking

Leaders sometimes face novel challenges for which no established solutions exist (Mumford & Connelly, 1991). Research has indicated that both positive and negative affect can be beneficial to an individual's creative thought processes. On one hand, positive affect facilitates exploration of procedures and possibilities in solving problems (Russ, 1993), insightful solutions (Isen, Daubman, & Nowicki, 1987), ideational fluency (Abele, 1992; Isen, 2003), and managerial problem solving (Staw & Barsade, 1993). Alternatively, negative affect facilitates certain aspects of creative problem solving, such as information search (Martin, Achee, Ward, & Harlow, 1993) and systematic information processing (Mackie & Worth, 1991).

Emotions are also relevant for creativity at the team level. When team climate is supportive and psychologically safe, teams are more creative and innovative (George & Zhou, 2002; Hunter, Bedell-Avers, & Mumford, 2007). Fostering creative problem solving at the team level requires leaders to manage their own emotional displays in ways that support a climate for creativity. They must also understand the influence of emotional states on

creative thinking well enough to know when followers' negative and positive emotional states will benefit their creative thinking. Certain processes
associated with creative thinking benefit from leaders being able to create
positive emotional states in themselves and in followers. However, given
that other creative processes can be enhanced by negative emotional states,
leaders may benefit from letting these states persist at certain points during
the creative process.

Research within and outside the leadership literature supports the influence of emotions and emotion management capabilities in these seven
domains of performance. As highlighted in a recent review by Gooty and
colleagues (2010), both positive and negative emotions have pros and cons
in leadership settings, implying that leaders must adapt emotion regulation efforts accordingly. The set of leader performance domains is a good
starting place, but may not be exhaustive. Considering the set of emotion-
related predictor constructs is also central to furthering our understanding
of the role of emotions in leadership contexts. The next section reviews
emotion management KSAs drawn from theories and empirical studies in
the areas of emotional intelligence, emotion perception, structure of emotion, emotion regulation, emotional labor, and emotional expression.

EMOTION MANAGEMENT KNOWLEDGE, SKILLS, AND ABILITIES

Emotion Knowledge

Emotion knowledge is the first category of constructs included in our
framework. Several theories of emotion and EI have emphasized the
importance of emotion knowledge (e.g., Izard 1971; Izard et al., 2001;
Salovey & Mayer, 1990). The present framework identifies four aspects of
emotion knowledge critical to emotion management, including types of
emotions, emotion norms, regulation methods, and processes and outcomes of emotions.

Knowledge of Types of Emotions
The first aspect of knowledge involves defining and characterizing different
types of affect, emotion traits, emotion states, and experiences. Salovey and
Mayer (1990) indicated that a key element of EI includes understanding

and labeling one's own emotions or those one perceives in others. While the perception of facial expressions depicting specific emotions is included in performance-based assessments of EI such as the Mayer Salovey Caruso Emotional Intelligence Test (MSCEIT), the ability model of EI does not articulate the possible ways of labeling and differentiating general affect, discrete emotions, mood, appraisals, emotion episodes, and other types of emotional experiences. For example, Frijda (1993) indicates that moods are distinguished from emotions by generally being less intense, longer in duration, and lacking a specific trigger. Emotions are characterized by subjective experience (e.g., feeling good), cognitive appraisal or interpretation of the event/circumstances triggering the emotion, physiological changes, and action readiness.

Several models of emotion such as the circumplex model (Russell, 1980) and the taxonomy of emotion developed by Shaver, Schwartz, Kirson, and O'Connor (1987) would also help leaders to develop a more complex vocabulary for emotion and to build emotion knowledge. The circumplex model of emotion characterizes emotions in terms of degree of negative or positive valence and degree of activation. Alternatively, Shaver and colleagues' (1987) taxonomy identifies six basic emotions: love, joy, anger, sadness, fear, and surprise. Blends or co-occurrences of these different emotions comprise lower levels of a hierarchy reflecting a variety of common but complex feelings such as hurt, disappointment, boredom, shame, and regret. Being able to better differentiate between emotions and blends of emotions is important to emotional awareness (Lane & Schwartz, 1987). Other research suggests that two emotions can occur either at the same time or in close succession (Izard, 1972; Tomkins, 1962). For example, an event can trigger an initial or primary emotion (e.g., anger regarding unreasonable demands from one's supervisor) and subsequently the experience of the primary emotion triggers a secondary emotion (e.g., shame or guilt about feeling angry at one's supervisor). Riggio and Lee (2007) point out that building emotion knowledge involves understanding the progression of emotions over time. A variety of complementary theoretical approaches exist that describe emotion concepts, each focusing on different ways emotions can be understood (Niedenthal, 2008). Some focus on defining categories of emotions (Shaver et al., 1987), others define emotions in terms of temporally structured scripts in people's minds that describe probabilistic features of an emotion (causes, beliefs, feeling states, physiological changes, actions) (Russell, 1991), and others view emotions as a semantic network of nodes (Bower, 1981). Each of these theories contributes a different perspective on emotion types.

Knowledge of Emotion Norms

Understanding emotion norms operating in organizational contexts is also important for leaders. Norms for expressing emotions at work are known as *display rules* (Grandey, 2000; Hochschild, 1983). Display rules indicate which emotions are appropriate to express and how emotions should be expressed (Dieffendorf & Richard, 2003). As Ashforth and Humphrey (1993) noted, emotional display rules are typically conveyed informally rather than through formal rule systems. Because of this, employee understanding of positive and negative display rules and the extent to which these are job requirements depends on a number of factors. Dieffendorf, Richard, and Croyle (2006) note that display rules can be communicated through job characteristics and requirements, but that it is still unclear the extent to which other factors such as training, leader communication, and organizational culture influence the acquisition of display rule information. Leaders have great potential to influence subordinates' perceptions of and adherence to emotional display rules. It is also important to bear in mind that while display rules in certain settings (e.g., customer service) are straightforward, many leadership situations are diverse and complex, requiring flexible display rules. Leaders must have knowledge of the likely consequences of positive, negative, and neutral emotional displays across different situational contexts and be able to communicate these expectations to subordinates (Seymour & Sandiford, 2005; Wilk & Moynihan, 2005).

Knowledge of Emotion Regulation

Understanding how people regulate emotions may also be central for leaders who want to develop emotion management skills in themselves and their employees. Gross's (1998b) model of emotion regulation identifies four categories of antecedent-focused regulation strategies, or those that operate prior to a person fully experiencing an emotion, and response-focused regulation strategies, or those employed after emotions have been experienced. Several points about emotion regulation are important to note. First, emotion regulation can occur both subconsciously and consciously (Gross, 1998a, 1998b). Second, recent research has revealed that different regulation strategies have different costs and benefits. For example, suppressing negative emotions is effective for decreasing emotional expression, but does not change what a person feels. Suppression also raises cortisol and stress levels and decreases oxygenation, resulting in negative consequences on an individual's physical health over time (Levenson, 1994; Thiruchselvam, Blechert, Sheppes, Rydstrom, & Gross, 2011). Additionally, suppression impairs memory of the emotional experience (Gross, 2002). Alternatively, cognitive reappraisal or changing the way a situation is construed decreases both the expression and experience of the emotion and does not adversely affect memory (Gross, 2002). Different regulation strategies rely on different parts of the brain and occur at different points in time during emotion regulation efforts (Ochsner & Gross, 2008). We do not yet understand all of the functional consequences of these differences. Still, developing an understanding of the different regulation strategies, the situations that call for particular strategies, and the known short-term and long-term trade-offs associated with the use of specific strategies is an essential part of preparing leaders to regulate emotions in themselves and others.

Knowledge of Emotion Processes and Outcomes

The fourth component of emotion knowledge is an understanding of emotion processes and outcomes (Mayer, Roberts, & Barsade, 2008; Salovey & Mayer, 1990). Lopes, Côté, and Salovey (2006) suggested that to manage emotions effectively one must first have knowledge of emotional processes. Knowledge of the emotion process includes understanding the causes, progression, experience, and potential outcomes associated with emotional experiences. Emotion researchers characterize emotional experience as comprised of physiological, cognitive, and behavioral elements (Ekman & Friesen, 1975; Gross, 1998b; Thompson, 1994). Understanding which physical sensations might be associated with experiencing emotion (e.g., increased pulse, flushed skin, fatigue) can provide valuable information for accurately identifying the emotions one might be experiencing.

Cognitive appraisal theories of emotion have suggested that emotional experiences are based on the appraisal, evaluation, and interpretation of events (Frijda, 1986; Lazarus, 1991; Ortony, Clore, & Collins, 1988; Roseman, Spindel, & Jose, 1990; Scherer, 1988; Smith & Ellsworth, 1985; Smith & Pope, 1992). Initially, a primary assessment is made to determine whether the event is good or bad with respect to goals and values, resulting in a general positive or negative feeling about an event or emotional trigger. Secondary appraisals incorporate the context surrounding the event with regard to factors such as the degree of personal control, coping potential, consequences of the event, and future expectations about the situation, resulting in the experience of more specific emotions such as anger, happiness, or fear. While there is no one agreed-upon list of appraisal dimensions, cognitive appraisal theories agree that different patterns of appraisals are associated with different discrete emotion states (Niedenthal, 2008).

Izard (1971; Izard et al., 2001) discusses the importance of identifying the causes or activators of emotions in oneself and others. While this component of Izard's model tends to resemble a skill, this is relevant to emotion knowledge. In order to effectively identify causes and activators of emotions, knowledge of events, situations, or issues that might cause emotions should help individuals develop this skill. Izard's model also emphasizes relationships among emotion, motivation, and behavior. More generally, this idea emphasizes the importance of understanding the outcomes associated with emotions. For instance, understanding that displaying anger could elicit a specific reaction in one's audience such as fear, guilt, or even reciprocated anger (Riggio & Lee, 2007) enables leaders to motivate followers in different ways to achieve objectives in combat situations. Along these lines, Saarni (1990) proposed that understanding the potential outcomes of emotions is important to emotional competence. More specifically, it is suggested that to manage emotions effectively, understanding how one's emotional behavior influences others is key. The construct of emotional contagion in a leadership context represents how followers observe a leader's emotional expression and subsequently, experience or "catch" the same emotion (Hatfield, Cacioppo, & Rapson, 1994). Leaders must understand how emotional contagion can influence their followers. The last part of this aspect of emotion knowledge involves understanding how emotions unfold and change over time, sometimes creating an emotion episode (Weiss & Cropanzano, 1996). Learning about these and other emotion process will help leaders better understand how emotions are experienced. However, knowledge alone does not guarantee that leaders will manage emotions effectively. Accordingly, this framework includes emotion recognition, regulation, and expression skills and abilities.

Emotion Recognition

Recognizing One's Own Emotions

Developing the capacity to recognize emotions one is experiencing is a common theme in many models related to emotion management. This is a core part of the ability model of EI (Mayer et al., 2008; Salovey & Mayer, 1990). Additionally, mixed models of EI have included a dimension labeled "self-awareness" (Dulewicz & Higgs, 1999, 2000; Goleman, 1995) or "emotional self-awareness" (Bar-On, 1997, 2006). Emotion theorists have also incorporated constructs related to self-awareness in their models, including Feldman (e.g., knowing one's self; 1999), Izard (e.g., recognize and label one's own emotions in varying circumstances; 1971; Izard et al., 2001), Lane and Schwartz (e.g., emotional awareness of self; 1987; Lane, Quinlan, Schwartz, & Walker, 1990), and Saarni (e.g., awareness of one's own emotional state; 1990). All of these models recognize the importance of accurately identifying what emotions one is experiencing.

Recognizing Emotions in Others

Recognizing others' emotions is also important to emotion management. Salovey and Mayer (1990) discussed the importance of perceiving emotions in oneself as well as in others. Jones and Rittman (2002) suggested that considering one's own emotional responses along with situational cues helps in interpreting others' emotional displays. Izard (1971; Izard et al., 2001) suggested in his model that it is essential to accurately perceive emotion signals in expressions, behaviors, and various contexts. Additionally, Feldman (1999) and Saarni (1990) indicated that reading others and detecting their emotions is critical for leaders.

Emotion Appraisal

Emotion appraisal, or the evaluation and interpretation of emotional responses, is also a key skill. Recognizing and decoding emotional information helps one appraise threats and opportunities in situations (Lopes et al., 2006), which in turn influences one's own emotional reaction (Gross, 1998a; Ochsner, Bunge, Gross, & Gabrieli, 2002; Ochsner et al., 2004). By appraising the situation, an individual can also become more accurate in understanding how others perceive emotions. Feldman (1999) differentiates between knowing oneself, reading others, and accurately appraising emotions. The latter involves attaching meaning and interpretation to the recognized emotion. For example, recognizing that another individual is angry is different from knowing how to respond. Only after understanding why the person is angry can a leader develop an appropriate response. Emotion recognition involves understanding and explaining emotions in light of the situation.

Emotion recognition can be positively influenced by emotion knowledge. In order to articulate emotions, one must first have a basic knowledge of the nature of emotions as mentioned earlier. Taylor (1985) argued that articulation of emotions can increase self-awareness and that emotional experience can be determined or shaped by one's understanding of emotions. Similarly, knowledge of common emotion cues and triggers is helpful in identifying what emotions others may be experiencing and attaching meaning to those emotions (Sander, Grandjean, Kaiser, Wehrle, & Scherer, 2007). Contextual knowledge about emotion norms and display rules in the organization is critical for accurate emotion recognition (Opengart, 2005).

Emotion Regulation

People use a variety of strategies to control or manage their experience of emotions (Gross, 1998a, 1998b; Gross & Thompson, 2007). Gross's (1998a) model of emotion regulation includes four categories of antecedent regulation strategies, or those occurring prior to a person fully experiencing an emotion. These include (1) situation selection, (2) situation modification, (3) attention deployment (distraction, concentration, rumination), and (4) cognitive change (defense mechanisms—denial, isolation, intellectualization, overly positive view of situation, downward social comparison, reappraisal). Gross also identified a fifth category of response-focused regulation strategies (e.g., suppression, enhanced expression, exercise, relaxation, drugs, food) or those occurring after one has experienced an emotion. Emotion regulation might occur consciously, subconsciously, or somewhere along this continuum (Gross, 2007). Furthermore, multiple strategies might be used at any given time. In this respect, the regulation strategies are not sequential in nature as originally conceptualized; rather, individuals might start regulating at any point in the process and switch between strategies as appropriate. The effectiveness of any given strategy depends on the context. Raising leaders' awareness of these strategies might enable more conscious application of a broader array of strategies for regulating emotions in themselves and their subordinates.

Some studies have evaluated the effectiveness of particular strategies as mentioned earlier. Gross (1998) examined reappraisal (an antecedent strategy) and suppression (a response strategy) as they influenced emotional response tendencies (behavioral, experiential, and physiological). He found that both strategies reduced behavioral expression of emotion, but only reappraisal reduced the experience of disgust. Additionally, suppression resulted in increased physiological activation (finger pulse, temperature, and skin conductance). Similarly, Gross and John (2003) found that different outcomes are associated with using suppression and reappraisal. Suppression has been associated with less desirable consequences than reappraisal such as decreased interpersonal functioning. This could be because those who use suppression do not like opening up and expressing their emotions to others, thus limiting their close social relationships. In contrast, reappraisal has been associated positively with interpersonal functioning and well-being but is more difficult to engage in, as it involves changing the way one views an emotionally charged situation.

In the kinds of social contexts leaders and subordinates face in organizational settings, one important behavioral aspect of emotion regulation is emotional expression. A number of emotion theories focus exclusively on this concept.

Emotional Expression

Emotional expression and emotional displays involve verbal and nonverbal responses to emotion stimuli and is one aspect of emotion regulation. Grandey (2000) suggested that the two types of emotional labor, surface acting and deep acting, have different implications for emotional expression. Surface acting involves suppressing the emotion one feels and faking the behavioral responses, resulting in an outcome-focused regulation strategy similar to Gross's (1998) response modulation. Deep acting requires changing the emotion one feels in order to display emotions that are likely to be more appropriate in the organizational context. Individuals want to express what is normatively acceptable, and thus will engage in either deep acting or surface acting to express emotions appropriately (Hochschild, 1983).

In a different model of emotional expression, Ekman and Friesen (1969, 1975) identified six aspects of expression management. These strategies for managing emotional expression include: (1) expressing the emotion in its true form, (2) expressing the emotion less strongly than experienced, (3) expressing the emotion at a heightened level, (4) expressing no emotion, (5) expressing the feeling with a verbal or nonverbal qualifier to modify the expression, and (6) displaying an opposite emotion.

Understanding how leaders express their emotions and how followers perceive and respond to this is important. Recent research suggests that leaders are required as part of their role to display or hide emotions (Clarke, Hope-Hailey, & Kelliher, 2007; Humphrey, Pollack, & Hawver, 2008) and that leader displays of emotion impact subordinate perceptions and performance (Connelly & Ruark, 2010; Waples & Connelly, 2008). Emotions can be expressed in a number of ways, such as authentic expression, adaptive expression, alternative expression, and modified intensity.

Authentic Expression

Authentic expression involves expressing the emotion as it is felt. Ekman and Friesen (1969, 1975) included this type of emotional expression in their model of expression management. This form of expression can be beneficial given that emotions are often sources of information about given situations. For instance, if a leader expresses negative emotions when providing negative performance feedback, the consistency of both the message and emotion provides clarity for followers, and potentially highlights the level of seriousness of the performance deficiency. Some research has shown that inconsistency between feedback content and valence of a leader's emotional expression results in poorer evaluations of the leader and less responsiveness to the feedback (Gaddis et al., 2004; Newcombe & Ashkanasy, 2002). Authentic expression of emotion might also facilitate the influence technique of authentic leadership such that the leader seeks to present a transparent picture of himself or herself and true beliefs and values (Avolio, Gardner, Walumbwa, Luthans, & May, 2004; Humphrey et al., 2008).

Adaptive Expression

Adaptive expression is similar to authentic expression in that the emotion displayed corresponds to the emotion that is felt, but it is displayed in an adaptive or socially acceptable way. This form of emotion expression often involves modifying the intensity of the experienced emotion, such as playing up one's anger to make a point with a subordinate (Lopes et al., 2006). Modifying the intensity of emotional displays was discussed decades ago as amplification and de-amplification by Ekman and Friesen (1969, 1975).

Alternative Expression

Contrary to authentic expression is the expression of an emotion that is different than the one that is felt. Much research on alternative emotional expression has delineated between expressing positive and expressing negative emotions (e.g., Brotheridge & Grandey, 2002; Gross & John, 1997; King & Emmons, 1990). Despite the fact that negative emotional displays are sometimes beneficial (Sy et al., 2005), the literature places greater emphasis on expressing positive emotions in work environments over negative ones. Thus, when a negative emotion is experienced, the situation or work environment might require the expression of a positive emotion. This form of emotion expression is also known as *surface acting*. For example, if a leader is frustrated or angered during negotiations with another party, the leader may show positive emotions or even humor if it is important to maintain or further develop the relationship with the other party. It is important to note, however, that this type of expression can result in emotional strain over time. It is fairly common for leaders to be put in situations requiring emotional labor (Clarke et al., 2007; Humphrey et al., 2008) as they might need to implement changes or take actions that they personally disagree with or that will cause negative reactions.

INDIVIDUAL DIFFERENCES AND LEADER EMOTION MANAGEMENT

Some leaders are more adept at managing emotions than others. A number of stable individual differences are likely to shape the development and expression of emotion KSAs. In addition to general traits such as cognitive ability, conscientiousness, and achievement motivation, which positively influence knowledge and skill acquisition in many areas (Campbell, 1988; Colquitt, LePine, & Noe, 2000; Tannenbaum & Yukl, 1992), other individual differences may influence the development of emotion management capabilities. Individual differences such as personality, trait affect, self-monitoring, empathy, and gender provide some clues about what emotion KSAs should be emphasized during training for different kinds of leaders.

Personality and Trait Affect

A number of studies have shown significant relationships of emotion management knowledge and skills to personality attributes. For example, Barchard and Hakstian (2004) found that extraversion, openness, and conscientiousness showed positive correlations with emotion recognition and regulation, while neuroticism showed negative correlations with these emotion capabilities. Agreeableness has also demonstrated positive relationships with emotion recognition, regulation, and expression (Davies, Stankov, & Roberts, 1998). Gross and John (1998, 2003) provided a similar pattern of evidence for how the Big 5 personality traits relate to emotion expression and emotion regulation.

Another aspect of personality that could potentially influence the development and expression of emotion management knowledge and skills is trait affect, or the tendency to experience and express positive or negative moods. John and Gross (2004) found that individuals with high positive affectivity were more likely to engage in cognitive reappraisal and less likely to engage in suppression, while individuals with high negative affectivity were just the opposite. Thus, trait affect is not related to whether or to what extent people regulate their emotion, but may influence their preferences in which strategies they apply. Future research could explore how positive and negative affectivity will influence an individual's capacity to learn other specific emotion management knowledge and skills, such as recognition. Trait affect also involves the intensity of one's typical affective reaction. Researchers have found that individuals with greater affect intensity tend to be better at interpreting emotional stimuli (Larsen, Diener, & Cropanzano, 1987). The relationship between affect intensity and emotion management is not as straightforward. Ben-Ze'ev (2002) suggested that individuals with low affect intensity may be better suited to regulating their emotions, but on the other hand less effective at recognizing emotions. By the same token, those that have high affect intensity may have more difficulty regulating emotions, yet will be more sensitive to recognizing emotions.

Cognitive Ability

Multiple studies have examined the relationship of cognitive ability to emotion management variables. For instance, in Barchard and Hakstian's (2004) study, cognitive ability was found to be positively related to a dimension similar to the present model's emotion knowledge. Further, Ben-Ze'ev (2002) pointed to intellectual ability as important to emotion knowledge in terms of calculating various implications or outcomes of different alternatives. Additionally, findings by Mayer and colleagues have indicated that verbal intelligence in particular is positively related to emotion knowledge and emotion recognition and regulation skills (Mayer, Caruso, & Salovey, 1999; Mayer et al., 2000). Further, emotion knowledge, recognition, and regulation have been found to be positively related to verbal SAT scores (Brackett & Mayer, 2003).

Self-Monitoring

Self-monitoring shares similarities to emotion regulation, but is more externally focused, reactive, and response driven. It focuses on observing and controlling how one appears to others (Lennox & Wolfe, 1984; Snyder, 1974). Schutte and colleagues (2001) showed positive correlations between self-monitoring and several emotion capabilities, including perceiving, understanding, regulating, and harnessing emotions adaptively. Gross and John (1998, 2003) have also demonstrated ties between self-monitoring and emotion management constructs. They found that self-monitoring was related to expressive confidence, which involves effectively expressing both positive and negative emotions. Additionally, their research showed that individuals higher in self-monitoring were more likely to engage in reappraisal as an emotion regulation strategy and less likely to engage in suppression as an emotion regulation strategy.

Empathy

Empathy is another stable individual difference potentially relevant to emotion management. Empathy involves being able to "comprehend another's feelings and to re-experience them oneself" (Salovey & Mayer, 1990, pp. 194–195). Schutte and colleagues (2001) found that those who demonstrated higher empathy also were better at understanding and regulating emotions in themselves and others. Empathetic perspective taking appears particularly helpful to skills related to emotion recognition and regulation (Hodgson & Wertheim, 2007; Ramos, Fernandez-Berrocal, & Extremera, 2007). Additionally, Kellett, Humphrey, and Sleeth (2006) suggested that, for leadership emergence and performance, empathy is related to both the ability to identify others' emotions (e.g., emotion recognition) as well as one's emotional expression.

Gender

Gender may also influence emotion-related knowledge and skills in important ways. Gender differences have been observed in a number of emotion-related experiences and behaviors (see Brody & Hall, 2008 for a review). Some research has indicated that women perceive emotions more accurately than men (Hall & Matsumoto, 2004). Women's ratings of facial displays of target emotions were higher and more accurate than men's ratings, regardless of whether the faces were presented for 10 seconds (indicating conscious processing) or for one second (on edge of conscious awareness). It is unclear whether this is due to differences in early socialization for men and women or the extent to which this is trait based. Research has also shown that women tend to self-report a wider range of emotions with greater intensity than men. Women also express emotion in different ways than men. For example, men's responses to anger have been found to be more aggressive than women's responses (Linden et al., 2003). Emotional expression in either gender does not always communicate what is actually felt. Kruml and Geddes (2000) found that women are more likely to feel differently than what their outward emotional expression would suggest, however, other research has shown no differences in men and women on emotional suppression (Erikson & Ritter, 2001).

Both genders regulate emotions, but do so differently. Men tend to rely on problem-solving, behavioral strategies (distraction, avoidance), suppression, and blaming others (Brody & Hall, 2008). Women tend to regulate their emotions through obtaining social support, internalizing or blaming themselves, and ruminating on the emotion instead of taking active steps. Both genders use cognitive reappraisal as a regulation strategy. Studies examining activation of different brain areas during reappraisal suggest that this process is less effortful for men than women, possibly because reappraisal is more automatic for men or because women engage positive emotions when reappraising, making the process more effortful (McRae, Ochsner, Mauss, Gabrieli, & Gross, 2008). These differences are important for male and female leaders to keep in mind when managing their own emotions as well as those of subordinates of the opposite gender. Additionally, training for emotion knowledge and skills can be targeted more effectively when strengths and weaknesses in emotion perception, expression, and regulation are taken into account. Finally, training should consider the fact that the same emotional expressions in male and female leaders evoke different reactions in followers (Lewis, 2000).

SITUATIONAL MODERATORS

The relationships of emotion management knowledge and skills to leader performance clearly do not exist in a vacuum. Rather, these relationships might be changed by aspects of the situation related to emotions, leader performance, or both. Several key situational characteristics are likely to moderate the effects of leaders' emotion management skills on performance. Uncertainty, stress and conflict, and follower characteristics (e.g., competence and emotionality) are three factors that could increase the need for emotion management and could change the nature of how emotion management skills relate to performance.

Uncertainty

Faced with sociotechnical complexity, economic pressure, and fast-paced organizational change, leaders must contend with a great deal of uncertainty. Uncertainty can arise from social as well as economic conditions that reduce employee feelings of personal control and increase disruption. Negative emotions often accompany uncertainty, especially when employees experience major shifts in job functions or employment prospects. Thus, during times of uncertainty, there may be a greater need for leaders' emotion management knowledge skills. Additionally, the relationship between leader emotion management and leader performance may well be stronger as uncertainty increases. During layoffs or shifts in markets and customers, leaders may need to communicate new display rules to subordinates as well as broaden their repertoire of emotion regulation strategies to align with those display rules. Unpredictability in the situation can also lead to overly pessimistic or optimistic assessments about what might happen in the future, which could differentially affect the level of risk taking. If the consequences of failing in high-risk situations are severe, leaders may want to suppress feelings of optimism (Lerner & Keltner, 2000). Cultural differences are another source of uncertainty requiring keen emotion management knowledge and skills. Butler, Lee, and Gross (2007) found that cultural values influenced the relationship between the suppression of emotion and subsequent social interactions such that individualistic cultures suffered degraded social interactions following suppression while collectivist cultures did not.

Stress and Conflict

The relationship between emotion management KSAs and leader performance might be stronger in the presence of greater stress and conflict. Ayoko and Härtel (2002) indicated that intragroup conflict can be both task and interpersonally based, and they explicitly redefined social conflict as emotional conflict. These authors suggest that emotional conflict elicits a clear set of emotional responses and can negatively affect subsequent social interactions and group performance. Leaders who can help their group or team members to effectively manage emotions will facilitate conflict resolution, enabling the team to refocus on the tasks at hand. When group social conflict is minimal, the relationships of leader emotion management knowledge and skills with performance may be smaller than when social conflict is present.

Stress is also an important aspect of organizational environments that may require a greater need for emotion management from leaders. In a recent meta-analysis on the relationship between intelligence and leadership, Judge, Colbert, and Ilies (2004) found that the positive relationship between intelligence and leadership is reduced under conditions of leader stress because of higher cognitive load and reduced cognitive resources. Regulating emotions during times of stress may free up cognitive resources. However, it is important to bear in mind that regulating emotional displays can also be a source of stress for employees, and that some regulation strategies are worse offenders than others in this regard (e.g., suppression). Bono, Foldes, Vinson, and Muros (2007) found that transformational leaders helped to minimize the negative effects of emotion regulation on job satisfaction.

Follower Attributes

Characteristics of a leader's followers might also influence the relationship between a leader's emotion management KSAs and performance. For instance, the performance of a leader that must manage the emotions of a team that is emotionally stable will be different than the performance of a leader that must lead a team in which the emotionality of followers is more varied. A recent study showed that follower emotional intelligence moderated the effects of leader emotional displays on followers (Waples & Connelly, 2008) such that those low in EI responded more positively to negative leader emotions than those high in EI.

The skills and general competence of the team can play a role in the relative importance placed on managing emotions within the team. Specifically, if the team is relatively unskilled, it might be more important that the leader focus on developing competence in other areas before focusing on developing emotion management. However, a team characterized with lower degree of skill might also be more likely to experience emotionally evocative situations, such as failing at a task. Accordingly it may be useful to examine follower emotional competence and task competence as moderators of leader emotion management capabilities and leader performance.

IMPLICATIONS FOR TRAINING LEADER EMOTION MANAGEMENT KSAs

The nature and variety of emotion-related knowledge, skills, and abilities suggests that many components of emotion management might improve through training and education interventions. In fact, emotional intelligence research offers initial evidence that emotional competencies respond favorably to training (Dulewicz & Higgs, 2004; Hopfl & Linstead, 1997). However, it is clear that much work remains with regard to understanding the relationships between emotion regulation and different aspects of leader performance. There is a lack of research on how to effectively develop emotion management, and conditions under which different emotion management strategies are most effective. Given this, training should provide practice with a variety of emotion-related skills, including increasing the accurate perception of emotions in others, regulating one's own and others' emotions, and tailoring emotional expression as part of goal-directed behavior under different conditions and in different situations.

Building Emotion Knowledge

Like many types of organizational knowledge, emotion knowledge can be acquired by leaders through a variety of formal and informal learning opportunities. An ever-expanding set of resources in psychological and organizational behavior literature describes relevant emotion theories, types of emotions, emotion norms (i.e., display rules), emotion processes, regulation strategies, and alternative forms of emotional expression. However, developing emotion knowledge requires more than simply providing leaders with a basic set of readings. Building complex emotion knowledge structures requires linking basic concepts, theories, and processes to see how these discrete pieces of information fit together to shape emotional experience. Emotion knowledge topics could easily be integrated into management and leadership educational curricula and could be developed through instructor-led training or self-study methods. Material could be learned in classroom settings, online, and through videos, demonstrations, and case studies to reinforce and apply what is learned from the readings.

A number of researchers have identified specific examples of training emotion knowledge. Lopes and colleagues (2006) discussed how understanding of emotions can be trained in a number of ways including discussing similarities and differences among emotions and triggers of emotions. Additionally, these researchers suggest that explicit discussion during training can facilitate understanding of emotion processes such as cognitive appraisal tendencies and emotion episodes. Along similar lines, other researchers have discussed how clarifying unspoken rules or norms for social interaction in the workplace might facilitate learning (Sternberg et al., 2000; Sternberg & Hedlund, 2002; Wagner & Sternberg, 1985). Others have proposed that individuals develop understanding of emotion norms within an organization in a number of ways, including training (Domagalski, 1999; Opengart, 2005).

Improving Emotion Perception and Regulation

Some empirical evidence indicates that people can improve their abilities to accurately perceive emotions and regulate emotions. For example, Elfenbein (2006) demonstrated that providing feedback on the accuracy of emotion identification based on photographs of facial expressions improved later emotion identification. Similarly, using a computerized emotion training program, other research has shown that individuals who have completed the training improve their scores on emotion identification and emotion differentiation tests (Silver, Goodman, Knoll, & Isakov, 2004).

With respect to emotion regulation, Schartau, Dalgleish, and Dunn (2009) examined the role of perspective taking in regulating emotional reactions. Training individuals on seeing the bigger picture reduced negative affective reactions to distressing stimuli and autobiographical memories. This kind of perspective-taking training for leaders could have benefits in areas beyond emotion regulation. The efficacy of other general approaches to self-regulation, such as meditation and mindfulness training, has also been shown. Tang and colleagues (2007) found that 20 minutes of meditation/mindfulness practice over five days significantly reduced trainees' anxiety, depression, and anger, and decreased stress-related cortisol levels.

Other organizational research is in line with these findings. Lopes and colleagues (2006) discussed emotion-related skill development with respect to Gross's (1998) model of emotion regulation, offering a number of practical ways leaders might apply different regulation strategies. They note that emotion regulation training can help leaders to question overly negative thoughts in order to prevent rumination, something that can worsen or prolong negative emotional states. Additionally, training can help leaders regulate their own and others' emotions through humor and emphasizing a positive work atmosphere.

Our proposed framework of leader emotion management has a number of implications for emotion management training. First, managing emotions does not simply imply suppressing or ignoring emotions. Organizational display rules and the goals of particular interactions will dictate whether emotional suppression is appropriate or authentic emotional expression is required. The number of different strategies applicable in any situation implies that training developed for emotion management needs to focus on increasing understanding of emotion norms, emotion triggers, and situational factors such as uncertainty so leaders can identify the most appropriate strategy for the situation at hand. Thus, increasing knowledge about emotions and emotion processes is likely an important starting point in training. Second, not all emotional processes are under an individual's conscious control. Training individuals on specific regulation strategies may result in small improvements. One approach to training emotion regulation is to first get leaders to recognize the strategies they rely on the most and determine how effective these are for the situations leaders face. The focus of training can be to work with one's effective strategies while developing alternative ones. Third, as with other types of training, stable individual differences will likely play a role in the development of emotion-related knowledge and skills. Some individuals will learn more, learn faster, and improve more overall compared to others. Personality could influence behaviors and strategies used in an emotionally laden situation (John & Gross, 2007) through selective awareness of and preference for some strategies over others. Finally, it is clear that much work remains with regard to understanding the relationships between emotion regulation and different aspects of job performance (Gross, 2007). There is a lack of research on how to effectively develop emotion management, and conditions under which different emotion management strategies are most effective. Given this, training should focus first on increasing basic emotion-related knowledge and vocabulary. Training should provide practice with a variety of emotion-related skills, including increasing the accurate perception of emotions in others, regulating one's own and others' emotions, and tailoring emotional expression as part of goal-directed behavior in specific situations. Experiential learning is likely key to effectively developing emotion management knowledge and skills in leaders. This base will allow individuals to adapt to a variety of performance contexts and use emotion management effectively to achieve desired goals.

CONCLUSION

Leadership scholars have long recognized the salience and influence of emotions and emotion management in leadership environments. However, many approaches assume that emotion management is needed in all leadership situations. This chapter argues that leaders' emotion-related capacities are more important in certain leader performance domains than others. The framework discussed here outlines various types of emotion knowledge, skills, and abilities critical for leader performance in seven areas of performance. This model advocates that leader knowledge concerning types of emotions, emotion norms, regulation methods, and emotion process and outcomes will facilitate the development and use of emotion-related abilities and skills. These abilities and skills in turn are expected to influence emotion-relevant leadership performance and their development and effective application is likely to depend on a number of individual traits and situational moderators. We hope this framework stimulates thinking with regard to the differential influence of emotion management across leadership performance domains and with regard to how organizations can foster the development of emotion management capabilities.

––––––––

ACKNOWLEDGMENT

This research was supported by a contract from the U.S. Army Research Institute (W91WAW-08-P-0438). The statements and opinions expressed in this chapter do not necessarily reflect the position or the policy of the U.S. government and no official endorsement should be inferred.

REFERENCES

Abele, A. (1992). Daily representations under the influence of positive and negative moods on task-related motivation. *Zeitschrift Fur Experimentelle und Angewandte Psychologie, 39,* 345.

Akerjordet, K., & Severinsson, E. (2010). The state of the science of emotional intelligence related to nursing leadership: An integrative review. *Journal of Nursing Management, 18,* 363–382.

Antonakis, J., Ashkanasy, N. M., & Dasborough, M. (2009). Does leadership need emotional intelligence? *Leadership Quarterly, 20,* 247–261.

Ashforth, B. E., & Humphrey, R. H. (1993). Emotional labor in service roles: The influence of identity. *Academy of Management Review, 18,* 88–115.

Ashkanasy, N. M., & Daus, C. S. (2002). Emotion in the workplace: The new challenge for managers. *Academy of Management Executive, 16,* 76–86.

Ashkanasy, N. M., & Humphrey, R. H. (2011). Current research on emotion in organizations. *Emotion Review, 3,* 214–224.

Avolio, B., Gardner, W., Walumbwa, F., Luthans, F., & May, D. (2004). Unlocking the mask: A look at the process by which authentic leaders impact follower attitudes and behaviors. *Leadership Quarterly, 15,* 801–823.

Ayoko, O. B., Callan, V. J., & Härtel, C. E. J. (2008). The influence of team emotional intelligence climate on conflict and team members' reactions to conflict. *Small Group Research, 39,* 121–149.

Ayoko, O. B., & Härtel, C. E. J. (2002). The role of emotion and emotion management in destructive and productive conflict in culturally heterogeneous workgroups. In N. M. Ashkanasy, W. J. Zerbe, & C. E. J. Härtel (Eds.), *Managing emotions in the workplace* (pp. 77–79). Armonk, NY: M. E. Sharpe.

Barchard, K. A., & Hakstian, A. R. (2004). The nature and movement of emotional intelligence abilities: Basic dimensions and their relationships with other cognitive ability and personality variables. *Educational and Psychological Measurement, 64,* 437–462.

Bar-On, R. (1997). *Bar-On Emotional Quotient Inventory (EQ-i): A test of emotional intelligence.* Toronto: Multi-Health Systems.

Bar-On, R. (2006). The Bar-On Model of Emotional-Social Intelligence (ESI). *Psicothema, 18,* 13–25.

Baron, R.A. (1990). Countering the effects of destructive criticism: The relative efficacy of four interventions. *Journal of Applied Psychology, 75,* 235–245.

Barry, B. (2008). Negotiator affect: The state of the art (and science). *Group Decision and Negotiation, 17,* 97–105.

Barsade, S.G., & Gibson, D.E. (2007). Why does affect matter in organizations? *Academy of Management Perspectives, 21,* 36–59.

Ben-Ze'ev, A. (2002). Emotional intelligence: The conceptual issue. In N.M. Ashkanasy, W.J. Zerbe, & C.E.J. Härtel (Eds.), *Managing emotions in the workplace* (pp. 164–183). Armonk, NY: M.E. Sharpe.

Bodtker, A.B., & Jameson, J.K. (2001). Emotion in conflict formation and its transformation: Application to organizational conflict management. *The International Journal of Conflict Management, 12,* 259–275.

Bono, J.E., Foldes, H.J., Vinson, G., & Muros, J.P. (2007). Workplace emotions: The role of supervision and leadership. *Journal of Applied Psychology, 92,* 1357–1367.

Bono, J.E., & Ilies, R. (2006). Charisma, positive emotions, and mood contagion. *Leadership Quarterly, 17,* 317–334.

Bower, G.H. (1981). Mood and memory. *American Psychologist, 36,* 129–148.

Boyatzis, R.E., & Sala, F. (2004). Assessing emotional intelligence competencies. In G. Geher (Ed.), *The measurement of emotional intelligence.* Hauppauge, NY: Nova Science.

Brackett, M.A., & Mayer, J.D. (2003). Convergent, discriminant, and incremental validity of competing measures of emotional intelligence. *Personality and Social Psychology Bulletin, 29,* 1147–1158.

Brody, L.R., & Hall, J. (2008). Gender and emotion in context. In M. Lewis, J.M. Haviland-Jones, & L. Feldman Barrett (Eds.), *Handbook of emotions* (3rd ed.). New York: Guilford Press.

Brotheridge, C.M., & Grandey, A.A. (2002). Emotional labor and burnout: Comparing two perspectives of "people work." *Journal of Vocational Behavior, 60,* 17–39.

Brown, M.E., & Trevino, L.K. (2006). Ethical leadership: A review and future directions. *Leadership Quarterly, 17,* 595–616.

Butler, E.A., Lee, T.L., & Gross, J.J. (2007). Emotion regulation and culture: Are the social consequences of emotion suppression culture-specific? *Emotion, 7,* 30–48.

Campbell, J.P. (1988). Training design for performance improvement: New perspectives from industrial and organizational psychology. In J.P. Campbell, R.J. Campbell, & Associates (Eds.), *Productivity in organizations* (pp. 177–216). San Francisco, CA: Jossey-Bass.

Cherniss, C. (2010). Emotional intelligence: Towards clarification of a concept. *Industrial and Organizational Psychology: Perspectives on Science and Practice, 3,* 110–126.

Clarke, C., Hope-Hailey, V., & Kelliher, C. (2007). Being real or really being someone else? Change, managers and emotion work. *European Management Journal, 25,* 92–103.

Colquitt, J.A., LePine, J.A., & Noe, R.A. (2000). Toward an integrative theory of training motivation: A meta-analytic path analysis of 20 years of research. *Journal of Applied Psychology, 85,* 678–707.

Connelly, S., Helton-Fauth, W., & Mumford, M.D. (2004). A managerial in-basket study of the impact of trait emotions on ethical choice. *Journal of Business Ethics, 51,* 245–267.

Connelly, S., & Ruark, G. (2010). Leadership style and activating potential as moderators of the relationship between leader emotional valence and outcomes. *Leadership Quarterly, 21,* 745–764.

Davies, M., Stankov, L., & Roberts, R.D. (1998). Emotional intelligence: In search of an elusive construct. *Journal of Personality and Social Psychology, 75,* 989–1015.

Dieffendorf, J.M., & Richard, E.M. (2003). Antecedents and consequences of emotional display rule perceptions. *Journal of Applied Psychology, 88,* 284–294.

Dieffendorf, J.M., Richard, E.M., & Croyle, M.H. (2006). Are emotional display rules formal job requirements? Examination of employee and supervisor perceptions. *Journal of Occupational and Organizational Psychology, 79,* 273–298.

Domagalski, T.A. (1999). Emotion in organizations: Main currents. *Human Relations, 52,* 833–853.

Druckman, D., & Olekalns, M. (2008). Emotions in negotiation. *Group Decision and Negotiation, 17*(1), 1–11.

Dulewicz, V., & Higgs, M. (1999). Can emotional intelligence be measured and developed? *Leadership and Organization Development Journal, 20,* 242–252.

Dulewicz, V., & Higgs, M. (2000). Emotional intelligence: A review and evaluation study. *Journal of Managerial Psychology, 15,* 341–372.

Dulewicz, V., & Higgs, M. (2004). Can emotional intelligence be developed? *International Journal of Human Resource Management, 15,* 95–111.

Eisenberg, N. (1998). Introduction. In N. Eisenberg (Vol. Ed.) & W. Damon (Series Ed.), *Handbook of Child Psychology, vol. 3, Social, Emotional, and Personality Development* (5th ed., pp. 1–24). New York: Wiley.

Ekman, P., & Friesen, W.V. (1969). Nonverbal leakage and clues to deception. *Journal for the Study of Interpersonal Processes, 32,* 88–106.

Ekman, P., & Friesen, W.V. (1975). *Unmasking the face: A guide to recognizing emotion from facial clues.* Oxford: Prentice-Hall.

Elfenbein, H.A. (2006). Learning in emotion judgments: Training and the cross-cultural understanding of facial expressions. *Journal of Nonverbal Behavior, 30,* 21–36.

Erez, A., & Isen, A. (2002). The influence of positive affect on the components of expectancy motivation. *Journal of Applied Psychology, 87,* 1055–1067.

Erez, A., Misangyi, V.F., Johnson, D.E., & LePine, M.A. (2008). Stirring the hearts of followers: Charismatic leadership as the transferal of affect. *Journal of Applied Psychology, 93,* 602–615.

Erickson, R.J., & Ritter, C. (2001). Emotional labor, burnout, and inauthenticity: Does gender matter? *Social Psychology Quarterly, 64,* 146–163.

Feldman, D.A. (1999). *The handbook of emotionally intelligent leadership: Inspiring others to achieve great results.* Falls Church, VA: Leadership Performance Solutions Press.

Frijda, N.H. (1986). *The emotions.* Cambridge: Cambridge University Press.

Frijda, N.H. (1993). Moods, emotion episodes, and emotions. In M. Lewis & J. Haviland (Eds.), *Handbook of emotions* (pp. 381–403). New York: Guilford Press.

Gaddis, B., Connelly, S., & Mumford, M. (2004). Failure feedback as an affective event: Influences of leader affect on subordinate attitudes and performance. *Leadership Quarterly, 15,* 663–686.

Gaudine, A., & Thorne, L. (2001). Emotion and ethical decision-making in organizations. *Journal of Business Ethics, 31,* 175–187.

George, J. (2000). Emotions and leadership: The role of emotional intelligence. *Human Relations, 53,* 1027–1055.

George, J. M., & Zhou, J. (2002). Understanding when bad moods foster creativity and good ones don't: The role of context and clarity of feelings. *Journal of Applied Psychology, 87*(4), 687–697.

Goleman, D. P. (1995). *Emotional intelligence: Why it can matter more than IQ for character, health, and lifelong achievement.* New York: Bantam Books.

Gooty, J. Connelly, S., Griffith, J., & Gupta, A. (2010). Leadership, affect, and emotions: A state of the science review. *Leadership Quarterly, 21,* 979–1004.

Grandey, A. A. (2000). Emotional regulation in the workplace: A new way to conceptualize emotional labor. *Journal of Occupational Health Psychology, 5,* 95–110.

Gross, J. J. (1998a). Antecedent- and response-focused emotion regulation: Divergent consequences for experience, expression, and physiology. *Journal of Personality and Social Psychology, 74,* 224–237.

Gross, J. J. (1998b). The emerging field of emotion regulation: An integrative review. *Review of General Psychology, 2,* 271–299.

Gross, J. J. (2002). Emotion regulation: Affective, cognitive, and social consequences. *Psychophysiology, 39,* 281–291.

Gross, J. J. (Ed.). (2007). *Handbook of emotion regulation.* New York: Guilford.

Gross, J. J., & John, O. P. (1997). Revealing feelings: Facets of emotional expressivity in self-reports, peer ratings, and behavior. *Journal of Personality and Social Psychology, 72,* 435–448.

Gross, J. J., & John, O. P. (1998). Mapping the domain of expressivity: Multi-method evidence for a hierarchical model. *Journal of Personality and Social Psychology, 74,* 170–191.

Gross, J. J., & John, O. P. (2003). Individual differences in two emotion regulation processes: Implications for affect, relationships, and well-being. *Journal of Personality and Social Psychology, 85,* 348–362.

Gross, J. J., & Thompson, R. A. (2007). Emotion regulation: Conceptual foundations. In J. J. Gross (Ed.), *Handbook of emotion regulation* (pp. 3–24). New York: Guilford Press.

Haidt, J. (2001). The emotional dog and its rational tail: A social intuitionist approach to moral judgment. *Psychological Review, 108,* 814–834.

Hall, J. A., & Matsumoto, D. (2004). Gender differences in judgments of multiple emotions from facial expressions. *Emotion, 4,* 201–206.

Harms, P. D., & Credé, M. (2010a). Emotional intelligence and transformation and transactional leadership: A meta-analysis. *Journal of Leadership and Organizational Studies, 17*(1), 5–17.

Harms, P. D., & Credé, M. (2010b). Remaining issues in emotional intelligence research: Construct overlap, method artifacts, and lack of incremental validity. *Industrial and Organizational Psychology, 3,* 154–158.

Hatfield, E., Cacioppo, J. T., & Rapson, R. L. (1994). *Emotional contagion: Studies in emotion and social interaction.* New York: Cambridge University Press.

Hochschild, A. R. (1983). *The managed heart.* Berkeley: University of California Press.

Hodgson, L., & Wertheim, E. (2007). Does good emotion management aid forgiving? Multiple dimensions of empathy, emotion management and forgiveness of self and others. *Journal of Social & Personal Relationships, 24,* 931–949.

Hopfl, H., & Linstead, S. (1997). Learning to feel and feeling to learn: Emotion and learning in organizations. *Management Learning, 28,* 5–12.

Humphrey, R. H., Pollack, J., & Hawver, T. H. (2008). Leading with emotional labor. *Journal of Managerial Psychology, 23,* 151–168.

Hunter, S. T., Bedell-Avers, K. E., & Mumford, M. D. (2007). The typical leadership study: Assumptions, implications, and potential remedies. *Leadership Quarterly, 18*, 435–446.

Isen, A. M. (2003). Positive affect as a source of human strength. In L. G. Aspinwall & U. M. Staudinger (Eds.), *A psychology of human strengths: Fundamental questions and future directions for a positive psychology* (pp. 179–195). Washington, DC: American Psychological Association.

Isen, A. M., Daubman, K. A., & Nowicki, G. P. (1987). Positive affect facilitates creative problem solving. *Journal of Personality and Social Psychology, 52*, 1122–1131.

Izard, C. E. (1971). *The face of emotion*. New York: Appleton-Century-Crofts.

Izard, C. E. (1972). *Patterns of emotions: A new analysis of anxiety and depression*. New York: Academic Press.

Izard, C. E., Fine, S., Schultz, D., Mostow, A., Ackerman, B., & Yountstrom, E. (2001). Emotional knowledge as a predictor of social behavior and academic competence in children at risk. *Psychological Science, 12*, 18–23.

John, O. P., & Gross, J. J. (2004). Healthy and unhealthy emotion regulation: Personality processes, individual differences, and life span development. *Journal of Personality, 72*, 1301–1333.

John, O. P., & Gross, J. J. (2007). Individual differences in emotion regulation. In J. Gross (Ed.), *Handbook of emotion regulation* (pp. 351–372). New York: Guilford Press.

Johnson, S. K. (2008). I second that emotion: Effects of emotional contagion and affect at work on leader and follower outcomes. *Leadership Quarterly, 19*, 1–19.

Johnson, E., & Tversky, A. (1983). Affect, generalization, and the perception of risk. *Journal of Personality and Social Psychology, 45*, 20–31.

Jones, R. G., & Rittman, A. L. (2002). A model of emotional and motivational components of interpersonal interactions in organizations. In N. M. Ashkanasy, C. E. J. Härtel, & W. J. Zerbe (Eds.), *Managing emotions in the workplace* (pp. 77–97). Armonk, NY: M. E. Sharpe.

Judge, T. A., Colbert, A. E., & Ilies, R. (2004). Intelligence and leadership: A quantitative review and test of theoretical propositions. *Journal of Applied Psychology, 89*, 542–552.

Kaplan, S., Cortina, J., & Ruark, G. (2010). Ooops…we did it again. Industrial-organizational's focus on emotional intelligence instead of its relationship to outcomes. *Industrial and Organizational Psychology: Perspectives on Science and Practice, 3*, 171–177.

Kellett, J. B., Humphrey, R. H., & Sleeth, R. G. (2006). Empathy and the emergence of task and relations leaders. *Leadership Quarterly, 17*, 146–162.

King, L. A., & Emmons, R. A. (1990). Ambivalence over expressing emotion: Physical and psychological correlates. *Journal of Personality and Social Psychology, 58*, 864–877.

Kligyte, V., Connelly, S., Thiel, C., & Devenport, L. (in press). The influence of anger, fear, and emotion regulation on ethical decision-making. *Human Performance*.

Kluger, A. N., & DeNisi, A. (1996). The effects of feedback interventions on performance: A historical review, a meta-analysis, and a preliminary feedback intervention theory. *Psychological Bulletin, 119*, 254–284.

Kruml, S. M., & Geddes, D. (2000). Exploring the dimensions of emotional labor: The heart of Hochschild's work. *Management Communication Quarterly, 14*, 8–49.

Lane, R. D., & Schwartz, G. E. (1987). Levels of emotional awareness: A cognitive-developmental theory and its application to psychopathology. *American Journal of Psychiatry, 144*, 133–143.

Lane, R. D., Quinlan, D. M., Schwartz, G. E., & Walker, P. A. (1990). The levels of emotional awareness scale: A cognitive-developmental measure of emotion. *Journal of Personality Assessment, 55*, 124–134.

Larsen, R. J., Diener, E., & Cropanzano, R. S. (1987). Cognitive operations associated with individual differences in affect intensity. *Journal of Personality and Social Psychology, 53,* 767–774.

Lazarus, R. S. (1991). Cognition and motivation in emotion. *American Psychologist, 46,* 352–367.

Lennox, R. D., & Wolfe, R. N. (1984). Revision of the self-monitoring scale. *Journal of Personality and Social Psychology, 46,* 1349–1364.

Lerner, J. S., & Keltner, D. (2000). Beyond valence: Toward a model of emotion-specific influences on judgment and choice. *Cognition and Emotion, 14,* 473–493.

Levenson, R. W. (1994). Emotional control: Variation and consequences. In P. Ekman & R. J. Davidson (Eds.), *The nature of emotion: Fundamental questions* (pp. 273–279). New York: Oxford University Press.

Lewis, K. M. (2000). When leaders display emotion: How followers respond to negative emotional expression of male and female leaders. *Journal of Organizational Behavior, 21,* 221–234.

Linden, W., Hogan, B. E., Rutlege, T., Chawla, A., Lenz, J. W., & Leung, D. (2003). There is more to anger coping than "in" or "out." *Emotion, 3*(1), 12–29.

Loewenstein, G., Weber, E. U., Hsee, C. K., & Welch, N. (2001). Risk as feelings. *Psychological Bulletin, 127,* 267–286.

Lopes, P. N., Côté, S., & Salovey, P. (2006). An ability model of emotional intelligence: Implications for assessment and training. In V. U. Druskat, F. Sala, & G. Mount (Eds.), *Linking emotional intelligence and performance at work: Current research evidence with individuals and groups* (pp. 53–80). Mahwah, NJ: Lawrence Erlbaum.

Mackie, D. M., & Worth, L. T. (1991). Feeling good, but not thinking straight: The impact of positive mood on persuasion. In J. Forgas (Ed.), *Emotion and social judgments* (pp. 201–219). Oxford: Pergamon Press.

Martin, L. L., Achee, J. W., Ward, D. W., & Harlow, T. F. (1993). The role of cognition and effort in the use of emotions to guide behavior. In R. S. Wyer & T. K. Srull (Eds.), *Advances in social cognition* (pp. 147–157). Hillsdale, NJ: Lawrence Erlbaum.

Mayer, J. D., Caruso, D. R., & Salovey, P. (1999). Emotional intelligence meets traditional standards for an intelligence. *Intelligence, 27,* 267–298.

Mayer, J. D., & Hanson, E. (1995). Mood-congruent judgment over time. *Personality and Social Psychology Bulletin, 21,* 237–244.

Mayer, J. D., Roberts, R. D., & Barsade, S. G. (2008). Human abilities: Emotional intelligence. *Annual Review of Psychology, 59,* 507–536.

Mayer, J. D., Salovey, P., & Caruso, D. R. (2000). Models of emotional intelligence. In R. J. Sternberg (Ed.), *The handbook of intelligence* (pp. 81–115). New York: Cambridge University Press.

McRae, K., Ochsner, K. N., Mauss, I. B., Gabrieli, J. D., & Gross, J. J. (2008). Gender differences in emotion regulation: An fMRI study of cognitive reappraisal. *Group Processes Intergroup Relations, 11,* 143–163.

Mumford, M. D., & Connelly, M. S. (1991). Leaders as creators: Leader performance and problem solving in ill-defined domains. *Leadership Quarterly, 2,* 289–315.

Mumford, M. D., Connelly, S., Brown, R. P., Murphy, S. T., Hill, J. H., Antes, A. L., Waples, E. P., & Devenport, L. D. (2008). A sensemaking approach to ethics training for scientists: Preliminary evidence of training effectiveness. *Ethics and Behavior, 18,* 315–339.

Newcombe, M., & Ashkanasy, N. (2002). The role of affect and affective congruence in perceptions of leaders: An experimental study. *Leadership Quarterly, 13,* 601–614.

Niedenthal, P. M. (2008). Emotion concepts. In M. Lewis, J. M. Haviland-Jones, & L. F. Barrett (Eds.), *Handbook of emotion* (3rd ed.). New York: Guilford.

Ochsner, K. N., Bunge, S. A., Gross, J. J., & Gabrieli, J. D. E. (2002). Rethinking feelings: An fMRI study of the cognitive regulation of emotion. *Journal of Cognitive Neuroscience, 14,* 1215–1229.

Ochsner, K. N., & Gross, J. J. (2008). Cognitive emotion regulation: Insights from social cognitive and affective neuroscience. *Currents Directions in Psychological Science, 17*(1), 153–158.

Ochsner, K. N., Ray, R. D., Cooper, J. C., Robertson, E. R., Chopra, S., Gabrieli, J. D. E., & Gross, J. J. (2004). For better or worse: Neural systems supporting the cognitive down- and up-regulation of negative emotions. *Neuroimage, 23,* 483–499.

Opengart, R. (2005). Emotional intelligence and emotion work: Examining constructs from an interdisciplinary framework. *Human Resource Development Review, 4,* 49–62.

Ortony, A., Clore, G. L., & Collins, A. (1988). *The cognitive structure of emotions.* New York: Cambridge University Press.

Pirola-Merlo, A., Härtel, C. E. J., Mann, L., & Hirst, G. (2002). How leaders influence the impact of affective events on team climate and performance in R&D teams. *Leadership Quarterly, 13,* 561–581.

Raghunathan, R., & Pham, M. T. (1999), All negative moods are not equal: Motivational influences of anxiety and sadness on decision making. *Organizational Behavior and Human Decision Processes, 79*(1), 56–77.

Ramos, N. S., Fernandez-Berrocal, P., & Extremera, N. (2007). Perceived emotional intelligence facilitates cognitive-emotional processes of adaptation to an acute stressor. *Cognition & Emotion, 21,* 758–772.

Riggio, R. E., & Lee, J. (2007). Emotional and interpersonal competencies and leader development. *Human Resource Management Review, 17,* 418–426.

Roseman, I. J., Spindel, M. S., & Jose, P. E. (1990). Appraisals of emotion-eliciting events: Testing a theory of discrete emotions. *Journal of Personality and Social Psychology, 59,* 899–915.

Russ, S. W. (1993). *Affect and creativity: The role of affect and play in the creative process.* Hillsdale, NJ: Lawrence Erlbaum.

Russell, J. A. (1980). A circumplex model of affect. *Journal of Personality and Social Psychology, 39,* 1161–1178.

Russell, J. A. (1991). Culture and the categorization of emotion. *Psychological Bulletin, 110,* 426–450.

Saarni, C. (1990). Emotional competence: How emotions and relationships become integrated. In R. A. Thompson (Ed.), *Nebraska Symposium on Motivation, 36 Socioemotional Development* (pp. 115–182). Lincoln: University of Nebraska Press.

Salovey, P., & Mayer, J. D. (1990). *Emotional intelligence: Imagination, cognition, and personality.* New York: Harper.

Sander, D., Grandjean, D., Kaiser, S., Wehrle, T., & Scherer, K. R. (2007). Interaction effects of perceived gaze direction and dynamic facial expression: Evidence for appraisal theories of emotion. *European Journal of Cognitive Psychology, 19,* 470–480.

Schartau, P. E., Dalgleish T., & Dunn, B. D. (2009). Seeing the bigger picture: Training in perspective broadening reduces self-reported affect and psychophysiological response to distressing films and autobiographical memories. *Journal of Abnormal Psychology, 118*(1), 15–27.

Scherer, K. R. (1988). Studying the emotion-antecedent appraisal process: An expert system approach. *Cognition and Emotion, 7,* 325–355.

Schroth, H. A., Bain-Chekal, J., & Caldwell, D. F. (2005). Sticks and stones may break bones and words can hurt me. *The International Journal of Conflict Management, 16,* 102–127.

Schutte, N.A., Malouff, J.M., Bobik, C., Coston, T.D., Greeson, C., Jedlicka, C., Rhodes, E., & Wendorf, G. (2001). Emotional intelligence and interpersonal relations. *The Journal of Social Psychology, 14,* 523–536.

Schwarz, N. & Clore, G.L. (1983). Mood, misattribution, and judgments of well-being: Informative and directive functions of affective states. *Journal of Personality and Social Psychology, 45,* 513–523.

Seymour, D., & Sandiford, P. (2005). Learning emotion rules in service organizations: Socialization and training in the UK public-house sector. *Work, Employment, and Society, 19,* 547–564.

Shaver, P., Schwartz, J., Kirson, D., & O'Connor, C. (1987). Emotion knowledge: Further exploration of a prototype approach. *Journal of Personality and Social Psychology, 52,* 212–232.

Silver, H., Goodman, C., Knoll, G., & Isakov, V. (2004). Brief emotion training improves recognition of facial emotions in chronic schizophrenia. A pilot study. *Psychiatry Research, 128,* 147–154.

Sinaceur, M., & Tiedens, L.Z. (2006). Get mad and get more than even: The benefits of anger expressions in negotiations. *Journal of Experimental Social Psychology, 42,* 314–322.

Smith, C.A., & Ellsworth, P.C. (1985). Patterns of cognitive appraisal in emotion. *Journal of Personality and Social Psychology, 48,* 813–838.

Smith, C.A., & Pope, L.K. (1992). Appraisal and emotion: The interactional contributions of dispositional and situational factors. In M.S. Clark (Ed.), *Emotion and social behavior. Review of personality and social psychology* (vol. 14, pp. 32–62). Newbury Park, CA: Sage.

Snyder, M. (1974). Self-monitoring of expressive behavior. *Journal of Personality and Social Psychology, 30,* 526–537.

Sonenshein, S. (2007). The role of construction, intuition, and justification in responding to ethical issues at work: The sense making-intuition model. *Academy of Management Review, 32*(4), 1022–1040.

Staw, B.M., & Barsade, S.G. (1993). Affect and managerial performance: A test of the sadder-but-wiser vs. happier-and-smarter hypotheses. *Administrative Science Quarterly, 38,* 304–331.

Sternberg, R.J., Forsythe, G.B., Hedlund, J., Horvath, J.A., Wagner, R.K., Williams, W.M., Snook, S.A., & Grigorenko, E.L. (2000). *Practical intelligence in everyday life.* New York: Cambridge University Press.

Sternberg, R.J., & Hedlund, J. (2002). Practical intelligence, g, and work psychology. *Human Performance, 15,* 143–160.

Sy, T., Côté, S., & Saavedra, R. (2005). The contagious leader: Impact of leader's mood on the mood of group members, group affective tone, and group processes. *Journal of Applied Psychology, 90,* 295–305.

Tang, Y., Ma, Y., Wang, J., Fan, Y., Feg, S., Lu, Q., . . . Posner, M. (2007). Short-term meditation training improves attention and self-regulation. *Proceedings of the National Academy of Sciences, 104,* 17152–17156.

Tangney, J.P., & Dearing, R.L. (2003). *Shame and guilt.* New York: Guilford Press.

Tangney, J.P., Stuewig, J., Mashek, D., & Hastings, M. (2011). Assessing jail inmates' proneness to shame and guilt: Feeling bad about the behavior or the self? *Criminal Justice and Behavior, 38,* 710–734.

Tannenbaum, S.I., & Yukl, G. (1992). Training and development in work organizations. *Annual Review of Psychology, 43,* 399–441.

Taylor, C. (1985). Human agency and language. *Philosophical papers* (vol. 1). Cambridge: Cambridge University Press.

Thiel, C., Connelly, S., & Griffith, J.A. (2011). The influence of ethical decision-making: Comparison of a primary and secondary appraisal. *Ethics and Behavior, 21,* 380–403.

Thiruchselvam, R., Blechert, J., Sheppes, G., Rydstrom, A., & Gross, J.J. (2011). The temporal dynamics of emotion regulation: An EEG study of distraction and reappraisal. *Biological Psychology, 87,* 84–92.

Thompson, R.A. (1994). Emotion regulation: A theme in search of definition. *Monographs of the Society for Research in Child Development, 59,* 250–283.

Tomkins, S.S. (1962). *Affect, imagery and consciousness, 1. The positive affects.* New York: Springer.

Van Kleef, G. (2008). Emotion in conflict and negotiation: Introducing the emotions as social information (EASI) model. In N. Ashkanasy & C. Cooper (Eds.), *Research companion to emotion in organizations* (pp. 392–422). Elgar Edward: Cheltenham, UK.

Van Kleef, G.A., de Dreu, C.K.W., & Manstead, A.S.R. (2004). The interpersonal effects of emotions in negotiations: A motivated information processing approach. *Journal of Personality and Social Psychology, 87,* 510–528.

Van Kleef, G.A., de Dreu, C.K.W., & Manstead, A.S.R. (2006). Supplication and appeasement in conflict and negotiation: The interpersonal effects of disappointment, worry, guilt, and regret. *Journal of Personality and Social Psychology, 91,* 124–142.

Wagner, R.K., & Sternberg, R.J. (1985). Practical intelligence in real-world pursuits: The role of tacit knowledge. *Journal of Personality and Social Psychology, 49,* 436–458.

Wang, X.T. (2006). Emotions within reason: Resolving conflicts in risk preference. *Cognition and Emotion, 20,* 1132–1152.

Waples, E.P., & Connelly, S. (2008). Leader emotions and vision implementation: Effects of activation potential and valence. In R.H. Humphrey (Ed.), *Affect and emotion—New directions in management theory and research* (pp. 67–96). Charlotte, NC: Information Age.

Weiss, H.M., & Cropanzano, R. (1996). Affective events theory: A theoretical discussion of the structure, causes and consequences of affective experiences at work. In B.M. Staw & L.L. Cummings (Eds.), *Research in organizational behavior: An annual series of analytical essays and critical reviews* (pp. 1–74). Greenwich, CT: JAI Press.

Westen, D. (1994). Toward an integrative model of affect regulation: Applications to social-psychological research. *Journal of Personality, 62,* 642–667.

Wilk, S.L., & Moynihan, L.M. (2005). Display rule "regulators": The relationship between supervisors and worker emotional exhaustion. *Journal of Applied Psychology, 90,* 917–927.

Wright, W.F., & Bower, G.H. (1992). Mood effects on subjective probability assessment. *Organizational Behavior and Human Decision Processes, 52,* 276–291.

Yukl, G. (2006). *Leadership in organizations.* Upper Saddle River, NJ: Prentice Hall.

Section III
Influence and Political Skills of the Leader

7

Leader Ethos

How Character Contributes to the Social Influence of the Leader

Peter L. Jennings and Sean T. Hannah

> The man who wishes to persuade people will not be negligent as to the matter of character [ethos]; no, on the contrary, he will apply himself above all to establish a most honorable name among his fellow-citizens; for who does not know that words carry greater conviction when spoken by men of good repute than when spoken by men who live under a cloud, and that the argument which is made by a man's life is more weight than that which is furnished by words?
>
> —Isocrates, *Antidosis* (cited in Hyde, 2004, pp. xiv–xv)

Leadership is typically understood as a social process, the essence of which is the influence a formal or informal leader has on others (Northouse, 2007). The majority of research on leader influence has focused on leader power, political savvy, influence tactics, skills, and leadership styles (Bass & Bass, 2008; Yukl, 2002). These approaches have thus focused primarily on what a leader *does* or on the power inherent in leaders' formal positions. Much less attention has been paid in research to who the leader *is* or the purposes and principles that define his or her character as a leader. While leader character is considered an essential aspect of the leadership process (Hannah & Avolio, 2011a, 2011b; Hannah & Jennings, 2013. Quick & Wright, 2011), little is known about how character specifically contributes to the social influence of a leader (Wright & Quick, 2011). This chapter examines this question through the concept of *ethos.*

Ethos has its roots in Aristotelian rhetoric—the art and science of persuasion through speech (Hyde & Schrag, 2004). An important dimension of ethos is the persuasive influence of a speaker's character in gaining credibility with an audience and making it receptive to his or her arguments. Aristotle theorized that ethos is the most important of three modes of persuasive influence—the other two being *pathos* (emotion/passion) and *logos* (logic/intellectual virtue) (Halloran, 1982). In this chapter, we adopt this Aristotelian concept of ethos to explain the theoretical significance of character to the social influence of a leader. We present a model that describes how leader ethos is socially constructed in and through the leadership process to establish the credibility and trust necessary for effective leadership (Hollander, 1993; Kouzes & Posner, 2002; Mayer, Davis, & Schoorman, 1995). We argue that the construction of leader ethos is not only essential to a leader's effectiveness in a practical sense in that it counts heavily toward others' willingness to follow, but it also promotes strong normative commitment among followers to support the leader's purposes and goals. This explains the central significance of character to leadership.

This chapter is organized as follows. We first frame leadership as a relational process between leaders and followers in which the leader's persuasive influence depends to a large extent on followers' perceptions of the leader's credibility. We then introduce the concept of ethos and present a theoretically derived model of the social construction of leader ethos in and through the dynamic leadership process. We conclude with a summary and discussion of key points and implications for research and practice.

THE RELATIONAL DYNAMICS OF LEADERSHIP AND THE RELEVANCE OF ETHOS

As a social process, leadership is not a particular quality or characteristic possessed by a leader so much as a particular quality or characteristic of the relationship established between leader and follower(s) (Hollander, 1993). A definitive characteristic of this relationship is the willingness of followers to be influenced by the leader. That is, what defines the leadership relationship is the voluntary acceptance and support followers give to leaders (Hollander, 1992, 1993). This perspective emphasizes the active role of followers in the leadership process: Whereas a leader is a person who exercises influence over others, a follower is a person who voluntarily accepts and supports this influence (DeRue & Ashford, 2010). In short, leadership is a relational process between those who aspire to lead and those who choose to follow (Kouzes & Posner, 2002). Over time some individuals form identities as leaders and others as followers (DeRue & Ashford, 2010). As Meindl noted in explaining his social constructionist approach to leadership, leadership emerges "when followers interpret their relationship as having a leadership-followership dimension" (1995, p. 332).

The implications of this relational perspective of leadership are four. First, it underscores the importance of followership as a necessary, interdependent, and reciprocal aspect of the leadership process. As Hollander stated, "Without followers, there plainly are no leaders or leadership" (1993, p. 29). Second, it recognizes that integral to followership is the decision or acceptance to follow a leader. That is, followership is by this definition an uncoerced, voluntary choice involving the act of providing or withdrawing support for the leader and his or her influence (Hollander, 1993). Third, because followership is a voluntary choice, a leader's success in gaining support depends less on the leader's formal authority to exercise coercive power over followers and more on the leader's personal capacity to exercise persuasive influence with followers (Hollander, 1985). Fourth, the effectiveness of a leader's persuasive influence in turn depends to a significant extent on followers' perceptions of the leader's credibility (Kouzes & Posner, 2002). Thus, crucial to the relational dynamics of leadership is the leader's persuasive influence, which is grounded in followers' perceptions of the leader's credibility and subsequent granting of influence to the leader (Bass & Bass, 2008).

Leader credibility refers to a leader's trustworthiness (Kouzes & Posner, 2002; Mayer et al., 1995). Credibility derives from the interaction between qualities demonstrated by a leader and followers' implicit theories and expectations about the qualities appropriate for a leader (Lord, Foti, & de Vader, 1984). Followers will provide or withdraw support for the leader based on their appraisal of the leader's fit or consistency in conforming to those qualities (Hollander, 1993; Lord & Maher, 1993). As a starting point, if we understand leader character broadly as the composite of good qualities possessed by the leader that are valued by his or her moral community, then it follows that character is central to followers' appraisal of the leader's fit and consistency in meeting their expectations, which in turn contributes to the leader's credibility and ultimately to the persuasive influence of the leader. We thus define leader character as a *purposeful and principled moral self that reflects the values, principles, and ideals of the collective to which the leader belongs.*

This discussion provides the broad outline of the relational dynamics involved in the leadership influence process that highlight the significance of leader character. The term that best captures these dynamics is *ethos*. Ethos has its roots in ancient Greek rhetoric—the science of persuasion through speech (Hyde & Schrag, 2004). As indicated earlier, it refers to the persuasive influence of a speaker's character in gaining credibility with an audience, making listeners receptive to his or her arguments. The concept of ethos was given its first formal expression by Aristotle (Hyde, 2004). In Aristotle's *Rhetoric, ethos* along with *pathos* and *logos* are theorized to be the three modes of persuasive influence: Ethos reflects the trustworthiness of the speaker's character; logos, the sheer logical force of the speaker's argument; and pathos, the emotion the speaker arouses in the audience (Halloran, 1982). For Aristotle, ethos is a mode of proof, a way for a speaker to offer evidence that the audience can believe what he or she says based on his or her moral character—the quality of the speaker's personhood— which in turn makes him or her and what he or she says trustworthy. Ethos therefore is a mode of proof that says, in effect: "Trust me because I am the kind of person you can trust" (Halloran, 1982). For example, Halloran notes that if at an academic conference, a presenter speaks with some persuasive effect, it is partly because he or she manages to look and sound the way professors are supposed to look and sound; he or she enacts and makes present in his or her presentation some important aspects of the "professorial ethos" (1982, p. 62). Similarly, a leader may exercise persuasive influence over followers in part because he or she enacts important aspects of what might be called the "leader ethos"—those qualities that fit followers' implicit expectations of the qualities appropriate for a leader (Lord, Foti, & de Vader, 1984).

Of the three modes of influence (ethos, pathos, and logos), Aristotle argued that ethos is the most powerful and is thus the dominant and controlling factor in persuasion (Smith, 2004). Since then, ethos has held a central position in the study of rhetoric. Empirical research generally supports Aristotle's proposition that ethos is the most potent means of persuasion, whether the goal of the communication effort be persuasion or the generation of understanding (McCroskey & Young, 1981). This connection between character, credibility, and persuasion makes ethos particularly helpful to understanding how character contributes to the social influence of the leader. To this end, we make a few brief points to clarify the relevance of a rhetorical concept to the study of leadership.

First, both rhetoric and leadership are understood as social influence processes that involve a relational dynamic: In rhetoric the process involves a speaker and the audience he or she seeks to influence; in leadership the process involves formal or informal leaders and their followers or others they seek to positively influence. Thus, the essential nature of the two social processes is similar. In addition, by rhetoric we commonly think of speech in terms of written or verbal communication. But rhetoric is not limited to these. In a broader sense, *rhetoric* refers to all forms of meaning giving, including physical presence and appearance; the tone, inflections, and accents of speech, as well as gestures and behaviors (Smith, 2004). This broader form of conveying meaning constitutes *enactment* whereby the leader in and through his or her "performance" gives public expression to his or her character and the values, principles, ideals, and other qualities that define it (Burke, 1962; Combs & Mansfield, 1976; Goffman, 1959). This public expression of meaning or sense giving is a critical aspect of effective leadership (Foldy, Goldman, & Ospina, 2008; Weick, 1988). Therefore, examining leadership through the rhetorical concept of ethos promises to shed light on our understanding of how character contributes to the social influence of the leader.

THE SOCIAL CONSTRUCTION OF LEADER ETHOS

At the most fundamental level, leader ethos is about the inherent moral worth of the leader as a person and the persuasive influence this inherent moral worth exerts on followers (Hyde, 2004; Smith, 2004). Every leader has a form of ethos, whether it be moral or immoral, noble or ignoble. For a leader's ethos to have a positive persuasive influence on followers, the leader must create among followers a strong and favorable impression of his or her character. *Leader ethos* refers to the public expression of leader character in a way that creates this strong and favorable impression. It involves a showing forth of a purposeful and principled moral self that evokes attributions of credibility and engenders trust among followers, which in turn make them receptive to the leader's persuasive influence (Hyde, 2004; Smith, 2004).

Leader ethos does not reside solely in the character of the leader nor does it reside solely in the perceptions of followers. On the contrary, as

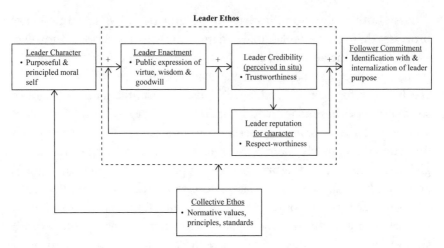

FIGURE 7.1

The social construction of leader ethos

suggested previously, leader ethos is a relational phenomenon that results from the interaction between a leader's public expression of his or her character and followers' perceptions of the leader's credibility and trustworthiness (Smith, 2004). Leader ethos is thus socially constructed in and through the leadership process. The key elements of this process are depicted in Figure 7.1. We briefly summarize the key aspects of this process before we elaborate each further in the remainder of the chapter.

The social construction of leader ethos begins at the collective level. Both leader character and follower perceptions are grounded in the normative values, principles, and ideals of the collective to which they belong. It is this *collective ethos* that shapes and forms a leader's character and also provides the point of reference from which followers judge the credibility and trustworthiness of the leader (Halloran, 1982). With this normative grounding, the process of constructing leader ethos proceeds to the character of the leader. We defined leader character as a purposeful and principled moral self that reflects the values, principles, and ideals of the collective to which the leader belongs. Leader character, in short, is the internalization of the collective ethos into the leader's self-understanding and identity as a leader. Leader character is in turn externalized and given public expression in and through the leader's decisions and actions such that the leader enacts the values, principles, and ideals of the collective in a way that creates a favorable impression of his or her character among followers (Burke,

1962; Combs & Mansfield, 1976; Goffman, 1959). This leader enactment is characterized by *virtue* (all around personal moral excellence), *practical wisdom* (good sense and judgment), and *goodwill* (genuine concern for others) (Smith, 2004; Solomon, 1992). This threefold Aristotelian conceptualization reflects three dimensions of character that people tend to value and admire (Smith, 2004). By manifesting them in and through his or her decisions and actions, a leader establishes personal credibility as one worthy of trust and respect, which in turn makes followers receptive to the leader's persuasive influence.

Over time, leaders who consistently demonstrate character in and through enactment of virtue, practical wisdom, and goodwill earn a reputation for character among their followers. This reputation for character has three recursive effects as depicted in Figure 7.1. The first strengthens the linkages between a leader's character and the enactment of character. The possession of character tends to produce strong self-consistency motives (Blasi, 1980, 2005; Verplanken & Holland, 2002)—the desire to ensure that one's behavior is consistent with the purposes and principles central to one's character—as well as the associated desire to maintain respect and a favorable reputation. The second strengthens the relationship between leader enactment and followers' positive perceptions of the leader's character and credibility. A leader who consistently enacts character in and through his or her decisions and actions earns a reputation for character among followers. This favorable reputation predisposes or biases followers to interpret the leader's future enactments favorably and predisposes them to be more receptive to his or her persuasive influence. The third strengthens the relationship between leader credibility in situ and follower commitment. A leader's strong reputation for character creates idealization among followers that strengthens followers' commitment when the leader acts with credibility in situ. Finally, when a leader enacts exceptional character that engenders positive attributions of credibility in situ, followers develop an especially strong commitment to the purposes and principles embodied by the leader. Follower commitment is the key outcome of leader ethos and represents the central significance of character to leader persuasive influence.

In sum, Figure 7.1 depicts the essential elements of the social construction of leader ethos. As conceptualized in this process, leader ethos is both a *source of credibility for* and a *praiseworthy effect of* the leader's character (Smith, 2004). With this conceptual framing of ethos, we now describe in greater detail the interpersonal dynamics associated with each of the dimensions depicted in Figure 7.1.

Collective Ethos: The Normative Grounding for Leader Ethos

The word *ethos* has both an individual and a collective meaning. It makes sense to speak of the ethos of this or that person, but it makes equally good sense to speak of the ethos of a group of people, an organization, culture, or even an era in history (Halloran, 1982). The earliest primordial uses of the term, in Homer and Hesiod, for example, emphasize its collective meaning. Etymological studies suggest that *ethos* derives from the Greek word for *custom, habit,* and *dwelling place,* which shares a close relation in meaning and usage to the Greek word for *character* (Hyde, 2004; Miller, 1974; Reynolds, 1993). These earliest usages derive from the notion of people regularly gathering together in a public place—a "habitual gathering place"—sharing experiences and in turn both experiencing and promulgating the values, beliefs, and mores of the community (Halloran, 1982, p. 60). It is here in this habitual gathering place of the community where the moral character of a person is shaped, formed, given expression, and in turn judged and evaluated by other members of the community (Hyde, 2004; Miller, 1974; Sattler, 1947).

These etymological roots suggest that *ethos* has a close connection to the social context surrounding the members of the community and entails the guiding values and beliefs that characterize or pervade the group or community. Over the centuries, the collective meaning of *ethos* as "habitual gathering place" became subsumed in the now conventional understanding of the word as *character* (Chamberlain, 1984). Nonetheless, the primordial social meaning of *ethos* remains an important if implicit and neglected aspect of the phenomenon that is important to understanding the significance of ethos to leadership.

Normative Grounding

The collective dimension of ethos emphasizes the characteristic spirit, prevalent tone, or genius of a community that is approved and respected by its members and motivates its ideas, customs, or practices (Geertz, 1973). These characteristics have a close similarity to folkways—that is, accepted and approved practices that define what it means to be a member of a community, including notions of warranted conduct that gain a person merit, praise, or honor as well as notions of unwarranted conduct regarded as wrong or intolerable (MacIntyre, 2007; Sattler, 1947). A collective's ethos—those values, beliefs, and mores vital to the social welfare—tends by definition to be highly normative in that it makes strong claims on members of the collective: It carries moral significance; it is authoritative; and it binds and obligates members of a community to certain kinds of conduct that add stability to and support the social structure and welfare of the collective (Korsgaard, 1996; Wren, 2010).

For example, military units tend to have strong norms around leaders' subordinating personal self-interests to duties and obligations attached to their role as a leader. This is because military leadership, especially in combat, is a grave responsibility and those entrusted with this responsibility often literally hold the lives of their fellow soldiers in their hands. Leaders who put their self-interests ahead of their responsibilities are a risk and threat not only to the mission, but to the lives of their soldiers. Therefore, the collective ethos of the military puts a strong emphasis on subordination of self-interests to the obligations of duty and the character of military leaders tends to reflect this strong sense of obligation to duty. Soldiers in turn expect their leaders to exhibit this strong commitment to duty in and through their leadership and will evaluate the credibility and trustworthiness of the leader in large part based on his or her consistency in upholding this and other collective norms.

Different moral communities thus establish unique systems of relationships and accountabilities through which members develop expectations and evaluations about the appropriateness of each other's actions (Tetlock & Mitchell, 2010). The collective dimension of ethos thus constitutes the normative grounding for the formation of leader character as well as the appraisal of leader character by potential followers within the leader's moral community.

Leader Character: Purposeful and Principled Moral Self

This social meaning of ethos underscores the fact that the ancient concept of character begins with the idea that people are first and foremost members of organized collectives with a collective ethos. Within this context, the ideal of character points toward public life, the life lived in that "gathering place" that serves as the root metaphor in the ancient usage of ethos (Halloran, 1982). From this perspective, character is understood as a complex set of characteristics acquired by an individual that reflect the values, beliefs, and mores of the community (Hunter, 2003). For a person to have character, therefore, is to have internalized the characteristics, qualities, or virtues most valued and respected by the culture in which one is embedded and belongs (Reynolds, 1993).

This conceptualization of character is thus socially constituted. It reflects a purposeful and principled moral self embedded in and in service to the collective. Such character is inculcated through social learning such as the observation of moral exemplars and the internalization of the ideals they model (Bandura, 1977, 1991; Walker & Henning, 2004). This differs from modern approaches to character grounded in personality psychology, which tend to foremost emphasize individualistic and autonomous traits possessed by an individual largely independent of the sociocultural context (Hunter, 2003). By contrast, the classical ideal of character is a socialized kind of character: It emphasizes the conventional rather than the idiosyncratic, the public rather than the private, the social rather than the personal (Halloran, 1982; Reynolds, 1993).

Character therefore involves a high degree of conformity with the values, beliefs, and mores of the collective. This conformity is not properly understood as blind conformity or merely doing what is expected based on socially imposed pressure or rewards. A leader who blindly conforms to role expectations and externally imposed obligations, who does what is expected of him or her out of fear of punishment or promise of reward, would not be recognized as having character. Leader character in the sense intended here is involved when a leader undertakes to become a full and productive member of a social group and becomes concerned with conducting himself or herself in accordance with the collective's ethos—because he or she has come to understand and accept the importance of this ethos and has taken on personal responsibility to preserve and sustain it (Power, Higgins, & Kohlberg, 1989; Wallace, 1996). Such leaders have what has been called a strong duty orientation, manifest in a drive toward fulfilling their duties to the collective, its missions and goals, and its codes and norms (Hannah, Jennings, Bluhm, Peng, & Schaubroeck, in press). Following up on the example of military combat leaders, combat leaders are willing to subordinate their self-interests to fulfill their obligations and duties as leaders because they have come to understand the grave responsibility of leading in combat and have in turn accepted and internalized into their self-understanding as leaders the collective norms around duty. Ultimately, the values, beliefs, and mores internalized as one's own tend to engage one's motivation more deeply and reveal character more thoroughly than do those that are externally imposed (Blasi, 1980, 2005; Verplanken & Holland, 2002). This internalized normative commitment manifests in leader enactment that gives public expression to the leader's character.

Leader Enactment: The Public Expression of Character

Leader ethos refers to the public expression of a leader's character in and through the leadership process. This involves an interaction between the leader's enactment and followers' perceptions of the leader's credibility based on that enactment. Leader enactment is therefore the pivotal point in the construction of leader ethos. In contrast to behavioral approaches to leadership, the enactment emphasized here does not refer to the surface behaviors or influence techniques used by a leader per se. Rather, it refers to how the surface behaviors express the substantive characteristics of the leader's character. Leader enactment involves a "showing forth" of the leader's underlying character—his or her purposeful and principled moral self (Hyde, 2004, p. xv). In the Aristotelian theory of ethos, the substantive characteristics necessary to show forth a purposeful and principled moral self are three: *virtue, practical wisdom,* and *goodwill* (Smith, 2004). These three characteristics are theorized to reveal the leader's underlying character, enhance followers' perceptions of the leader's credibility, and ultimately make followers receptive to his or her persuasive influence.

Virtue

Leader ethos puts a primary emphasis on virtue, where virtue is defined as "all-round personal excellence" in service to the collective (Solomon, 1992, p. 103). Aristotle defined virtue as a stable state of character—an acquired and therefore malleable disposition that manifests in certain characteristic ways of thinking, feeling, and acting (Kupperman, 1991; Sherman, 1989). This stable state of character is best understood not as a single unitary excellence of a person, but more of a constellation of related excellences or virtues that are important to a particular social practice (Solomon, 1992). For example, we can think of the martial virtue of a military leader that may include such virtues as duty, courage, and loyalty. Or we may think of the virtues of an athlete that include physical prowess, competitive spirit, and sportsmanship. In this way a leader's character is comprised of a constellation of related virtues relevant to his or her role and position in the collective. The character of the leader is revealed by the way these virtues "hang together" to form what is recognized as "good" character—a purposeful and principled moral self in service to the particular collective (Solomon, 1992, p. 107).

The concept of virtue provides the conceptual linkage between the leader's character and the collective ethos of his or her community. Virtues are, as Solomon (1992) describes, essential aspects of a leader's character on one hand; on the other hand, they constitute the excellences required of a particular social practice in a certain society, community, or organization— for example, the duty, courage, and loyalty the military requires of leaders or the physical prowess, competitiveness, and sportsmanship that sports require of athletes. Thus, virtues are "social traits": They reflect the ethos of a particular community and allow one to "fit in" and excel in a particular social practice (Solomon, 1992, p. 107). Virtues are therefore a way of summarizing the ideals of a community that define good character; they are the guiding light of leader ethos (Solomon, 1992).

However, what distinguishes virtue from the related notion of character traits is the close link they have to motivation and performance. Zagzebski, for instance, defines a virtue as "a deep and enduring acquired excellence of a person involving a *characteristic motivation* to produce a certain *desired end* and *reliable success* in bringing about that end" (1996, p. 137; italics added). By *characteristic motivation* she refers to a person's basic tendency to be moved or motivated to act for certain kinds of reasons. These reasons have to do with achieving a certain end or goal. This suggests that virtues are teleological or purpose driven: They are in some way in service to the collective as described earlier (Solomon, 1992). Virtue also implies what Zagzebski describes as *reliable success* in achieving the desired purpose or goal. To ascribe a virtue to someone is to suggest (among other things) that he or she tends to perform very well (excellently) in a particular social practice; to ascribe a vice (the antithesis of a virtue) is to say that he or she tends to perform badly (Zagzebski, 1996). Thus the notion of virtue has a close link to motivation and goal-driven performance toward socially valued outcomes that is typically not associated with the more global and static notion of character traits.

Practical Wisdom
The second component involved in the public manifestation or enactment of leader character involves what in Aristotelian terms is called *phronesis* or practical wisdom—good sense, sagacity, expertise, intelligence (Schwartz,

2011). Aristotle thought that the most routine social practices such as leadership demanded choices—for example, when to be loyal to a boss, or how to be fair to a subordinate, or how to confront an ethical violation, or when and how to be angry. These kinds of choices demand virtue in general and practical wisdom in particular (Schwartz, 2011). For example, with regard to anger, the concern for Aristotle was not whether anger was good or bad; it was the particular and concrete question of how to appropriately (i.e., excellently) express anger in a particular circumstance: who to be angry at, for how long, in what way, and for what purpose (Schwartz, 2011). Schwartz emphasizes that the wisdom to answer such questions and to act rightly is "distinctly practical" (2011, p. 4). It depends on the ability to perceive a situation, to have the appropriate feelings or motivations about it, to deliberate about what is appropriate in these circumstances, and to act (Sherman, 1989).

From this perspective, practical wisdom is less about moral judgments about what is right to do in a particular circumstance and more about performing a particular social practice well, which involves not only *knowing what* the right thing to do is, but also *knowing how* to go about doing the right thing in a particular circumstance, with a particular person at a particular time (Schwartz, 2011). The capability for individualized consideration as evident in transformational leadership (Avolio & Bass, 1988; Bass, 1985), self-awareness as evident in authentic leadership (Avolio, Gardner, Walumbwa, Luthans, & May, 2004; Hannah, Walumbwa, & Fry, 2011), and social awareness as evident in emotional intelligence (Goleman, Boyatis, & McKee, 2002) may thus be underpinned by practical wisdom. This practical wisdom is an expansive combination of principled moral judgment and practical moral skill or competence.

Practical wisdom is of great importance to the manifestation of character and specifically the practice of virtue (Solomon, 1992). None of the virtues in particular or virtue in general can be exercised without practical wisdom (Sherman, 1989). The practice of virtue is concerned with motivations and actions that lie on a continuum running from excess to deficiency, either end being a vice, with the intermediate or mean position being a virtue (Smith, 2004). Courage, for example, is a moral virtue that manifests in performance reflecting something between cowardice (vice of deficiency of courage) and recklessness (vice of excess of courage). That is, courageous decisions and actions are neither rash nor cowardly but well motivated and productive of praiseworthy performance (Schwartz, 2011;

Smith, 2004). The vices thus fall short of or exceed what is right concerning motivations and actions, while virtue reflects the mean, which is not the average, but the right amount and requires practical wisdom (Schwartz, 2011).

Goodwill

Aristotle argues that when considering the three performance characteristics of ethos, even though leaders may have virtue and wisdom, if they lack goodwill they may not be trusted (Smith, 2004). Based on attribution theory, observers will not just judge the actions of others, but also infer whether the intentions for their actions sought pro-social or benevolent ends (Jones & Davis, 1965; Kelley, 1972). There are two dimensions to the notion of goodwill: goodwill directed toward others, which is synonymous with benevolence (Smith, 2004); and goodwill directed toward the values, principles, and ideals of the collective (Sherman, 1989; Wallace, 1996). First, goodwill is wishing good for others for their sake without any expectations of reciprocation (Smith, 2004). For example, a leader would demonstrate goodwill if he directed his followers to do something that would benefit them but not him or her. Second, goodwill is the disposition to decide and act in the best interests of the collective and to uphold its mission, values, and principles. This aspect of goodwill reflects an individual's deep understanding and appreciation of the mores of the community (Sherman, 1989; Wallace, 1996). It is grounded in the notion of respect. To respect something is to understand and appreciate its value, to regard it as important and worth taking seriously, and to give it appropriate weight in influencing one's behavior (Darwell, 1977). The manifestation of goodwill is thus grounded in a deep dispositional commitment to respect the central values, beliefs, and mores of the community to which one belongs.

Leader Choice

A crucial aspect of the substantive characteristics of leader enactment concerns the choices a leader makes. Aristotle emphasized that one certain way to convey character is through effective deliberate choice (Sattler, 1947). A leader merits credit for voluntary choices that affirm the values, principles, and ideals of the collective. These voluntary choices are perceived to reflect the good character of the person (Smith, 2004).

Choice is inherent and explicit in the dynamics between virtue and practical wisdom; specifically these dynamics involve deliberate choice in finding and choosing the mean between excess and deficiency that will lead to or reinforce the values, principles, and norms of the community. But leader choice involves more than rational deliberate choice. It also involves the ability to control the irrational or emotional aspects of the self (Sherman, 1989). Choice here includes the capacity to have and to avoid certain emotions—the ability to discriminate in what one feels. It involves the ability to feel the right emotions at the right times, with reference to the right objects or people (Sherman, 1989).

Additionally, character is conveyed through the choice of behavioral style (Smith, 2004). Leaders project a sense of character when they choose a style appropriate to the circumstances they face. For example, there are times and places where bravery or humor are demanded and others where each would be entirely inappropriate. Thus the leader's behavioral style is another way in which character is conveyed through choice.

The Deep Structure of Leader Choice

But leader choice is not limited to the virtuous mean, emotional control, and behavioral style enacted in particular situations a leader faces, but also concerns choices of the leader in the larger context of his or her career as a leader (Solomon, 1992). This suggests that an important aspect of leader choice is his or her conception of success. From this broader perspective, leaders can be motivated to lead for noble or ignoble reasons; for selfish and self-serving reasons; or for reasons that reflect a commitment to projects, causes, and ideals greater than themselves. These kinds of choices reflect the deep structure of leader choice (Wren, 1991). They reveal the inner motivational core of the leader that governs his or her day-in-and-day-out decisions and actions at the most fundamental level. For a leader of character, choice from this deep structure level involves the development of the kind of self—a purposeful and principled moral self— who attaches his or her long-term self-interest to noble, just, worthy, and right objects subsumed under the concept of *the good* (Murdoch, 2009). It involves choosing and having reliable and praiseworthy motives, expressed in chosen actions over time that produce and preserve the fundamental values, principles, and ideals of the community and that have come to have intrinsic value to the leader such that he or she is self-determined in his or her enactment of those values, principles, and ideals (Deci & Ryan, 2000; Solomon, 1992).

Summary

The pivotal point in the construction of leader ethos is leader enactment, which refers to the public expression of character in and through the leader's decisions and actions. Leader enactment that projects character involves three substantive characteristics: virtuous action, which involves the rejection of vice and affirming of virtue; practical wisdom, which involves basing decisions on sound deliberation and practical knowledge; and goodwill, which involves acting for the benefit of others for their own sake and acting on the best interests of the collective to uphold its core values and principles. In the manifestation of leader character, choice emerges as a dominant factor: deliberate choice in finding the virtuous mean, controlling emotions, and selecting the appropriate behavioral style. The deep structure of leader choice involves choosing and having reliable and praiseworthy motives, expressed in chosen actions over time that have come to have intrinsic value to the leader. Character from this deeper perspective reveals to others a purposeful and principled moral self motivated by the desire to produce and preserve the good—the fundamental values, principles, and ideals of the community. These characteristics of leader enactment are theorized to reveal the leader's underlying character, enhance followers' perceptions of the leader's credibility, and ultimately make followers receptive to the leader's persuasive influence.

Follower Perceptions of Leader Credibility and Trustworthiness

Leader ethos is about establishing, in the process and enactment of leading, a character that merits credibility as a leader. Credibility is often asserted to be the foundation of leadership: "People want leaders who are credible" (Kouzes & Posner, 2002, p. 32). In rhetorical theory, this aspect of ethos is referred to as *source credibility* (Hovland, Janis, & Kelley, 1953). Source credibility refers to the trustworthiness of a leader as perceived by followers, which is derived from the interaction between qualities demonstrated by a leader in a particular situation and their expectations about the qualities appropriate for a leader in that situation. Followers will tend to provide or withdraw support for the leader based on their appraisal of the leader's fit in conforming to those qualities (Hollander, 1993; Lord et al., 1984; Lord & Maher, 1993).

In demonstrating the three substantive characteristics of leader enactment, a leader constructs an ethos that gains credibility because virtue, practical wisdom, and goodwill are "favorable dispositions" that people tend to find trustworthy (Cooper, 1932, p. xxii) and consistent with their expectations about the qualities appropriate for a leader (Hollander, 1993; Lord et al., 1984; Lord & Maher, 1993). To underscore this point, it is worthwhile to highlight the correspondence between the three substantive characteristics of leader enactment and empirical research identifying the primary characteristics associated with trustworthiness (Colquitt, Scott, & LePine, 2007; Mayer et al., 1995). Although research on trustworthiness has tended to focus on dyadic forms of trust and not the culturally embedded normative context that underpins ethos, it nonetheless has relevance to our understanding of leader ethos.

This research suggests that trustworthiness is based on three primary characteristics of the trustee (leader): *ability, integrity,* and *benevolence.* Ability or competence captures the knowledge and skills needed to do a specific job along with the interpersonal skills and general wisdom needed to succeed in an organization (Gabarro & Athos, 1978; cited in Colquitt et al., 2007). Ability corresponds in many ways to the leader enactment of practical wisdom. Practical wisdom is a combination of principled moral judgment and practical moral skill or competence, the essence of which is the capacity to figure out the right thing to do in a particular situation as well as the right way to go about doing it. Integrity captures the extent to which a trustee is believed to adhere to sound moral and ethical principles that the follower finds acceptable (Mayer et al., 1995). Integrity corresponds in part to the leader enactment characteristic of virtue. Virtue reflects the values, principles, and ideals of a particular community and involves the characteristic motivation to realize these values, principles, and ideals in performance. Finally, benevolence captures the extent to which a trustee is believed to want to do good to the trustor apart from any self-interested or egotistic motive. Benevolence thus corresponds to the leader enactment characteristic of goodwill. Goodwill involves acting for the benefit of others for their own sake. Goodwill also involves acting on the best interests of the collective to uphold its core values and principles, which overlaps with integrity.

Thus the substantive characteristics of leader enactment that express character also have a close correspondence with the primary characteristics that make a person worthy of trust. The act of trusting involves uncertainty and risk to the degree that a leader's credibility is uncertain. A leader, however, who successfully enacts virtue, practical wisdom, and goodwill in and through his or her decisions and actions mitigates this uncertainty and will gain credibility because followers tend to find these characteristics trustworthy (Smith, 2004). The enactment of virtue, practical wisdom, and goodwill therefore constitutes a mode of proof—a way for a leader to offer evidence of trustworthiness (Smith, 2004). As a mode of proof, the public expression of character in and through the enactment of virtue, practical wisdom, and goodwill communicates an implicit but substantive message to followers that says, in effect: "Trust me because I am the kind of person you can trust" (Halloran, 1982).

This is the second pivotal point in the social construction of leader ethos. Whether or not a leader is successful in establishing credibility hinges on whether followers are persuaded by this character-based proof of his or her trustworthiness. To the degree to which followers are positively persuaded, the relationships between leader and followers will be characterized by an emergent state of trust (Burke, Sims, Lazzara, & Salas, 2007). The consequences of this state of trust include a number of follower attitudinal and behavior outcomes essential to the leadership relationship including: confidence in the character of the leader, willingness to rely on the leader, receptivity to the leader's influence, acceptance of the leader's guidance and direction, and willingness to work toward achieving the leader's purposes (Burke et al., 2007). These first-order outcomes are necessary and definitive of leadership as a relationship between those who aspire to lead and those who choose to follow: They reflect the willingness of followers to voluntarily support and follow the leader.

Over time, leaders who consistently demonstrate character in and through the enactment of virtue, practical wisdom, and goodwill earn a reputation for character among their followers. This reputation for character reinforces the construction and emergence of leader ethos and promotes the emergence of certain second-order outcomes, the most significant of which involves follower identification with the leader and commitment to the purposes of the leader. In the next two sections, we address these final aspects of the social construction of leader ethos.

Leader Reputation for Character

Leader reputation is defined as the identity of a leader as perceived by others (Hall, Blass, Ferris, & Massengale, 2004). In our terms, the leader's reputation for character reflects followers' perceptions of the leader as built through observation over time, as a purposeful and principled moral person. Respect is at the heart of a leader's reputation for character. Three dimensions of respect are relevant to a leader's reputation for character: appraisal respect, recognition respect, and identification respect (Clarke, 2011). Each has significant implications for the construction of leader ethos.

Appraisal Respect

A leader's reputation grounded in appraisal respect reflects what followers admire about a leader. It is a measure of esteem for higher-than-usual performance or achievement (Clarke, 2011; Darwall, 1977). It reflects what followers as a community believe and value most in leaders—their collective implicit theory of exemplary leaders—and involves evaluations of a leader's performance over time and his or her success in enacting what followers value most in leaders.

In terms of the social construction of leader ethos, appraisal respect has its most significant influence on the leader himself or herself. As members of a moral community, leaders desire and seek a degree of moral approbation from their followers (Jones & Ryan, 1997; Ryan & Riordan, 2000). A junior leader in the fire services, for example, will want to prove himself to and receive approbation from his firemen that he has what it takes to lead in tough and dangerous situations. Appraisal respect provides a kind of affirmation and social reward for merit. It reflects the external aspect of a leader's ethos—excellence in performance; but that excellence is an expression of an internal asset—namely the leader's character. Because this kind of respect and the good reputation that accompanies it is an intrinsic reward and considered a valuable asset to the leader, the leader is motivated to ensure that his or her current and future performance does not risk or damage the respect and reputation he or she has earned (Burke et al., 2007). Thus, appraisal respect acts as a reinforcement that, as depicted in Figure 7.1, strengthens the linkage between leader character and the leader's enactment of that character.

Recognition Respect

Next, a leader's reputation for character is bound up in followers' recognition that the leader's character is not just admirable but authoritative. That is, a leader's reputation for character becomes a source of legitimacy for a leader over and above legitimacy based on his or her formal position or authority as a leader. That is, character has moral authority that evokes a sense of obligation among followers to accept and support the leader and his or her influence. This is what is meant by recognition respect. It consists of recognizing and giving appropriate consideration to the qualities of a leader that make him or her worthy of leadership and to act accordingly (Clarke, 2011; Darwall, 1977). For example, followers will tend to feel a sense of obligation to support the direction of a leader who has demonstrated that he or she consistently subordinates his or her self-interest for the good of the organization and its members. On the other hand, followers will tend to feel less obligated to support the direction of a leader who has demonstrated that he or she acts out of self-interest.

Recognition respect is a function of the extent to which the leader is perceived as acting in a manner consistent with the values, principles, and ideals of the community (Clarke, 2011). If so, recognition respect for a leader's character creates an implicit obligation among followers to accept and support his or her purposes, particularly concerning a leader in a formal leadership position. Thus, as depicted in Figure 7.1, recognition respect for a leader's character acts as a reinforcement that strengthens the linkage between leader enactment and follower perceptions of leader credibility and the decision to trust and willingly allow the leader to exert influence.

Over time, as the leader gains a reputation for enacting character, followers would tend to form expectancies that the leader will act with character in the future. This is in part because people normally have a confirmation bias (see Nickerson, 1998), in that they seek out information that confirms their existing beliefs and hypotheses while paying less attention to information that counters those beliefs. Therefore, followers will readily seek and be very sensitive to cues that confirm that a leader who has a reputation for character (or lack of) is indeed acting again with character (or lack of) as opposed to looking for disconfirming cues.

Identification Respect

Last, a leader's reputation for character manifests in a respect that is based on followers' identification with the purposes and principles of the leader (Atwell, 1981; Clarke, 2011). This form of respect—identification respect—reflects the personal attachment of followers to the values, principles, and ideals embodied in the leader's character and manifested in and through the leader's enactment. It reflects an alignment between the purposes and principles of the leader and his or her followers. This kind of respect involves followers in a far more active level of engagement with the leader (Clarke, 2011). Thus, as depicted in Figure 7.1, identification respect for a leader strengthens the linkage between follower perceptions of leader credibility and follower commitment, and influences a number of second-order attitudinal and behavioral outcomes including increased follower job satisfaction, increased performance, increased organizational commitment, and decreased turnover (Dirks & Ferrin, 2002). However, most significant among the various second-order outcomes is increased follower commitment to the purposes and goals set by the leader.

Self-Consistency Motives

The three forms of respect provide extrinsic motivation for a leader to ensure that his or her performance consistently enacts and gives public expression to his or her character. Yet, we suggest that leaders also form a personal narrative of their prior behaviors that drives them intrinsically to enact their character. Leaders over time form a life story, a personal narrative of who they are, authentically, as a leader (Shamir & Eilam, 2005). Such a narrative creates self-consistency motives to act in alignment with core aspects of their self—such as their character and moral identity (Hannah, Avolio, & May, 2011; Stahlberg, Peterson, & Dauenheimer, 1999; Verplanken & Holland, 2002). This is because people seek to maintain self-esteem and a consistent self-view, and acting inconsistently with the moral self creates cognitive disequilibrium and damages self-esteem and sense of self-worth (Blasi, 1980; Hannah et al., 2011).

Follower Commitment

Rhetorical theory suggests that the construction of a leader ethos grounded in the substantive characteristics of virtue, practical wisdom, and goodwill can have social influence effects that go beyond the willingness of followers to voluntarily support and follow the leader. On the contrary, leader ethos can be a catalyzing influence that motivates a strong sense of commitment among followers. This commitment is characterized by followers' strong affective attachment to the purposes, principles, and goals of the leader and to their role as followers in relation to those purposes, principles, and goals, apart from any instrumental or extrinsic motives or incentives—that is, formal or informal rewards or punishments (Buchanan, 1974). This commitment reflects a decisive moral choice to support the leader that results from followers' strong identification with and internalization of the leader's ethos, which generates internalized normative pressures to act in a way that supports the leader (Wiener, 1982). This internalized normative pressure motivates several second-order relational outcomes that share similarity with the outcomes associated with a charismatic or transformational leadership relationship (Bass, 1985; Howell & Shamir, 2005). As Shamir and Howell noted:

> Followers who share a charismatic relationship with a leader are willing to transcend self-interests for the sake of the collective (team or organization), to engage in self-sacrifice in the interest of the mission, to identify with the vision articulated by the leader, to show strong emotional attachment to the leader, to internalize the leader's values and goals, and to demonstrate strong personal or moral (as opposed to calculative) commitment to those values or goals. (2005, p. 99)

These follower outcomes associated with a charismatic leadership relationship, or idealized influence as included in transformational leadership theory (Bass, 1985), parallel the outcomes we associate with the catalyzing influence of leader ethos. The quality and strength of these charismatic outcomes depend in large part on the strength of followers' normative commitment, which is grounded in their identification with and internalization of the leader's ethos—that is, the purposes, principles, and goals that constitute the leader's character. Leader ethos thus constitutes the normative foundation of leadership as a relational process.

DISCUSSION

In this chapter we have applied the Aristotelian concept of ethos to explain the significance of character to the social influence of leadership. We presented a model describing how leader ethos is socially constructed and establishes the credibility necessary for effective leadership. This framework has important implications for research and practice.

Implications for Research

The predominance of research on leader influence has focused on concepts such as leader power, political savvy, influence tactics, skills, and leadership styles (Bass & Bass, 2008; Yukl, 2002). Largely neglected, particularly from an empirical perspective, is an understanding of how and through which processes leader character creates and sustains leader influence. We believe that a deeper understanding of what constitutes leader ethos will enrich our theoretical models of leadership processes.

First, scholars have called in the literature for placing more emphasis on leadership as a relational phenomenon and to recognize the active role followers have in reacting to and interpreting leader qualities (Hollander, 1992; Uhl-Bien & Pillai, 2007). Further, there have been numerous calls in the literature to make context more explicit in models of leadership (Avolio, 2007; Porter & McLaughlin, 2006). Our conceptualization of leader ethos attempts to account for both of these emphases. The social construction of leader ethos suggests that it resides neither solely in the character of the leader (as typically assumed in moral psychology approaches to character) nor solely in the perceptions of followers with regard to source credibility (as frequently assumed in rhetorical theory). Rather, ethos is a relational concept residing at the intersection of the character of the leader and the perception of leader credibility in followers, both of which are grounded in the normative values, principles, and ideals of the community—the collective ethos—in which they belong. This collective ethos provides the point of reference by which people develop character and by which others judge the credibility of character. Leader ethos thus reflects the character of the relational dynamics between the leader, the followers, and the communal context in which they are located. It reflects a coming together and having or sharing the same values, principles, and ideals that are embodied in the character and enactment of the leader and recognized, respected, and supported by followers (Burke, 1962; Sullivan, 1993). In this respect, leader ethos serves as a kind of organizing principle that bonds together those who aspire to lead and those who choose to follow, and infuses this relationship with a strong normative commitment to the purposes and principles embodied by the leader (McEvily, Perrone, & Zaheer, 2003; Selznick, 1957).

Second, scholars have called for researchers to explore how leaders and followers interact to create meaning in the workplace (Shamir, 1991). We suggest that the conceptualization of leader ethos as an organizing principle offers insights into how followers make sense and interpret meaning in the workplace, which is thought to be central to followers' engagement and performance (May, Gilson, & Harter, 2004). Organizing principles are ways of solving problems of interdependence and uncertainty (McEvily et al., 2003). They involve certain logics and associated heuristics for how leaders and followers process information and select appropriate behaviors for coordinating their actions (McEvily et al., 2003; Zander & Kogut, 1995). With leader ethos, we begin to better understand how collective values, principles, and ideals embodied and enacted by a leader create a framework of meaning or lens through which followers as well as leaders perceive and interpret leaders' behaviors and how those behaviors in turn serve to enhance or deter attributions of credibility and resulting commitments.

Third, leader ethos provides a framework to help distinguish what is often taken for granted in leadership research: the distinction between *power* and *influence*. Traditionally, power is associated with organizational authority and refers to the ability of a formal leader to exert some degree of coercive control over other persons, things, or events (Hollander, 1993). By contrast, influence involves persuasion in which the subordinate retains some degree of autonomy and control over his or her decisions and actions (Hollander, 1993). Hollander notes that leaders' reliance on power can be "highly dysfunctional"—provoking negative attitudes and counterproductive behaviors among followers (1985, p. 485). Effective leaders thus emphasize persuasion instead of the full power at their disposal by virtue of their formal authority (Bass, 1985; Hollander, 1985). The persuasive influence of a leader in turn will depend in large part on informal legitimacy based on followers' appraisals of the leader's credibility and their decision to accept and support the leader's influence (Hollander, 1993). Our framework of leader ethos can help inform this persuasive influence process.

Fourth, leader ethos may enhance the understanding of both implicit leadership theory (ILT; Lord & Maher, 1993) and leader-member exchange theory (LMX; Graen & Uhl-Bien, 1995). Research on ILT has shown that followers not only encode into memory a leader prototype but also a leader *anti-prototype*, reflecting their prototype of what constitutes negative leader qualities (e.g., unethical, self-serving, incompetent, etc.) as a separate cognitive categorization (Epitropaki & Martin, 2004). We suggest that collective ethos, through social learning and socialization processes, informs followers' formation of these dual prototypes and followers' determinations of what is exemplary and distasteful in leaders. Further, our framework describes how the enactment of leader character is viewed through these normative prototypes. Additionally, our framework for leader ethos describes how leader enactment, when it is consistent (inconsistent) with followers' prototypes, engenders (reduces) respect and perceptions of credibility. As respect and trust are components of LMX (Graen & Uhl-Bien, 1995), the social processes of leader ethos may inform phenomenon operating at the lower range of LMX. Specifically, when a leader matches followers' anti-prototype related to expected character, they may not just experience low levels of LMX, but negative LMX (Uhl-Bien & Maslyn, 2003). Negative LMX would not reflect concepts such as trust, liking, and respect; but distrust, disliking, and disrespect, and result in negative forms of social exchange between leader and follower (Sparrowe & Liden, 1997).

Fifth, understanding the social phenomenon of leader ethos can help to advance research on character as applied to leadership and the workplace. Character has largely been studied from a descriptive approach, and research has tended to conceptualize character as an intrapersonal phenomenon (Wright & Goodstein, 2007). We have developed a framework placing leader character as a social, not merely intrapersonal phenomenon, and have provided logic for how character is situated within normative constraints. This is important as models of leadership have more often than not neglected relevant levels of theory and analysis (Yammarino, Dionne, Uk Chun, & Dansereau, 2005). The leader ethos framework operates across three levels. At the micro/individual level, the framework describes how leader character manifests in enactment. At the dyad and meso levels, the framework describes how leader enactment is interpreted and attributed by others and groups. At the macro level, the framework describes how both the micro and meso processes are situated in the normative context of collective ethos. The current framework for leader ethos thus offers logic for numerous hypotheses that could be developed and tested to advance multilevel leadership frameworks for the study of character in organizations.

Sixth, our conceptualization of what constitutes leader credibility extends beyond current conceptualizations of trustworthiness and thus provides new opportunities for trust research. First, we ground trustworthiness in the leader's character, based on the leader's virtue, practical wisdom, and goodwill. These broader constructs extend beyond the concepts of ability-based, benevolence-based, and integrity-based trust, which have been the focus of trust research to date (Colquitt et al., 2007; Mayer et al., 1995). Our approach also situates trust not just at the dyad level, but operating across levels situated in the normative context of collective ethos. Further, we build the concept of time into our process model (Figure 7.1) and describe how leader trustworthiness feeds the leader's reputation for character over time. This links trust to appraisal, recognition, and identification forms of respect (Clarke, 2011) that constitute the leader's reputation for character and thus open new logics that can be formulated into hypotheses and tested to advance both the trust and respect literatures.

Implications for Practice

An understanding of leader ethos has important implications for leader development. Specifically, leader development programs that focus on skills and competencies alone may have significant shortcomings in aiding organizational leaders to exercise persuasion and influence in the workplace. Our framework suggests that followers will assess not just the message, but the messenger when deciding whether they will allow the leader influence over them. Without establishing character-based credibility, followers will not be confident that the leader will use his or her skills for pro-social and ethical aims and not for self-gain or manipulative purposes, and may thus tend to not fully commit to the leader's purpose. This places character development at the center of leader development, yet research syntheses have shown that the leadership field has not focused on character in development frameworks (Avolio, Reichard, Hannah, Walumbwa, & Chan, 2009).

The framework for leader ethos also has significant implications for socialization programs. To be effective, leaders must understand the collective ethos and followers' corresponding character-based ILT. They must also have internalized the ethos to ensure they manifest it in practice in order to gain credibility and follower commitment.

We have also brought attention to the importance of leaders developing a reputation for character in the workplace and emphasized that reputation not only influences the external realm related to followers' perceptions and attributions, but also the internal realm—the intrapersonal processes that drive the leader himself or herself to enact character. This framework thus has implications for ethical leadership theory (Brown & Treviño, 2006). Ethical leadership distinguishes a *moral person* (a leader with ethical traits) from a *moral manager* (a leader who takes purposive actions to discipline and reward based on (un)ethical behaviors and communicates ethics in the workplace). This theory proposes that a leader can be a highly moral person, but be seen as ethically ambivalent by followers if he or she does not project that morality into the workplace as a moral manager. Our framework for leader ethos can inform the processes through which this projection occurs and is received and interpreted by followers.

Finally, leader ethos can inform the development of ethical climate and ethical culture as well as multilevel models of ethical leadership (Treviño, 1986; Treviño & Youngblood, 1990; Victor & Cullen, 1988). Specifically, research has shown that ethical culture and ethical leadership operate across organizational levels to influence ethical thoughts and behaviors of followers at lower levels (Schaubroeck et al., 2012). The concept of collective ethos may inform the mechanisms through which such cross-level effects occur. Collective ethos informs what normative values, principles, and standards are esteemed in a given culture and the lens through which followers will assess the adequacy and credibility of leaders, and thus the likelihood that their influence will cascade across levels. The concept of leader reputation for character and the three forms of respect it engenders (appraisal respect, recognition respect, and identification respect) may also inform how leaders can positively influence not only their immediate followers, but also followers at two or more organizational levels below them as determined by Schaubroeck and colleagues (2012). This is because a leader's reputation has informational value and when followers at lower levels receive the directives of higher leaders they respect, they would be more likely to attribute those decisions to a source of character, increasing perceptions of credibility and thus influence. Further, understanding the formation of collective ethos can inform how shared values, principles, and standards are formed across levels and are reinforced through the exemplification of those shared beliefs by leaders. In summary, an understanding of what constitutes leader ethos can inform how formal and informal leader behaviors and culture create leadership *systems* that build and sustain character.

CONCLUSION

We adopted the Aristotelian concept of ethos to explain the theoretical significance of character to the social influence of the leader. We presented a model that describes how leader ethos is socially constructed in and through the leadership process to establish the credibility and trust necessary for effective leadership. We argued that the construction of leader ethos is not only essential to a leader's effectiveness in a practical sense in that it counts heavily toward others' willingness to follow, but it also promotes strong normative commitment among followers to support the leader's purposes and goals. We conclude that the social construction of leader ethos constitutes the essence of leader character as a social and not just a psychological phenomenon and explains the central significance of character to leadership.

REFERENCES

Atwell, J. (1981). Kant's notion of respect for persons. *Tulane Studies in Philosophy, 31*, 17–30.

Avolio, B.J. (2007). Promoting more integrative strategies for leadership theory building. *American Psychologist, 62*, 25–33.

Avolio, B.J., & Bass, B.M. (1988). Unlocking the essence of individualized consideration: A view from the inside out in replies to Conger and Locke. In F. Dansereau & F.J. Yammarino (Eds.), *Leadership: The multi-level approaches* (pp. 93–102). Stamford, CT: JAI Press.

Avolio, B. J., Gardner, W. L., Walumbwa, F. O., Luthans, F., & May, D. R. (2004). Unlocking the mask: A look at the process by which authentic leaders impact follower attitudes and behaviors. Leadership Quarterly, 15, 801–823.

Avolio, B.J., Reichard, R. J., Hannah, S.T., Walumbwa, F. O., & Chan, A. (2009). 100 years of leadership intervention studies: A meta-analysis. *Leadership Quarterly, 20*, 764–784.

Bandura, A. (1977). *Social learning theory.* Englewood Cliffs, NJ: Prentice-Hall.

Bandura, A. (1991). Social cognitive theory of moral thought and action. In W.M. Kurtines & J.L. Gewitz (Eds.), *Handbook of moral behavior and development* (vol. 1, pp. 45–103). Hillsdale, NJ: Erlbaum.

Bass, B.M. (1985). *Leadership and performance beyond expectations.* New York: Free Press.

Bass, B.M., & Bass, R. (2008). *The Bass handbook of leadership.* New York: Free Press.

Blasi, A. (1980). Bridging moral cognition and moral action: A critical review of the literature. *Psychological Bulletin, 88*, 1–45.

Blasi, A. (2005). Moral character: A psychological approach. In D.K. Lapsley and F.C. Power (Eds.), *Character psychology and character education* (pp. 67–100). Notre Dame, IN: University of Notre Dame Press.

Brown, M.E., & Treviño, L.K. (2006). Ethical leadership: A review and future directions. *Leadership Quarterly, 17*, 595–616.

Buchanan, B. (1974). Building organizational commitment: The socialization of managers in work organizations. *Administrative Sciences Quarterly, 19*, 533–546.

Burke, C.S., Sims, D.E., Lazzara, E.H., & Salas, E. (2007). Trust in leadership: A multi-level review and integration. *Leadership Quarterly, 18*, 606–632.

Burke, K. (1962). *A rhetoric of motives.* Berkeley: University of California Press.

Chamberlain, C. (1984). From "haunts" to "character": The meaning of ethos and its relation to ethics. *Helios, 11*, 99–103.

Clarke, N. (2011). An integrated model of respect in leadership. *Leadership Quarterly, 22*, 316–327.

Colquitt, J. A., Scott, B. A., & LePine, J. A. 2007. Trust, trustworthiness, and trust propensity: A meta-analytic test of their unique relationships with risk taking and job performance. Journal Of Applied Psychology, 92, 909–927.

Combs, J. E., & Mansfield, M. W. (1976). *Drama in life: The uses of communication in society.* New York: Hasting House.

Cooper, L. (1932). *The rhetoric of Aristotle.* New York: Appleton-Century-Crofts.

Darwall, S. L. (1977). Two kinds of respect. *Ethics, 88,* 36–49.

Deci, E. L., & Ryan, R. M. (2000). The "what" and "why" of goal pursuits: Human needs and the self-determination of behavior. *Psychological Inquiry, 11,* 227–268.

DeRue, D. S., & Ashford, S. J. (2010). Who will lead and who will follow? A social process of leadership identity construction in organizations. Academy of Management Review, 35(4), 627–647.

Dirks, K. T., & Ferrin, D. L. (2002). Trust in leadership: Meta-analytic findings and implications for research and practice. *Journal of Applied Psychology, 87,* 611–628.

Epitropaki, O., & Martin, R. (2004). Implicit leadership theories in applied settings: Factor structure, generalizability, and stability over time. *Journal of Applied Psychology, 89.*

Foldy, E. G., Goldman, L., & Ospina, S. (2008). Sensegiving and the role of cognitive shifts in the work of leadership. *Leadership Quarterly, 19,* 514–529.

Gabarro, J. J., & Athos, J. (1978). The development of trust, influence, and expectations. In A. G. Athos & J. J. Gabarro (Eds.), *Interpersonal behaviors: Communication and understanding in relationships* (pp. 290–303). Englewood Cliffs, NJ: Prentice Hall.

Geertz, C. (1973). *The interpretation of cultures.* New York: Basic Books.

Goffman, E. (1959). *The presentation of self in everyday life.* New York: Doubleday.

Goleman, D., Boyatzis, R., & McKee, A. (2002). *Primal leadership: Realizing the power of emotional intelligence.* Cambridge, MA: Harvard Business School Press.

Graen, G. B., & Uhl-Bien, M. (1995). Relationship-based approach to leadership: Development of leader-member exchange (LMX) theory of leadership over 25 years: Applying a multi-level multi-domain perspective. *Leadership Quarterly, 6,* 219–247.

Hall, A. T., Blass, F. R., Ferris, G. R., & Massengale, R. (2004). Leader reputation and accountability in organizations: Implications for dysfunctional leader behavior. *Leadership Quarterly, 15,* 515–536.

Halloran, S. M. (1982). Aristotle's concept of ethos, or if not his somebody else's. *Rhetoric Review, 1,* 58–63.

Hannah, S. T., & Avolio, B. J. (2011a). The locus of leader character. *Leadership Quarterly, 22,* 979–983.

Hannah, S. T., & Avolio, B. J. (2011b). Leader character, ethos, and virtue: Individual and collective considerations. *Leadership Quarterly, 22,* 989–994.

Hannah, S. T., Avolio, B. J., & May, D. R. (2011). Moral maturation and moral conation: A capacity approach to explaining moral thought and action. *Academy of Management Review, 36*(4), 663–685.

Hannah, S. T. & Jennings, P. L. (2013) Leader ethos and big-C character. Organizational Dynamics, 42, 8–16.

Hannah, S. T., Jennings, P. L., Bluhm, D., Peng, A. C., & Schaubroeck, J. M. (in press). Duty orientation: Theoretical Development and Preliminary Construct Testing. Organizational Behavior and Human Decisions Processes.

Hannah, S. T., Walumbwa, F. O., & Fry. J. (2011). Leadership in action teams: Team leader and members' authenticity, authenticity strength, and performance outcomes. *Personnel Psychology, 64,* 771–801.

Hollander, E. P. (1985). Leadership and power. In G. Lindzey & E. Aronson (Eds.), *handbook of social psychology* (3rd ed., vol. 2, pp. 485–537). New York: Random House.

Hollander, E. P. (1992). Leadership, followership, self, and others. *Leadership Quarterly, 3*(1), 43–54.

Hollander, E. P. (1993). Legitimacy, power, and influence: A perspective on relational features of leadership. In M. M. Chemers & R. Ayman (Eds.), *Leadership theory and research: Perspectives and directions* (pp. 29–47). San Diego, CA: Academic Press.

Hovland, C. I., Janis, I. L., & Kelley, H. H. (1953). *Communication and persuasion.* New Haven, CT: Yale University Press.

Howell, J. M., & Shamir, B. (2005). The role of followers in the charismatic leadership process: relationships and their consequences. *Academy of Management Review, 30,* 96–115.

Hunter, J. D. (2003). *The death of character.* New York: Basic Books.

Hyde, M. J. (2004). Rhetorically, we dwell. In M. J. Hyde & C. O. Schrag (Eds.), *The ethos of rhetoric* (pp. xiii–xxviii). Columbia: University of South Carolina Press.

Hyde, M. J., & Schrag, C. O. (2004). *The ethos of rhetoric.* Columbia: University of South Carolina Press.

Jones, E. E., & Davis, K. E. (1965). From acts to dispositions: The attribution process in person perception. In L. Berkowitz (Ed.), *Advances in experimental social psychology* (vol. 2, pp. 219–266). New York: Academic Press.

Jones, T. M. & Ryan, L. V. (1997). The link between ethical judgment and action in organizations: A moral approbation approach. *Organization Science, 8,* 663–680.

Kelley, H. H. (1972). Attribution in social interaction. In E. E. Jones, D. E. Kanouse, H. H. Kelley, R. Nisbett, S. Valins, & B. Weiner (Eds.), *Attribution: Perceiving the causes of behavior* (pp. 1–26). Morristown, NJ: General Learning Press.

Korsgaard, C. M. (1996). *Sources of normativity.* Cambridge: Cambridge University Press.

Kouzes, J. M., & Posner, B. Z. (2002). *The leadership challenge.* San Francisco, CA: John Wiley.

Kupperman, J. (1991). *Character.* New York: Oxford University Press.

Lord, R. G., Foti, R. J., & de Vader, C. L. (1984). A test of leadership categorization theory: Internal structure, information processing, and leadership perceptions. *Organizational Behavior & Human Performance, 34,* 343.

Lord, R. G., & Maher, K. J. (1993). *Leadership and information processing: Linking perceptions and performance.* London: Routledge.

MacIntyre, A. C. (2007). *After virtue.* Notre Dame, IN: Notre Dame University Press.

May, D. R., Gilson, R. L., & Harter, L. M. (2004). The psychological conditions of meaningfulness, safety and the engagement of the human spirit at work. *Journal of Occupational and Organizational Psychology, 77,* 11–37.

Mayer, J. H., Davis, J. H., & Schoorman, D. F. (1995). An integrative model of organizational trust. *Academy of Management Review, 20,* 709–734.

McCroskey, J. C., & Young, T. J. (1981). Ethos and credibility: The construct and its measurement after three decades. *Central States Speech Journal, 32,* 24–34.

McEvily, B., Perrone, V., & Zaheer, A. (2003). Trust as an organizing principle. *Organization Science, 14,* 91–106.

Meindl, J. R. (1995). The romance of leadership as a follower-centric theory: A social constructionist approach. *Leadership Quarterly, 6,* 329–341.

Miller, A. B. (1974). Aristotle on habit and character: Implications for the rhetoric. *Speech Monographs, 41,* 309–316.

Murdoch, I. (2009). *The sovereignty of good.* New York: Routledge.

Nickerson, R.S. (1998). Confirmation bias: A ubiquitous phenomenon in many guises. *Review of General Psychology; Review of General Psychology, 2*(2), 175.

Northouse, P.G. (2007). *Leadership theory and practice* (4th ed.). Thousand Oaks, CA: Sage.

Porter, L.W., & McLaughlin, G.B. (2006). Leadership and the organizational context: Like the weather. *Leadership Quarterly, 17,* 559–576.

Power, F.C., Higgins, A., & Kohlberg, L. (1989). The habit of the common life: Building character through just community schools. In L. Nucci (Ed.), *Moral development and character education: A dialogue.* Berkeley, CA: McCutchan.

Quick, J.C., & Wright, T.A. (2011). Character-based leadership, context and consequences. *Leadership Quarterly, 22,* 984–988.

Reynolds, N. (1993). Ethos as location: New sites for understanding discursive authority. *Rhetoric Review, 11,* 325–338.

Ryan, L.V., & Riordan, C.M. (2000). The development of a measure of desired moral approbation. *Educational and Psychological Measurement, 60,* 448.

Sattler, W.M. (1947). Conceptions of ethos in ancient rhetoric. *Speech Monographs, 14,* 55–65.

Schaubroeck, J., Hannah, S.T., Avolio, B.J., Kozlowski, S.W.J., Lord, R.L., Treviño, L.K., Peng, A.C., & Dimotakas, N. (2012). Embedding ethical leadership within and across organization levels. *Academy of Management Journal, 55,* 1053–1078.

Schwartz, B. (2011). Practical wisdom and organizations. *Research in Organizational Behavior, 31,* 3–23.

Selznick, P. (1957). *Leadership in administration.* New York: Harper & Row.

Shamir, B. (1991). Meaning, self, and motivation in organizations. *Organization Studies, 12,* 405–424.

Shamir, B., & Eilam, G. (2005). "What's your story?" A life-stories approach to authentic leadership development. *Leadership Quarterly, 16,* 395–417.

Sherman, N. (1989). *The fabric of character: Aristotle's theory of virtue.* New York: Oxford University Press.

Smith, C.R. (2004). Ethos dwells pervasively: A hermeneutic reading of Aristotle on credibility. In M.J. Hyde & C.O. Schrag (Eds.), *The ethos of rhetoric,* pp. 1–19. Columbia: University of South Carolina Press.

Solomon, R.C. (1992). *Ethics and excellence: Cooperation and integrity in business.* New York: Oxford University Press.

Sparrowe, R.T., & Liden, R.C. (1997). Process and structure in leader-member exchange. *Academy of Management Review, 22,* 522–552.

Stahlberg, D., Peterson, L., & Dauenheimer, D. (1999). Preferences for and evaluation of self-relevant information depending on the elaboration of the schema involved. *European Journal of Social Psychology, 29,* 489–502.

Sullivan, D. (1993). The ethos of epideictic encounter. *Philosophy and Rhetoric, 26,* 113–133.

Tetlock, P.E., & Mitchell, G. (2010). Situated social identities constrain morally defensible choices: Commentary on Bennis, Medin, & Bartels (2010). *Perspectives on Psychological Science, 5,* 206–208.

Treviño, L.K. (1986). Ethical decision making in organizations: A person-situation interactionist model. *Academy of Management Review, 11,* 601–617.

Treviño, L.K., & Youngblood, S.A. (1990). Bad apples in bad barrels: A causal analysis of ethical decision-making behavior. *Journal of Applied Psychology, 75,* 378–385.

Uhl-Bien, M., & Maslyn, J.M. (2003). Reciprocity in manager-subordinate relationships: components, configurations, and outcomes. *Journal of Management, 29,* 511–532.

Uhl-Bien, M., & Pillai, R. (2007). The romance of leadership and the social construction of followership. *Follower-centered perspectives on leadership: A tribute to the memory of James R. Meindl* (pp. 187–209). Information Age Publishing: Greenwich, CT.

Verplanken, B., & Holland, R.W. (2002). Motivated decision making: Effects of activation and self-centrality of values on choices and behavior. *Journal of Personality and Social Psychology, 82,* 434–447.

Victor, B., & Cullen, J.B. (1988). The organizational bases of ethical work climates. *Administrative Science Quarterly, 33,* 101–125.

Walker, L.J., & Henning, K.H. (2004). Differing conceptions of moral exemplarity: Just, brave, and caring. *Journal of Personality and Social Psychology, 86,* 629–647.

Wallace, J.D. (1996). *Ethical norms, particular cases.* Ithaca, NY: Cornell University Press.

Weick, K.E. (1988). Enacted sensemaking in crisis situations. *Journal of Management Studies, 25,* 305–317.

Wiener, Y. (1982). Commitment in organizations: A normative view. *Academy of Management Review, 7,* 418–428.

Wren, T.E. (1991). *Caring about morality, philosophical perspectives in moral psychology.* Cambridge, MA: MIT Press.

Wren, T.E. (2010). *Moral obligations: Action, intention, and valuation.* New Brunswick, NJ: Transaction.

Wright, T.A., & Goodstein, J. (2007). Character is not "dead" in management research: A review of individual character and organizational-level virtue. *Journal of Management, 33,* 928–958.

Wright, T.A., & Quick, J.C. (2011). The role of character in ethical leadership research. *Leadership Quarterly, 22,* 975–978.

Yammarino, F.J., Dionne, S.D., Uk Chun, J., & Dansereau, F. (2005). Leadership and levels of analysis: A state-of-the-science review. *Leadership Quarterly, 16,* 879–919.

Yukl, G. (2002). *Leadership in organizations* (5th ed.). Upper Saddle Creek, NJ: Prentice-Hall.

Zagzebski, L.T. (1996). *Virtues of the mind.* Cambridge: Cambridge University Press.

Zander, U.B., & Kogut, B. (1995). Knowledge and the speed of the transfer and imitation of organizational capabilities: An empirical test. *Organization Science, 1,* 76–92.

8

Leader Political Skill and Team Effectiveness

The Positioning of Political Skill in the Framework of Leader Competencies

Darren C. Treadway, Ceasar Douglas, B. Parker Ellen III, James K. Summers, and Gerald R. Ferris

The topic of leadership remains one of the most actively researched areas in the organizational sciences, and has for many years. Some of the earliest efforts to understand leadership were the "great man theories" focusing on the traits possessed by individuals who generally were perceived as effective leaders. Unfortunately, such early trait approaches tended to relate leader traits to measures of leadership effectiveness virtually devoid of any attempts to explain how or why these traits made a difference (e.g., Yukl, 2006). In recent years, we have witnessed renewed interest in the trait view approach, but this new work has focused on multistage models that more precisely articulate the intermediate linkages or mediating processes that occur between leader traits/characteristics and leadership effectiveness (e.g., DeRue, Nahrgang, Wellman, & Humphrey, 2011; Van Iddekinge, Ferris, & Hefner, 2009; Zaccaro, 2007; Zaccaro, Kemp, & Bader, 2004).

A body of work related to the renewed interest in trait theories has been the political perspective on leadership. In response to an appeal for theory and research in this area by House and Aditya (1997), Ammeter, Douglas, Gardner, Hochwarter, and Ferris (2002) proposed a political theory of leadership, which articulated the leader traits/characteristics, behaviors, and contextual factors contributing to leadership effectiveness. Political skill was a focal leader characteristic proposed in this theory, which is reflective of a synergistic set of social competencies argued to bring adaptability and situationally appropriate influence behavior to interactions with followers, inspiring trust and confidence, through which both leaders and followers can realize effectiveness (e.g., Ferris, Davidson, & Perrewé, 2005; Ferris, Treadway, Brouer, & Munyon, 2012; Ferris et al., 2005; Ferris et al., 2007).

DeRue and colleagues recently proposed "an integrative trait-behavioral model of leadership effectiveness," which positioned political skill as one of the "leader traits and characteristics" believed to impact leadership effectiveness through the demonstration of specific leader behaviors (2011, p. 7). Previous research on leader political skill has demonstrated direct relationships with leadership effectiveness (Ahearn, Ferris, Hochwarter, Douglas, & Ammeter, 2004; Douglas & Ammeter, 2004; Semadar, Robins, & Ferris, 2006), but no investigation of mediators of those relationships were examined, or even proposed, despite appeals to do so (i.e., Ahearn et al., 2004; Ammeter et al., 2002; Treadway et al., 2004).

Therefore, clear deficiencies remain in our understanding of leader political skill and how it exercises its effects on leadership effectiveness outcomes. Specifically, we need to take a lesson from the scholars promoting the renewed research interest in trait views of leadership, which have proposed multistage models that more precisely articulate the mediating processes that occur between leader traits/characteristics and leadership effectiveness (e.g., DeRue et al., 2011; Van Iddekinge et al., 2009; Zaccaro, 2007; Zaccaro et al., 2004).

The present chapter expands theory in this area by developing a model suggesting that leader political skill operates through the leader behaviors demonstrated and team processes, which then impact team and leadership effectiveness. In so doing, the proposed conceptualization expands upon recent work on trait views, political perspectives on, and relational approaches to leadership (e.g., Ammeter et al., 2002; Carmeli, Ben-Hador, Waldman, & Rupp, 2009; DeRue et al., 2011; Uhl-Bien, 2006). Furthermore, this research responds to appeals in these areas collectively to provide a more integrated model of leadership that develops a more informed understanding of the mechanisms underlying the nature of the relationships between leader characteristics and leadership and team effectiveness (e.g., Avolio, 2007; DeRue et al., 2011).

Leadership effectiveness is a broad term that represents the various ways we can construe leadership outcomes to reflect increased performance and effectiveness of leaders, followers, and teams. Indeed, scholars have argued that organizational environments are changing with regard to the structure and design as well as the nature and definition of work, and that team-based work structures are increasingly replacing work designed at the individual job level (e.g., Bridges, 1994; Cascio, 1995; Daft & Lewin, 1993). Thus, the perspective taken in the proposed conceptualization is to articulate how leader political skill works through intermediate linkages to influence the effectiveness of teams.

Our framework follows the traditional I-P-O (i.e., Input-Process-Output) model (e.g., Hackman, 1987), in that inputs (i.e., leader political skill and leader behaviors) influence team processes and then effectiveness. Specifically, we propose that political skill directly affects the leader's ability to enact specific team leadership behaviors. The enactment of team-directed leadership behaviors impacts team processes, and finally, team effectiveness criteria. This framework follows the appeal of Ahearn and colleagues (2004), who found that leader political skill was associated with team effectiveness, but did not measure, and thus could only speculate about, the intermediate linkages that explained this important relationship.

LEADERSHIP IN THE TEAM CONTEXT

More than a half century ago, Stogdill said, "leadership is always associated with the attainment of group objectives. Leadership implies activity, movement, getting work done. The leader is the person who occupies a position of responsibility in coordinating the activities of the members of the group in their task of attaining a common goal" (1948, p. 64). To say that the use of groups and teams to accomplish organizational goals is prevalent today would be an understatement. As Morgeson, DeRue, and Karam pointed out, "Structuring work around teams has become a fact of organizational life" (2010, p. 6).

Flatter organizations, more specialized skill sets, project-based approaches to work, growth in the number of remote work arrangements, and increases in turnover suggest that the increased use of team-based work is unlikely to reverse (e.g., Mathieu, Maynard, Rapp, & Gilson, 2008; Tannenbaum, Mathieu, Salas, & Cohen, 2012). As such, there is a growing interest in the research area of teams that is accompanied by the need for a better understanding of the necessary skills, behaviors, and functions for leaders to be effective in the team context. Furthermore, we suggest that some competencies equip leaders to better demonstrate the requisite behaviors that address the key functions that will contribute to teams being effective. Indeed, this is the focus of the proposed framework.

Nature of Work, Performance, and Effectiveness in the Team Context

Organization and Conduct of Work

It is important to distinguish between the concept of *groups* and *teams* when discussing the nature of collective work. Although both *groups* and *teams* refer to a assemblage of individuals working toward a common goal, the context is distinct. *Group* refers to a collective that shares a common goal, but that performs work in an environment characterized by lower task complexity and interaction. In these settings, group success largely is a function of the aggregate performance of the individual group members. *Team* refers to a more structured, complicated, and often intricate set of performance interactions among members (Kozlowski, Gully, McHugh, Salas, & Cannon-Bowers, 1996). Therefore, teamwork is the accomplishment of goals through a group of people working together in a manner that enables them to achieve more than they could with uncoordinated individual actions. So, the nature of work through teams can be characterized by the mutually dependent interaction of its members.

Team Work Outcomes: Performance and Effectiveness

As Kozlowski and colleagues pointed out, "In team situations, effectiveness hinges on the ability of team members to integrate their individual performances to meet coordination demands," and "Team performance is the result of a complex network of linkages among individual tasks, roles, and goals" (1996, p. 257). Team effectiveness, or success, is then not simply a function of individual team member ability, but also involves the *processes* employed to facilitate the interaction of team members necessary to perform the work. These interactions take place throughout recurring cycles that can be described as episodes by specific action and transition periods (Marks, Mathieu, & Zaccaro, 2001; Zaccaro, Rittman, & Marks, 2001).

The transition phase is the period of time when the team is focused on group membership, structure, goal setting, work planning, and evaluation of work performed during previous action phases. The action phase is the period of time when the team is focused on the performance of task/work that directly contributes to goal attainment. Team performance occurs through the repetition of these transition and action phase cycles over time (Morgeson et al., 2010).

As teams repeatedly work through the transition and actions phases, they are likely to experience tensions that can thwart team member and collective team performance by hindering team member ability to regulate goal-directed behavior. The challenge of working through these tensions creates needs that must be satisfied for the team to achieve its goals. In agreement with Morgeson and colleagues (2010), we argue that team performance and effectiveness are achieved through leadership qualities and characteristics that translate into effective leader behaviors, which in turn contribute to teams becoming more effective.

THEORETICAL FOUNDATIONS AND MODEL

We propose that leader political skill represents a set of critical social competencies that can contribute meaningfully to the performance and effectiveness of teams. Furthermore, we introduce a multistage mediation model in the following sections that suggests how leader political skill affects team outcomes. The model is presented in Figure 8.1, and essentially it argues that leader political skill contributes to the demonstration of particular leader behaviors that influence team processes which, in turn, affect team performance and effectiveness. The following sections examine each of the model's components in greater detail.

Nature of Leader Political Skill and Leadership Effectiveness

Political Skill Construct Overview
Political skill was first introduced in the organizational sciences literature by Pfeffer (1981). This notion of a political perspective on organizations was

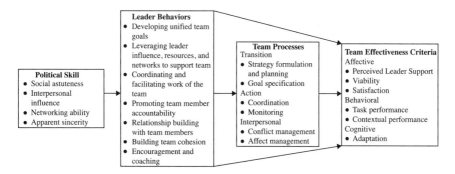

FIGURE 8.1
Multistage framework of leader political skill and team effectiveness

shared and put forth independently by Mintzberg (1983, 1985). The political skill construct conceived by both scholars involves the ability to acquire and effectively use power and influence to achieve goals, and Pfeffer (1981) indicated that political skill was necessary to succeed in organizations. This initial characterization of political skill largely dealt with notions of formal power, but subsequent work demonstrated its effectiveness in the exercise of influence in the absence of formal authority (Perrewé et al., 2004).

Early empirical work on political skill focused on the investigation of the use of influence tactics in organizations, but in the late 1990s and 2000s, the focus turned from the "what" of influence to the "how" of influence (Ferris et al., 2012). This program of research led to the conceptualization of political skill as a complex multidimensional construct consisting of four dimensions (i.e., social astuteness, interpersonal influence, networking ability, and apparent sincerity). Ferris and colleagues characterized the construct as "a comprehensive pattern of social competencies, with cognitive, affective, and behavioral manifestations, which have both direct effects on outcomes, as well as moderating effects on predictor-outcome relationships" (2007, p. 291). Furthermore, Ferris and colleagues initially defined the political skill construct as "the ability to effectively understand others at work, and to use such knowledge to influence others to act in ways that enhance one's personal and/or organizational objectives" (2005, p. 127). They also provided more specificity concerning the four dimensions of political skill.

Political Skill Dimensions

Social astuteness. Politically skilled individuals possess a heightened awareness of their social surroundings. They understand the intricacies of their environment, including the interrelated nature of their motivations and the motivations of others. This level of social awareness enables them to correctly interpret and identify with the behavior of others (Ferris et al., 2012), which Pfeffer (1992) claimed was integral to the ability to influence others effectively.

Interpersonal influence. The politically skilled are experts at the art of subtly influencing others through a communication and interaction style that puts those around them at ease (Ferris et al., 2012), and are characterized by what Pfeffer (1992) referred to as "flexibility," which enables them to adapt to the needs of the environment in ways that elicit desired responses from others.

Networking ability. Politically skilled individuals are experts at building and maintaining diverse social networks with valuable assets, which they can then leverage for individual and organizational success. Further, the politically skilled are adept at resolving conflict and handling negotiations, which reinforces the bonds they have formed with others (Ferris et al., 2012). Effective networking skills also enable these individuals to be properly positioned (e.g., are always at the right place at the right time) to take advantage of opportunities (Ferris et al., 2005; Pfeffer, 1992).

Apparent sincerity. Politically skilled individuals are perceived by others as displaying high levels of integrity, and as being honest and open (Ferris et al., 2005). Because they are considered authentic, politically skilled individuals' influence attempts are viewed as trustworthy and genuine. This is an essential component to the ability to influence, as it allows the politically skilled to mask any ulterior motives if they are present. Because of this, the politically skilled are not seen as manipulative or coercive, and their influence attempts are more likely to be successful (Jones, 1990).

Leader Political Skill and Leader Effectiveness

Given the nature of the four political skill dimensions outlined earlier, a politically skilled leader (i.e., charged with acquiring and employing the resources needed to guide and direct others toward the attainment of objectives) is equipped to realize effectiveness through an enhanced ability to understand people and situations, adapt and calibrate behavior to elicit desired responses, and leverage social resources, all while conveying an appropriate level of sincerity (Douglas, Ferris, & Perrewé, 2005). As Treadway, Bentley, and Williams (in press) pointed out, the four dimensions do not imply that a person high in political skill is expected to engage in subversive acts of manipulation, but that they are effective at meeting goals through social means.

Admittedly, there is some commonality between the dimensions of political skill and other concepts present in the field of leadership. Some of these related constructs include:

- Social Intelligence: "an ability to successfully engage in fundamentally four cognitive and behavioral processes—social awareness, social acumen, response selection, and response enactment" (Zacarro, 2002, p. 38)

- Political Intelligence: "accurately reads political currents, understands patterns of relationships quickly . . . builds relationships with peers and subordinates" (Ciampa, 2005, p. 51)
- Sociopolitical Intelligence: "enables leadership because it is the key to social skill and thus the ability to build a team" (Hogan & Hogan, 2002, p. 79)
- Interpersonal Acumen: "refers to the ability to decipher underlying intentions in other people's behavior" (Aditya & House, 2002, p. 218)
- Successful Intelligence: "the ability to achieve success by one's own standards, given one's sociocultural context" (Sternberg, 2002, p. 10)
- Leader Self-Regulation: "how a leader uses his or her own abilities in the domain of leadership" (Murphy, 2002, p. 164)
- Leader Charisma: the ability to "inspire subordinates toward both strong commitment to team tasks and high satisfaction with membership on the team" (Balkundi, Kilduff, & Harrison, 2011, p. 1210)

Although somewhat similar, and perhaps sharing modest construct domain space, each of these leadership constructs is distinct from political skill. For example, in a recent empirical assessment, Balkundi and colleagues (2011) tested two models to examine the impact of charisma on team effectiveness. The first model used network centrality to mediate the relationship between leader charisma and team effectiveness. In this conceptualization, leader charisma positioned them at the center of the advice network, which facilitated team effectiveness. The second model used charisma to mediate the relationship between network centrality and team effectiveness. The authors found support for the charisma-mediating model, suggesting that leader presence in the center of an advice network was associated with attributions of charisma from the followers.

We argue that the superior networking ability of politically skilled leaders contributes to their position at the center of the team's advice network, which leads to attributions of charisma and affects team performance. This is consistent with findings by Douglas and Ammeter (2004), where data on leader effectiveness ratings and work group performance were predicted by a two-factor political skill model that included the dimensions of networking ability and interpersonal influence. Even after the inclusion of leader education, gender, self-efficacy, and self-monitoring as control variables, networking ability explained significant variance in leader performance ratings.

Further, Semadar and colleagues (2006) demonstrated the distinctiveness of political skill by examining its predictive power for managerial effectiveness in direct competition with self-monitoring, emotional intelligence, and leadership self-efficacy. Neither self-monitoring nor leadership self-efficacy was found to be a significant predictor of managerial performance, and while emotional intelligence was found to be a significant predictor it accounted for very little variance beyond that explained by political skill. In addition to being the strongest predictor of managerial effectiveness, political skill was a key factor that distinguished top performers from their peers.

In a recent two-study investigation, Brouer, Douglas, Treadway, and Ferris (2012) examined the impact of political skill on leadership effectiveness through a social exchange perspective, showing that leaders realize effectiveness through increasing followers' perceptions of higher-quality leader-follower relationships. They argued that politically skilled leaders are considered more trustworthy (Treadway et al., 2004), and thus able to encourage followers to develop mutual obligations by using their sincerity to make followers feel that it is more likely that their behaviors will be reciprocated (Ferris et al., 2007).

While Brouer and colleagues (2012) examined leader and follower contextual performance (individual level of analysis), Ahearn and colleagues demonstrated the effects of leader political skill on objective performance measures at the team level (2004, p. 317). In this investigation, performance was operationalized as "permanency rate" among teams of case workers at a child welfare agency (i.e., "successful placement of children into final living arrangements"). Even after controlling for leader and team variables, leader political skill was shown to account for a significant increment in team performance variance.

These results indicate that political skill is a differentiator among leaders. Research has shown that leader political skill ultimately demonstrates effects on performance, but has yet to show more precisely how this occurs. Understandably, the desire to illuminate the "black box" of leadership effectiveness has led to appeals calling for exploration of intermediate linkages to explain better how political skill works (Ahearn et al., 2004; Brouer et al., 2012; House & Aditya, 1997; Treadway et al., in press).

Leader Behaviors and Team Reactions as Dual Mediators of the Leader Political Skill—Team Effectiveness Relationship

Although prior studies have theoretically and empirically linked leader political skill to team effectiveness, the conceptual argument cannot be made that team performance stems directly from a leader's possession of political skill. As Burke and colleagues (2006) noted, it is leadership behaviors in teams that matter when seeking to achieve team performance outcomes. Thus, politically skilled leaders must demonstrate specific behaviors that ultimately lead to enhanced performance.

For example, in their qualitative investigation of managers, Smith, Plowman, Duchon, and Quinn (2009) found that politically skilled managers were able to influence subordinates in ways that positively influenced organizational outcomes by developing trust, leading by example, and creating accountability in their subordinates. Additionally, these leaders focused on processes such as goal setting, influencing and learning from below, and empowering their subordinates (Ferris et al., 2012). Therefore, we argue that team effectiveness emerges from the performance of specific behaviors indicative of politically skilled leaders that positively influence team processes, ultimately leading to enhanced team performance and effectiveness.

Leader Political Skill → Leader Behaviors

Ferris, Davidson, and Perrewé (2005) identified political skill as "the necessary precondition for effective behavior" for leaders. Because of social astuteness, networking ability, interpersonal influence, and apparent sincerity, politically skilled leaders are able to effectively read people and situations, build effective relationships, select appropriate behaviors, and execute in a manner that is regarded as sincere, genuine, and authentic. The sections that follow outline how leader political skill leads to the effective utilization of specific behaviors. These behaviors overlap with many of the functions Morgeson and colleagues (2010) presented in their taxonomy of leader functions necessary for positive team performance.

Developing unified team goals. In order to meet or exceed performance criteria, it is necessary for the team to have established goals that it can work to accomplish. Goal-setting theory states that challenging and clearly established goals are important determinants of individual motivation toward achieving performance targets and, as Morgeson and colleagues (2010) reported, multiple studies have shown the same to hold true in the team context. The goal-setting process involves leaders actively working with their teams to articulate the specific measures by which they will be evaluated. To do so, leaders must first successfully understand and interpret the organizational context within which the team operates to determine, craft, and communicate the team mission and vision. Team cohesion can be built around the vision (Dionne, Yammarino, Atwater, & Spangler, 2004), and, with challenging goals, can serve as an overarching sense of purpose for the team.

Politically skilled leaders, possessing social astuteness and the ability to effectively leverage personal networks, are equipped to successfully interpret broader organizational expectations for the team, which can aid in setting appropriate goals. Additionally, because politically skilled leaders possess an increased ability for interpersonal influence, they can effectively persuade team members to adopt the vision and accept challenging and unifying performance goals.

Leveraging leader influence, resources, and networks to support the team. Regardless of individual team member capability or superior leadership skill, no team can accomplish its tasks without necessary resources (Hackman, 1987). One of the primary responsibilities for team leaders is to secure the "informational, financial, material and personnel resources" (Morgeson et al., 2010) that the team needs so that it can perform effectively. Locating these resources requires broad access inside and outside the organization. This access is achieved through extensive networks; however, simple access to a vast and resource-rich network isn't always enough.

Leaders often need to employ interpersonal influence to achieve commitment of resources needed for teams to meet their performance expectations. In addition to being essential to task accomplishment, the provision of key resources also is instrumental in developing feelings of perceived leader support. When leaders use their personal networks and influence to provide for the team, it signifies that the leader supports the team, reinforces beliefs that the team goals, and therefore the team's work, are important, and motivates the team to perform (Morgeson et al., 2010).

As Ferris and colleagues noted, "politically skilled individuals are argued to be able to more effectively utilize, present, and leverage resources at their disposal" (2012, p. 507). First, politically skilled leaders, noted for superior networking ability, are likely to have access to extensive, diverse, and resource-rich networks. Second, increased interpersonal influence equips politically skilled leaders to convince members of the network to provide the resources necessary for team success. As pointed out in a study of politically skilled football recruiters (Treadway et al., in press), this can enable politically skilled leaders to leverage organizational (e.g., head coach and team) performance to secure commitment of key resources.

Coordinating and facilitating work of the team. Whereas establishing goals and securing resources determines the "what" of team performance, the task of coordinating and facilitating the work of teams addresses the "how" (i.e., methods that will be employed to do the work), the "who" (i.e., which team members), and the "when" (i.e., specific sequencing of the work tasks) of team performance. Coordinating and facilitating behaviors mark the move from the transition phase to the action phase of the team performance cycle, and are concerned with the actual execution of the work. Burke and colleagues referred to these behaviors as task-focused actions used to initiate structure. These can involve assigning specific tasks to particular team members, specification of processes to be utilized, and establishment of communication channels (Burke et al., 2006).

The effective assignment of tasks and definition of roles for team members requires an awareness of their individual capabilities as related to the specific goals established for the team. The social astuteness of politically skilled leaders increases the awareness of team member ability and a high degree of interpersonal influence, and enables politically skilled leaders to successfully convince team members to accept roles and tasks that may be new, unfamiliar, more difficult, or less glamorous than they desire, but that are necessary to accomplish team objectives. Further, because politically skilled leaders are known to be high in apparent sincerity, it is more likely that they will be able to perform these coordinating and facilitating behaviors in a manner that makes team members believe their specific assignments are what is best for effective team performance.

Promoting team member accountability. To ensure that they perform up to their potential, teams must be monitored as they carry out their work. Monitoring is critical in that it provides information to leaders regarding team performance that informs leaders and facilitates successful execution of other leader behaviors (Morgeson et al., 2010). This includes evaluating team member performance to gauge what, within the team, is working effectively and what is not so that decisions and adjustments can be made to ensure goal attainment. Once discovered, this information must be presented to the team in the form of feedback. Feedback enables the team to assess its past and current performance against objectives and adapt as necessary (Morgeson et al., 2010). Because feedback often has a critical component, it can be difficult for the team to hear.

Smith and colleagues (2009) found that politically skilled managers, because of humility and affability, were able to create accountability in their followers, and Ferris and colleagues (2007) noted that the politically skilled were able to inspire trust and confidence in others. This enables leaders to deliver feedback in a manner that team members will accept, and to translate it into the changes necessary to ensure adequate progress toward goals (Morgeson et al., 2010). By demonstrating that critical feedback can be delivered in a sensitive manner, politically skilled leaders create an environment of safety for the team. This sets the tone that accountability is necessary for success, and that feedback can be delivered humanely. In this environment, team members may be more likely to mimic leader behavior, and this can foster a culture of mutual accountability within the team.

Relationship building with team members. Though definitions of leadership vary, a consistent theme among them is the notion that leaders are people of influence (Ferris, Davidson, & Perrewé, 2005). The leadership behaviors discussed previously certainly are consistent with a conceptualization of interpersonal influence and, as evident in the descriptions, the effective performance of those behaviors involves more than a formal authoritative relationship between leaders and individual team members. Effective leadership is built upon successful influence, and successful influence requires savvy and subtlety (Ferris, Davidson, & Perrewé, 2005), which suggests that an interpersonal relationship must exist between leaders and individual team members. Leaders can build relationships with team members by showing respect, exhibiting warmth, and demonstrating concern for them (Morgeson et al., 2010; Schminke, Wells, Peyrefitte, & Sebora, 2002). In some of the earliest behavioral leadership research efforts, these behaviors were labeled "consideration" (Judge, Piccolo, & Ilies, 2004), and refer to actions used to maintain close social relationships (Burke et al., 2006).

Politically skilled leaders are able to employ the behaviors outlined earlier because they possess the social astuteness needed to identify and understand the social needs of team members. Additionally, because of apparent sincerity, politically skilled leaders can act in a manner that convinces team members that the leader is genuinely respectful and concerned about team member well-being and leader-member relations.

Building team cohesion. Throughout the life cycle of the team, the leader needs to be aware of and tend to the team's social environment. This can involve effectively addressing conflicts that emerge between team members that threaten team cohesion and that could adversely affect the team's ability to achieve its goals (Morgeson et al., 2010). Because conflicts may not always be presented to leaders, or even be readily apparent, leaders must possess the ability to effectively read team members and evaluate their interactions. Politically skilled leaders are socially astute and equipped to identify and understand underlying conflicts between team members. Additionally, politically skilled leaders possess the interpersonal influence and apparent sincerity necessary to resolve conflicts in a manner that preserves team member relationships and maintains team cohesion.

Encouragement and coaching. Even if the team environment is free of interpersonal conflict, it is unlikely that all of the task work will be completed and objectives accomplished without teams facing some sort of obstacle, errors, or mistakes. Because challenges can discourage teams, it is necessary for leaders to encourage and coach them through these rough spots. These behaviors empower team members and build efficacy. In their meta-analysis of effective team leader behaviors, Burke and colleagues (2006) presented coaching as a person-focused leader behavior aligned with empowerment. Politically skilled leaders, through social astuteness, are able to identify when the team needs encouragement and, through interpersonal influence, are effective in convincing team members to adjust approaches and press forward through difficult stretches.

Leader Behaviors → Team Processes

As noted in the previous section, the specific behaviors indicative of politically skilled leaders overlap in many ways with the key team leadership functions outlined by Morgeson and colleagues (2010). While they cited a number of studies that show links between the team leadership behaviors and team effectiveness, more attention is needed regarding the explanation of why these behaviors lead to higher team effectiveness. The nature of these team effectiveness criteria is dependent on the quality of execution by leaders in the manifestation of teamwork. The more effective leaders are at performing the relevant leader behaviors, the more positive and productive teams will be working together effectively by managing both interdependencies and personalities.

Marks and colleagues argued (2001, p. 357), and LePine and colleagues meta-analytically supported (LePine, Piccolo, Jackson, Mathieu, & Saul, 2009), the notion that team processes (i.e., defined as members' interdependent acts that convert inputs to outcomes through cognitive, verbal, and behavioral activities directed toward organizing task work to achieve collective goals) can be clustered into three higher-order categories differentiated by content domain. These broad processes occur through-out periods of episodic performance (i.e., teams are actively engaged in various forms of tasks at different phases of task accomplishment) referred to as transition and action phases. These three higher-order processes are (1) transition-phase processes, (2) action-phase processes, and (3) inter-personal processes.

Transition-phase processes. Transition phases are periods of time when teams concentrate mainly on evaluation and planning activities to guide their accomplishment of team goals or objectives. Strategy formulation and planning, key processes during this phase, represent the development of alternative courses of action for mission accomplishment. These involve decision making about how team members will go about achieving their missions, discussion of expectations, relay of task-related information, pri-oritization, role assignment, and the communication of plans to all team members (Hackman & Oldham, 1980; Stout, Cannon-Bowers, Salas, & Milanovich, 1999). Another important process that stems from the tran-sition phase is goal specification, which refers to the recognition and prioritization of goals and subgoals for mission completion. It accounts for the development and assignment of comprehensive mission goals and subgoals that specify what and how much must be completed by a speci-fied time and within a particular quality measure (Marks et al., 2001).

Team leaders should demonstrate effective behaviors that enhance team transition-phase processes. One particular leader behavior that should improve team transition-phase processes is that of building team cohesion. Specifically, as team cohesion increases, they tend to plan more efficiently and develop more appropriate performance strategies (Hackman, 1987; Hackman & Morris, 1975). Developing unified team goals also helps teams during transition-phase processes, as Klein and colleagues concluded that communicating the overall plan in a manner that elicited a unified response from team members more clearly specified team goals as well as their abil-ity to successfully formulate plans (Klein, Ziegert, Knight, & Xiao, 2006). Coaching also contributes to transition-phase processes (Edmondson, 1999), as team leaders can clarify the direction the team needs to follow as well as provide relevant information (Hackman, 2002). Further, leader ability to leverage resources allows teams to formulate strategies with more certainty, as they have a much better understanding of the resources they have at their discretion.

Action-phase processes. Next, action-phase processes are intervals of time when teams perform behaviors leading directly to goal accomplishment. Action-phase processes consist primarily of coordination activities and monitoring behaviors (Marks et al., 2001). Coordination is the process of managing interdependencies between activities and workflow (Malone & Crowston, 1994), whereas monitoring behaviors include behaviors such as monitoring progress toward goals, systems monitoring, and team monitoring and backup behaviors (Cannon-Bowers, Tannenbaum, Salas, & Volpe, 1995; Fleishman & Zaccaro, 1992; Jentsch, Barnett, Bowers, & Salas, 1999).

Perhaps the most obvious leader behavior affecting action-phase processes is when leaders facilitate work and assist the team in coordinating its behavior. Leaders should encourage members to interact and bond in order to increase coordination. Because team tasks can place a heavy burden on member resources that exceed their current capabilities, leaders must be prepared to coach and intervene as necessary by prompting coordination among team members (Kozlowski, Watola, Nowakowski, Kim, & Botero, 2009).

To positively impact team monitoring, team leaders can promote team member accountability, which will allow team members not only to keep track of their own behavior, but also to manage interdependencies, as team members must rely on one another for workflow and resources (Saavedra, Earley, & Van Dyne, 1993). This is accomplished by team members monitoring one another to ensure they are adhering to their roles and responsibilities (Barker, 1993).

Interpersonal processes. Last, interpersonal processes occur throughout both transition and action phases, and are utilized to manage member relationships within teams. Marks and colleagues (2001) described processes that govern interpersonal activities, including conflict management and affect management. Working in teams imparts an interpersonal context in which conflict occurs, and successfully managing conflicts is necessary for teams to function properly (Jehn, 1995; Jehn, Greer, Levine, & Szulanski, 2008). Specifically, we focus on conflict management and affect management as two integral interpersonal processes (Marks et al., 2001).

Conflict management refers to both preemptive (i.e., establishing conditions to prevent, control, or guide team conflict before it occurs) and reactive (i.e., working through task and interpersonal disagreements among team members) mechanisms for handling conflict (Cannon-Bowers et al., 1995; Jehn, 1995; Simons & Petersen, 2000). Affect management, then, involves regulating member emotions during teamwork including, but not limited to, social cohesion, frustration, and excitement (Cannon-Bowers et al., 1995). Interpersonal processes are present and necessary at all phases of team operations (Arrow, McGrath, & Berdahl, 2000), and so they require constant attention by team leaders.

Relationship building with team members creates close ties (Ferris et al., 2009) and psychological safety (Edmondson, 1999), creating a more supportive and open environment, which allows leaders to be more effective when encouraging team members. By developing relationships with team members, trusted leaders (Ferris et al., 2009) are in a better position to mediate conflicts, as team members are more likely to compromise, more open and flexible, and more willing to accept differences in opinion (Pace, 1990). Team leaders also are more capable of positively shaping affect management after developing relationships as they have a better understanding of the team and individual team members. Thus, leaders have a better understanding of proper techniques to regulate emotions in both good times and bad by being able to successfully encourage team members.

Team ability to manage conflict and affect also is influenced by leader ability to build team cohesion (Harrison, 1983). By successfully building cohesive teams, leaders develop environments where team members are more comfortable dealing with conflict (Patten, 1981), managing team affect (Harrison, 1983), and improving relations among team members (Bechhard, 1983). Further, through building cohesion, team leaders can demonstrate productive mechanisms (e.g., breaking tension, joking, relaxing, complaining), which facilitate team ability to manage conflict and emotion (Marks et al., 2001).

Leader Behaviors and Team Processes → Team Effectiveness
The last linkage in the model describes the impact that leader behaviors and team processes have on team effectiveness. Extant research has posited and empirically examined the roles that leader behaviors (Burke et al., 2006; Morgeson et al., 2010) and team processes (LePine et al., 2008; Marks et al., 2001) play in team effectiveness, which is a multifaceted construct (Hackman & Morris, 1975; McGrath & Altman, 1966). Morgeson and colleagues (2010) outlined three broad categories of team effectiveness: (1) affective, (2) behavioral, and (3) cognitive.

Pertinent to our present conceptualization, the affective outcomes we examine are perceived leader support, viability, and satisfaction. The behavioral outcomes identified in the literature as critical to overall team effectiveness are task and contextual performance, whereas the cognitive outcome conjectured is adaptation (Morgeson et al., 2010). We are not positing that leader behaviors and team processes affect team outcomes equally. Instead, we argue that leader behaviors and team processes can have an impact on team effectiveness. Thus, the next section outlines how leader behaviors and team processes impact team effectiveness.

Affective Team Effectiveness Criteria

Perceived leader support. It is likely that perceived leader support will be more influenced by leader behaviors than team processes, although team processes should have a moderate impact. As for leader behaviors, those behaviors that focus on the personnel side of the team should have a greater positive effect on perceived leader support. Specifically, perceived leader support can be a result of leaders assisting the team in task and goal accomplishment. This can be realized by composing the team (e.g., getting the new members that existing members believe are necessary), training and developing the team so that team efficacy is fostered, and providing necessary resources (Burke et al., 2006). Leader support also is enhanced as leaders engage in active problem solving as issues arise and by performing team tasks to demonstrate commitment (Hackman, 2002).

Further, actively managing team boundaries creates an environment in which team members are more likely to support leaders. Managing team boundaries involves communicating both politically oriented communication that increases the resources available to the team and networking communication that expands the amount and variety of information available to the team (Brown & Eisenhardt, 1995). This type of leader behavior also involves collaborating with others outside the team, scanning the environment, and negotiating resources for the team (Hirst & Mann, 2004). Thus, providing these behaviors to the team increases leader support.

Team processes also can have a positive effect on perceived leader support. Each of the three categories of team processes can impact perceived leader support. To the extent that teams function smoothly and in a well-coordinated manner, are well prepared by effective planning, and have a clear strategic direction, team members will have more support for their leader. Further, exchanges where leaders provide praise and rewards build support for the leader (Burns, 1978).

Viability. Although team viability has been long considered an important attitudinal outcome of team effectiveness, little research has addressed this important criterion variable (Mathieu et al., 2008). Assuring that a team is capable of future success is critical given the nature of most organizational teams (Hackman, 1987). Specifically, teams in today's organizations tend to exist for long periods of time, manage bundles of activities rather than one specific task (Marks et al., 2001), and are dynamic systems that experience change over time (e.g., in membership, roles, and tasks; Summers, Humphrey, & Ferris, 2012), making team viability, or "the capacity for the sustainability and growth required for success in future performance episodes" (p. 276), a principal consideration when leading organizational teams (Bell & Marentette, 2011).

Politically skilled leaders are in the unique position to ensure the sustainability and growth of work teams. Such leaders have more capability to ensure the sustained performance and growth of team members by anticipating and securing highly valued resources, which facilitates a team's ability to continue performing. Leaders also can positively influence a team's willingness or its members' desire to work together in the future. Politically skilled leaders effectively build cohesion and develop lasting relationships among team members (Morgeson et al., 2010), which positively impacts team viability.

Team processes, specifically interpersonal and transition processes, also should affect team viability. Team viability research focused on interpersonal processes and the related affective reactions of team members suggests a moderate to strong relationship between interpersonal processes and team viability (e.g., Jehn, 2008; Tekleab, Quigley, & Tesluk, 2009). Transition processes are where teams reflect on previous team accomplishments as well as prepare for future actions. These processes also should have a strong relationship with team viability because of their specific focus on attaining success in future performance episodes (Bell & Marentette, 2011).

Satisfaction. Although team satisfaction most likely is correlated with team viability, these are two distinct constructs; that is, satisfaction focuses on the positive attitude the team presently holds about itself whereas viability focuses on continued team existence (Bell & Marentette, 2011). Team satisfaction likely is affected by both leader behaviors and team processes. Because we are discussing general or global team satisfaction, team member relationships with leaders as well as team member interactions with other team members should influence attitudes toward the team. First, leaders can affect team satisfaction via several of the outlined leader behaviors. Building team cohesion can have a powerful influence on team satisfaction. As leaders build team cohesion, team members feel a higher sense of commitment to the team, which relates to team satisfaction (Zaccaro et al., 2001).

Second, team processes also impact team satisfaction. Perhaps one of the most influential team processes impacting team satisfaction is conflict management. Conflict is very detrimental to general team attitude about the nature of the team. There has been some debate regarding the type of conflict that impacts satisfaction (see De Dreu & Weingart, 2003). However, both task and relationship conflict have been found to negatively relate to team member satisfaction (e.g., Amason & Schweiger, 1997; Jehn, 1995). Thus, the ability to manage team conflict is critical to team satisfaction.

Behavioral Team Effectiveness Criteria

Task performance. Researchers recognize that at least two distinguishable dimensions contribute independently to overall performance, consisting of task performance and contextual performance (e.g., Borman & Motowidlo, 1993; Conway, 1996; Van Scotter & Motowidlo, 1996). Task performance bears a direct relation to the organization's technical core, either by executing its technical processes or by maintaining and servicing its technical requirements (Borman & Motowidlo, 1993). The most researched outcome of teams is that of task performance (for a recent meta-analysis, see LePine et al., 2008), which is a primary mechanism for assessing team results (Arrow et al., 2000). Many factors contribute to team task performance (for review, see Mathieu et al., 2008). However, we focus on the role of leader behaviors (Morgeson et al., 2010) and team processes (Marks et al., 2001) on task performance.

As for leader behaviors, one of the most relevant behaviors is that of building team cohesion, as cohesion has been found to be positively correlated with team performance (Webber & Donahue, 2001). Specifically, as leaders build cohesion, team members are likely to be more committed to tasks and devote more effort to their accomplishment. Additionally, developing team cohesion sets and enforces more stringent performance norms that compel effort (Zaccaro & McCoy, 1988), thus increasing task performance.

Promoting team member accountability also likely positively impacts team task performance. Accountability pressures lead team members to exert more effort and take more risks than when they are not under pressure from leaders (cf. Carnevale, Pruitt, & Seilhemier, 1981). Further, team members who are accountable to leaders for attaining a particular outcome are less likely to give up, and more likely to expect more out of one another, than are team members who are not accountable (Carnevale, Pruitt, & Britton, 1979).

Team processes also impact team task performance (LePine et al., 2008). Broadly speaking, higher-order processes (i.e., transition, action, and interpersonal processes) as well as narrow team processes (i.e., strategy formulation and planning, goal specification, coordination, monitoring, conflict management, and affect management) impact team task performance (Marks et al., 2001). Results from a recent meta-analysis demonstrate that both higher-order and narrow team processes are positively and significantly related to team task performance (LePine et al., 2008).

Contextual performance. In contrast to task performance, contextual performance supports the broader, organizational, social, and psychological environment in which the technical core must function (Mohammed, Mathieu, & Bartlett, 2002). Very similar to Organ's (1997) conceptualization of organizational citizenship, contextual performance includes volunteering to carry out task activities that are not formally part of the job, helping and cooperating with others, and following rules and procedures even when personally inconvenient (Borman & Motowidlo, 1993, 1997). Contextual performance is critical for team success because it captures many of the interpersonally oriented behaviors that support the social and motivational context in which organizational work is accomplished (e.g., Borman & Motowidlo, 1993; LePine, Hanson, Borman, & Motowidlo, 2000; Van Scotter & Motowidlo, 1996).

Leader behaviors should play a major role in contextual performance, as extant research has emphasized the leader behaviors—contextual performance relationship, with no prior research to our knowledge linking team processes to contextual performance. As for leader behaviors having an impact on contextual performance, building cohesion and relationships and encouragement would appear to all positively affect contextual performance. Leader behaviors that build a cohesive unit, focusing on developing relationships and encouragement, motivate team members by getting them to internalize and prioritize a larger collective cause over individual interests (Smith, Organ, & Near, 1983). Team members who are intrinsically motivated to fulfill a collective vision without expecting immediate personal and tangible gains may be inclined to contribute toward achieving the shared workplace goal in ways that their roles do not prescribe (Wang, Law, Hackett, Wang, & Chen, 2005).

Cognitive Team Effectiveness

Adaptation. Nearly half a century ago, Terreberry (1968) predicted increasing turbulence in organizational environments and claimed that adaptability would become increasingly critical for organizational effectiveness. Those assertions are omnipresent in today's organizations as they utilize teams to adapt to a constantly changing economic landscape (Burke et al., 2006). Moreover, because teams are supposed to increase an organization's flexibility, responsiveness, and self-management, their ability to adapt to a diverse set of dynamic and often ambiguous problems becomes of paramount importance for organizations (Kozlowski, 1998). Thus, the next section describes the role of leader behavior and team processes in adaptation.

Leaders can play a valuable role in team adaptation (Burke et al., 2006). Coaching and encouragement has been found to increase team ability to successfully adapt. If leaders encourage team members to adapt and be forward looking, then team members are more likely to support one another in such endeavors (Tyler & Lind, 1992). Further, leader ability to acquire and leverage resources reduces insecurity and defensiveness, which increases the team propensity to take risks and explore new options (Edmondson, 1999).

Team processes also likely promote effective team adaptation. First, the action-phase process of monitoring has long been researched within the teams' domain as promoting adaptability (Swezey & Salas, 1992). Furthermore, monitoring has been argued to allow teams to self-correct more efficiently when it is combined with back-up behavior such as the provision of feedback (Salas, Sims, & Burke, 2005).

Second, the transition-phase process of strategy formation and planning also should affect team adaptability, as it is the development of alternative courses of action that form mission accomplishment. As teams work to complete tasks, they must move back and forth from action-phase processes to transition-phase processes. In order to successfully adapt, teams must readdress decision making about how team members will go about achieving their missions, discuss changing expectations, relay new task-related information, reprioritize tasks, reassign roles, and then communicate new plans to all team members (Hackman & Oldham, 1980; Stout et al., 1999).

CONTRIBUTIONS AND IMPLICATIONS OF THE CONCEPTUALIZATION

Nearly a decade ago, Ahearn and colleagues (2004) reported the results of a study demonstrating that leader political skill explained significant incremental team performance variance, even after controlling for several team and leader variables. The authors suggested that these results would make contributions to the literatures on leader political skill, and team-based work structures in organizations, noting that leader characteristics and behaviors apparently can facilitate team performance and effectiveness beyond mere empowerment of team members.

Ahearn and colleagues (2004) suggested that it might be increased trust in leader by team members, greater perceptions of leader credibility, and enhanced team cohesion that mediated the relationships between leader political skill and team performance. Furthermore, they argued that politically skilled leaders might inspire team members to greater team performance, and that such leaders might orchestrate political dynamics of team member interactions in productive ways by channeling resources and effort toward effectiveness instead of dysfunctional outcomes. Unfortunately, although Ahearn and colleagues (2004) suggested and discussed potential mechanisms through which leader political skill affected team effectiveness, such intermediate linkages were not actually measured. Therefore, they appealed for future research to more clearly articulate and assess the intervening variables through which leader political skill influences team performance and effectiveness.

The renewed interest in the trait view of leadership has focused on multistage models that more precisely specify the intermediate linkages or mediating processes that occur between leader traits/characteristics and leadership effectiveness. DeRue and colleagues (2011) specifically proposed an integrative model of leadership effectiveness that discussed leader political skill as one of the "leader traits and characteristics" believed to impact leadership and team effectiveness mediated by specific leader behaviors. The present chapter expands theory in this area by presenting a model that suggests leader political skill operates through demonstrated leader behaviors and team processes, which then impact team and leadership effectiveness. Specifically, we propose that political skill directly affects a leader's ability to enact specific team leadership behaviors and that the enactment of these team-directed leadership behaviors impact team processes and, ultimately, team effectiveness criteria.

DIRECTIONS FOR FUTURE RESEARCH

The obvious immediate direction for future research in this area is to conduct partial or full tests of the multistage model of leader political skill and team process and effectiveness. Additionally, it is noteworthy to suggest that some of this future research investigates leader political skill at the dimension level of analysis, in order to expand theory in this area regarding the differential predictability of the different political skill dimensions. Most of the political skill research to date has examined the construct at the overall composite level, so we know little about the relative impact of the individual dimensions on leadership effectiveness criteria. Such research would contribute greatly not only to theory and research on political skill, but also to team leadership and effectiveness as well.

Tannenbaum and colleagues (2012) recently published a quite interesting conceptual article that makes the argument that "teams are changing." They suggested that there are new and different research needs in the area of teams because the very nature of teams and the environments within which they operate have undergone substantial change. More specifically, they identified three main areas of change that are affecting teams: dynamic composition, technology and distance, and empowerment and delayering. With respect to dynamic composition, they argued that traditional teams were more static in nature, and conditions and members didn't change very much or very often. They argue that today there is much more dynamism and fluidity in team membership, with members coming and going more frequently. Besides the implications of this change for the validity of our proposed model, it also seems to resonate well with Summers and colleagues' (2012) notion of "flux" in team process and its implications for team effectiveness.

The second change, technology and distance, raises the issue of virtual teams and the ability to interact and function well at a physical distance.

Certainly, this has important implications for how team leaders communicate, interact, and influence at a distance. Thus, it might have important implications for the role of leader political skill in not only team processes but also team effectiveness. Interestingly, there has been some, but quite limited theory and research on the role of distance in organizational behavior (e.g., Antonakis & Atwater, 2002; Napier & Ferris, 1993). Some of what we know from this work is that rather than exclusively a linear relationship between distance and effectiveness (i.e., either more is always better or less is always better), it has been argued that distance can reflect a nonlinear relationship with effectiveness outcomes (Napier & Ferris, 1993). Therefore, the objective is to accurately identify the inflection in the curve and the optimum level of distance.

The third change area Tannenbaum and colleagues (2012) identified is empowerment and delayering, and this area strikes directly at the nature of team leadership and who actually makes decisions and is responsible for how the team operates and performs. As teams move to greater self-management and are empowered to a greater extent in work environments, it might suggest that team leaders are simply not needed anymore. However, it seems that a key function of team leaders in these new environments, and working with teams who are empowered to a greater extent, is to monitor and regulate the degree of responsibility that can be allocated to particular team members so as to use such experiences as developmental in nature, and not allow for increasing member responsibility inappropriately in ways that could overwhelm the individual member and hinder team effectiveness. Again, the investigation of traits and characteristics, like political skill, that facilitate these types of behavior required to address the changing nature of teams seems increasingly important. Collectively, it seems like overlaying the Tannenbaum and colleagues (2012) perspective on the testing of our proposed model might provide some useful and enlightening findings.

THE ACQUISITION OF POLITICAL SKILL

As evidenced by the theme of the present volume, soft skills are critical to the modern leadership landscape. Further, as discussed in this chapter, political skill research is among the most critical of these leadership skills.

Thus, it is not surprising that political skill research is flourishing in the organizational sciences. The most dominant themes of this research have been outlined in this chapter, and include research that indicates political skill impacts leader effectiveness, job performance, and job stress in ways that enhance both employee and organizational functioning. Absent from this growing research stream is an understanding of how, and perhaps even if, training impacts employee political skill.

Generally, it is accepted that a lack of political skill or political awareness is a key determinant in the derailing of executive's careers (Van Velsor & Leslie, 1995). More pointedly, limited access to established networks and resource channels has been posited as an explanation for the limited promotions of female managers (Mainiero, 1994). Although, in our unpublished data, we have not observed that demographic minorities possess significantly lower levels of political skill than their white male counterparts, research indicates that political skill is more effective when used with gender-stereotyped soft influence tactics for women (Shaughnessy, Treadway, Breland, Williams, & Brouer, 2011). Taken together, we feel it is important to consider the role of formal mentoring programs in organizations in general, and for minorities in particular, as it relates to the development of political skill. We feel that when coupled with an effectively designed skills training program, these mentoring relationships may provide the ongoing feedback and behavior modeling necessary to solidify transfer of training.

But what does an effective political skill training program encompass? The abundance of research on social skills training exists within the developmental literature. These studies focus primarily on assisting individuals who have accentuated skill deficits and demonstrates how skills training programs can improve the participant's quality of life. For example, social skills training has been shown to be effective in improving job performance of schizophrenic patients (Tsang & Pearson, 2001); life skills training has been shown to have a positive impact on adolescents' future substance abuse patterns (Botvin & Griffin, 2004); and social competence training to reduce aggression in children (Darjan & Lustrea, 2010). Although this research is promising in providing evidence that soft skills training is both achievable and effective, the utility of applying training to individuals at the upper range of social skill, which we would expect to see in managers rather than to those that have pronounced social skill deficiencies, has not yet been established. It is reasonable to assume that the benefits of such training may not be as easily achieved or demonstrably seen.

The most extensive discussion of political skill training was covered in Ferris, Davidson, and Perrewé's (2005) *Political Skill at Work*. In this book, the authors suggested that whereas political skill is, to some degree, an innate ability, it could, on the margin, be developed. Leaning on the dramaturgical underpinnings of the impression management and politics literature, they postulated that drama-based training might be helpful in generating increases in political skill levels. Such training includes participants engaging in role-playing exercises that take them out of their traditional relationships and roles. An advantage of this type of training is the opportunity for participant reflection during the role-playing activity. By asking participants to portray roles that are outside of their work context, scripted behavior is replaced with raw interpersonal behavior. Thus, the nature of the exercise reduces the scripted behavior that may be implicit in responses undertaken if the participants were forced or allowed to remain within the dynamics of their typical work-related role.

Whereas Ferris and colleagues' (2005) framework serves as a useful starting point for discussions of how best to train or develop political skill, impediments still exist in developing and assessing these training programs. One of the challenges of developing political skill training programs is defining the behaviors through which political skill is demonstrated. Typical training programs seek to move behavioral indicators of performance or demonstrations of the behavior. However, political skill theory argues that whereas one can be educated about the influence behaviors that result in enhanced performance for the actor, improved political skill functioning creates a level of behavioral flexibility and contextual matching that makes measurement of such behaviors difficult at best. Thus, the process of training political skill only can be measured through the enhanced outcomes that are resultant of this training (performance, follower trust, etc.).

CONCLUSION

The renewed interest in trait view research today has focused on multistage models that more precisely articulate the intermediate linkages between leader characteristics and leadership effectiveness (e.g., DeRue et al., 2011; Van Iddekinge et al., 2009; Zacarro, 2007). This chapter expanded theory in this area by developing a model suggesting that leader political skill operates through the leader behaviors demonstrated and team processes, which then impact team effectiveness, integrating work on trait views, political perspectives on, and relational approaches to leadership, along with team process dynamics.

Furthermore, this research responds to appeals in these areas collectively to provide a more integrated model of leadership that develops a more informed understanding of the mechanisms underlying, and multiple intermediate linkages between, the relationships between leader characteristics and leadership and team effectiveness (e.g., Avolio, 2007; DeRue et al., 2011). Scholars have argued that organizational environments are changing, and that team-based work structures are increasingly replacing work designed at the individual job, thus necessitating a greater understanding of team processes, outcomes, and leadership of teams. The perspective taken here is to articulate how leader political skill works through intermediate linkages to influence the performance and effectiveness of teams. We hope this conceptualization inspires further research in this important area.

REFERENCES

Aditya, R., & House, R. J. (2002). Interpersonal acumen and leadership across cultures: Pointers from the GLOBE study. In R. E. Riggio, S. E. Murphy, & F. J. Pirozzolo (Eds.), *Multiple intelligences and leadership* (pp. 215–240). Mahwah, NJ: Lawrence Erlbaum.

Ahearn, K. K., Ferris, G. R., Hochwarter, W. A., Douglas, C., & Ammeter, A. P. (2004). Leader political skill and team performance. *Journal of Management, 30*, 309–327.

Amason, A. C., & Schweiger, D. M. (1997). The effects of conflict on strategic decision making effectiveness and performance in organizational teams. *Personnel Psychology, 53*, 625–642.

Ammeter, A. P., Douglas, C., Gardner, W. L., Hochwarter, W. A., & Ferris, G. R. (2002). Toward a political theory of leadership. *Leadership Quarterly, 13*, 751–796.

Antonakis, J., & Atwater, L. (2002). Leader distance: A review and proposed theory. *Leadership Quarterly, 13*, 396–402.

Arrow, H., McGrath, J. E., & Berdahl, J. L. (2000). *Small groups as complex systems.* Thousand Oaks, CA: Sage.

Avolio, B. J. (2007). Promoting more integrative strategies for leadership theory-building. *American Psychologist, 62*(1), 25–33.

Balkundi, P., Kilduff, M., & Harrison, D. A. (2011). Centrality and charisma: Comparing how leader networks and attributions affect team performance. *Journal of Applied Psychology, 96*(6), 1209–1222.

Barker, J. R. (1993). Tightening the iron cage: Concertive control in self-managing teams. *Administrative Science Quarterly, 38*, 408–437.

Bechhard, R. (1983). Optimizing team building efforts. In W. L. French, V. Bell, Jr., & R. A. Zawacki (Eds.), *Organizational development: Theory, research, and practice* (pp. 152–157). Plano, TX: Business.

Bell, S.T., & Marentette, B.J. (2011). Team viability for ongoing and organizational teams. *Organizational Psychology Review, 1,* 275–292.

Borman, W.C., & Motowidlo, S.J. (1993). Expanding the criterion domain to include elements of contextual performance. In N. Schmitt et al. (Eds.), Personnel selection in organizations. San Francisco, CA: Jossey-Bass.

Borman, W.C., & Motowidlo, S.J. (1997). Task performance and contextual performance: the meaning for personnel selection research. *Human Performance, 10,* 99–109.

Botvin, G.J., & Griffin, K.W. (2004). Life skills training: Empirical findings and future directions. *The Journal of Primary Prevention, 25,* 211–232.

Bridges, W. (1994, September 19). The end of the job. *Fortune, 62,* 64, 68, 72, 74.

Brouer, R.L., Douglas, C., Treadway, D.C., & Ferris, G.R. (2012). Leader political skill, relationship quality, and leader effectiveness: A two-study model test and constructive replication. Manuscript under review.

Brown, S.L., & Eisenhardt, K.M. (1995). Product development: Past research, present findings, and future directions. *Academy of Management Review, 20,* 343–378.

Burke, C.S., Stagl, K.C., Klein, C., Goodwin, G.F., Salas, E., & Halpin, S.M. (2006). What type of leadership behaviors are functional in teams? A meta-analysis. *Leadership Quarterly, 17,* 288–307.

Burns, J.M. (1978). *Leadership.* New York: Harper & Row.

Cannon-Bowers, J.A., Tannenbaum, S.I., Salas, E., & Volpe, C.E. (1995). Defining competencies and establishing team training requirements. In R.A. Guzzo, E. Salas, & Associates (Eds.), *Team effectiveness and decision making in organizations* (pp. 333–380). San Francisco, CA: Jossey-Bass.

Carmeli, A., Ben-Hador, B., Waldman, D.A., & Rupp, D.E. (2009). How leaders cultivate social capital and nurture employee vigor: Implications for job performance. *Journal of Applied Psychology, 94,* 1553–1561.

Carnevale, P., Pruitt, D., & Britton, S. (1979). Looking tough: The negotiator under constituent surveillance. *Personality and Social Psychology Bulletin, 5,* 118–121.

Carnevale, P., Pruitt, D., & Seilhemier, S. (1981). Looking and competing: Accountability and visual access in integrative bargaining. *Journal of Personality and Social Psychology, 40,* 111–120.

Cascio, W.F. (1995). Whither industrial and organizational psychology in a changing world of work. *American Psychologist, 50,* 928–939.

Ciampa, D. (2005, January). Almost ready: How leaders move. *Harvard Business Review,* 46–53.

Conway, J.M. (1996). Additional construct validity for the task/contextual performance distinction. *Human Performance, 9,* 309–329.

Daft, R.L., & Lewin, A.Y. (1993). Where are the theories for the "new" organizational forms? An editorial essay. *Organization Science, 4,* i–iv.

Darjan, I., & Lustrea, A. (2010). Promoting social competence development to reduce children's social aggression. *Social and Behavioral Sciences, 2,* 3297–3302.

DeRue, D.S., Nahrgang, J.D., Wellman, N., & Humphrey, S.E. (2011). Trait and behavioral theories of leadership: An integration and meta-analytic test of their relative validity. *Personnel Psychology, 64,* 7–52.

De Dreu, C.K.W., & Weingart, L.R. (2003). Task versus relationship conflict, team performance, and team member satisfaction: A meta-analysis. *Journal of Applied Psychology, 88,* 741–749.

Dionne, S.D., Yammarino, F.J., Atwater, L.E., & Spangler, W.D. (2004). Transformational leadership and team performance. *Journal of Organizational Change Management, 17,* 177–193.

Douglas, C., & Ammeter, A. P. (2004). An examination of leader political skill and its effect on ratings of leader effectiveness. *Leadership Quarterly, 15,* 537–550.

Douglas, C., Ferris, G. R., & Perrewé, P. L. (2005). Leader political skill and authentic leadership. In W. L. Gardner, B. J. Avolio, & F. O. Walumbwa (Eds.), *Authentic leadership theory and practice: Origins, effects, and development* (vol. 3, pp. 139–154 of the *Monographs in Leadership Management* series, J. G. Hunt, senior editor). Oxford: Elsevier Science.

Edmondson, A. (1999). Psychological safety and learning behavior in work teams. *Administrative Science Quarterly, 4,* 350–383.

Ferris, G. R., Davidson, S. L., & Perrewé, P. L. (2005). *Political skill at work: Impact on work effectiveness.* Mountain View, CA: Davies-Black.

Ferris, G. R., Liden, R. C., Munyon, T. P., Summers, J. K., Basik, K., & Buckley, M. R. (2009). Relationships at work: Toward a multidimensional conceptualization of dyadic work relationships. *Journal of Management, 35,* 1379–1403.

Ferris, G. R., Treadway, D. C., Brouer, R. L., & Munyon, T. P. (2012). Political skill in the organizational sciences. In G. R. Ferris & D. C. Treadway (Eds.), *Politics in organizations: Theory and research considerations* (pp. 487–528). New York: Routledge/Taylor and Francis.

Ferris, G. R., Treadway, D. C., Kolodinsky, R. W., Hochwarter, W. A., Kacmar, C. J., Douglas, C., & Frink, D. D. (2005). Development and validation of the political skill inventory. *Journal of Management, 31*(1), 1–28.

Ferris, G. R., Treadway, D. C., Perrewé, P. L., Brouer, R. L., Douglas, C., & Lux, S. P. (2007). Political skill in organizations. *Journal of Management, 33,* 290–320.

Fleishman, E. A., & Zaccaro, S. J. (1992). Toward a taxonomy of team performance functions. In R. W. Swezey & E. Salas (Eds.), *Teams: Their training and performance* (pp. 31–56). Norwood, NJ: Ablex.

Hackman, J. R. (1987). The design of work teams. In J. L. Lorsch (Ed.), *Handbook of organizational behavior* (pp. 315–342). Englewood Cliffs, NJ: Prentice-Hall.

Hackman, J. R. (2002). *Leading teams: Setting the stage for great performances.* Boston, MA: HBS Press.

Hackman, J. R., & Morris, C. G. (1975). Group tasks, group interaction process, and group performance effectiveness: A review and proposed integration. In L. Berkowitz (Ed.), *Advances in experimental social psychology* (pp. 45–99). New York: Academic Press.

Hackman, J. R., & Oldham, G. R. (1980). *Work redesign.* Reading, MA: Addison-Wesley.

Harrison, R. (1983). When power conflicts trigger team spirit. In W. L. French, V. Bell, Jr., & R. A. Zawacki (Eds.), *Organizational development: Theory, research, and practice* (pp. 183–191). Plano, TX: Business.

Hirst, G., & Mann, L. (2004). A model of R&D leadership and team communication: The relationship with project performance. *R&R Management, 34,* 147–160.

Hogan, J., & Hogan, R. (2002). Leadership and sociopolitical intelligence. In R. E. Riggio, S. E. Murphy, & F. J. Pirozzolo (Eds.), *Multiple intelligences and leadership* (pp. 75–88). Mahwah, NJ: Lawrence Erlbaum.

House, R., & Aditya, R. N. (1997). The social scientific study of leadership: Quo vadis? *Journal of Management, 23*(3), 409–473.

Jehn, K. A. (1995). A multimethod examination of the benefits and detriments of intragroup conflict. *Administrative Science Quarterly, 40,* 256–282.

Jehn, K. A. (2008). Diversity, conflict, and team performance: Summary of program of research. *Performance Improvement Quarterly, 12*(1), 6–19.

Jehn, K.A., Greer, L., Levine, S., & Szulanski, G. (2008). The effects of conflict types, dimensions, and emergent states on group outcomes. *Group Decision and Negotiation, 17,* 783–808.

Jentsch, F., Barnett, J., Bowers, C.A., & Salas, E. (1999). Who is flying this plane anyway? What mishaps tell us about crew member role assignment and air crew situational awareness. *Human Factors, 41,* 1–14.

Jones, E.E. (1990). *Interpersonal perception.* New York: W.H. Freeman.

Judge, T.A., Piccolo, R.F., & Ilies, R. (2004). The forgotten ones: The validity of consideration and initiating structure. *Journal of Applied Psychology, 89*(1), 36–51.

Klein, K.J., Ziegert, J.C., Knight, A.P., & Ziao, Y. (2006). Dynamic delegation: Shared, hierarchical, and deindividualized leadership in extreme action teams. *Administrative Science Quarterly, 51,* 590–621.

Kozlowski, S.W.J. (1998). Training and developing adaptive teams: Theory, principles, and research. In J.A. Cannon-Bowers & E. Salas (Eds.), *Decision making under stress: Implications for training and simulation* (pp. 115–153). Washington, DC: APA Books.

Kozlowski, S. W. J., Gully, S. M., McHugh, P. P., Salas, E., & Cannon-Bowers, J.A. (1996). A dynamic theory of leadership and team effectiveness: Developmental and task contingent leader roles. In G.R. Ferris (Ed.), *Research in personnel and human resources management* (vol. 14, pp. 253–305). Greenwich, CT: JAI Press.

Kozlowski, S.W.J., Watola, D.J., Nowakowski, J.M., Kim, B.H., & Botero, I.C. (2009). Developing adaptive teams: A theory of dynamic team leadership. In E. Salas, G.F. Goodwin, & C.S. Burke (Eds.), *Team effectiveness in complex organizations: Cross-disciplinary perspectives and approaches* (pp. 113–156). New York: Psychology Press.

LePine, J.A., Hanson, M.A., Borman, W.C., & Motowidlo, S.J. (2000). Contextual performance and teamwork: Implications for staffing. *Research in Personnel and Human Resource Management, 9,* 53–90.

LePine, J.A., Piccolo, R.F., Jackson, C.L., Mathieu, J.E., & Saul, J.R. (2008). A meta-analysis of teamwork processes: Tests of a multidimensional model and relationships with team effectiveness criteria. *Personnel Psychology, 61,* 273–307.

Mainiero, L.A. (1994). On breaking the glass ceiling: The political seasoning of powerful women executives. *Organizational Dynamics, Spring,* 5–20.

Malone, T.W., & Crowston, K. (1994). The interdisciplinary theory of coordination. *ACM Computing Surveys, 26,* 87–119.

Marks, M.A., Mathieu, J.E., & Zaccaro, S.J. (2001). A temporally based framework and taxonomy of team process. *Academy of Management Review, 26*(3), 964–971.

Mathieu, J., Maynard, M.T., Rapp, T., & Gilson, L. (2008). Team effectiveness 1997–2007: A review of recent advancements and a glimpse into the future. *Journal of Management, 34,* 410–476.

McGrath, J.E., & Altman, I. (1966). *Small group research: A synthesis and critique of the field.* New York: Holt, Rinehart, & Winston.

Mintzberg, H. (1983). *Power in and around organizations.* Englewood Cliffs, NJ: Prentice-Hall.

Mintzberg, H. (1985). The organization as political arena. *Journal of Management Studies, 22,* 133–154.

Mohammed, S., Mathieu, J.E., & Bartlett, A.L. (2002). Technical-administrative task performance, leadership task performance, and contextual performance: Considering the influence of team- and task-related composition variables. *Journal of Organizational Behavior, 23,* 795–814.

Morgeson, F.P., DeRue, D.S., & Karam, E.P. (2010). Leadership in teams: A functional approach to understanding leadership structures and processes. *Journal of Management, 36*(1), 5–39.

Murphy, S.E. (2002). Leader self-regulation: The role of self-efficacy and multiple intelligences. In R.E. Riggio, S.E. Murphy, & F.J. Pirozzolo (Eds.), *Multiple intelligences and leadership* (pp. 163–186). Mahwah, NJ: Lawrence Erlbaum.

Napier, B.J., & Ferris, G.R. (1993). Distance in organizations. *Human Resource Management Review, 3,* 321–357.

Organ, D.W. (1997). Organizational citizenship behavior: It's construct cleanup time. *Human Performance, 10*(2), 85–97.

Pace, R.C. (1990). Personalized and depersonalized conflict in small group discussions. *Small Group Research, 21,* 79–96.

Patten, T.H., Jr. (1981). *Organizational development through teambuilding.* New York: Wiley.

Perrewé, P.L., Zellars, K.L., Ferris, G.R., Rossi, A.M., Kacmar, C.J., & Ralston, D.A. (2004). Neutralizing job stressors: Political skill as an antidote to the dysfunctional consequences of role conflict stressors. *Academy of Management Journal, 47,* 141–152.

Pfeffer, J. (1981). *Power in organizations.* Boston, MA: Pitman.

Pfeffer, J. (1992). *Managing with power.* Boston, MA: Harvard University Press.

Saavedra, R., Earley, P.C., & Van Dyne, L. (1993). Complex interdependencies in task-performing groups. *Journal of Applied Psychology, 78,* 61–72.

Salas, E., Sims, D.E., & Burke, C.S. (2005). 25 years of team effectiveness in organizations: Research themes and emerging needs. In C.L. Cooper & I.T. Robertson (Eds.), *International review of industrial and organizational psychology* (pp. 47–91). New York: Wiley & Sons.

Schminke, M., Wells, D., Peyrefitte, J., & Sebora, T.C. (2002). Leadership and ethics in work groups. *Group and Organizational Management, 27,* 272–293.

Semadar, A., Robins, G., & Ferris, G.R. (2006). Comparing the validity of multiple social effectiveness constructs in the prediction of managerial job performance. *Journal of Organizational Behavior, 27*(4), 443–461.

Shaughnessy, B.A., Treadway, D.C., Breland, J.W., Williams, L.M., & Brouer, R.L. (2011). Influence and promotability: Importance of female political skill. *Journal of Managerial Psychology, 26,* 584–603.

Simons, T.L., & Petersen, R.S. (2000). Task conflict and relationship conflict in top management teams: The pivotal role of intragroup trust. *Journal of Applied Psychology, 85,* 102–111.

Smith, A.D., Plowman, D., Duchon, D., & Quinn, A. (2009). A qualitative study of high-reputation plant managers: Political skill and successful outcomes. *Journal of Operations Management, 27,* 428–443.

Smith, C.A., Organ, D.W., & Near, J.P. (1983). Organizational citizenship behavior: Its nature and antecedents. *Journal of Applied Psychology, 68,* 653–663.

Sternberg, R.J. (2002). Successful intelligence: A new approach to leadership. In R.E. Riggio, S.E. Murphy, & F.J. Pirozzolo (Eds.), *Multiple intelligences and leadership* (pp. 9–28). Mahwah, NJ: Lawrence Erlbaum.

Stogdill, R.M. (1948). Personal factors associated with leadership: a survey of the literature. *Journal of Psychology: Interdisciplinary and Applied, 25,* 35–71.

Stout, R.J., Cannon-Bowers, J.A., Salas, E., & Milanovich, D.M. (1999). Planning, shared mental models, and coordinated performance: An empirical link is established. *Human Factors, 41,* 61–71.

Summers, J.K., Humphrey, S.E., & Ferris, G.R. (2012). Team member change and flux in coordination and performance: Effects of strategic core roles, controllability, and cognitive ability. *Academy of Management Journal, 55*(2), 314–338.

Swezey, R.W., & Salas, E. (Eds.). (1992). *Teams: Their training and performance.* Norwood, NJ: Ablex.

Tannenbaum, S.I., Mathieu, J.E., Salas, E., & Cohen, D. (2012). Teams are changing: Are research and practice evolving fast enough? *Industrial and Organizational Psychology: Perspectives on Science and Practice, 5*(1), 2–24.

Terreberry, S. (1968). The evolution of organizational environments. *Administrative Science Quarterly, 12,* 590–613.

Tekleab, A.G., Quigley, N.R., & Tesluk, P.E. (2009). A longitudinal study of team conflict, conflict management, cohesion, and team effectiveness. *Group and Organization Management, 34,* 170–205.

Treadway, D.C., Adams, G., Hanes, T.J., Perrewé, P.L., Magnusen, M.J., & Ferris, G.R. (in press). The roles of recruiter political skill and performance resource leveraging in NCAA football recruitment effectiveness. *Journal of Management.*

Treadway, D.C., Bentley, J.R., & Williams, L.M. (in press). The skill to lead: The role of political skill in leadership dynamics. In D.V. Day (Ed.), *Oxford handbook of leadership and organizations.* Oxford: Oxford University Press.

Treadway, D.C., Hochwarter, W.A., Ferris, G.R., Kacmar, C.J., Douglas, C., & Ammeter, A.P. (2004). Leader political skill and employee reactions. *Leadership Quarterly, 15,* 493–513.

Tsang, H.W., & Pearson, V. (2001). Work-related social skills training for people with schizophrenia in Hong Kong. *Schizophrenia Bulletin, 27*(1), 139–148.

Tyler, T.R., & Lind, E.A. (1992). A relational model of authority in groups. *Advances in Experimental Social Psychology, 25,* 115–191.

Uhl-Bien, M. (2006). Relational leadership theory: Exploring the social processes of leadership and organizing. *Leadership Quarterly, 17*(6), 654–676.

Van Iddekinge, C.H., Ferris, G.R., & Hefner, T.S. (2009). Test of a multi-stage model of distal and proximal predictors of leader performance. *Personnel Psychology, 62,* 461–493.

Van Scotter, J.R., & Motowidlo, S.J. (1996). Interpersonal facilitation and job dedication as separate facets contextual performance. *Journal of Applied Psychology, 81,* 525–531.

Van Velsor, E., & Leslie, J.B. (1995). Why executives derail: Perspectives across time and cultures. *Academy of Management Executive, 9,* 62–72.

Wang, H., Law, K.S., Hackett, R.D., Wang, D., & Chen, Z.X. (2005). Leader-member exchange as a mediator of the relationship between transformational leadership and followers' performance and organizational citizenship behavior. *Academy of Management Journal, 48,* 420–432.

Webber, S.S., & Donahue, L.M. (2001). Impact of high and less job-related diversity on work group cohesion and performance: A meta-analysis. *Journal of Management, 27,* 141–162.

Yukl, G. (2006). *Leadership in organizations* (6th ed.). Upper Saddle River, NJ: Pearson-Prentice Hall.

Zaccaro, S.J. (2002). Organizational leadership and social intelligence. In R.E. Riggio, S.E. Murphy, & F.J. Pirozzolo (Eds.), *Multiple intelligences and leadership* (pp. 29–54). Mahwah, NJ: Lawrence Erlbaum.

Zaccaro, S.J. (2007). Trait-based perspectives of leadership. *American Psychologist, 62*(1), 6–16.

Zaccaro, S. J., Kemp, C., & Bader, P. (2004). Leader traits and attributes. In J. Antonakis, A. T. Cianciolo, & R. J. Sternberg (Eds.), *The nature of leadership* (pp. 101–124). Thousand Oaks, CA: Sage.

Zaccaro, S. J., & McCoy, M. C. (1988). The effects of task and interpersonal cohesiveness on performance of a disjunctive group task. *Journal of Applied Social Psychology, 18,* 837–851.

Zaccaro, S. J., Rittman, A. L., & Marks, M. A. (2001). Team leadership. *Leadership Quarterly, 12,* 451–483.

9

Social Identity Framing

A Strategy of Social Influence for Social Change

Viviane Seyranian

History is replete with examples of leaders who, together with their groups, have influenced and directed the course of social change in some significant way. Mahatma Gandhi, Martin Luther King Jr., and Nelson Mandela successfully led social movements to eradicate oppression in the form of colonization, racial segregation, and apartheid. Noble Peace Prize laureates Rigoberta Menchú and Aung San Suu Kyi have respectively called world attention to discrimination in Guatemala and political repression in Burma, and continue to champion social change in spite of exile and house arrest. How do leaders and groups accomplish these enormous feats of social change? In what ways do leaders garner follower support for their visions? What strategies of social influence do they use? How do followers react to leaders? Although leadership has received considerable research attention, relatively little is known about *how* leaders and groups can effectively institute social change (Fiol, Harris, & House, 1999; Meindl, 1992; Seyranian & Bligh, 2008). The aim of this chapter is to fill this gap by outlining *Social Identity Framing* (Seyranian, 2011, 2012; Seyranian & Bligh, 2008). Social identity framing draws on social psychological insights from intergroup relations, leadership, and persuasion in proposing a strategy of social influence—an intergroup communication process—that implicates social identity (Tajfel & Turner, 1986; Turner, 1985) to promote social change.

To provide a contextual framework for social identity framing, the chapter begins by briefly defining leadership and detailing the role of intergroup communication in the leadership-followership relationship. Then, it provides an overview of social identity theory (Tajfel & Turner, 1986) and the theory's formal extension into the realm of leadership (Hogg,

2001; Van Knippenberg & Hogg, 2003) and communication (Hogg & Reid, 2006; Reicher & Hopkins, 2001). Building on this literature and research, social identity framing is delineated through an exposition of the specific communication tactics leaders employ to garner support for social change (Seyranian & Bligh, 2008). Follower reactions and facilitating intergroup conditions for social identity framing are then discussed. Finally, ethical aspects of leadership and social influence are considered in relation to social identity framing.

LEADERSHIP AND SOCIAL INFLUENCE

Social identity framing theory defines *leadership* as a formal or informal role within a group that capacitates an individual's ability to effectively shape, influence, motivate, and represent the group (to outgroups) toward the achievement of shared group vision and goals. While the leader's role exists at the apex of social influence capacity within a group, followers are not impotent forces of influence. The social influence capacity of a leader *depends* on followers and how much trust and credibility they attribute to the leader. Therefore, there is a dynamic bidirectional social influence relationship between leaders and followers whereby leaders and followers reciprocally influence each other through a feedback loop. One by-product of the leader-follower influence process is the creation and perpetual negotiation of a dynamic and ever-evolving sense of who the group is, that is, its identity. The ingroup negotiation process of the group's identity is a fundamental aspect of group life—it defines not only who the group is and where it is going, but also how the group is represented in the intergroup circle and its influence potential with other groups. Although the roles of both the leaders and followers in this ingroup negotiation process are important to consider to gain a complete understanding of the influence process, the concern here consists solely of delineating the social influence potential encapsulated by the leadership position and its effect on followers.

How do leaders exert social influence in their groups? Social identity framing holds that a leader's main vehicle of social influence is communication (Fiol, 2002; Hogg & Tindale, 2005), particularly intergroup communication where the "transmission or reception of messages is influenced by the group memberships of the individuals involved" (Harwood, Giles, & Palomares, 2005, p. 3). Intergroup communication does not imply communication between groups, but communication *involving* or pertaining to group membership. Leaders may strategically employ intergroup communication both within groups and between groups as a mechanism of social influence; that is, to confer and alter the meaning of ingroup or outgroup goals, norms, values, and behaviors and create a sense of positive distinctiveness (see Brewer, 1991) from the outgroup. This idea leads to several critical questions that get to the heart of social identity framing: What is the essence of intergroup communication? Is there a pattern in message content that leaders engage in to encourage group change?

The answers to these questions may be partially gleaned from the leadership literature, which supports the idea that leaders, particularly charismatic ones, employ intergroup communication tactics. Studies show that charismatic leaders do in fact use particular communication tactics (e.g., Conger, 1991; Conger & Kanungo, 1998; Emrich, Brower, Feldman, & Garland, 2001; Fiol et al., 1999; Holladay & Coombs, 1993, 1994) involving leader-follower group memberships (e.g., Bligh, Kohles, & Meindl, 2004; Reicher, Haslam, & Hopkins, 2005; Reicher & Hopkins, 1996a; Seyranian & Bligh, 2008; Seyranian, Rast, & Bligh, 2012; Shamir, Arthur, & House, 1994; Shamir, House, & Arthur, 1993). This work implies that *what is being communicated is important to consider in the influence process.* Yet the leadership literature lacks a cohesive theory or prescriptive model of how leaders may formulate transformational and influential rhetoric. Social identity theory may provide substantive direction for the development of such a prescriptive model, especially one addressing leaders' intergroup communication.

SOCIAL IDENTITY THEORY

Social identity framing extends social identity theory to explain leaders' intergroup communication en route to social change. *Social identity* refers to "that part of an individual's self-concept which derives from his knowledge of his group membership of a social group (or groups) together with the emotional significance attached to that membership" (Tajfel, 1974, p. 69). In other words, social identity is an individual's self-definition (i.e., who I am) related to a specific group membership (e.g., female). The content of a particular social identity consists of the norms (e.g., females wear high heels), attitudes (e.g., females are pro-choice), attributes (e.g., females are verbose), and behaviors (e.g., females gossip) that define the group and distinguish it from another group (Hogg & Abrams, 2001; Turner, 1985). Social identity content is also known as ingroup *prototypes* or "the position that best represents the group as a whole" (Turner, 1991, p. 165). The more individuals identify with a group, the more they conform to the prototypes that typify that group (Abrams & Hogg, 2010). They are also more likely to scrutinize the extent to which individual group members represent these prototypes (Hogg & Van Knippenberg, 2003). Invariably, some group members are more likely to embody the group's prototypes than others (Hogg & Abrams, 2001; Turner, 1985). Individuals who diverge markedly from the group prototypes—that is, who are distinctive or counternormative—are more likely to be seen as minorities and deviants (Hogg & Reid, 2006; Seyranian, Atuel, & Crano, 2008). On the other hand, individuals who closely represent the group prototype tend to be the most influential group members and to assume the mantle of leadership (Hogg, 2001; Turner, 1991).

LEADERSHIP AND SOCIAL IDENTITY

The social identity theory of leadership (Hogg, 2001, 2010; Hogg & Van Knippenberg, 2003; Turner, 1991; Van Knippenberg, Van Knippenberg, De Cremer, & Hogg, 2004) develops the idea that leaders influence followers' self-concepts. The key idea is that leadership effectiveness and influence is related to how closely the leader represents the group's prototypes, especially when group members strongly identify with the group. In support of this proposition, research has shown that the individual who most typically personifies the group's prototype is more likely to emerge as a leader (Hogg, Hains, & Mason, 1998), to be viewed as effective (Fielding & Hogg, 1997; Hains, Hogg, & Duck, 1997), to appear powerful and influential (Haslam, Oakes, McGarty, Turner, & Onorato, 1995), and to possess influence over followers (Seyranian, 2011). Hogg (2001) attributes the increased influence potential of prototypical leaders to their social attraction, that is, the fact that they are popular and liked within the group. As a result of their appeal, they are endowed with special qualities such as charisma (Hogg, 2001; Platow, Van Knippenberg, Haslam, Van Knippenberg, & Spears, 2006). This distinguishes the prototypical leader from the rest of the group and fosters perceptions of status and prestige.

Prototypical leaders are also ascribed with more legitimacy (Tyler, 1997), trust (Giessner & Van Knippenberg, 2008), and fairness (De Cremer & Tyler, 2005) than non prototypical leaders. They have a heightened ability to gain follower compliance (Hogg, 2001, 2010) and to advance change within the group (Platow et al., 2006; Van Knippenberg & Van Knippenberg, 2005). In addition, leaders viewed as prototypical influence followers' values, stereotypes, and attitudes in the same direction as their own views (Seyranian, 2011). Their influence potential can be far reaching; they may be endorsed (under some conditions) even if they act in autocratic and tyrannical ways (Rast, Hogg, & Giessner, in press).

Because prototypicality is determined by social context, over time, a leader's prototypicality may wax and wane. To regain prototypicality and assure their leadership position, Hogg (2001) suggests that leaders may use rhetoric and polemics to recentralize themselves as representing the group prototype. This may be accomplished through three tactics: (a) reaffirming the existing ingroup prototype; (b) ostracizing ingroup deviants; and (c) demonizing an appropriate outgroup. Not only can leaders use rhetoric to sustain their leadership position, but they may also employ rhetoric to communicate about norms (Hogg & Giles, 2012; Hogg & Reid, 2006) and mobilize their group members toward social change (Reicher, Hopkins, Levine, & Rath, 2005; Seyranian, 2012).

SOCIAL IDENTITY CONSTRUCTIONS

Reicher and Hopkins's (2001) analysis complements the social identity theory of leadership by advancing the idea that leaders are "entrepreneurs of identity." That is, they bring about transformation by mobilizing people toward action by using rhetoric that shapes perceptions of norms, goals, and values. This is accomplished by reinterpreting group definitions (Tajfel, 1981). Leaders define who is included in the group category (e.g., who is "American") and they describe category content (e.g., the meaning of "American"). In doing so, they concomitantly represent themselves as the prototype of the category, which helps secure their leadership position and affords them the opportunity to direct the power of the group (e.g., human capital, material resources) to actuate in reality their understanding of the group's identity (Reicher, Hopkins et al., 2005; Seyranian, 2012). They also bring this identity to life by performing the constructed identity and embedding it into materials artifacts (Haslam, Reicher, & Platow, 2011).

Research supports the idea that leaders actively construct identity through their communications. Reicher and Hopkins (1996a) used discourse analysis to provide evidence for social identity constructions in Margaret Thatcher and Neil Kinnock's speeches concerning the British miners' strike in 1984–1985. Their analysis revealed that each speaker portrayed the miners' strike as being about "Britishness" and attempted to persuade the audience that their respective policy was congruent with the definition of what it means to be British. This type of social identity construction has also been evidenced in the rhetoric of American presidents (Seyranian & Bligh, 2008; Seyranian et al., 2012), in the political mobilization attempts of British Muslims concerning voting or abstaining from British elections (Hopkins, Reicher, & Kahani-Hopkins, 2003), in anti-abortion speeches (Hopkins & Reicher, 1997; Reicher & Hopkins, 1996b), in the preservation of hunting in the United Kingdom by focusing on the connection of nation and place (Wallwork & Dixon, 2004), in Scottish politicians' speeches (Reicher & Hopkins, 2001), in Patrice Lumumba's speeches during the Congolese decolonization from Belgium (Klein & Licata, 2003), and by a prisoner attempting to mobilize both prisoners and guards against management during the BBC prison study experiment (Reicher, Haslam et al., 2005). This work makes a contribution to the leadership literature by underlining the idea that leaders may use rhetoric to construct social identities en route to mobilizing the group toward collection action. However, the idea of social identity construction does not fully delineate how leaders redefine who the group is and what it stands for. It leaves us wondering about the *process* of social identity construction and what specific rhetorical devices leaders may employ en route to social change. It also only focuses on constructions of ingroup identity without considering that leaders may also construct outgroup identities. Social identity framing theory (Seyranian, 2011, 2012; Seyranian & Bligh, 2008) addresses all of these points.

VISION AS THE BASIS OF SOCIAL IDENTITY FRAMING

The core idea underlying social identity framing is that social change emanates from the leader's vision of a better future for the group. Many scholars acknowledge the important role that visions play in leadership (e.g., Bass, 1985; Baum, Locke, & Kirkpatrick, 1998; Bennis & Nanus, 1985; Conger & Kanungo, 1998; Hartog & Verburg, 1997; Holladay & Coombs, 1993, 1994; Shamir et al., 1993; Yukl, 2012). Visions allude to a "mental image of some desired and possible future state" (Bennis & Nanus, 1985). Holding this mental image in mind helps leaders delineate short-term and long-term goals and strategies to achieve this desire future state, and provides group members with the necessary impetus to expend effort toward actualizing group goals.

Conger and Kanungo (1998) affirm that visions are usually not the figment of the leader's imagination alone, but depend on the communication of future goals that are meaningful to followers in their current environmental context. Building on this idea, it may be argued that for a vision to be compelling to followers, it should aim to put to rights that which is *problematic* for the group within its environmental context. That is, the vision should aim to redress grievances, dissatisfactions, and uncertainties a group faces in some way. For example, a vision may seek to overturn social subjugation endured by the group; it could outline how a corporation may regain its competitive edge; or delineate steps as to how a country can win a war. Visions not only address the group's perceived needs within its environmental context, but they should also paint a better picture of the future. That is, visions should aim to ameliorate the group's state within its context in some novel way, acting as a proverbial light at the end of the tunnel.

Because leaders' visions are inherently embedded within an environmental context and are concerned with how the group is functioning within that context, visions evoke social identity concerns insofar as they provide meaning and direction to group membership and identity. Visions often directly relate to (re)definitions of who the group is, what it stands for, and where it is headed as a group; that is, social identity concerns. As fellow and possibly prototypical group members, leaders are in a position to voice a vision that meets perceived group needs and the demands of the group context. By tuning in to the group's environmental context and interpreting it, a leader's vision both *influences* and *is influenced by* the group's environmental context. For leaders to maximize their influence potential within the group, visions need to address central collective concerns in an innovative way and be combined with articulations of realistic yet challenging goals and strategies.

To bring about the vision, a leader's function includes: (a) articulating a vision that addresses shared group membership issues within its group context; (b) highlighting the compatibility of the vision with social identity and values (Shamir et al., 1993); (c) persuading followers about the viability of the vision with optimism and confidence (Shamir et al., 1993); (d) delineating practical means of vision attainment (Berson, Shamir, Avolio, & Popper, 2001); and (e) helping to organize the group to accomplish it (Conger & Kanungo, 1998). The successful articulation of a vision allows the vision to become mutually shared and negotiated among group members and internalized as a part of the group's social identity. In turn, implicating social identities and securing collective identification motivates collection action toward vision realization (Shamir et al., 1993).

Some visions may be incompatible with the content of a group's social identity, that is, how the group views itself and its prototypes. When a group's preexisting social identity is incongruent with the leader's vision, it could hamper vision acceptance (Shamir et al., 1993) and curb collective action. In this case, it may be particularly important to reframe the social identity of the group so that the proposed vision falls in line with group's view of itself. The leader's vision needs to be innovative and novel in addressing perceived group problems without appearing so radically distinctive that the vision is disregarded and the leader is recast as an outgroup member (Turner, 1991) or a wishful thinker (Berson et al., 2001). In other words, the vision needs to be located within the group's latitude of acceptance (Sherif & Hovland, 1961). Visions must also not signal the possibility of ingroup dissolution or pose a threat to ingroup functioning or maintenance, as this may incite considerable backlash from highly identified group members. Take, for example, promoting a vision of a "fossil-fuel free America" to employees of ExxonMobil Oil. This vision may be met with considerable resistance because it may result in major losses for ExxonMobil (and consequently employees' jobs), unless ExxonMobil revamps its raison d'être. While the status quo is serving group interests and no immediate problems are perceived, there may be little incentive for ExxonMobil to revamp its organizational objectives.

This point is particularly pertinent for more established high-status groups whose group members are less likely to embrace change, as the status quo may be adequate in meeting the needs of the group members. In fact, high-status majority groups may be the least amenable to change, seeking more conventional leaders to sustain the status quo rather than to institute change. High-status majority groups may only be open to a vision of change under conditions of major crisis (Seyranian et al., 2012) or uncertainty (Seyranian, 2012). Under these conditions, a leader may have considerably more leeway to propose social change and reframe social identity.

Altering social identity may be also be vital for groups that possess pre-existing social identities that are negative and represent low status—that is, stigmatized minority groups. Unlike high-status groups, low-status minority groups may not need a precipitating crisis event to trigger uncertainty, thereby creating a perceived need for social change. Minority group members operate within psychological fields of uncertainty where grievances abound as they are mistreated and downtrodden. Social identity theory predicts that minority group members are looking to either exit the group via upward mobility or to engage in collective action to ameliorate the lot for their group (Tajfel, 1981). One obstacle to collective action may be an internalization of negative perceptions of the ingroup (Mummendey, Kessler, Klink, & Mielke, 1999). In these cases, minority leaders who can alter a stigmatized social identity into a relatively more positive representation may be able to successfully mobilize followers to act for the group.

Majority and minority group status in the intergroup circle and the role of social identity framing in these different groups will be considered in greater detail later on. Prior to this, let us address the critical question of how a leader can alter social identity to promote social change. I detail the central features of the social identity framing communication process in the following section.

SOCIAL IDENTITY FRAMING

The very act of communicating a vision entails framing (Hartog & Verburg, 1997). *Framing* refers to employing particular interpretive schemas to organize and make sense of events into a meaningful picture that helps to guide action (Goffman, 1974). Leaders gain support for their visions and ideas by communicating through frames at every opportunity (Fairhurst & Sarr, 1996). Charismatic leaders, in particular, frame their visions of change (Conger & Kanungo, 1998). They may also change, through framing, the group's shared values and identities into a *different social identity* that is compatible with the leader's vision. Specifically, social identity alteration is proposed to occur through communication tactics that form frames that unfreeze, move, and refreeze (Lewin, 1951) followers' sense of group identity. This three-phase change process is termed *social identity framing.*

Social identity framing draws on Lewin's (1951) field theory. Field theory postulates that when a force for change concerning a group standard is applied to a group member, the resulting change is determined by the counterforce of resistance. The more a group member values a group standard, the greater resistance will be evidenced toward change. Resistance to change may be lessened with a process that either reduces the strength of the value of the group standard (i.e., perceiving that the old standard no longer works) or changes what is perceived as having social value (i.e., an alternate group standard has social value). In the latter case, because the group is presumably valued by group members, perceived change in the group standard is accepted (i.e., "group carried change"; Lewin, 1951). Therefore, the first step involved in group change entails reducing resistance by lessening the social value of the group standard or changing what is valued (unfreezing). The necessity of this step depends on the level of resistance group members display. The next step involves detailing the change and moving the group standard to a new level (moving). In the final step, it is necessary to secure the new group standard to ensure permanency of the change (refreezing). In sum, field theory postulates that a successful change entails three steps: unfreezing the present level, changing to a new level, and refreezing group life on that level. In social identity framing, these three steps are termed *social identity unfreezing* (phase 1), *social identity moving* (phase 2), and *social identity freezing* (phase 3). (Note that the terminology associated with each phase here differs from the terminology used by Seyranian and Bligh (2008). It is updated here to emphasize the framing and evolution of social identity.) It is assumed that these three phases occur in a variety of ways including in a temporal sequence or in a direct sequence, depending on the extent and degree of social identity alteration. However, this assumption may be qualified by future research.

During each phase of this change process, social identity framing proposes that leaders may employ a set of specific communication tactics to realign the group's identity in line with a transformative vision. Not only do leaders employ communication as a means of influencing the group (Fiol, 2002; Hogg & Tindale, 2005), but language also reflects and provides one gauge of leaders' visions, agendas, and worldviews. As Krauss and Chiu affirm, how people "define the social situation, their perceptions of what others know, think, and believe, and the claims they make about their own and others' identities will affect the form and content of their acts of speaking" (1998, p. 41). As such, social identity framing assumes that one way that social identity alterations are evident is through leaders' communication content.

Social identity reframing tactics proposed here are based, to a large extent, on previous research on the rhetorical devices used by charismatic leaders (Seyranian & Bligh, 2008). Because leaders viewed as charismatic are visionary and transformative (Yukl, 2012), able to implicate follower's social identities (Shamir et al., 1993; Shamir et al., 1994), and theorized to represent the group's prototype (Hogg, 2001), the specific content of social identity alteration may be gleaned from analyzing the rhetoric of charismatic leaders. That is, charismatic leaders may be especially adept at the skill of social identity framing. In fact, the ability to reframe the group's shared values and identities into an alternate representation that more closely aligns with the leader's vision may promote follower perceptions of charisma and instill perceptions that the leader is prototypical of the newly framed social identity of the group.

A growing body of literature shows that charismatic leaders do indeed use different language than noncharismatic leaders (e.g., Berson et al., 2001; Bligh et al., 2004; Conger, 1991; Emrich et al., 2001; Fiol et al., 1999; Mio, Riggio, Levin, & Reese, 2005; Seyranian & Bligh, 2008). Seyranian and Bligh's (2008) research found that charismatic communication tactics not only differed from those of noncharismatic leaders, but some tactics also differed across different framing phases. In a computerized content analysis of 112 speeches by 17 American presidents in the 20th century, Seyranian and Bligh (2008) compared rhetorical devices employed by charismatic ($n = 5$) versus noncharismatic ($n = 12$) presidents during each framing phase outlined previously. Following the methodology of Fiol and colleagues (1999), at least six speeches were selected for each president: two or more from the beginning of the presidency to represent the *unfreezing* phase, two or more from the middle of the presidency to represent the *moving* phase, and two or more from the end of the presidency to represent the *refreezing* phase. As such, these speeches represented Lewin's (1951) three phases of change over the course of each president's first term in office. Results showed that compared to noncharismatic leaders, charismatic leaders used language to emphasize their similarity to their followers (familiarity, leveling) during the unfreezing phase. That is, they used familiar everyday language (e.g., "this," "that"). They also used leveling or words that ignore individual differences and build a sense of completeness and assurance (e.g., "everyone," "anybody"). Charismatic leaders were also more likely to use negation (e.g., "not," "nobody") during the moving phase than noncharismatic leaders. All leadership types used increasingly active and tangible language as they moved from phase 1 to 2 to 3. Active language represents words that denote aggression (e.g., "conquest," "overcome"), accomplishment (e.g., "succeed," "agenda"), subtracted by words that indicate passivity (e.g., "allow," "submit"), and ambivalence (e.g., "perhaps," "might)." Tangible language is represented by concrete terms (e.g., "airplane," "courthouse") and insistence (e.g., a calculation of repetition of key terms). Across phases, charismatic leaders used language that elicited imagery (e.g., "road," "wave") and stressed inclusion (e.g., "we," "us"), while utilizing less concept-based language (e.g., "measure," "thought") referring to abstract, logical, and reality-oriented terms (for sample quotations of these rhetorical constructs, refer to Seyranian & Bligh, 2008). Overall, the results of this study suggested that leaders employed charismatic communication tactics in a three-phase sequence to encourage social change. Building on previous research and theory (e.g., Bligh et al., 2004; Fiol et al., 1999; Hogg, 2001; Lewin, 1951; Reicher, Hopkins et al., 2005; Shamir et al., 1993), Seyranian and Bligh (2008) outlined social identity framing by theorizing that these communication tactics create three frames that ultimately alter the group's social identity. In the next section, I further develop social identity framing and revise some of the propositions put forth in Seyranian and Bligh (2008).

SOCIAL IDENTITY FRAMING COMMUNICATION TACTICS

During each phase of the social identity alteration process, social identity framing outlines various leadership framing goals and a set of corresponding communication tactics that may help to accomplish these goals. The

TABLE 9.1

Social Identity Framing Leader Goals

Phase 1: Social Identity Unfreezing

    a) Render group membership salient

    b) Increase identification with leader, thereby building trust and credibility

    c) Create perceptions of leader prototypicality

    d) Underline uncertainty and dissatisfaction with status quo

    e) Highlight main group problems that need to be addressed

Phase 2: Social Identity Moving

    a) Present new vision of social change that addresses group problems

    b) Negate components of previous framing of social identity

    c) Relay new social identity content including norms, values, attitudes, and behavior

    d) Positively affirm new framing of social identity content

Phase 3: Social Identity Freezing

    a) Positively affirm new framing of social identity content

    b) Reaffirm vision and tie it to utopian outcomes

    b) Encourage vision commitment and follower action

---

complete model may be found in Table 9.1 and Table 9.2. The communication tactics outlined in Table 9.2 are drawn either from previous research and theory (Seyranian & Bligh, 2008) or from communication constructs outlined in the Diction 5.0 text analysis program.

Social Identity Unfreezing

The purpose of social identity unfreezing is to loosen followers' resistance to social change by seeking to unfreeze the group's current social identity. This may be accomplished by highlighting problems and uncertainty concerning the status quo, linking these problems with the group's current social identity, and cultivating a perceived need for change. For leaders' framing of group problems to be persuasive, leaders must first secure followers' identification and build a sense of legitimacy and credibility. This may be accomplished by promoting the perception that the leader is a prototypical group member (Hogg, 2001). This is important because (as mentioned earlier) prototypical leaders possess substantial influence potential in the group because they are seen as trustworthy group members

TABLE 9.2

Ingroup Social Identity Framing Communication Strategies

Social Identity Unfreezing	Social Identity Moving	Social Identity Freezing
Inclusion	*Inclusion* Vision *Imagery* *Less Conceptual*	*Inclusion* Vision *Imagery* *Less Conceptual*
Past and Present	Present and Future	Present and Future
Tangibility (low)	*Tangibility* (moderate)	*Tangibility* (high)
Action (low)	*Action* (moderate)	*Action* (high)
Similarity to followers	*Negation* Positive Group Identity (optimism)	Positive Group Identity (optimism)
Limited Self-Reference	Identity-Relevant Values	Follower Cooperation
Negative Emotions		Positive Emotions
Crises		Motion
Uncertainty		Utopian outcomes
Liberation		

Note: Communication tactics in italics denote strategies that were empirically supported by Seyranian and Bligh (2008). The remaining tactics (in standard print) are propositions awaiting verification by future research.

who represent the core prototypes of the group (Hogg & Van Knippenberg, 2003). To increase their perceived prototypicality in the group, leaders may use communication that emphasizes *inclusive language, similarity to followers,* and *self-references.*

Past research suggests that inclusive language ("we," "us," "collective," "our," "group") primes representations of the self that are more inclusive (Brewer & Gardner, 1996; Seyranian & Bligh, 2008; Seyranian, 2011), increases a sense of familiarity (Housley, Claypool, Garcia-Marques, & Mackie, 2010), and produces positive reactions (Perdue, Dovidio, Gurtman, & Tyler, 1990; Seyranian, 2011). Building on this research, social identity framing suggests that inclusive language serves as a core communication strategy that evokes social identity and directly connects the leader and follower through the common bond of group membership. This type of language also helps to communicate normative social identity content such as injunctive norms (Seyranian, 2011). As such, it would be worthwhile for leaders to employ inclusive language not only to increase their prototypicality during social identity unfreezing, but also during all phases of social identity alteration. Note that in line with Seyranian and Bligh's (2008) findings, leaders may employ inclusion during each phase to continually raise the salience of group membership, thereby mustering support and commitment.

Another way for leaders to increase their perceived prototypicality is to stress their similarity to followers (Bligh et al., 2004) and to the group. Similarity to followers consists of a combination of familiar language (i.e., most common words in English such as "that," "this") and leveling language (i.e., ignores individual differences, "everyone," "anybody"). Language emphasizing similarity to followers highlights a sense of shared experience and mutual understanding between the leader and follower. It also accentuates joint adherence to group prototypes. Previous research suggests that perceived similarity increases liking (Bersheid & Reis, 1998; Hogg, Cooper-Shaw, & Holzworth, 1993), and augments influence (Oldmeadow, Platow, Foddy, & Anderson, 2003) and agreement with the leader's message (Silvia, 2005).

Self-references may provide the leader with the opportunity to build on leader-follower similarity by stressing how the leader embodies group prototypes and serves as an exemplary group member and role model. For example, the leader could point out personal stories of success to advance the group's agenda, highlight sacrifices made for the group to achieve this success, or showcase anecdotes when the leader clearly demonstrated prototypical attitudes, values, and behaviors. In this way, leaders build an image of themselves as a prototypical leader that followers can trust, like, and seek to emulate to become "good group members."

Being seen as prototypical and rendering group membership salient will ultimately empower the leader with sufficient influence potential to unfreeze followers' attachment to the status quo and current social identity in preparation for social change. To facilitate this process, it may be also fruitful for the leader to use language alluding to *liberation,* which utilizes terms that maximize individual choice and reject social conventions (e.g., "unencumbered," "released").

Lewin suggests that to unfreeze people's attachment to the status quo, it may sometimes be necessary to deliberately bring about an "emotional stir-up" (1951, p. 229). Leaders may stir up followers' emotions by expressing *negative emotion* (e.g., "worry," "anger") about the status quo. Additionally, they may use language that arouses subjective *uncertainty* (Hohman, Hogg, & Bligh, 2010) concerning the *past and the present* while relaying a sense of *urgency* (e.g., "urgent," "immediate," "now") to resolve or change the status quo. This may be accomplished by emphasizing a sense of crisis (political, international, environmental, social, or economic), highlighting problems that the group is facing, underlining the group's minority status in an intergroup circle, or stressing outgroup competitions, threats, or wars. When leaders evoke a sense of subjective uncertainty, followers experience a highly aversive state of negative emotions such as anxiety and fear (Hogg, 2007; Seyranian, 2012). To reduce their anxiety and fear, followers may become more open to the possibility of changing the status quo to restore their emotional equilibrium. As such, uncertainty may promote consideration of a new vision of change that may potentially redefine how group members see themselves (Seyranian, 2012).

Social Identity Moving

During social identity moving, followers are encouraged to support the leader's vision of change for the group. Toward this end, leaders may engage in high levels of *negation* to derogate parts of the social identity that conflict with their vision of change (Fiol et al., 1999; Seyranian & Bligh, 2008; see also Mayo, Schul, & Burnstein, 2004). In this way, they build on the uncertainty aroused during unfreezing and seek to eradicate support for specific policies, rules, norms, or conventions that are incompatible with their vision.

To move followers toward the vision of social change, leaders may engage in rhetoric that highlights social identity (*inclusive* language) and connects social identity to a vision of the future. The leader may reframe social identity by using the following communication tactics: (a) describing a positive vision of the future with pictorial representations; that is with *imagery*, less *conceptual* language, and increasing references to the *present* and *future*; (b) raising the salience of specific group-level *values* (e.g., freedom, equality) that support the vision (Shamir et al., 1993); (c) relating group values to social identity (e.g., "we stand for freedom"); (d) connecting specific attitudes, norms, policies, and behaviors that are relevant to the values with the social identity (e.g., "because we support freedom, we should do enact this policy"); (e) and stressing the *positivity of this altered social identity* with language that stresses *optimism*.

Optimistic language endorses some person, group, concept or event (in this case, the group and social change) and underlines its positive elements (e.g., "delightful," "mighty," "pride").

Note that in line with Seyranian and Bligh's (2008) findings, leaders may make references to their vision with imagery and less conceptual language during each phase. However, leaders likely articulate their vision most thoroughly during social identity moving to help move social identity. It is also suggested that action and tangibility are increasingly used starting from unfreezing to moving to freezing phases. During social identity moving in particular, leaders may connect the vision to specific goals through *action* and *tangible* terms to ensure that the vision seems tenable and to convince followers that there is an action plan to accomplish the vision. As the vision seems more achievable, followers may feel an increased sense of collective efficacy, inspiration, and optimism about the prospect of social change, which will likely encourage followers to exert action on behalf of the collective.

Through social identity moving rhetorical tactics, followers will begin to internalize the leader's values and social identity related to the vision, which will motivate them to act toward the vision for the collective interest. Moreover, presenting social identity and followers' behaviors as connected to the leader's positive vision of the future imbues followers with increased collective self-esteem (Luhtanen & Crocker, 1992) and collective efficacy to accomplish the vision. However, moving followers toward a reframed social identity based on the leader's vision is insufficient to secure long-term change. In the next phase, leaders must ensure the permanency of the changes set during the social identity moving phase.

Social Identity Freezing

Social identity freezing rhetoric entails solidifying the group's altered social identity and channeling motivations set up in social identity moving into follower commitment and action. To solidify social identity, leaders may once again employ *inclusion* to make social identity salient. They may positively affirm the group's newly framed social identity by stressing the positivity of the social identity with *optimistic language* and expressing *positive emotions* related to fulfilling the leader's vision. Leaders must continue to emphasize the importance of vision attainment by stressing the *present and the future* and linking vision attainment with utopian outcomes. In speaking about *utopian outcomes*, leaders may use vivid *imagery* of a positive future and language that alludes to *safety* (e.g., "security," "refuge") and *tenacity* (words connoting confidence and totality e.g., "must").

To mobilize follower commitment and action, additional communication tactics may be necessary. Lewin posited that moving followers' motivations in the desired direction is insufficient for freezing change because motivation often fails to lead to action. Rather, "decision links motivation to action and, at the same time, seems to have a 'freezing' effect which is partly due to the individual's tendency to 'stick to his decision' and partly to the 'commitment to a group'" (1951, p. 233). To instill perceptions of a group decision to act toward the vision, the leader may reframe preexisting personal and group accomplishments and actions in terms of how they fulfill goals related to the vision. This proposition is in line with Seyranian and Bligh's (2008) study showing that all leaders used a high level of *action* (aggression, accomplishment, less passivity, and less ambivalence) and *tangibility* (concreteness, insistence) during refreezing. To harness perceptions of group action toward the vision, leaders may use language that emphasizes *motion* (e.g., "momentum," "bustle," "job") and *follower cooperation*. Follower cooperation consists of words that accentuate behavioral interactions among people for the purpose of creating a group product (e.g., "network," "teamwork," "self-sacrifice").

Communicating follower cooperation and accomplishments during refreezing in particular may serve several important functions. First, referring to *group accomplishments* and *actions* in *tangible* terms that emphasize *motion* and *cooperation* may create a sense of group commitment to the vision as well as increase followers' sense of collective efficacy (Shamir et al., 1993), even if crucial steps toward the vision have yet to be successfully achieved. Perceptions of group commitment and collective efficacy may be translated into follower motivation to expend time and effort toward the vision. Failing to act on this group commitment may cause followers to experience cognitive dissonance because of their need to be consistent and to stick to decisions (Lewin, 1951; Shamir et al., 1993). Second, language referring to the leader's *personal accomplishments* and *actions* in *tangible* terms may demonstrate the leader's personal efficacy and commitment to the vision. In positioning themselves as committed and active group members who are making strides for the collective, leaders continually emphasize that they embody the prototype of the reframed social identity, thereby ensuring their leadership position and influence (Hogg, 2001), even during change. Pointing out personal accomplishments also presents a behavioral exemplar that followers can emulate; for instance, leaders may cite examples of their personal sacrifices for the collective (Shamir et al., 1993) and their selflessness. Third, highlighting personal and group achievements toward the vision may also serve the purpose of burning bridges to the past to refreeze the reframed social identity. When actions are perceived to successfully contribute toward the vision, a return to old conventions and social identity may no longer be seen as viable. As such, the desire for social change may become the convention and the reframed social identity that is in line with the leader's vision permanently replaces the former social identity and status quo.

MESSAGE CONTENT AND DELIVERY

Social identity framing may be facilitated by strong message delivery. As we have seen, the communicative substance of a leader's message is clearly of importance in persuasive contexts (Awamleh & Gardner, 1999; Bligh et al., 2004; Conger, 1991; Den Hartog & Verburg, 1997; Emrich et al., 2001; Fiol et al., 1999; Holladay & Coombs, 1994; Seyranian & Bligh, 2008; Shamir et al., 1994), but cumulative evidence suggests that it can be obscured by delivery and presentation of speech (see Awamleh & Gardner, 1999; Holladay & Coombs, 1993, 1994; Howell & Frost, 1989). For example, body gestures, posture, vocal fluency, eye contact (Holladay & Coombs, 1993), speed of speech (Miller, Maruyama, Beaber, & Valone, 1976), nonverbal communications such as expressiveness (Friedman, Riggio, & Casella, 1988), and prosody of speech (Argyle, Salter, Nicholson, Williams, & Burgess, 1970) comprise important aspects of delivery. Followers' preconceived notions (prototypes) of an effective leader (Lord, Foti, & de Vader, 1984) likely include expectations of strong communication and delivery. Weak delivery may violate this prototype and distract followers from the message, thereby impairing their ability to process its content (Petty & Wegener, 1998). Strong delivery may act as a heuristic cue that fits with leadership prototypes, thereby summoning inferences of source characteristics such as credibility, trust, a sense of authority, and even expertise. Perceptions of these source characteristics are known to enhance persuasive effects of a message during low-effort message processing, and even during close message scrutiny by biasing information processing in the direction advocated by the source (Petty & Wegener, 1998).

FOLLOWERS' REACTIONS

Even the most eloquently phrased and inspirational communication is futile without amenable recipients. Aside from leader communication, how followers react to leader messages is an important consideration in determining whether social identity change ensues and even whether communication was effective. Despite a wealth of literature on attitude change (Forgas, Cooper, & Crano, 2010) and coping with social change (Duncan, 2012), there is little social psychological theory and research that directly delineates how followers react to leaders and how social identity change occurs from recipients' or followers' perspective. As Reicher and colleagues note, "social identity models of leadership need to be developed in order to account for the active manner in which (a) leaders seek to shape identities; and (b) followers respond to these attempts" (2005, p. 549). It is suggested here that the process of social identity content change from a follower's perspective may be likened, at least in part, to that of stereotype change and attitude change. As noted earlier, when a particular social identity is made salient, people's sense of self becomes depersonalized (Hogg, 2001). Individuals think, feel, behave, and define themselves through group attributes, characteristics, and norms instead of individual characteristics (Terry & Hogg, 1996). That is, people act in ingroup stereotypic ways (Hogg & Turner, 1987). When social categories, group attributes, values, attitudes, and norms are represented differently by a trusted, liked, and influential member of the group (prototypical leader), internalization (Kelman, 1958) of these social identity definitions will likely result in changed perceptions of the collective self. What is the process of internalization of the leader's message that leads to social identity alteration? To address this question, let us consider the cognitive and emotional aspects related to the internalization of the leader's message.

Cognitive Processing

A key question necessitating empirical clarification is whether followers must engage in effortful processing of the leader's message for social identity reframing to occur. According to the Elaboration Likelihood Model of Persuasion (ELM, Petty & Cacioppo, 1986), an attitude object (in this case position) is evaluated based on a continuum of how much an individual is motivated and able to assess information. When one is sufficiently motivated and able to process a message (high elaboration likelihood), central route processing is employed to carefully scrutinize all of the available information concerning the attitude object. As such, individuals compare the message content to their previous knowledge and evaluate its merit. This type of intense and effortful message consideration not only induces attitude change, but it could also potentially induce social identity change in the context of intergroup communication. High elaboration may also produce stronger and more coherent social identity content and strong identity-related attitudes with extensive supportive information as a result of message exposure, especially if these messages are repeated (Cacioppo & Petty, 1979). A clear and consensual social identity may partly explain followers' staunch dedication and loyalty to charismatic leaders (Seyranian, 2012). Similar to attitudes, social identities formed as a result of high elaboration may not only be strong, but they are more resistant to change, persistent over time, and predictive of behavior (Martin, Hewstone, & Martin, 2003). As such, they may provide the necessary impetus to prompt followers to bring the leader's vision into fruition.

When one is insufficiently motivated or unable to process a message (low elaboration likelihood), a less effortful cognitive processing strategy called peripheral route processing is employed. Instead of closely scrutinizing message content, peripheral cues such as source credibility or leader prototypicality are used to assess the validity of the overall gist of the message. If attitudes change ensues at all, it is relatively weak. Applied to the case of low elaboration of intergroup communication, if social identity change were to occur, it is unlikely that these changes would be profound or long lasting.

The motivation to engage in high or low elaboration is determined by a confluence of factors, but researchers have reached substantial agreement that the personal relevance or vested interest (Crano, 1995) of a message increases elaboration likelihood (Petty & Wegener, 1998). For individuals who are highly identified with a group, intergroup communication by leaders will be regarded as personally relevant as it concerns their group membership, thereby bolstering the elaboration likelihood of the leader's message and subsequent attitude (and identity) change. In this regard, inclusive such as "we" or "us" should be critical in cueing the personal relevance and prompting close message scrutiny (Brewer & Gardner, 1996).

Evaluation of Leader Source Cues

In the attitude change literature, source cues such as attractiveness, exper-tise, trustworthiness, and power are known to increase influence most markedly during low elaboration likelihood (Crano & Prislin, 2006). Follower observations of leader source cues may also facilitate influence during high elaboration. Perceived leader source cues may operate as cues in the minds of followers that add to the impact of high-effort process-ing by providing additional information about the value of the message (Petty & Wegener, 1998). That is, leader source cues may not actually bolster the elaboration likelihood, but these factors may be viewed as rel-evant information in judging the overall merit of the message. As such, source cues may bias processing in the direction advocated by the leader during high elaboration. Leader source cues include: (a) prototypicality (hence, liked and attractive) and perceptions that the leader adequately represents the group in its current context or within a particular frame of reference (Hogg, 2001); (b) perceptions that the leader is procedurally just, legitimate, competent, and trustworthy (Tyler & De Cremer, 2005; see also Pillai, Scandura, & Williams, 1999); and (c) a strong oratory style. Distant followers (Shamir, 1995) may be particularly influenced by leader source cues because they do not have direct interactions with the leaders and rely on exposure to leader speeches, other group members, and in some cases, media portrayals to form evaluations of the leader.

Emotional Reactions and Identification

Cognitive processing of leader messages by followers only evidences a par-tial picture of the influence process. Leaders and their communications arouse emotional reactions in followers that can facilitate the influence process. Charismatic leadership theories postulate that followers of char-ismatic leaders exhibit profound emotional states: They are inspired by the leader, feel affection toward him or her, are hopeful and optimistic, and are emotionally invested and excited by the leader's vision (Bass & Avolio, 1993; Yukl, 2012). Several scholars hold that charismatic (transfor-mational) leaders actually *influence* their followers toward change through their ability to provoke intense emotions (Bass & Avolio, 1993), immense passion (Reicher & Hopkins, 2003), strong emotional attachments (House, Spangler, & Woyke, 1991), and personal and social identifications (Con-ger, Kanungo, & Menon, 2000; Kark, Shamir, & Chen, 2003; Shamir et al.,

1993). One way to achieve these emotional reactions in followers may be by using emotion-based communication that directly appeals to followers' emotions and boosts self-worth (Emrich et al., 2001; House et al., 1991). Together, this suggests that rote processing of leader messages may not be sufficient to impel followers toward social change. Emotional processes must be implicated in the influence process, especially in relation to social identities (Reicher & Hopkins, 2003).

Social identity includes an emotional component (Tajfel, 1974) and follower identifications with the leader and group are essentially levels of emotional attachment. Group members who are emotionally invested in the group may experience strong emotional reactions if they perceive relative ingroup disadvantage compared with the outgroup. Research shows that identification is important in predicting emotional reactions of fraternal deprivation and group efficacy (Mummendey et al., 1999; Walker & Pettigrew, 1984). *Fraternal deprivation* refers to a group member's feelings of resentment stemming from perceiving ingroup disadvantage compared to an advantaged outgroup (Brewer, 2003; Runciman, 1966). Feelings of fraternal deprivation could translate into perceptions of the illegitimacy of the status quo (Tajfel, 1981) and contribute to the negative emotional reactions necessary to pave the way for change.

Social identity unfreezing entails the stirring up of shared uncertainty and negative emotions associated with the former social identity and conventions such as fear, anxiety, urgency, resentment, dissatisfaction, disappointment, anger, frustration, irritation, and annoyance. This emotional upheaval shapes the motivational base or the "commonly felt deprivation, frustrations and rising aspirations" (Sherif & Sherif, 1969; Simon & Klandermans, 2001), which forms a momentum and shared climate for change. These negative emotional reactions help destabilize followers from accepting the status quo and create the need to alleviate this perceived negativity. In turn, followers may be more susceptible to subsequent influence attempts, such as social identity moving communications. A growing body of research suggests that negative affect spurs high elaboration and analytic processing (Forgas, 2008), which, as mentioned earlier, may be necessary for the internalization of the leader's message and to prompt followers toward action. The leader's positive vision of the future purports improvement from this negative emotional state. The leader's vision (and reframing of social identity) may empower followers with a sense of comfort, certainty, courage, hope, passion, optimism, and confidence to achieve an alternate reality. Therefore, social identity moving and refreezing phases may be characterized by progressively more positive follower emotions associated with the vision and the reframed social identity and progressively lower levels of negative emotions and resistances concerning change (but not necessarily the status quo).

MAJORITY AND MINORITY GROUPS

Leaders who seek change during unfavorable circumstances may meet considerable group resistance that may threaten their leadership position in the group. As a consequence, it is important to note group conditions that are flag posts signaling ripe change contexts that may facilitate social identity alteration. A central group condition that may affect social identity framing is the group's majority or minority status within its wider intergroup context (Moscovici, 1976, 1994; Tajfel, 1981). Recent research has identified four prominent majority and minority group types (Seyranian et al., 2008): the *Moral Majority,* the *Elites,* the *Powerless Populace,* and the *Subjugated.* The *Moral Majority* is powerful and large in number. It is a dominant group in the intergroup circle that is able to wield considerable power and influence over other groups. Examples include European Americans (in the United States), heterosexual people, men, and able-bodied individuals. *Elites* also possess power, but they are relatively small in number. However, because of their power, elites are perceived and treated by other groups as if they were dominant and powerful majorities. Examples include the apartheid rulers of South Africa, the British in 19th-century India, leadership cliques of political regimes, and the highly educated. The *Powerless Populace* is numerically large but holds little power in the intergroup circle. It is an exploited group that is treated much like a minority. That is, it bears the brunt of ill treatment by other groups because its group members possess distinctive or counternormative attributes. Examples include members of the untouchable caste in India or women in some parts of the world. Finally, the *Subjugated* are small in size and hold little power in the intergroup circle. As a result, they are often the target of negative treatment (e.g., expulsion, subjugation, discrimination) by other groups. Examples include homeless people, the lesbian, gay, bisexual, and transgender (LBGT) community in many countries, and people with disabilities.

Majority Groups

Different group conditions and processes may impel majority and minority groups toward social change. In the intergroup setting, majority groups such as the moral majority and the elites set wider societal norms, possess a positive social identity (high status), and aim to sustain the status quo (Moscovici, 1976; Tajfel, 1981) to maintain their advantageous position. Majority groups will likely resist any proposed change that challenges the status quo and appears to compromise their high status (Tajfel, 1981). Not only will other groups that challenge the majority's positive status face avid resistance, but ingroup leaders of majority groups who propose radical changes that may appear to threaten the group's status and power in the intergroup setting will likely be derogated and outcast. As indicated earlier, an outgroup threat to the viability of the ingroup that is perceived as a real or potential crisis, however, may mitigate these reactions. This may be particularly true of the elites group, who may be more prone to perceive threat from other groups because of their relatively small numerical size. When majority groups perceive such a threat, whether from an outgroup or because of environmental circumstances, social change may be deemed necessary as a crisis response to sustain the group and adapt to changing conditions. During crises, leaders who propose a vision that legitimizes and promotes the restoration, maintenance, or enhancement of the group's positive status and power (Tajfel, 1981) and reduces subjective uncertainty (Hogg, 2007) may be met with enthusiasm, even if this vision requires alternate redefinitions of what and who the group is in terms of norms and self-stereotypes. Leaders of majority groups may be attributed with charisma, but this type of leadership may be more akin to crisis-responsive charisma (e.g., Winston Churchill) than visionary charisma (Hunt, Boal, & Dodge, 1999). Visionary charisma may be more likely to occur in minority groups (e.g., Martin Luther King Jr.) because a reversal of subjugation may require a strong and compelling leader who espouses a powerful and radically different vision in such a way as to inspire follower courage to move past the status quo and collectively confront the powerful majority group.

Minority Groups

Minorities are likely to possess negative social identity content (i.e., stigmatized, inferior) both in terms of how the majority views them and how they view themselves (Schmitt, Spears, & Branscombe, 2003). As a result, minority groups such as the powerless populace and the subjugated are not necessarily open to engaging in collective action to ameliorate their subjugated status in the intergroup setting. Social identity theory predicts that some minority group members will attempt to individually exit the group if group boundaries are permeable (Tajfel, 1981). When group boundaries are not permeable, minority group members may also resist social change if they perceive that their relatively powerless and subjugated status is legitimate and stable. Minority groups must first switch from acceptance to rejection of their intergroup status by viewing the current state of affairs as illegitimate and/or unstable (Tajfel, 1981). Therefore, perceptions of the illegitimacy of the intergroup relationship are "socially and psychologically the accepted and acceptable level for social and social change in intergroup behavior . . . it provides a basis for the shared and durable ideologizing of arousal, discontent or frustration" (Tajfel, 1981, p. 267). This implies that minority groups who view the status quo as illegitimate (and/or unstable) are more likely to feel anger and resentment at the status quo and to process and internalize the leader's communications of social change. Extensive social identity unfreezing may not be necessary in this condition, as followers are already open to change and amenable to the impact of social identity framing. Leaders may also provoke rejection of the status quo, perceptions of the illegitimacy of current intergroup relations, and stimulate emotional reactions from followers who are still in acceptance of the status quo by encouraging effortful processing of unfreezing communications.

Whereas leaders of majority groups utilizing social identity framing may reaffirm and increase the groups' already valued positive status and self-stereotypes, minority group leaders employing social identity moving communication may need to alter the negative content of the group's identity (e.g., self-stereotypes) to a positive comparative image (e.g., "Black is beautiful"; see social creativity, Tajfel, 1981) to provide minority group members with the collective esteem and sense of efficacy to achieve the leaders' vision of a better future. A positive redefinition of the group may be especially critical for a numerically small subjugated minority group that does not possess the strength of numbers and therefore requires additional impetus to impel followers toward collective action. This idea is a departure from social identity theory, which posits that positive social identities emerge as a *consequence* of social change and acknowledgment from other groups. When Gandhi called for a nonviolent response to the British, did he and his followers who gave up their lives in nonviolent ways believe that Indians were not worthy of independence? When Rosa Parks refused to give up her seat, was her act of defiance consistent with believing that African Americans were inferior and should sit in the front of the bus? When the French stormed the Bastille, did they believe that the majority of the hungry population did not deserve to "eat cake"? When minorities pick up a picket sign or go on strike, do they think that their group is inferior and unworthy of what they are demanding? This appears highly improbable. These groups not only progressed from acceptance of the status quo to rejection, but they also experienced a redefinition of the group that included a new and more positive social identity that may have resulted from social identity framing-type rhetoric. That is, these minorities ceased to see themselves through the eyes of the majority. As a result, new social identity frames may have provided the springboard for social action, which eventually altered intergroup relations and social reality.

INGROUP AND OUTGROUP SOCIAL IDENTITY FRAMING

The discussion to this point has focused primarily on how leaders may use communication to promote social change within their groups via reframing ingroup social identity. It is also important to note that under some circumstances, leader may also reframe outgroup social identities en route to social change. *Outgroup social identity framing* involves redefining ingroup perceptions of social identity of the outgroup. Outgroup social identity framing may be necessary under circumstances where intergroup relations (i.e., "us" versus "them" frames) are salient. This may be particularly likely: (a) during a crisis or times of uncertainty that involves hostile or threatening relations with the outgroup such as in cases of terrorism, wars, threats, or territorial disputes (Seyranian, 2012); or (b) when a low-status minority group is attempting to gain equal footing with a majority group (Crano & Seyranian, 2009). In these situations, the ingroup leader is expected to interpret the intentions and actions of the outgroup and outline an agenda for how the ingroup should react. To gain support from the group for his or her agenda, the leader may reframe the outgroup's social identity for the ingroup as a means of justifying the leader's proposed actions and vision in handling the crisis, perceived threat, or the outgroup's subjugated status. For example, the leader may outline who the outgroup is, what it stands for, what its intentions are toward the ingroup, and how it plans to interact with the ingroup in the future. While a low-status minority group leader may need to engage in *both* ingroup social identity framing (to redefine the ingroup in more positive terms) and outgroup social identity framing (to redefine the outgroup in terms of equal status), this may not be necessarily the case in all instances. For example, during a major crisis involving an outgroup, it may be critical for the leader to focus on the threat from the outgroup. In this case, the leader may engage in less ingroup social identity framing and more outgroup social identity framing as a part of crisis-response communication. Support for this proposition is provided by a computerized content analysis of 196 speeches by eight 20th-century American presidents who faced international crises (Seyranian et al., 2012). Results indicated that presidents used language that focused more on the outgroup and less on the ingroup following a major international crisis. This study provides evidence of outgroup social identity framing and supports the idea that intergroup relations (i.e., crises provoked by the outgroup) may act as an environmental contingency that affects the content of leadership rhetoric.

ETHICAL LEADERSHIP AND SOCIAL IDENTITY FRAMING

Leadership and social influence scholars face the moral dilemma of uncovering the means to effective leadership and social influence and laying it in front of those who may employ it for self-interested pursuits and gain (Price, 2002; Reicher et al., 2005; Yukl, 2012). Pursuing a strict code of ethical behavior is particularly important for leaders who aim to bring about social change through social identity framing as changing group-level self-definitions can be profound for followers (for a discussion of extremist leadership and social identity framing, see Seyranian, 2012). Leaders tread a fine line between ethical and unethical behavior. For this reason, it is imperative to consider the ethical aspects of leadership and influence after laying out a prescriptive model of leadership communication such as social identity framing.

It is held here that ethical leadership aims to serve the group and nurture and empower followers in an altruistic capacity based on a solid foundation of moral values. This type of leadership does not advocate change for the group for self-interested gain. That is, ethical leaders would not attempt to modify the group's prototype to maintain leadership position and power

(Hogg, 2001). Ethical leaders who engage in social identity framing are able to tune into and articulate a vision that is grounded in altruistic values, that is available to all group members, and that aims to ameliorate the group's situation and create a more positive future in some way. They raise the consciousness of followers and guide them down an avenue toward some collective good. What represents a collective good for one group does not represent a zero-sum game in intergroup relations such that it is necessary to downgrade the dignity, status, or well-being of other groups or organizations to achieve a collective good. In other words, ingroup love does not imply outgroup hate (Brewer, 1999). Ethical leaders are not involved in promoting or imposing direct or indirect harm on other groups or organizations, creating enemies, perpetuating a perpetrator-victim ideology, or demonizing an outgroup. They are not under the impression that they are above the law and they do not employ repressive means to secure legitimate ends (Price, 2002). Price (2002) draws an important distinction between authentic and pseudo-transformational leaders that should be highlighted here: Authentic transformational leaders champion some type of social change that they perceive would be of collective benefit based on a moral foundation of *altruistic values.* More important, their behavior, actions, and policies are congruent with these altruistic values. Hence, the behaviors, actions, and policies of a leader should be consistent with the values they espouse. A disparity between what is advocated and how the leader acts should set off a siren for the presence of a pseudo-transformational leader (Price, 2002). It is not likely that social identity framing by pseudo-transformational leaders will last long because time will expose the fruits of their labor. It is relatively easy to craft transformational rhetoric such as social identity framing. The challenge is in walking the talk. To persevere and navigate through challenging circumstances to make a vision attainable without compromising altruistic values is truly the essence of extraordinary leadership.

CONCLUDING REMARKS

Without loyal followers who are willing to work toward achieving a leader's vision of social change for the ingroup, a leader is like a lock without a key, a business without a customer, a captain without a vessel, or a seed without soil. He or she has stagnant potential that cannot come to fruition. Consequently, the ability of a leader to influence followers and to gain support is crucial. In fact, it can be argued that a key function of leaders is to persuade followers to adopt a vision for the future and to encourage followers to work together as a collective to bring that vision into fruition. Articulating a vision that attracts followers and translates follower support for the vision into real-time efforts can be tricky. This is where social identity framing has the potential to make both a theoretical and practical contribution.

Drawing on social identity theory, social identity framing suggests that a key variable in gaining follower support for a vision of social change is to use a specific type of communication that implicates the group's social identity. Social identity framing outlines a series of leadership goals in a three-phase sequence and corresponding communication tactics that may help to achieve social change. Preliminary research suggests that social identity framing communication tactics provide a promising line of inquiry (e.g., Seyranian, 2011; Seyranian & Bligh, 2008; Seyranian et al., 2012). Ideally, these ideas will stimulate empirical verification in the field of leadership and limitations will be exposed and revised. With continued empirical verification and correction, social identity framing has the potential to contribute to the sparse literature on *how* leaders can strategically harness their influence potential to bring about social change and how followers may respond to these social influence attempts. It also has the potential to inform a wide array of leaders (e.g., corporate, political, community) on how to communicate a vision of change that will succeed in garnering follower support and collective action. Overall, it is my hope that the insights garnered from social identity framing will enable us all to direct the course of social change with increased awareness and a vision of a bright and hopeful future.

REFERENCES

Abrams, D., & Hogg, M.A. (2010). Social identity and self-categorization. In J.F. Dovidio, M. Hewstone, P. Glick, & V.M. Esses (Eds.), *The SAGE handbook of prejudice, stereotyping, and discrimination* (pp. 179–193). London: Sage.

Argyle, M., Salter, V., Nicholson, H., Williams, M., & Burgess, P. (1970). The communication of inferior and superior attitudes by verbal and nonverbal signals. *British Journal of Social and Clinical Psychology, 9,* 222–231.

Awamleh, R., & Gardner, W.L. (1999). Perceptions of leader charisma and effectiveness: The effects of vision content, delivery, and organizational performance. *Leadership Quarterly, 10,* 345–373.

Bass, B.M. (1985). *Leadership and performance beyond expectations.* New York: Free Press.

Bass, B.M., & Avolio, B. (1993). Transformational leadership: A response to critiques. In M.M. Chemers & R. Ayman (Eds.), *Leadership theory and research: Perspectives and directions* (pp. 49–80). New York: Academic Press.

Baum, J.R., Locke, E.A., & Kirkpatrick, S.A. (1998). A longitudinal study of the relation of vision and vision communication to venture growth in entrepreneurial firms. *Journal of Applied Psychology, 83,* 43–54.

Bennis, W.G., & Nanus, B. (1985). *Leadership: The strategies for taking change.* New York: Harper & Row.

Berscheid, E., & Reis, H.T. (1998). Attraction and close relationships. In D. Gilbert, S.T. Fiske, & G. Lindsey (Eds.), *The handbook of social psychology* (4th ed., vol. 2, pp. 193–281). New York: McGraw-Hill.

Berson, Y., Shamir, B., Avolio, B.J., & Popper, M. (2001). The relationship between vision strength, leadership style, and context. *Leadership Quarterly, 12,* 53–73.

Bligh, M.C., Kohles, J.C., & Meindl, J.R. (2004). Charisma under crisis: Presidential leadership, rhetoric, and media responses before and after 9/11. *Leadership Quarterly, 15,* 211–239.

Brewer, M.B. (1991). The social self: On being the same and different at the same time. *Personality and Social Psychology Bulletin, 86,* 307–324.

Brewer, M.B. (1999). The psychology of prejudice: Ingroup love or outgroup hate? *Journal of Social Issues, 5,* 429–444.

Brewer, M.B. (2003). *Intergroup relations* (2nd ed.). Buckingham, UK: Open University Press.

Brewer, M.B., & Gardner, W. (1996). Who is this "we"? Levels of collective identity and self representations. *Journal of Personality and Social Psychology, 71,* 83–93.

Cacioppo, J.T., & Petty, P.E. (1979). Effects of message repetition and position on cognitive responses, recall, and persuasion. *Journal of Personality and Social Psychology, 37,* 97–109.

Conger, J.A. (1991). Inspiring others: The language of leadership. *Academy of Management Executive, 5,* 31–45.

Conger, J.A., & Kanungo, R.N. (1998). *Charismatic leadership in organizations.* Thousand Oaks, CA: Sage.

Conger, J.A., Kanungo, R.N., & Menon, S.T. (2000). Charismatic leadership and follower effects. *Journal of Organizational Behavior, 21,* 741–767.

Crano, W.D. (1995). Attitude strength and vested interest. In R. Petty & J. Krosnick (Eds.), *Attitude strength: Antecedents and consequences* (pp. 131–157). Hillsdale, NJ: Erlbaum.

Crano, W.D., & Prislin, R. (2006). Attitudes and persuasion. *Annual Review of Psychology, 57,* 345–374.

Crano, W.D., & Seyranian, V. (2009). How minorities prevail: The context/comparison-leniency contract model, *Journal of Social Issues, 65,* 335–363.

De Cremer, D., & Tyler, T.R. (2005). Managing group behavior: The interplay between procedural fairness, self, and cooperation. In M.P. Zanna (Ed.), *Advances in experimental social psychology* (vol. 37, pp. 151–218). San Diego, CA: Academic Press.

Den Hartog, D.N., & Verburg, R.M. (1997). Charisma and rhetoric: Communicative techniques of international business leaders. *Leadership Quarterly, 8,* 355–391.

Duncan, L.E. (2012). The psychology of collective action. In K. Deaux & M. Snyder (Eds.), *Oxford handbook of personality and social psychology* (pp. 781–803). New York: Oxford University Press.

Emrich, C.G., Brower, H.H., Feldman, J.M., & Garland, H. (2001). Images in words: Presidential rhetoric, charisma, and greatness. *Administrative Science Quarterly, 46,* 527–557.

Fairhurst, G. T., & Sarr, R. A. (1996). *The art of framing: Managing the language of leadership.* San Francisco, CA: Jossey-Bass.

Fielding, K. S., & Hogg, M. A. (1997). Social identity, self-categorization, and leadership: A field study of small interactive groups. *Group Dynamics: Theory, Research, and Practice, 1,* 39–51.

Fiol, C. M. (2002). Capitalizing on paradox: The role of language in transforming organizational identities. *Organization Science, 13,* 653–666.

Fiol, C. M., Harris, D., & House, R. (1999). Charismatic leadership: Strategies for effecting social change. *Leadership Quarterly, 10,* 449–482.

Forgas, J. (2008). The role of affect in attitudes and attitude change. In W. D. Crano & R. Prislin (Eds.), *Attitudes and attitude change.* New York: Psychology Press.

Forgas, J., Cooper, J., & Crano, W. D. (2010). *The psychology of attitudes and attitude change* (Sydney Symposium in Social Psychology). New York: Psychology Press.

Friedman, H. S., Riggio, R. E., & Casella, D. F. (1988). Non-verbal skill, personal charisma, and initial attraction: The affective communication test. *Journal of Personality and Social Psychology, 39,* 333–351.

Giessner, S. R., & Van Knippenberg, D. (2008). "License to fail": Goal definition, leader prototypicality, and perceptions of leadership effectiveness after leader failure. *Organizational Behavior and Human Decision Processes, 105,* 14–35.

Goffman, E. (1974). *Frame analysis.* Cambridge, MA: Harvard University Press.

Hains, S. C., Hogg, M. A., & Duck, J. M. (1997). Self-categorization and leadership: Effects of group prototypicality and leader stereotypicality. *Personality and Social Psychology Bulletin, 23,* 1087–1099.

Harwood, J., Giles, H., & Palomares, N. A. (2005). Intergroup theory and communication processes. In J. Harwood & H. Giles (Eds.), *Intergroup communication: Multiple perspectives* (pp. 1–17). New York: Peter Lang.

Haslam, S. A., Oakes, P. J., McGarty, C., Turner, J. C., & Onorato, S. (1995). Contextual changes in the prototypicality of extreme and moderate outgroup members. *European Journal of Social Psychology, 25,* 509–530.

Haslam, S. A., Reicher, S. D., & Platow, M. J. (2011). *The new psychology of leadership: Identity, influence, and power.* New York: Psychology Press.

Hogg, M. A. (2001). A social identity theory of leadership. *Personality and Social Psychology Review, 5,* 184–200.

Hogg, M. A. (2007). Uncertainty-identity theory. In M. P. Zanna (Ed.), *Advances in experimental social psychology* (vol. 39). San Diego, CA: Academic Press.

Hogg, M. A. (2010). Leadership and influence. In D. Gilbert, S. Fiske, & G. Lindsey (Eds.), *The handbook of social psychology* (5th ed., vol. 2, pp. 1166–1207). Hoboken, NJ: John Wiley & Sons.

Hogg, M. A., & Abrams, D. (2001). Intergroup relations: An overview. In M. A. Hogg & D. Abrams (Eds.), *Intergroup relations* (pp. 1–14). New York: Psychology Press.

Hogg, M. A., Cooper-Shaw, L., & Holzworth, D. W. (1993). Group prototypicality and depersonalized attraction in small interactive groups. *Personality and Social Psychology Bulletin, 19,* 452–465.

Hogg, M. A., & Giles, H. (2012). Norm talk and identity in intergroup communication. In H. Giles (Ed.), *The handbook of intergroup communication* (pp. 373–387). New York: Routledge.

Hogg, M. A., Hains, S. C., & Mason, I. (1998). Identification and leadership in small groups: Salience, frame of reference, and leader stereotypicality effects on leader evaluations. *Journal of Personality and Social Psychology, 75,* 1248–1263.

Hogg, M.A., & Reid, S.A. (2006). Social identity, self-categorization, and the communication of group norms. *Communication Theory, 16*, 7–30.

Hogg, M.A., & Tindale, R.S. (2005). Social identity, influence, and communication in small groups. In J. Harwood & H. Giles (Eds.), *Intergroup communication: Multiple perspectives* (pp. 141–163). New York: Peter Lang.

Hogg, M.A., & Turner, J.C. (1987). Intergroup behavior, self stereotyping and the salience of social categories. *British Journal of Social Psychology, 26*, 325–340.

Hogg, M.A., & Van Knippenberg, D. (2003). Social identity and leadership processes in groups. In M.P. Zanna (Ed.), *Advances in experimental social psychology* (vol. 35, pp. 1–52). San Diego, CA: Academic Press.

Hohman, Z.P., Hogg, M.A., & Bligh, M.C. (2010). Identity and intergroup leadership: Asymmetrical political and national identification in response to uncertainty. *Self and Identity, 9*, 113–128.

Holladay, S.J., & Coombs, W.T. (1993). Communicating visions: An exploration of the role of delivery in the creation of leader charisma. *Management Communication Quarterly, 6*, 405–427.

Holladay, S.J., & Coombs, W.T. (1994). Speaking of visions and visions being spoken: An exploration of the effects of content and delivery on perceptions of leader charisma. *Management Communication Quarterly, 8*, 165–189.

Hopkins, N., & Reicher, S. (1997). Social movement rhetoric and the social psychology of collective action: A case study of anti-abortion mobilization. *Human Relations, 50*, 261–286.

Hopkins, N., Reicher, S., & Kahani-Hopkins, V. (2003). Citizenship, participation, and identity construction: Political mobilization amongst British Muslims. *Psychologica Belgica, 43–1/2*, 33–54.

House, R.J., Spangler, W.D., & Woyke, J. (1991). Personality and charisma in the U.S. presidency: A psychological theory of leader effectiveness. *Administrative Science Quarterly, 36*, 364–396.

Housley, M.K., Claypool, H.M., Garcia-Marques, T., & Mackie, D.M. (2010). "We" are familiar but "It" is not: Ingroup pronouns trigger feelings of familiarity. *Journal of Experimental Social Psychology, 46*, 114–119.

Howell, J.M., & Frost, P.J. (1989). A laboratory study of charismatic leadership. *Organizational Behavior and Human Decision Processes, 43*, 243–269.

Hunt, J.G., Boal, K.B., & Dodge, G.E. (1999). The effects of visionary and crisis-responsive charisma on followers: An experimental examination of two kinds of charismatic leadership. *Leadership Quarterly, 10*, 423–448.

Kark, R., Shamir, B., & Chen, G. (2003). The two faces of transformational leadership: Empowerment and dependency. *Journal of Applied Psychology, 88*, 246–255.

Kelman, H.C. (1958). Compliance, identification, and internalization: Three processes of attitude change. *Journal of Conflict Resolution, 2*, 51–60.

Klein, O., & Licata, O. (2003). When group representations serve social change: The speeches of Patrice Lumumba during the Congolese decolonization. *British Journal of Social Psychology, 42*, 571–593.

Krauss, R.M., & Chiu, C. (1998). Language and social behavior. In D. Gilbert, S. Fiske, & G. Lindsey (Eds.), *The handbook of social psychology* (vol. 2, pp. 41–88). New York: Oxford Press.

Lewin, K. (1951). *Field theory in social science.* New York: Harper.

Lord, R.G., Foti, R.J., & de Vader, C.L. (1984). A test of leadership categorization theory: Internal structure, informational processing, and leadership perceptions. *Organizational Behavior and Human Performance, 34*, 343–378.

Luhtanen, R., & Crocker, J. (1992). A collective self-esteem scale: Self-evaluation of one's social identity. *Personality and Social Psychology Bulletin, 18,* 302–318.

Martin, E., Hewstone, M., & Martin, P.Y. (2003). Resistance to persuasive messages as a function of majority and minority source status. *Journal of Experimental Social Psychology, 39,* 585–593.

Mayo, R., Schul, Y., & Burnstein, E. (2004). "I am not guilty" vs. "I am innocent": Successful negation may depend on the schema used for its encoding. *Journal of Experimental and Social Psychology, 40,* 433–449.

Meindl, J.R. (1992). Reinventing leadership: A radical, social psychological approach. In K. Murnighan (Ed.), *Social psychology in organizations: Advances in theory and research* (pp. 89–118). Englewood Cliffs, NJ: Prentice-Hall.

Miller, N., Maruyama, G., Beaber, R., & Valone, K. (1976). Speed of speech and persuasion. *Journal of Personality and Social Psychology, 12,* 109–119.

Mio, J.S., Riggio, R.E., Levin, S., & Reese, R. (2005). Presidential leadership and charisma: The effects of metaphor. *Leadership Quarterly, 16,* 287–294.

Moscovici, S. (1976). *Social influence and social change.* London: Academic Press.

Moscovici, S. (1994). Three concepts: Minority, conflict, and behavioral style. In S. Moscovici, A. Mucchi-Faina, & A. Maass (Eds.), *Minority influence* (pp. 233–251). Chicago, IL: Nelson-Hall.

Mummendey, A., Kessler, T., Klink, A., & Mielke, R. (1999). Strategies to cope with negative social identity: Predictions by social identity theory and relative deprivation theory. *Journal of Personality and Social Psychology, 76,* 229–245.

Oldmeadow, J.A., Platow, M.J., Foddy, M., & Anderson, D. (2003). Self-categorization, status and social influence. *Social Psychology Quarterly, 66,* 138–152.

Perdue, C.W., Dovidio, J.F., Gurtman, M.B., & Tyler, R.B. (1990). Us and them: Social categorization and the process of intergroup bias. *Journal of Personality and Social Psychology, 59,* 475–486.

Petty, R., & Cacioppo, J.T. (1986). The elaboration likelihood model of persuasion. In L. Berkowitz (Ed.), *Advances in Experimental Social Psychology* (vol. 19, pp. 123–205). New York: Academic Press.

Petty, R., & Wegener, D.T. (1998). Attitude change: Multiple roles for persuasion variables. In D. Gilbert, S. Fiske, & G. Lindsey (Eds.), *The handbook of social psychology* (vol. 2, pp. 323–390). New York: Oxford Press.

Pillai, R., Scandura, T.A., & Williams, E.A. (1999). Leadership and organizational justice: Similarities and differences across cultures. *Journal of International Business Studies, 30,* 763–779.

Platow, M.J., Van Knippenberg, D., Haslam, S.A., Van Knippenberg, B., & Spears, R. (2006). A special gift we bestow on you for being representative of us: Considering leader charisma from a self-categorization perspective. *British Journal of Social Psychology, 45,* 303–320.

Price, T.L. (2002). The ethics of authentic transformational leadership. *Leadership Quarterly, 14,* 67–81.

Rast, D.E., III, Hogg, M.A., & Giessner, S.R. (in press). Leadership under uncertainty: The appeal of strong leaders and clear identities. *Self & Identity.*

Reicher, S., Haslam, S.A., & Hopkins, N. (2005). Social identity and the dynamics of leadership: Leaders and followers as collaborative agents in the transformation of social reality. *Leadership Quarterly, 16,* 547–568.

Reicher, S.D., & Hopkins, N. (1996a). Self-category constructions in political rhetoric: An analysis of Thatcher's and Kinnock's speeches concerning the British miners' strike (1984–85). *European Journal of Social Psychology, 26,* 353–372.

Reicher, S.D., & Hopkins, N. (1996b). Seeking influence through characterizing self-categories: An analysis of anti-abortionist rhetoric. *British Journal of Social Psychology, 35*, 297–311.

Reicher, S.D., & Hopkins, N. (2001). *Self and nation.* London: Sage.

Reicher, S.D., & Hopkins, N. (2003). On the science of the art of leadership. In D. van Knippenberg & M.A. Hogg (Eds.), *Leadership and power: Identity processes in groups and organizations* (pp. 197–209). London: Sage.

Reicher, S.D., Hopkins, N., Levine, M., & Rath, R. (2005). Entrepreneurs of hate and entrepreneurs of solidarity: Social identity as a basis for mass communication. *International Review of the Red Cross, 87*, 621–637.

Runciman, W.C. (1966). *Relative deprivation and social justice: A study of attitudes to social inequality in twentieth century England.* Berkeley: University of California Press.

Schmitt, M.T., Spears, R., & Branscombe, N.R. (2003). Constructing a minority identity out of shared rejection: The case of international students. *European Journal of Social Psychology, 33*, 1–12.

Seyranian, V. (2011). *Social identity framing: Leader communication for social change* (PhD dissertation). ProQuest Information and Learning database. (AAI3445777)

Seyranian, V. (2012). Constructing Extremism: Uncertainty provocation and reduction by extremist leaders. In M.A. Hogg & D. Blaylock (Eds.), *The psychology of uncertainty and extremism* (pp. 228–245). Malden, MA: Wiley-Blackwell.

Seyranian, V., Atuel, H., & Crano, W.D. (2008). Dimensions of majority and minority groups. *Group Processes and Intergroup Relations, 11*, 21–37.

Seyranian, V., & Bligh, M.C. (2008). Presidential charismatic leadership: Exploring the rhetoric of social change. *Leadership Quarterly, 19*, 54–76.

Seyranian, V., Rast, D., & Bligh, M.C. (2012). *Outgroup social identity framing: International crises and the changing rhetoric of American presidents.* Manuscript in preparation.

Shamir, B. (1995). Social distance and charisma: Theoretical notes and exploratory study. *Leadership Quarterly, 10*, 257–283.

Shamir, B., Arthur, M.B., & House, R.J. (1994). The rhetoric of charismatic leadership: A theoretical extension, a case study, and implications for research. *Leadership Quarterly, 5*, 25–42.

Shamir, B., House, R.J., & Arthur, M.B. (1993). The motivational effects of charismatic leadership: A self-concept based theory. *Organization Science, 4*, 577–594.

Sherif, M., & Hovland, C.I. (1961). *Social judgment: Assimilation and contrast effects in communication and attitude change.* New Haven, CT: Yale University Press.

Sherif, M., & Sherif, M.C.W. (1969). *Social psychology.* New York: Harper and Row.

Silvia, P.J. (2005). Deflecting reactance: The role of similarity in increasing compliance and reducing resistance. *Basic and Applied Social Psychology, 27*, 277–284.

Simon, B., & Klandermans, B. (2001). Politicized collective identity. *American Psychologist, 56*, 319–331.

Tajfel, H. (1974). Social identity and intergroup behavior. *Social Science Information, 13*, 65–93.

Tajfel, H. (1981). *Human groups and social categories.* Cambridge: Cambridge University Press.

Tajfel, H. & Turner, J.C. (1986). The social identity theory of intergroup behavior. In S. Worchel & W.G. Austin (Eds.), *Psychology of Intergroup Relations* (2nd ed., pp. 7–24). Chicago, IL: Nelson-Hall.

Terry, D.J., & Hogg, M.A. (1996). Group norms and the attitude-behavior relationship: A role for group identification. *Personality and Social Psychology Bulletin, 22*, 776–793.

Turner, J.C. (1985). Social categorization and the self-concept: a social cognitive theory of group behavior. *Advances in Group Processes, 2,* 77–121.

Turner, J.C. (1991). *Social influence.* Buckingham, UK: Open University Press.

Tyler, T.R. (1997). The psychology of legitimacy: A relational perspective on voluntary deference to authorities. *Personality and Social Psychology Review, 1,* 323–345.

Tyler, T.R., & De Cremer, D. (2005). Process-based leadership: Fair procedures and reactions to organizational change. *Leadership Quarterly, 16,* 529–545.

Van Knippenberg, B., & Van Knippenberg, D. (2005). Leader self-sacrifice and leadership effectiveness: The moderating role of leader prototypicality. *Journal of Applied Psychology, 90,* 25–37.

Van Knippenberg, D., & Hogg, M.A. (2003). *Leadership and power: Identity processes in groups and organizations.* London: Sage.

Van Knippenberg, D., Van Knippenberg, B., De Cremer, D., & Hogg, M.A. (2004). Leadership, self, and identity: A review and research agenda. *Leadership Quarterly, 15,* 825–856.

Walker, I., & Pettigrew, T.F. (1984). Relative deprivation theory: An overview and conceptual critique. *British Journal of Social Psychology, 23,* 303–310.

Wallwork, J., & Dixon, J.A. (2004). Foxes, green fields, and Britishness: On the rhetorical construction of place and national identity. *British Journal of Social Psychology, 43,* 21–39.

Yukl, G. (2012). *Leadership in organizations* (8th ed.). Upper Saddle River, NJ: Prentice Hall.

Section IV

Implementing and Developing Leader Interpersonal and Influence Skills

10

Leveraging the Science of Memory to Enhance the Efficacy of Leader Communications

Jay A. Conger

The ability to communicate effectively has long been associated with leadership. As Pondy (1978) noted some time ago, one of the most vital roles of a leader is to make activity meaningful. Through their communications, effective leaders provide an understanding to their followers of why they are doing what they are doing. Through leaders' choice of words, imagery, and portrayals of future organizational outcomes, they can deploy language to directly influence their followers' motivations, decisions, and identities. Their communications set standards as to what are appropriate follower attitudes, behaviors, and values. For these reasons, the topic of leadership communications is a critical one for practitioners and scholars alike. In this chapter, I examine one of the least explored dimensions—the use of communications techniques to ensure recall of the leader's messages. These techniques leverage certain dynamics of human memory that encourage retention and recall of information. In an age of information overload, the ability to communicate in memorable ways is an imperative for leaders.

THE RESEARCH ON LEADERSHIP AND COMMUNICATIONS

To date, the scholarly literature has focused primarily on three dimensions of leader communications: the use of language to motivate followers, the actual content of communications related to organizational goals or visions advocated by leaders, and the means that leaders use to articulate their messages.

Early theory on the use of communications to motivate followers focused almost exclusively on the role of language to reduce uncertainty among organizational members. It was assumed that if followers were uncertain about how to accomplish goals, they would become demotivated in the pursuit of those goals. The purpose of much of a leader's communications was therefore to lessen uncertainties and strengthen the motivation to achieve desirable but challenging outcomes. Communications was a vehicle for leaders to help their followers construct mental models of a world that provided clear goals, strong intrinsic meaning to their work, and convincing justifications for actions. In particular, a process called *frame amplification* is considered an essential step (Snow, Rochford, Worden, & Benford, 1986). To motivate, leaders need to frame or highlight values and goals that are deeply appealing to their followers. By framing their overarching organizational visions around such appeals, leaders provide a meaningful endeavor and build identification with the mission. In other words, such frames trigger a strong motivational response from followers.

The second research area focused on how leaders shape the content of their messages—again largely around the topic of their organizational visions (Conger & Kanungo, 1998). Using frames of sharp contrast, the leader could heighten the attractiveness of the future state versus the current state. This is accomplished primarily by constructing images of reality that emphasize the positive features of the future vision while simultaneously highlighting the negative features of the current context. The aim is to depict the status quo as so unattractive or threatening that it creates disenchantment. This negative portrayal of the status quo unfreezes attachments to the current state and in turn lowers resistance to whatever changes the leader is advocating. It also heightens the probability that followers will abandon behaviors, values, and beliefs that are perceived as ineffective to reach the new order (Beer, 1980).

The final topic of research—articulation techniques—explored the means by which leaders can and do project their assertiveness, conviction, expertise, and concern for followers' needs (Conger & Kanungo, 1998). In any communications act, an audience must ascertain whether the speaker is trustworthy and his or her message credible. In the case of leadership, many factors shape followers' perceptions of leaders' credibility—for example, the leaders' prior successes, their demonstrated expertise, and their history of relationships with followers. Nonetheless, leaders can use language to further reinforce the credibility not only of themselves but of the initiatives they are advocating. For example, we know from persuasion theory that audiences place trust in a speaker's message depending on their interpretations of the individual's character (Hauser, 1986) that is discerned in part by the habits the leader reveals through his or her communications. As Miller (1956) has shown, habits are discerned by the causes an individual advocates, the values he or she endorses, and the actions he or she advises. We also know from persuasion theory that audiences evaluate a speaker's credibility by assessing three specific categories of habits that manifest themselves in intellectual, moral, and emotional qualities. The more admirable an audience finds these qualities in a presenter, the more credible that individual will appear (Hauser, 1986). Specifically, intellectual or mental habits are revealed through the appearance of the speaker being well informed, skillful at reasoning, and able to overcome objections by providing compelling evidence. Speakers demonstrate moral habits through the confidence they exhibit in understanding what is right, through their courage of convictions, and through the virtues and values they extol. Finally, an individual's emotional habits are discerned through the speaker's disposition of either goodwill or ill will toward their audience. Goodwill is typically demonstrated through a speaker's concern for the audience's interests. Hauser (1986) highlights the types of expressions that audiences typically interpret as reflective of a speaker's goodwill: For example, speakers are angry at people who insult or harm an audience; they are fearful of impending dangers an audience perceives; they are joyful at the successes of the audience. An audience further tests the sincerity of speakers' feelings in terms of the personal stakes they have in the outcomes of what they propose. An audience is well disposed to speakers when their advice is not necessarily in their best interests, though it is in the audience's.

While the explorations described earlier have extended our knowledge of leadership communications, the field is still in its infancy. One particularly overlooked topic is the leader's deployment of techniques to ensure that followers retain and recall communications long after information is communicated. In ages past when the vast majority of the world's population was illiterate, leaders deployed parables, stories, and analogies to ensure that their goals and values would be remembered and acted on. In this age when we suffer from information overload, leaders face the dilemma that their communications will be crowded out by the flood of information that their followers digest in a day. It is highly probable that followers may find themselves so overwhelmed with daily information that they easily forget important messages around the goals, actions, and values their leader communicates. In addition, we have come to rely on the outsourcing of our memory to storage devices ranging from books and notepads to digital devices like phones and laptops. We no longer feel a need to literally store information in human memory. One recent study entitled "Google Effects on Memory: Cognitive Consequences of Having Information at Our Fingertips" demonstrates that when individuals have access to search engines like Google they remember less information because they know they can rely on a readily available shortcut (Sparrow, Liu, & Wenger 2011). Similarly, our laptops, desktops, and phones are where we today store information. We have been cultivating lazy memories.

Finally, we live in an age when our leaders are no longer nearby physically. They may be thousands of miles away in global corporations. In large organizations, senior leaders may communicate to organizational members infrequently, say once a month or a quarter. The scenarios I have described demand that leaders be capable of instilling their important communications in enduring or memorable ways so as to shape the behaviors and decisions of their followers in their absence.

THE DYNAMICS OF MEMORY: THE INFORMATION RETENTION HURDLE FACING LEADERS

While we think of memory as a single term or phenomenon, the construct refers to multiple human capabilities. Scientific studies into memory reveal no simple classification system for memory (Roediger, Marsh, & Lee 2002). For example, there are important variations in where memories are stored within the physical brain, how long the memory of certain information is retained, why certain types of information and experiences are completely lost to consciousness, and why others can be recalled. Science has yet to even trace an actual memory from start to storage to recall. Given the emphasis of this chapter on information retention and recall, we focus on the aspects of research into memory that appear to be most relevant to leadership communications.

From the standpoint of followers being able to recall information conveyed by leaders, two particular studies stand out in the history of memory science. The first concerns working memory. This is a temporary memory system in which information is maintained and considered consciously for a short period of time by our minds (Baddeley, 2000). Harvard psychologist George Miller discovered in 1956 that our ability to process information in working memory is limited by an important constraint. We can retain only up to seven, eight, or nine items at a time. He called this dynamic the "law of seven plus or minus two." In addition, those seven things are not retained for long. Working memory is interrupted every 10 or so minutes by fatigue or distraction. A portion of what was retained in the previous working memory cycle is then lost. In other words, incoming information replaces existing information in our working memories. Using simple strings of letters or numbers, tests consistently demonstrate the inability of our working memories to retain more than seven or eight letters or numbers that are communicated to us at one time. The implication for leaders communicating information is both simple and profound. Most of the content that is communicated to followers will not be retained longer than a few minutes. Given that leaders are influencing their followers to embrace certain values, behaviors, and decision-making guidelines, this lack of retention in short term memory becomes a critical problem.

From the standpoint of longer-term memory, the research of another memory pioneer, Hermann Ebbinghaus (1885), shed light on how poorly we retain information at all. With the goal to quantify the process of forgetting, he consciously memorized three-letter nonsense syllables like YAT or DAX. At set time intervals, he would test to see how many of these syllables he had forgotten and how many he had retained. He discovered that within the first hour of memorizing his nonsense syllables, more than half were forgotten—even after consciously committing them to memory. By the next day, an additional 10% were gone from memory. Another 14% were lost after a month. He called this process the "curve of forgetting." Time erodes long-term memory.

These studies confirm that the vast majority of information we hear and see is soon lost. But it appears that under very specific conditions certain types of information, however, receive preferential treatment from our memory. We are not only more likely to retain that information but also to recall it. Ebbinghaus documented something called the "serial position effect"—where information is positioned when it is communicated affects its retention and recall. The two main concepts in the serial position effect are "recency" and "primacy." The "recency" effect shows a higher probability of recall of the most recently or last communicated information. It is retained in the short-term memory for a longer duration. The "primacy" effect refers to the greater likelihood that the first set of information that is shared will also be remembered. This information not only comes first, but it may be repeated in the subsequent communications so as to reinforce it as the opening point. In other words, there are more opportunities for listeners to remember and in turn to commit the information to long-term memory. Ebbinghaus also discovered a phenomena he called "savings." This refers to the amount of information retained in the subconscious even after this information can no longer be consciously accessed. Ebbinghaus would commit a list of items to his memory until he had perfect recall of them. He would then allow time to pass so that he forgot or could no longer recall any of its items. He then would relearn the list and compare the new learning curve to the learning curve of his previous memorization of the list. The second list was memorized more rapidly. This difference between the two learning curves is what Ebbinghaus called "savings." Later studies on the repetition of information would support these findings. The more we are exposed to the same information, the probability increases that we will remember it.

These early studies in memory strongly suggest that leaders need to take into very serious consideration how they communicate. They need to possess a keen understanding of the relevant aspect of human memory as they construct and convey their messages. A failure to consider this dimension will mean that the influence of their communications will be minimal given how quickly information is lost in both short-term and long-term memory.

LEVERAGING MEMORY SCIENCE TO ENSURE THAT LEADER COMMUNICATIONS ARE MORE MEMORABLE

Research on memory suggests that how information is presented can significantly impact the probability that individuals—in this case, a leader's followers—will recall it. For example, findings include the importance of the repetition of information, the use of concrete descriptors, picture superiority, the active involvement of listeners with information, and distinctiveness of materials presented. In this section, we explore the implications of these findings for how leaders can more memorably communicate their messages to followers.

Repetition

We know that repeated information is more effectively remembered than items mentioned only once (Crowder, 1976). The spacing of repetitions also matters. Tests of long-term retention show that "spaced repetition" is most effective. In other words, when information is repeated between time and other information intervals, it is retained with greater frequency than when it is repeated in succession. It appears that the greater the lag or spacing, the stronger the retention (Dempster, 1988; Melton, 1970).

While there are several theories as to why repetition and spacing increase the retention of information, one of the more appealing possibilities is the following. There is a value to forgetting, which is to prevent the nervous system from running out of memory storage. The benefit to remembering, however, comes from strengthening memories so that the most frequently encountered tasks are always remembered. In real life, a twice-encountered task is more likely to be encountered again than a once-encountered task. We might call this a *utility model of memory*. The optimum action of our memory is to increase the strength of retrieving the appropriate memory each time a similar task is encountered. The habituation of memories that follows a repetition seems to ensure that the brain maximizes the average probability of reencountering the remembered tasks, that is, it maximizes the usefulness of memories (Wozniak, 1995).

For this reason, repetition enhances retention and recall. So what are the implications for leaders? Leaders can create memorable phrases that they repeat that remind their followers of certain behaviors to follow or how decisions should be made or mindsets that are essential. For example, Horst Schulze, the former president of the Ritz-Carlton, deployed his famous Ritz-Carlton motto, "Ladies and Gentlemen Serving Ladies and Gentlemen," repeatedly to remind Ritz-Carlton associates of their empowered status.

This simple motto would become the core of the Ritz-Carlton culture.

Similarly, simple strategic objectives can be repeated to ensure recall of organizational targets. For example, Carlos Ghosn, CEO of Nissan Motor Company, began his tenure in 1999 with a goal called the Plan 180. As he traveled to Nissan's global operations, he repeated the essentials of the Plan 180 to ensure that every employee would focus on its attainment. In the plan, the "1" represented 1 million cars to be sold within three years. The "8" stood for 8% operating margins, and the "0" was zero debt by 2003. These simple three numbers repeated over and over again formed a highly memorable means to ensure that employees across the globe would remember their most essential goals. In addition, Ghosn was using another memory retention device—Miller's law of seven plus or minus two pieces of information. He has chosen three pieces of information—an extreme minimum to be retained in memory.

Concrete Information

Concrete materials are more readily retained than abstractions. Studies show that the mind grasps and retains concrete concepts far more successfully than abstract ones (Paivio, Yuille, & Rogers, 1969). By concrete, we mean information that can be examined and understood through one's senses. Leaders who can explain abstractions by using a concrete analogy and examples can make their communications not only easier to understand but more memorable.

There is an added dilemma with abstractions. As Heath and Heath (2007) have noted, abstractions make it more difficult to coordinate activities with others, who may interpret the meaning of the abstraction in very different ways. When a leader says that "the organization must operate as *one team*," he or she is expressing the desire to see greater coordination between specific functions around very specific activities. The mandate of "one team" is far too abstract and therefore easily misinterpreted. Instead the leader needs to offer very specific examples of where coordination has had a positive impact and needs to be undertaken. The leader can instead describe in short but rich illustrations what concrete actions individuals have taken and how their coordination paid off. Detailed examples would not only be more memorable but offer far more precise guidance to followers.

One of the most easily retained pieces of concrete material is pictorial illustration (Paivio & Csapo, 1973). In the 1970s, researchers carried out experiments in which they asked their subjects to remember 10,000 visual images. The test involved displaying one image briefly to each participant only once. The test took place over an entire week because of the enormous volume of images shown. The participants then had to choose between two images—the original they had been shown and another image. The researchers discovered that individuals could recall more than 80% of the images that they had seen (Standing, 1973). A more recent study was performed with 2,500 images. Participants were asked to choose between images that differed in a tiny detail. Individuals were still able to remember 90% of the images they had originally been shown (Brady, Konkle, Alvarez, & Oliva, 2008). These studies strongly suggest that leaders need to incorporate far more visual material in their communications whether that be actual images or rich pictorial descriptions of information. For example, a leader could communicate strategic market dynamics through pictorial descriptions of customer segments or competitors. They could also illustrate appropriate behaviors through images of those same behaviors.

Narratives

Information conveyed in story form has a significantly higher probability of retention and recall (Heath & Heath, 2007). Stories contain numerous features that ensure recall. They almost always are composed around concrete information. Well-told stories include rich imagery to convey characters and context. They are designed to stimulate listeners with their twists and turns throughout a plot. Often listeners experience something unexpected. Finally, there is an emotional dimension that has been shown to enhance retention significantly (McGaugh, 2006).

Herb Kelleher, former CEO of Southwest Airways, shared this story with *Fortune* to describe the "secret" to the company's people-oriented culture:

> [T]hey basically wanted to know how we hired, how we trained, and how we motivated. And so we would tell them. And many of them, I think, were looking for some formula, you know, that you could put on the blackboard. The concept is simple, but the execution takes a lot of work and a lot of attention. If you're going to pay personal attention to each of your people, for instance, and every grief and every joy that they suffer in their lives, you really have to have a tremendous network for gathering information.
>
> We want to show them they're important to us as who they are, as people. And by the way, one ramp agent—I have not disclosed this—sent me a note one day which I've never publicized, and I think you'll understand why. He said, "Herb, I finally got it. You're making work fun, and home is work." [Laughter.] I think you'll understand why I did not publicize that widely.
>
> It's not formulaic. The way I describe it is this huge mosaic that you're always adding little pieces to make it work. And it's not a job that you do for

six months and then you just say, "Well, that's behind us." It's something you do every day. (Fortune, "Southwest's Herb Kelleher: Still crazy after all these years," January 14, 2013)

Through this simple story of companies searching for a best practice from Southwest, Kelleher illustrates the day-to-day striving required to build a strong culture—that no one best practice is sufficient. Kelleher could have simply stated that point. Instead he deployed this story. Enhancing the overall story's paradox is the ramp agent's comment that work had become fun and home had become work.

CONCLUSION

In summary, leaders need to pay far greater attention to the retention dimension of their communications. Given the information demands on followers as well as their propensity to rely on the "outsourced memory" offered by digital technologies, it is highly likely that a leader's communications will be drowned out by competing information and by time. Memory research demonstrates time and time again the fragility of memory when it comes to information retention and recall. That said, research also highlights the fact that certain forms have a significantly higher probability of retention. As we have discussed in this chapter, these include information that is repeated, concrete, visual, distinctive, and in narrative forms. Leaders today have an obligation to deploy these vehicles to make their communications more memorable and in turn more influential. Otherwise, their goals, values, and decision rules will be diluted or lost thanks to the forgetfulness of their followers.

REFERENCES

Baddeley, A. D. (2000). The episodic buffer: A new component of working memory? *Trends in Cognitive Science, 4*(11), 417–423.

Beer, M. (1980). *Organizational change and development: A systems view.* Santa Monica, CA: Goodyear.

Brady, T. F., Konkle, T., Alvarez, G. A., & Oliva, A. (2008). Visual long-term memory has a massive storage capacity for object details. *Proceedings of the National Academy of Sciences USA, 38*(105), 14325–14329.

Conger, J.A., & Kanungo, R.N. (1998). *Charismatic leadership in organizations.* Thousand Oaks, CA: Sage.

Crowder, R.G. (1976). *Principles of learning and memory.* Oxford: Lawrence Erlbaum.

Dempster, F.N. (1988). The spacing effect: A case study in the failure to apply the results of psychological research. *American Psychologist, 43*(8), 627–634.

Ebbinghaus, H. (1885). *Über das Gedächtnis. Untersuchungen zur experimentellen Psychologie* [*Memory: A contribution to experimental psychology*]. Trans. H. A. Ruger & C. E. Bussenius. Leipzig, Germany: Duncker & Humblot.

Hauser, G.A. (1986). *Introduction to rhetorical theory.* New York: Harper Books.

Heath, C., & Heath, D. (2007). *Made to stick: Why some ideas survive and others die.* New York: Random House.

McGaugh, J.L. (2006). Make mild moments memorable: Add a little arousal. *Trends in Cognitive Sciences, 10*(8), 345–347.

Melton, A.W. (1970). The situation with respect to the spacing of repetitions and memory. *Journal of Verbal Learning and Verbal Behavior, 9*(5), 596–606.

Miller, G.A. (1956). The magical number seven, plus or minus two: Some limits on our capacity for processing information. *Psychological Review, 63,* 81–97.

Paivio, A., & Csapo, K. (1973). Picture superiority in free recall: Imagery or dual coding? *Cognitive Psychology, 5*(2), 176–206.

Paivio, A., Yuille, J.C., & Rogers, T.B. (1969). Noun imagery and meaningfulness in free and serial recall. *Journal of Experimental Psychology, 79*(3), 509–514.

Pondy, L.R. (1978). Leadership is a language game. In M.W. McCall & M.M. Lombardo (Eds.), *Leadership: Where else can we go?* (pp. 87–99). Durham, NC: Duke University Press.

Roediger, H.L., Marsh, E.J., & Lee, S.C. (2002). Kinds of memory. In H. Pashler & D. Medin (Eds.), *Steven's handbook of experimental psychology* (3rd ed., vol. 2, pp. 1–41). Hoboken, NJ: John Wiley & Sons.

Snow, D.A., Rochford, E.B., Worden, S.K., & Benford, R.D. (1986). Frame alignment processes, micromobilization, and movement participation. *American Sociological Review, 51*(4), 464–481.

Sparrow, B., Liu, J., & Wegner, D.M. (2011). Google effects on memory: Cognitive consequences of having information at our fingertips. *Science, 333,* 476–478.

Standing, L. (1973). Learning 10,000 pictures. *The Quarterly Journal of Experimental Psychology, 25*(2), 207–222.

Wozniak, P.A. (1995). *Economics of learning* (PhD dissertation). University of Economics, Wroclaw, Poland.

11

Developing Capacity for Responsible Leadership

The Interactive Role of Identity and Competence Development

Craig R. Seal, Joanna Royce-Davis, Krystal Miguel, and Adrianna Andrews-Brown

The focus of this chapter is to propose an integrative model of student leadership, called *responsible leadership development,* which builds on the interdisciplinary work of leadership identity development and social emotional competence. The model is in response to increased pressure for college accountability and the need for an understanding of leadership that addresses limitations of current leadership models and programs in higher education. In particular, existing concepts of leadership generally fail to account for the unique developmental context of college students. In addition, programs of leadership often view leadership as a position for a select few students, rather than as a process for all students. In this chapter, we highlight the push for greater accountability in higher education and the limitations of current approaches to leadership development, and present our integrated model of responsible leadership development.

For institutions of higher education, the ability to justify the time and money invested in higher education by demonstrating the value added benefits of a college degree is particularly important, as colleges and universities are under political and economic pressure to validate the efficacy of their programs. In a 2008 address to the Wharton Business School, Chairman of the Joint Chiefs of Staff Navy Admiral Mike Mullen spoke about the importance of accountability in a business school program. Admiral Mullen reminded students that "leadership is about understanding accountability and being held accountable." Similarly, in the 2013 State of the Union Address, President Obama discussed the need for higher education to demonstrate "value," becoming more accountable to parents and taxpayers in terms of cost and impact. President Obama announced that his administration "will release a new 'College Scorecard' that parents and students can use to compare schools based on a simple criteria: where you can get the most bang for your educational buck." This increased pressure of accountability, for colleges in general and business schools in particular, is growing. In response, schools have been positioning the accountability discussion around the question of value-added learning outcomes that are developed during the college experience and that contribute to student success post-graduation, such as career opportunities, community engagement, and quality of life (Bogue & Hall, 2012; Lattimore, D'Amico, & Hancock, 2012). One learning outcome in particular that colleges and universities are promoting is the goal of student leadership development (Bing et al., 2012; Crossan, Mazutis, Seijts, & Gandz, 2011). Scan the mission statements and messages from schools of business across the country, and a consistent theme will emerge: "We are educating the next generation of leaders" (Dean Thomas Robertson, the Wharton School of the University of Pennsylvania).

Although introducing leadership development into curricular and co curricular programs for college students is not new, the underlying theories and methods of understanding and developing leadership are still in question. It is one thing to claim your institution develops leaders, but it is quite another to provide evidence of leadership development and to have an integrative theory to explain the design and impact of leadership development programs.

Despite the multitude of models and practices available, finding a reliable and valid theory and method of leadership development for college students is a fundamental challenge (Dugan, 2006). Contemporary leadership models such as charismatic (Conger & Kanungo, 1998), authentic (Avolio & Gardner, 2005), and transformational (Bass & Riggio, 2006) consider leadership from the perspective of management. Therefore, incorporating recent approaches to leadership development that address (or at least acknowledge) the unique dimensions of college-aged student development need to be considered (Komives et al., 2009; Seal, Naumann, Scott, & Royce-Davis, 2010).

In addition to the issues of a theory grounded in student development, another challenge is in implementation of leadership programs. In our experience, we often find leadership development in higher education to be fragmented across campuses or spread out between academic and student affairs. In academic affairs, leadership is generally provided through theoretical readings (i.e., Aristotle) and programs (i.e., honors) that impact a limited number of students. In student affairs, leadership is generally provided through an office or program that focuses on administrative support and reflective activities for positional student leaders on campus. In both cases, there is little integration between theory and practice to provide intentional learning across settings. In addition, even when attempting to broaden the settings of leadership development, the scope of programs is generally restricted to those students who have already self-selected to participate. Given this limited scope, the lack of integration, and the increasing demand for leadership development, a more responsive, flexible, and integrative model for student leadership development is needed (Komives et al., 2009; Seal et al., 2010).

What is needed is an approach to leadership development that overcomes the current theoretical and programmatic limitations by integrating theory and practice, adjusting for the unique population and environment of college, supporting leadership development for a broader scope of potential students. In short, the practice and conceptualization of leadership development in higher education may need to be reframed as an integrative construct that includes student development theory, considering student identity formation, as well as leadership skill development, considering student competence capacity, to better serve students in their leadership learning (Dugan, 2006; Pascarella & Terenzini, 2005).

RESPONSIBLE LEADERSHIP

In this chapter, we build on the interdisciplinary literature of student success and emotional intelligence to propose a new framework called *responsible leadership development*. *Responsible leadership* is defined as an ethical act of inspiring others toward effecting positive change through the accomplishment of a common goal. The construct emerges from the intersection of leadership identity development and social emotional competence development. *Leadership identity development* (LID) involves engaging with learning opportunities in one's environment over time to build one's awareness and efficacy to engage in leadership (Komives, Owen, Longerbeam, Mainella, & Osteen, 2005). *Social emotional development* (SED) is the desirable, sustainable enhancement of personal capacity to utilize emotional information, behaviors, and traits to facilitate desired social outcomes (Seal et al., 2010). Responsible leadership development is a function of leadership identity development and social emotional development that results in the self-efficacy and personal-interpersonal capacity to be responsive to issues and audiences within multiple contexts. Specifically, responsible leadership development assumes that social emotional competencies moderate the relationship between leadership identity emergence and leadership effectiveness. Scholars and practitioners may use this construct to better understand and improve individual leadership efficacy and capacity of students within a collegiate context.

The proposed model of responsible leadership development posits that social emotional competencies moderate the relationship between leadership identity emergence and leadership effectiveness. There are three aspects that influence this model, drawn from contemporary considerations of leadership, student success, and emotional intelligence. First, as argued by Kouzes and Posner (2003), and supported by the literature on student involvement (Astin, 1993), leadership is for everyone. Second, part of leadership development is the process of self-discovery (Komives, Lucas, & McMahon, 2007) and the influence of self-awareness and self-efficacy (Murphy, 2002). Third, leadership effectiveness may be considered a set of competencies that can be developed (Goleman, Boyatzis, & McKee, 2004).

A key assumption of responsible leadership development is that leadership is for everyone. Kouzes and Posner (2003) and other leadership researchers (Bass & Riggio, 2006; Boyatzis & McKee, 2005; Hunt & Baruch, 2003) have been working to debunk the myth that leadership is only reserved for a few charismatic men and women. Rather, leadership is everyone's business—and opportunity. In a 1996 report exploring the need for integrating social and emotional skills into undergraduate learning by the U.S. Department of Education Office of Educational Research and Improvement, the final recommendation calls for "creating collaborative learning environments and situations where all students have opportunities to contribute" (Cove & Love, 1996). This call for the integration of intellectual, social, and emotional skill training is referred to as "holistic" or "whole student" learning (Bernard, 2006; Cove & Love, 1996), and the need for its implementation in university training has been championed by well-known student success researchers (Astin, 1993; Pascarella & Terenizini, 2005; Tinto, 1993). One aspect of student success is based on the concept of student involvement

(Astin, 1993; Kuh, Kinzie, Buckley, Bridges, & Hayek, 2006). Leadership programs, as an explicit form of involvement, provide the opportunity to focus student success on developmental outcomes that focus on the potential leadership capabilities within each student. This view of leadership considers the broader impact of cultivating skills and capacities of all students, not just to influence potential leader effectiveness, but also to engage all students as part of the college learning community.

In considering the challenge and opportunity of leadership development in college, the student success literature provides an important lens for the concept of responsible leadership. The research on student success considers college as a time of significant self-discovery, including the development of a more expansive and refined sense of self, through the process of student involvement (Evans, Forney, Guido, Patton, & Renn, 2010; Pascarella & Terenzini, 2005). College is a time and context where students find and affirm their purpose and consider how they will influence and impact the world. Part of the self-discovery journey includes developing a more mature relationship with the self, which results in both a defined sense of self and developed self-awareness. Leaders must be aware of their own strengths and limitations, as well as able to acknowledge the corresponding strengths and limitations in others. Komives and colleagues (Komives, Longerbeam, Owen, Mainella, and Osteen, 2006) describe leadership as the outcome of relationships between people that are engaged together to achieve goals that benefit others. In other words, leaders emerge when they see a need and believe they have the capacity to bring people together to respond to the challenge at hand. Leaders must be self-aware enough to recognize their ability to influence the outcome of a situation. Leadership, therefore, is not just strong interpersonal skills, but also about the relationship with self and others to find mutually beneficial goals. Therefore, self-efficacy becomes a core element of leadership, as those who see themselves as strong leaders are more likely to perform better as leaders than those who do not feel as capable (Murphy, 2002).

Finally, after recognizing that leadership is for everyone and that student success provides a starting point, there is the contribution of social and emotional competence development to help frame the concept of responsible leadership. Goleman, Boyatzis, and McKee (2004), as well as other emotional intelligence scholars, have been working to identify core competencies associated with commonly identified indicators of leadership success. Leadership is seen as a set of interpersonal and intrapersonal skills that may be improved through training and development (Boyatzis & Saatcioglu, 2008; Cherniss,

2010; Riggio, Riggio, Salinas, & Cole, 2003). In other words, not only is leadership for everyone that involves a journey of self-discovery, but in addition the underlying skills may be trained through targeted intervention, which is particularly ripe for development during the college experience. Based on the belief that leadership involves a core set of skills that can be learned, responsible leadership provides a common framework and systematic approach to helping students develop their leadership identities and competencies.

Responsible leadership is an interpersonal act of relationship and shared purpose between people that may be intentionally developed. Responsible leadership is related to relational leadership, the leadership framework used in the development of leadership identity development theory, through a shared focus on process, group achievement, and goal orientation (Komives et al., 2007). Responsible leaders emerge when they are self-aware enough to recognize their ability to positively impact the outcome of a situation, their capacity to activate the social and cultural capital in a group, and act to do so in an ethical manner. This process involves learning how to become responsible leaders in both personal and professional contexts. Implicit in the model of responsible leadership is the idea that leadership potential lives within each student, albeit differently based on a unique combination of background, skills, and experiences (Boyatzis & McKee, 2005). It is also believed that by developing leadership identity as well as developing a set of core competencies, one can begin to realize his or her leadership potential. To achieve leadership potential, responsible leadership development proposes that leadership identity development and social emotional development results in the capacity to be responsive to issues and audiences within cultural contexts. The definition captures the essence of the prior definitions while also acknowledging the college environment as learning context. The model is grounded by the student development theories that shape our understanding of how students change, grow, and learn during their college years.

LEADERSHIP IDENTITY DEVELOPMENT

The first part of the model builds on leadership awareness. Leadership identity development (LID) involves engaging with learning opportunities in one's environment over time to build one's awareness and efficacy to engage in leadership (Komives et al., 2005). LID is based on Komives and colleagues' (2005) grounded theory study that resulted in the identification of a six-stage developmental process of how students situate themselves in the construct of leadership over time. This process is based on an in-depth exploration of the life experiences, related to leadership of a select but diverse group of student leaders that led to an understanding of leadership identity development specific to college students. This developmental approach entails moving from simple to more complex dimensions of growth in self-understanding using both the curricular and co curricular environments to serve the goals of integrated learning. LID provides the theoretical underpinning to responsible leadership education.

This approach to leadership emergence begins with first recognizing leadership in others, then seeing oneself as a leader, and finally developing leadership in others. Using a grounded theory approach, Komives and colleagues (2006) detailed a six-stage model of leadership identity development, based on the LID theory. The model includes six distinct stages of development:

1. *Awareness.* In the Awareness stage, the student believes that leadership is practiced by others, but that the student himself or herself is not a leader.
2. *Exploration/Engagement.* In the Exploration/Engagement stage, the student is beginning to move toward active participation in leadership activities.
3. *Leader Identified.* In the Leader Identified stage, the student views leadership as a position, such as club president.
4. *Leader Differentiated.* In the Leader Differentiated stage, the student recognizes that leadership is a process.
5. *Generativity.* In the Generativity stage, the student accepts that leadership is to develop others.
6. *Integration/Synthesis.* In the Integration/Synthesis stage, the student focuses energy toward personal development.

Movement through each stage is impacted by five categories, including: (1) a broadening view of leadership; (2) developing self; (3) group influences; (4) developmental influences; and (5) the changing view of self with others. These categories both challenge and affirm students as they move through the LID stages (Komives et al., 2006). For example, affirmation and encouragement by adults is a key developmental influence that impacts movement from awareness (stage 1) to exploration/engagement (stage 2).

In order to move through each stage, it is helpful to consider each developmental stage as having two distinct phases (Komives et al., 2006). During the first phase, the student is completely immersed in the stage, exhibiting the ways of thinking and behaviors that define the stage. During the second phase, the student is in transition and begins to display characteristics of the subsequent phase. The transition phase is marked by letting go of old ways of thinking and trying new ways of acting.

As students move through the stages of the LID model, experiences or circumstances may cause students to revisit stages they have already progressed through, albeit at a higher or more complex level. In this way, LID is a helix model of development, rather than a simple linear progression. For example, a resident assistant who is currently in the Leader Identified stage of development sees herself as a leader because of the position she holds. However, a resident assistant who is currently in the Generativity stage of development may still feel that his position provides him with an authority to lead, or that others will expect him to be a leader because of his position, while still understanding that all students may practice leadership.

The most complex transition in the model occurs between stage 3 Leader Identified and stage 4 Leader Differentiated. This transition marks a movement toward interdependence and a major shift in thinking from leadership as a position to leadership as a process. It is helpful to remember that prior to college, most students trust external authorities to decide what to believe, and follow the advice of others. In the early stages, external voices drown out the development of a reliable internal voice. This move from reliance on external authority to intrinsic voice is echoed across the self-efficacy, cognitive development, and career development research literature (Bandura, 1977; Baxter-Magolda, Creamer, & Meszaros, 2010; Gecas & Schwalbe, 1983; Kitchener & King, 1990; Perry, 1981). So it comes as no surprise that the development of leadership identity and leadership capacity follows a similar trajectory. Pre college students generally view leadership from a positional perspective that involves a formal dance between a leader and his or her followers. As a result of external influences and a wide variety of high school experiences, it is generally believed that most undergraduate students enter college at a key transition point somewhere between stages three and four (Komives et al., 2005).

Most curricular and co curricular college experiences range throughout the various LID stages (stages 1–5). Often students find themselves in different roles that range from simple solo assignments and group participation experiences, to more sophisticated mentor and program facilitator roles. In providing leadership coaching to students, it is helpful to keep in mind the LID stage that the experience will provide to the individual student and to provide the appropriate balance of challenge and support. For example, a student elected as a student group president may develop her or his leadership identity as a result of encouragement to view the success of the group as collaborative, even though he or she holds a positional leadership role. In this example, the experience may illicit stage 3 thinking and behaviors, even if the student is already transitioning to stage 4 or is at another stage of development.

Many colleges create programs or courses designed to develop student leaders already in a position. The LID model can serve as a framework for creating holistic leadership development programs designed to help all students' progress to more complex stages (Komives et al., 2009). The opportunity embedded in the LID model is that it is not designated for any particular group of students or delivery by individuals holding any particular role at the university. It allows for powerful individualization of learning that is simultaneously inclusive of all learners by virtue of the learning taking place within the context of community and being made accessible to all students. In addition to providing an outline for program progression, the LID model can also serve as a basis for assessment. Formative assessment tools, such as reflective journaling or e-portfolios, may be used to understand what stage students are currently engaged in, as well as to provide evidence of growth through a stage or between stages. Although no formal assessment tool is currently associated with the LID model, evaluating formative assessments through the lens of the LID model will likely yield valuable insight (Komives et al., 2009).

Although LID provides a developmental sequencing of identity development, the model on its own does not provide enough specificity for the development of targeted curriculum designed to facilitate development and build capacity. LID does not detail clear skill blocks that may be used by students at each level or define related opportunities for development. As with most human performance endeavors, recognition of a problem is only part of the solution, and by itself is a necessary but not sufficient condition without the requisite competencies to realize identity potential.

SOCIAL EMOTIONAL DEVELOPMENT

The second part of the model builds on skill development. Social emo-tional development (SED) is the desirable, sustainable enhancement of personal capacity to utilize emotional information, behaviors, and traits to facilitate desired social outcomes (Seal & Andrews-Brown, 2010). SED is the integration of the theory of social intelligence (Gardner, 1983), emo-tional intelligence (Salovey & Mayer, 1990), and competence development (Boyatzis, 2009) applied toward educational practice. This developmental approach entails moving from rudimentary skill levels to more complex mastery of interaction, as students discover and develop greater capacity to impact their environment. SED provides the practical underpinning to the responsible leadership education. This approach to leadership effectiveness includes managing different sets of competencies toward recognizing and responding to emotional and social challenges. In subsequent data analysis, Seal, Beauchamp, Miguel, and Scott (2011) detailed a four-factor model of social emotional development, based on the SED model. The model includes four interdependent clusters of competencies.

1. *Self-Awareness* is the knowledge and understanding of your emo-tions and aptitudes, integrating the ability to identify and ascer-tain the cause of emotions and knowledge of one's own strengths, weaknesses, and preferences.
2. *Consideration of Others* is the regard for the person and situation before thinking and acting. Employing empathy through under-standing and scaled valuation and the ability to recognize and regulate one's own behavior and response to stimuli.
3. *Connection to Others* is the ease and effort in developing rapport and closeness with others. It is the ability to create and develop interpersonal relationships.
4. *Influence Orientation* is the propensity to seek leadership opportu-nities and move others toward change. A regard for position and intention as well as motivation is necessary to inspire action.

The model is additive, with each factor contributing toward an individ-ual's capacity to respond to various social and emotional challenges. The first two factors (awareness and consideration) comprise the knowledge component of the model, impacting understanding of both self and other. The second two factors (connection and influence) comprise the behavior component of the model, impacting actions to relate and motivate others.

The model provides two key pieces of valuable information from a development perspective. First, this approach serves as a diagnostic tool for understanding why a particular course of action (either currently, in the past, or planned for the future) may or may not be effective. Second, this model acts as an intervention for identifying the knowledge or skills that are likely to be most amenable to sustainable change.

Each factor is both independent and interdependent; that is, they may stand alone as a particular strength (or limitation) for the person, but at the same time, each factor may influence the other in terms of providing an increase in effective information and action. For example, being highly considerate of others would help inform how best to improve a relationship or motivate others toward a shared goal.

In addition, the model is designed as compensatory; that is, although the ideal is for students to develop in each factor, the reality is students who are strong in one area may be able to compensate for an area of vulnerability in another factor. For example, someone who is highly self-aware may be able to use the understanding of their own emotions and talents to better position himself or herself into successful situations (playing to his or her strengths).

Although in practice you may be able to intervene at any point in the model, the preferred focus is to start with the two knowledge dimensions of self-awareness (to provide insights into current strengths and limitations) and consideration of others (to better understand others) and then move to the two behavioral dimensions of connection to others (to provide a stronger relationship) and influence orientation (to inform what actions to take to initiate and inspire action). In college, preliminary research indicates students generally follow a predictable pattern of scoring higher on self-awareness, moderately on consideration and connection, and relatively lower on influence orientation (Seal et al., 2011). This highlights the importance of moving beyond simple activities of self-discovery and into more complex activities that help to establish consideration, connection, and ultimately influence orientation.

In terms of skill development, two key mechanisms may be used. The first is to use the elements of the model to reflect on social and emotional events to better understand and improve future capabilities. The second is to use the model as a framework for peer coaching whereby students help one another to consider and overcome potential challenges. Boyatzis and McKee (2005) discuss the potential to develop through a process of intentional change, through a process of realizing the ideal self, the real self, creating a learning agenda, developing opportunities for experimentation and practice, while leveraging interpersonal relationships for support. In terms of effectiveness, recent research indicates a measurable positive correlation between the development of social emotional competencies and increased well-being (Boyatzis & Saatcioglu, 2008), increased capacity to meet life challenges (Kuh, Kinzie, Schuh, Whit, & Associates, 2010), and workplace performance (Seal, Boyatzis, & Bailey, 2006).

Although SED provides a potential roadmap for skill development, it does not necessarily empower students to understand when and where to use those skills. In particular, by itself, it lacks the ethical acumen for when and how to use the skills of leadership effectiveness. However, when partnered with leadership identity development, the two constructs create a more robust, integrative, and useful model for student leadership emergence and effectiveness.

RESPONSIBLE LEADERSHIP DEVELOPMENT

Responsible leadership is defined as an ethical act of inspiring others toward effecting positive change through the accomplishment of a common goal. The process for responsible leadership development is based on three assumptions: (1) that leadership is for everyone, not just positional leaders; (2) that it is a process of self-discovery, culminating in leadership identity development; and (3) that the process includes the development of a set of learned social and emotional competencies. Responsible leadership, therefore, is both a common framework and systematic approach to helping all students develop their leadership identity and competence.

The responsible leadership development process involves learning how to become a responsible leader in both personal and professional contexts by engaging students in a process of self-discovery and skill mastery to maximize leadership potential. That is, responsible leadership development is a function of leadership identity development and social emotional development that results in an increased capacity to be responsive to diverse issues and audiences. Specifically, social emotional development moderates the relationship between leadership identity development and leadership effectiveness.

Leadership identity development involves engaging with learning opportunities in one's environment over time to build one's awareness and efficacy to engage in leadership, the cornerstone of leader emergence that indicates how students situate themselves in the construct of leadership over time. Social emotional development involves building the capacity to navigate social and emotional challenges, the cornerstone of leader effectiveness that indicates the capacity students have for motivating themselves and others to action.

The interaction effect of leadership identity and competency has three hypothesized results. First, the interaction effect multiplies the impact on current leadership emergence and effectiveness, than would normally be explained by one factor (identity or competence) alone. Second, the interaction effect provides a scaffolding approach and framework to foster an increase in leadership capacity development. Third, it is our belief that the process of identity and competence development, together, facilitates authenticity on the relationship between leaders and followers.

In terms of leadership emergence (being recognized by others as a leader) and leader effectiveness (helping others to achieve mutually desired goals), the model provides a more comprehensive lens for better understanding both leadership outcomes. Specifically, "leadership competence" (underlying leadership skills) influences the strength of "leadership identity" (current leadership responsibility) and subsequent emergence and effective leadership performance.

In terms of leader development, the trajectory whereby students may develop leadership effectiveness may be accelerated by intentionally accounting for both identity and competence in designing learning experiences and contexts. Each occurs in tandem, as students move between dependence, independence, and interdependence within the identity model; and development, threshold, competence, and mastery within the competence model.

We believe that the development process also includes an underlying assumption of authenticity on the part of the appropriately matched leader and followers' interactions that manifests in the responsible (positive change through the accomplishment of a common goal) part of the definition. Rather than manifest as some random or egocentric goal attainment, responsible leadership assumes intrapersonal and interpersonal harmony that resonates with both leader and follower, resulting in an ethical act of inspiring others toward goal attainment. Authenticity of self and others is needed to maximize the potential of responsible leadership developmental. It is also assumed that this harmony may be measured as an increase in understanding between leaders and followers as well as a reduction in potential relationship or dysfunctional conflict. The impetus to act with sincerity is the root of authenticity and this authenticity, as it is repeated, establishes an ethical habitus, an integrity schema, that becomes a new framework shaping perceptions and actions, producing a personal ethic defined by integrity of self and others. This integrative foundation of identity and competence, which impacts leader emergence and effectiveness, influences the developmental process, and manifests as a proclivity toward ethical behaviors, is the central focus of the responsible leadership development construct.

PRACTICAL APPLICATIONS

As a learned construct, leadership must be practiced to develop efficacy and mastery. As Baxter-Magolda, Creamer, and Meszaros (2010) suggested, a key condition for making learning relevant and real for students is to situate the learning within their real-world experiences. Fortunately, the college environment provides a safe space and extensive opportunities for experiential learning that could be proactively cultivated. Toward that end, both the LID and SED models lend themselves to the design of curriculum that is focused on active learning and engagement with the immediacy of student's lives. The authors will provide a few examples to help highlight how the responsible leadership development model may be applied.

First, one of the most important factors in assisting individuals to find their internal voices and embark on desired, sustained learning involves the presence of a helping, honest, and supportive relationship (Boyatzis & McKee, 2005). An intervention well suited to demonstrate the potential of a helping relationship to develop responsible leadership is a collaborative peer-coaching training model structured to facilitate identity and competence development. Through the practice of a collaborative helping relationship, the training requires students to engage their emotions, consider different perspectives, evaluate relationship dynamics, and develop leadership skills. The training method is conducted with triads of students, with each student alternating through the various roles of participant, coach, and observer. The participant states a real problem or opportunity he or she would like the coach to help him or her explore. The coach, through a series of structured dialogues helps the participant to assess the situation, challenges underlying assumptions, and supports the participant in understanding and responding to the participant. The observer, through a series of structured feedback sessions, helps the coach to develop greater self-discovery and skill development in helping others. Although the premise is on assisting the participant, in truth, the training is designed to develop the capacity of the coach. As the process unfolds, each student becomes invested in the positive development of each member of the triad. The peer relationship helps to add synergy to the process that enhances the feelings of resonance within the interactions, and expands the self-efficacy and skill capacity of each member as they shift perspectives and roles. The coaching intervention allows each participant to engage each problem from not only the various positions in the coaching process but from each component of the competency development model (i.e., awareness, consideration, connection, and influence). The participants are provided the opportunity to participate in joint problem solving as they assess, challenge, and support their peers. As part of the development process, the peer-coaching method allows coach, participant, and observer to foster their own development by supporting the success of others through empathic consideration (Baxter-Magolda, 2009).

In a second example, the authors associated with a medium-sized comprehensive private university designed a common syllabus service-learning course (that integrated staff from student life and faculty from academic affairs). The course was offered as both a section in the credit bearing first year seminar core that was required of all students and as a non-credit-bearing workshop series facilitated by peer advisors and staff for first year advising students. This course, and its equivalent modules, intentionally focused on challenging students to describe and examine aspects of their identity, including leadership identity, and to begin to define purpose and then integrate identity and purpose through feedback and coaching from peers and professionals. Students practiced this integration while also receiving conceptual instruction and operational coaching in SED and LID while together working on community-based projects. Students assessed their movement in the development of leadership identity and competence through assessments, reflection activities, and feedback from mentors and peers. This focus on identity and competency development through the class had the potential to influence other areas of student success by creating a safe space and shared language for students to understand and impact their learning, campus community, and surrounding environment. The hope was to provide an avenue for broader involvement, which is critical to student persistence and success (Astin, 1993; Kuh et al., 2006).

In a third example, during orientation new students are introduced to and asked to practice guidelines for intercultural interaction and relationship that incorporate the development of SED competencies. One guideline, *acknowledging both intent and impact,* asks students to become conscious of intention when engaging in an interaction (self-awareness) and also the [often unintentional] impact that another person might experience based on that person's history and background (consideration of others). The act of acknowledgment becomes both an act of self-management in avoiding the excuse supplied by intent and an act of relationship in honoring the perspective and experience of another. This simple guideline or agreement brings all of the SED competencies together as named skills necessary for effective and meaningful relationship and, by extension, responsible leadership influence.

Finally, SED and LID may serve as a lens for responding to student conduct issues in the first year. By asking students key questions about what they hoped to achieve with particular behaviors, what impression they hoped to make, or what impact they hoped to have, students are more often able to engage in educational conversations that set the stage for increased self and social awareness and improved effectiveness in relationships and positive influence with peers. This approach has borne out with fewer students repeating the same infractions and more students able to articulate the motivation behind and the community impact of their decisions. As indicated by each example, having a more integrative, student-centered model of leadership provides opportunities and avenues for fostering student success and subsequent learning outcomes.

DISCUSSION

The theoretical framework presented here provides a systematic approach to accelerate college students' development of efficacy and capacities necessary for responsible leadership. The responsible leadership model contributes to the existing theoretical literature by connecting evolving thinking about leadership development with emerging understandings of the role of social and emotional competence in leadership effectiveness and student success. By fostering student self-awareness and social emotional skills, responsible leadership provides an opportunity to better equip students to understand and respond to problems and challenges from real-world contexts in an authentic schema that features positive, mutual goal attainment. The next step is to confirm the potential of the model, translate theory into practice, and design best practice experiences that integrate leadership identity development and social emotional development for students.

Ultimately, leadership development is about creating safe spaces where intentional focus on development of leadership identity and coaching for social emotional development may take place. These spaces are already found in many existing learning contexts that create opportunities for exposure to leadership interaction and challenge by virtue of the activities already in place. Group projects and other collective learning experiences, such as residential learning communities, are ripe for adding the purposeful overlay of reflection on leadership identity and the use of social emotional competencies. Future research should study the relationship between leadership identity and social emotional development, particularly the kinds of leadership competencies essential to development of responsible leadership.

As indicated at the beginning of the chapter, there is a push, through accreditation, for institutions of higher learning to demonstrate value-added benefits of a college education. For better or worse, universities will need to consider what is the range of knowledge, skills, and abilities that students develop while in school, in other words, what students, parents, and society should expect from their investment. In addition, institutions will need to consider what types of assessments are used to measure those knowledge, skills, and abilities. And finally, institutions will need to consider how best to leverage in-class and outside-class learning experiences to maximize student growth and development. The area of leadership development, a promised outcome of student investment, is already being promoted by institutions of higher education. The key will be to reflect on those promises and to design integrative models and measures to meet those promises. We believe that the responsible leadership development model provides an integrative, inclusive, and student-centric framework to help educators and administrators better conceptualize, plan, and potentially measure leadership development.

As the world has become more interconnected and interdependent, modern understandings of leadership place leadership not in a position but in the interactions in the networks between people. The leaders of organizations are not always those at the top of the hierarchy and modern conceptualizations help explain this phenomenon. This is a hopeful place in which to consider a model of responsible leadership. Hope, because everyone can share in the leadership process without waiting for someone else to take the lead. Hope, because each person has the potential to improve leadership capacity without assuming that his or her limits are preset. The bottom line is that there is a generation's worth of difficult problems waiting to be tackled by today's students. The concept of responsible leadership provides hope for the future. Hope that everyone has potential to lead and may participate in the leadership process.

REFERENCES

Astin, A. (1993). *What matters in college.* San Francisco, CA: Jossey-Bass.

Avolio, B. J., & Gardner, W. L. (2005). Authentic leadership development: Getting to the root of positive forms of leadership. *Leadership Quarterly, 16,* 315–338.

Bandura, A. (1977). Self-efficacy: Toward a unifying theory of behavioral change. *Psychological Review, 84*(2), 191–215.

Bass, B. M., & Riggio, R. E. (2006). *Transformational leadership.* (2nd ed.). Mahwah, NJ: Lawrence Erlbaum.

Baxter-Magolda, M. B. (2009). The activity of meaning making: A holistic perspective on college student development. *Journal of College Student Development, 50*(6), 621–639.

Baxter-Magolda, M. B., Creamer, E. G., & Meszaros, P. S. (2010). *Development and assessment of self-authorship: Exploring the concept across.* Stylus Sterling, VA.

Bernard, M. E. (2006). It's time we teach social-emotional competence as well as we teach academic competence. *Reading & Writing Quarterly, 22*(2), 103–119.

Bing, M. N., Davison, H. K., Vitell, S. J., Ammeter, A. P., Garner, B. L., & Novicevic, M. M. (2012). An experimental investigation of an interactive model of academic cheating among business school students. *Academy of Management Learning & Education, 11*(1), 28–48.

Bogue, G., & Hall, K. (2012). Business, political & academic perspectives on higher education. Accountability policy. *College and University Journal, 87*(3), 14–23.

Boyatzis, R. E. (2009). Competencies as a behavioral approach to emotional intelligence. *Journal of Management Development, 28*(9), 749–770.

Boyatzis, R. E., & McKee, A. (2005). *Resonant leadership: Renewing yourself and connecting with others through mindfulness, hope and compassion.* Boston, MA: Harvard Business School Press.

Boyatzis, R.E., & Saatcioglu, A. (2008). A 20-year view of trying to develop emotional, social and cognitive intelligence competencies in graduate management education. *Journal of Management Development, 27*(1), 92–108.

Cherniss, C. (2010). Emotional intelligence: Toward clarification of a concept. *Industrial and Organizational Psychology: Perspectives on Science and Practice, 3,* 110–126.

Conger, J.A., & Kanungo, R.N. (1998). Charismatic leadership in organizations. Thousand Oaks, CA: Sage.

Cove, P., & Love, A. (1996). Enhancing student learning: Intellectual, social, and emotional integration. Washington, DC: ERIC Clearinghouse on Higher Education; George Washington University, Graduate School of Education and Human Development.

Crossan, M., Mazutis, D., Seijts, G., & Gandz, J. (2011). Developing leadership character in business programs. *Academy of Management Learning & Education.* doi: 10.5465 /amle.2011.0024.

Dugan, J.P. (2006). Involvement and leadership: A descriptive analysis of socially responsible leadership. *Journal of College Student Development, 47*(3), 335–343.

Evans, N.J., Forney, D.S., Guido, F.M., Patton, L.D., & Renn, K.A. (2010). *Student development in college: Theory, research, and practice.* San Francisco, CA: Jossey-Bass.

Gardner, H. (1983). *Frames of mind: The theory of multiple intelligences.* New York: Basic Books.

Gecas, V., & Schwalbe, M.L. (1983). Beyond the looking-glass self: Social structure and efficacy-based self-esteem. *Social Psychology Quarterly, 46*(2), 77–88.

Goleman, D., Boyatzis, R.E., & McKee, A. (2004). *Primal leadership: Learning to lead with emotional intelligence.* Boston, MA: Harvard Business School Press.

Hunt, J.W., & Baruch, Y. (2003). Developing top managers: The impact of interpersonal skills training. *Journal of Management Development, 22,* 729–752.

Kitchener, K.S., & King, P.M. (1990). The reflective judgment model: Transforming assumptions about knowing. In J. Mezirow (Ed.), *Fostering critical reflection in adulthood* (pp. 159–176). San Francisco, CA: Jossey-Bass.

Komives, S.R., Longerbeam, S.D., Mainella, F.C., Osteen, L., Owen, J.E., & Wagner, W. (2009). Leadership identity development: Challenges in applying a developmental model. *Journal of Leadership Education, 8,* 11–47.

Komives, S.R., Longerbeam, S.D., Owen, J.E., Mainella, F.C., & Osteen, L. (2006). A leadership identity development model: Applications from a grounded theory. *Journal of College Student Development, 47,* 401–418.

Komives, S.R., Lucas, N., & McMahon, T.R. (2007). *Exploring leadership: For college students who want to make a difference* (2nd ed.). San Francisco, CA: Jossey-Bass.

Komives, S.R., Owen, J.E., Longerbeam, S.D., Mainella, F.C., & Osteen, L. (2005). Developing a leadership identity: A grounded theory. *Journal of College Student Development, 46,* 593–611.

Kouzes, J.M., & Posner, B.Z. (2003). Challenge is the opportunity for greatness. *Leader to Leader, 28,* 16–23.

Kuh, G.D., Kinzie, J., Buckley, J.A., Bridges, B.K., & Hayek, J.C. (2006). What matters to student success: A review of the literature. Commissioned report for the National Symposium on Postsecondary Student Success: Spearheading a Dialog on Student Success. http://nces.ed.gov/npec/pdf/kuh_team_report.pdf.

Kuh, G.D., Kinzie, J., Schuh, J.H., Whit, E.J., & Associates (2010). *Student success in college: Creating conditions that matter.* San Francisco, CA: Jossey-Bass.

Lattimore, J. B., D'Amico, M. M., & Hancock, D. R. (2012). Strategic responses to accountability demands: A case study of three community colleges. *Community College Journal of Research and Practice, 36*(12), 928–940.

Murphy, S. E. (2002). Leadership self-regulation: The role of self-efficacy and multiple intelligences. In R. Riggio, S. Murphy, & F. Pirozzolo (Eds.), *Multiple intelligences and leadership* (pp. 63–186). Mahwah, NJ: Lawrence Erlbaum.

Pascarella, E. T., & Terenzini, P. T. (2005). *How college affects students: A third decade of research.* San Francisco, CA: Jossey-Bass.

Perry, W. G. (1981). Cognitive and ethical growth: The making of meaning. In A. W. Chickering & Associates, *The Modern American College* (pp. 76–116). San Francisco, CA: Jossey-Bass.

Riggio, R. E., Riggio, H. R., Salinas, C., & Cole, E. J. (2003). The role of social and emotional communication skills in leader emergence and effectiveness. *Group Dynamics: Theory, Research, and Practice, 7*(2), 83–103.

Salovey, P., & Mayer, J. D. (1990). Emotional intelligence. *Imagination, Cognition & Personality, 9,* 185–211.

Seal, C. R., & Andrews-Brown, A. (2010). An integrative model of emotional intelligence: emotional ability as a moderator of the mediated relationship of emotional quotient and emotional competence. *Organization Management Journal, 7*(2), 143–152.

Seal, C. R., Beauchamp, K., Miguel, K., & Scott, A. N. (2011). Development of a self-report instrument to assess social and emotional development. *Journal of Psychological Issues in Organizational Culture, 2*(2), 82–95.

Seal, C. R., Boyatzis, R. E., & Bailey, J. R. (2006). Fostering emotional and social intelligence in organizations. *Organization Management Journal, 3,* 190–209.

Seal, C. R., Naumann, S. E., Scott, A., & Royce-Davis, J. (2010). Social emotional development: A new model of learning in higher education. *Research in Higher Education Journal, 10,* 1–13.

Tinto, V. (1993). *Leaving college: Rethinking the causes and cures of student attrition* (2nd. ed.). Chicago, IL: University of Chicago Press.

12

Soft Skills Training

Best Practices in Industry and Higher Education

Susan Elaine Murphy, Stefanie Putter, and Stefanie K. Johnson

> "I certainly have not the talent which some people possess," said Darcy, "of conversing easily with those I have never seen before. I cannot catch their tone of conversation, or appear interested in their concerns, as I often see done."
>
> —Mr. Darcy, from the novel *Pride and Prejudice*
> (Austen, 1813/1980, pp. 169–170)

In Jane Austen's *Pride and Prejudice,* one of the main characters, Mr. Fitzwilliam Darcy, is criticized by casual acquaintances in the early 19th-century English countryside because of his prejudiced and prideful behaviors. His harsh judgment of those not of his social class and his arrogant remarks are off-putting to others to say the least. Later in the book as we learn more about Mr. Darcy, we see that he explains this inability to behave well in groups of people with which he is unacquainted is based on a lack of talent, a fact that to a modern observer might suggest a missing ingrained trait. Miss Elizabeth Bennet, the object of his affection, disagrees with his assessment. She offers that her piano playing is similarly lacking, not because she is untalented, but because she does not practice—suggesting that Darcy's social failings are due to a lack of practice of the important skills required for effective social interaction.

Research and popular articles today suggest that particular industries are replete with individuals who have Mr. Darcy's difficulty in interacting with others. The example of the uncaring physician, the out-of-touch engineer, or the unethical financial manager may be overgeneralizations, but unfortunately many fit these stereotyped characterizations. Some of Mr. Darcy's same intense, logical, Mr. Spock-like behaviors are the characteristics necessary for individuals today to succeed in many occupations that require a high level of technical skill and a single-minded drive. Stories of Steve Jobs and other Internet moguls suggest that the technical side plays an important role in their success, but when it comes to understanding others or practicing a more nuanced form of influence, these individuals' efforts fall flat.

Current employment contexts demand that many types of workers develop the skills for connecting effectively with others. High levels of interpersonal skills are necessary for the multitude of service workers, team-based workforces, and the global community, where much work is accomplished virtually. All of these situations require that individuals understand the rules of interacting with coworkers. This high level of complexity is also important for individuals working together in synchronous or asynchronous teams (e.g., Thompson, 2007) and for those leading these teams (e.g., Kahai, 2013). Many universities have recognized that it is not enough to provide education in technical skills, but instead understand that the purpose of education is to prepare the whole person for life after college whether it is through liberal arts curriculum or through courses that augment what is learned through application. Accordingly these skills include written and verbal communication, the ability to solve complex problems, to work well with others, and to adapt in a changing workplace. However, again, not all students will be involved in a curriculum that focuses on gaining these skills.

Moreover, some believe that the students enrolled in today's colleges and universities lack many of these more general skills because of the current focus by primary and secondary schools on standardized tests. Some educators in fact argue that much of classroom time is spent on a narrow curriculum that maps to the standardized test, or what is more commonly known as "teaching to the test" (Bushweller, 1997). A focus on test performance may reduce the time spent learning the nuances of social skills that in the past may have been emphasized both inside and outside of the classroom. A recent study suggests that the focus on standardized tests is one contributor to declining levels of creativity over the past 20 years (Kim, 2011). In addition, the author cites the structured play environment of many students as another creativity killer. Some fear that this overemphasis on structured play has left young children without time to learn conflict resolution and other important interpersonal skills (Murphy & Reichard, 2011). Therefore, an emphasis on soft skills training in college and later in the workplace becomes very important to address the deficit.

—————

"BUSINESS CASE" FOR SOFT SKILLS

Have jobs changed? The answer is yes. The increase in service jobs has resulted in a commensurate need for training in soft skills. Gone are the days when employees might work with a machine or along an assembly line with little contact with others on the job. The ideas of "high touch, high tech" characterize many of today's jobs rather than the large percentage of manufacturing jobs that once characterized the labor force. Projections to the year 2020 indicate that we will see increases in the service sector in health care as well as other professions and a further decline in manufacturing (Henderson, 2012). In addition to changing types of jobs, individuals are asked to work in organizations that are more diverse with respect to gender, race, and nationality than they once were. Navigating these heterogeneous groups in which individuals may value different things, as well as use different communication and conflict resolution styles, requires increased soft skills than working in groups where everyone is similar in these personal aspects. And finally, many organizations operate in a global environment in which individuals interact with people from many different countries.

We only need to look to the hiring process to observe the premium afforded those with good "people skills." One survey of CFOs showed that people skills were more important than software/technology skills or industry-specific experience (*Deloitte CFO Journal,* 2012). These skills show up in hiring interviews when applicants are asked to give examples of how they handled interpersonal issues in the past with coworkers, customers, or bosses. A recent survey of hiring decision makers found that a full 84% of their new hires do not have the skills necessary to succeed in their organizations (ACICS, 2011). When drilling down as to what specific skills are lacking from the perspective of hiring companies, the most important skills identified were interpersonal skills, which showed a large gap between the importance of the skill and the actual performance of recent hires. The other gap that was as large was the importance and performance of problem-solving skills. The hiring managers responding to the survey were split, though, as to whether these skill gaps could be closed with more technical training or more broad-based training. When asked to think about important skills for the future, social intelligence (defined by the survey as "the ability to connect to others in a deep and direct way, to sense and stimulate reactions and desired interactions") was near the top of the list just after novel-thinking ability. The gap between the current skill level for social intelligence and what was needed for the future was viewed as quite large. Are hiring managers correct in the need for soft skills for success in today's jobs? Many studies suggest this is true when we consider the long-term impact of soft skills. One study showed that 75% of long-term job success depends on people skills, while only 25% depends on technical knowledge (Klaus, 2010).

Have workers changed? There is some argument that today's workforce consisting of many millennial workers (those born between 1977 and 1992, who range from the late teens to the early 30s in age), have communicated electronically almost since they were born (think AOL instant messenger circa 1997), or at least since college. Their experiences may be as different from today's older workers' experiences as those of someone who did not grow up communicating over a telephone with someone who did. How has the use of electronic communication such as email, text messages, and instant messages influenced millennials' soft skills? Would one expect generational differences to occur in the way soft skills are acquired and utilized at work? Perhaps. There is some evidence that communications practices may differ. Anecdotes abound in which companies complain that they must train the millennials in their workforce not to compose emails with text message abbreviation/acronyms. Hartman and McCambridge (2011) suggest that communication instruction that moves away from the sender's understanding to a focus on the audience's understanding is one method of increasing millennials' interpersonal communication skills.

Why are soft skills especially important for leaders? Leaders must influence others toward organizational goals and most of that influence is interpersonal. Although there is a strong case for the need for developing soft skills, there is some lack of agreement on what should be included in soft skills development and how to develop these skills in employees. Pichler and Beenen (this volume) introduced a model of managerial interpersonal skills that looks at the shortcomings of management education for building interpersonal skills (Rubin & Dierdorff, 2009, 2011) as well as analysis of data collected by the Graduate Management Admissions Council (GMAC) of MBA program admissions officers. Their model includes: managing self, communicating, supporting, motivating others, and managing conflict. Their model also underscores some of the underlying constructs that enable managers to be effective in these interpersonal dimensions such as emotional and social intelligences or self-management for skill deployment and development.

One way of understanding how these intrapersonal skills/soft skills develop is focusing on to what extent individuals engage in self-management practices and possess emotional intelligence. For example, individuals who manage their own emotional reactions and understand the emotions of others in social interactions would be practicing self-management on an intrapersonal level. We also make the point in this chapter that training of soft skills is not enough to fully develop these skills unless individuals are simultaneously encouraged to develop the underlying skills of self-management to transfer that training and continue to develop it over time. Self-management has been studied as a general concept of human behavior and specifically to issues of workplace behavior such as leadership, careers, and reducing ineffective behaviors (Latham & Frayne, 1989). Indeed, self-management skills are essential for leader development and encouraging leaders to self-develop can be an invaluable business strategy (Reichard & Johnson, 2011).

For the purposes of this chapter we adopt the definition of interpersonal skills from Klein, DeRouin, and Salas:

> goal-directed behaviors, including communication and relationship-building competencies, employed in interpersonal interaction episodes characterized by complex perceptual and cognitive processes, dynamic verbal and nonverbal interactive exchanges, diverse roles, motivations, and expectancies. (2006, p. 81)

We tie interpersonal skills to leadership skills by focusing on interpersonal skill development practices among the top external leadership training companies ("2012 Top 20 Leadership Training Companies," 2012) and the best internal companies for leaders ("Ten Best Companies for Leaders," 2012). After this review, and some research on some of the more effective techniques, we review what colleges and universities within the specific areas of business education, engineering, and medicine are doing with respect to interpersonal skill training. Finally, we end with additional ways to improve interpersonal and soft skills training for both contexts.

TRAINING LEADER SOFT SKILLS IN ORGANIZATIONS

Interpersonal skills are largely considered critical elements of workplace success, with research demonstrating positive relationships between leader social skills and performance and salary on the job (Ferris, Witt, & Hochwarter, 2001). For example, an American Society for Training and Development (ASTD; 2000) survey found that more than 33% of individuals believe that excellent communication and interpersonal skills are essential characteristics in a high-quality boss, and a 2004 survey by Munson, Phillips, Clark, and Mueller-Hanson demonstrated that Society for Industrial and Organizational Psychology (SIOP) practitioners deem interpersonal skills and teamwork important qualities in successful interns. Together, along with estimates that approximately 50% of organizational training budgets are used for interpersonal skills development (*US Banker,* 2000), there is considerable evidence that organizations place high value on interpersonal skills training.

More recently, in 2008, Linkage Inc. surveyed practitioners to better understand organizational best practices around leader development (Giber, Lam, Goldsmith, & Bourke, 2009). Beyond revealing that leadership development remains a key focus across companies in all industries, these survey results suggest that organizations focus on the following core leadership competencies: strategic thinking, communication, building relationships, and developing talent. Although leadership practitioners gave strategic thinking top priority, it is quite evident that interpersonal leadership skills (e.g., communication, building relationships) are of high importance as well. Further, these survey findings indicate that the most common leader development methodologies were 360-degree feedback, leader development programming, facilitated discussions, individual development plans, and team building. Such findings demonstrate a clear trend toward hands-on and customized learning solutions. In the following sections, we highlight how these themes around leader interpersonal skills development are embedded in today's top internal and external leadership training organizations.

Best Practices in Interpersonal Skills Development

To identify best practices in organizational training of leader soft skills, we targeted our research on the best internal and external leadership training organizations, according to trainingindustry.com and chiefexecutive

.net (referring to 2012 rankings only). We conducted a small-scale study of 30 top-ranked organizations (see Appendix A for a full list), gathering information from company websites and through personal interviews with organizational leaders. Interviews were conducted with company representatives from the following companies: American Management Association International, Impact International, InsideOut Development, and Wilson Learning Corporation. To the extent possible, we explored the "what" (the types of interpersonal skills trained), the "how" (the training methodologies utilized), and the "why" (evidence of training effectiveness) of interpersonal skills training at each of these companies. Although our search was limited, the themes and best practices identified shed light on current organizational practices around interpersonal skill development.

Interpersonal Skills Training Content

Using our earlier definition of interpersonal skills, we target leadership training and development around communication and relationship building competencies for our present analysis. Based on our research, the top leadership training organizations offer extensive learning and development opportunities on these particular areas of skill development. Specifically, we found that organizations tend to focus on developing the following communication skills: communicating effectively and with authenticity; overcoming common barriers to effective communication (e.g., differing communication styles, interacting with difficult people, running with assumptions); understanding the psychology of influence and persuasion; and becoming a better listener. As examples, AchieveGlobal offers a one-day workshop entitled "Connecting with others: Listening and speaking," which helps develop leaders' active listening and communication skills and influencing others, and Forum Corporation offers a four-hour program called "Skillful Conversations," which focuses on checking assumptions, understanding intentions, and bringing out others' ideas.

In terms of relationship building, we discovered that organizations commonly teach leadership skills that involve strengthening interpersonal relationships (through building trust, handling conflict, and giving feedback), working collaboratively with others, and building internal and external networks. For example, Wilson Learning Corporation offers a course entitled "Building Relationship Versatility" that helps leaders learn how to manage interpersonal conflict and foster productive relationships, and Hemsley Fraser offers a workshop called "Interpersonal Effectiveness for Managers" that helps participants understand how to improve working relationships. Taken together, it is evident that today's top companies place high value in providing training and development opportunities on leader interpersonal skills.

Interpersonal Skills Training Approaches

In terms of the "how," leader interpersonal skills can be developed through a variety of training approaches. Our research has found that the top leadership training organizations typically utilize at least one of the following: face-to-face training, online/virtual training, blended learning approaches, coaching/mentoring, on-the-job experiences, and action learning. Next, we discuss each of these approaches in more detail.

Classroom learning. Classroom learning typically involves instructor-led trainings, seminars, or workshops. This type of programming may utilize facilitators who are either internal to an organization (who are certified to teach the training content), or external and hired through a consulting firm. Best practice organizations typically go beyond just lecture and actively involve their participants in the learning process through engagement in hands-on, experiential learning opportunities. On the other hand, some organizations also utilize *online or virtual* training, which provides added flexibility and learner control (this learning is commonly self-guided) to the training process. Online or virtual training resources may include e-learning libraries, electronic books and resources, or webinars and webcasts with experts in the field. Best practice organizations commonly provide e-learning modalities as support after a more in-depth learning experience, in order to help sustain learning and foster transfer back on the job (e.g., Wilson Learning).

Important, research supports the efficacy of face-to-face (or classroom based) approaches to teaching soft skills (Arthur, Bennett, Edens, & Bell, 2003) and management skills defined as self-awareness skills, human relations skills, and general management skills (Burke & Day, 1986). Further, the use of more active learning techniques is supported by evidence that the benefits of lecture can be further enhanced when combined with discussion (Arthur et al., 2003; Burke & Day, 1986) and additional interactive learning strategies such as behavioral modeling and role plays (Beard, Salas, & Prince, 1995; Salas, Burke, & Cannon-Bowers, 2001). Practice seems to be key to learning new skills (Baldwin, 1992; Goldstein & Sorcher, 1974; May & Kahnweiler, 2000). It is also relevant to note that the use of e-learning modalities is supported by research (Holsbrink-Engels, 1997;

Salas, Burke, Bowers, & Wilson, 2001; Smith-Jentsch, Griffin, & Onye-jiaka, 2006). For example, Smith-Jentsch and colleagues (2006) created a 40-minute multimedia platform that demonstrated positive effects on assertive communication skills. In sum, research supports the use of classroom-based learning, particularly when combined with more active learning techniques, and even when delivered virtually.

Coaching and mentoring. Further, coaching and mentoring are useful approaches for developing leader interpersonal skills. It is common for organizations to offer coaching both during and after a learning experience, in either one-on-one or small group formats (e.g., Impact International). Many best practice companies also match leaders with strong mentors who will challenge, support, and stretch them to accelerate the learning process. Both coaching and mentoring can help facilitate leader development and personal growth. The use of coaching and mentoring to teach soft skills is also supported by research (Klein, 2009). For example, Baron and Morin (2010) found that executive coaching enhanced self-efficacy for leader soft skills. To the extent that these methods utilize high levels of feedback, there is evidence for their effectiveness at teaching soft skills (Tews & Tracey, 2008). Feedback provides the necessary information required for the individual to change his or her soft skill behavior (Klein et al., 2006).

On-the-job experiences. A third category of training methodology targets on-the-job experiences. Through providing early responsibility, challenging learning opportunities, and rotating job assignments, best practice organizations help strengthen leadership skills while leaders are on the job. Such opportunities help expand the depth and breadth of leaders' expertise, helping accelerate the development and learning process. For example, Cardinal Health provides leaders with early development experiences through the EMERGE program. This program is "designed to offer leadership development to participants in an environment where they can rotate through different departments and locations. Participants are provided an ideal opportunity to continue exploring careers within their discipline while gaining valuable work experience needed to succeed in the future." On-the-job experiences are invaluable for strengthening leader interpersonal skills.

Further, organizations typically leverage action learning projects as training opportunities for leader interpersonal skills. Action learning opportunities allow learners to work together to tackle real organizational problems. Thus, training is all about current leadership and business challenges that leaders are facing. Impact International, for example, has leaders engage in business action learning projects that involve real-time, interactive, scenario-based leadership simulations. Individuals tackle real issues in order to develop and strengthen their leadership skills.

There is also evidence of the effectiveness of on-the-job experiences as a method of developing leadership skills (McCall, Lombardo, & Morrison, 1988; McCauley, Ruderman, Ohlott, & Morrow, 1994). DeRue and Wellman (2009) found that the more challenging the on-the-job experience, the more beneficial it was for leader development. We can also draw evidence from the effectiveness of process interventions, such as team building and sensitivity training, as types of on-the-job training. Meta-analysis suggests that sensitivity training (Burke & Day, 1986) and team-building improve soft skills (Klein et al., 2009). On-the-job training should be particularly effective because it eases the transfer process. It is believed that the transfer of soft skills is lower than hard skills (Foxon, 1993; Georgenson, 1982; Kupritz, 2002), so maximizing the similarity between the training environment and the job environment can encourage transfer (Laker & Powell, 2011).

Blended learning. Finally, another common way to train leader soft skills is through the use of *blended learning* approaches. Best practice organizations commonly blend various approaches together (e.g., face-to-face training, online training, action learning, etc.), depending on the needs and interests of the client (for external organizations) or their people (for internal organizations). As an example, GE offers developmental opportunities that combine real-world experiences with formal, classroom-based learning. Overall, best practice organizations train leader interpersonal skills using a variety of approaches. A commonality across these different methodologies is a heavy reliance on adult learning principles that posit that learning is most successful when individuals are actively engaged in the learning process, self-directing or guiding their own development, exposed to immediate practice opportunities, and learning relevant content (Knowles, 1990; Knowles, Holton, & Swanson, 2005). Thus, despite the specific approach, it is critical that interpersonal skills training leverage adult learning concepts, so that learning can be optimally effective.

Interpersonal Skills Training Evaluation

Evaluation is an important piece of any successful leader development experience. It is critical for any organization (whether internal or external) to evaluate the effectiveness of its programming in order to make informed decisions about the quality of its services (i.e., decision making), provide feedback to trainers, developers, and participants, and assist with marketing and business development (Kraiger, 2002). In general, evaluation criteria for interpersonal skills training vary, depending on the interests of the organization, as well as available metrics. Most of the time, companies can't enforce evaluation, but offer such services as an additional benefit.

A variety of evaluation models and taxonomies are being studied in academia and utilized in practice (e.g., Kirkpatrick, 1994; Kraiger, Ford, & Salas, 1993; Phillips & Phillips, 2007). Some commonly examined training criteria include trainee reactions, trainee self-efficacy, learning, behavior/performance change, and organizational results. Best practice organizations commonly utilize multiple evaluation criteria, collected at multiple points in time (such as pre- and postassessments) to examine training and development effectiveness. For example, American Management Association International evaluates its leader development program effectiveness by assessing trainee reactions (e.g., Did participants enjoy the learning experience?); knowledge transfer and learning (e.g., Did participants increase their knowledge in the desired content area?); behavior and performance changes (e.g., What were the behavioral or performance impacts of training?); and company metrics (e.g., What is the return on expectations (ROE)?).

Additionally, best practice organizations also have training participants complete ongoing assessments in order to (1) evaluate the effectiveness of their development experience, and (2) help sustain learning over time. For example, InsideOut Development has individuals fill out a technology-based tool, post training, on a regular basis to demonstrate what they are doing and whether it has an impact on business critical issues. This process provides an ongoing opportunity for individuals to reflect on professional growth and maintain engagement in the learning process. Further, Impact International uses online technology to facilitate an ongoing dialogue between individuals and their managers regarding personal development and growth after going through training. Generally speaking, ongoing evaluation and assessment is essential for maintaining training quality, sustaining learning over time, and demonstrating the return on investment (ROI) of leader development efforts.

Summary

Overall, we have examined trends among 30 of the top external and internal leadership training companies. Our research suggests a variety of themes among the best *external* leadership consulting firms, including a view that leader development is a lifelong process rather than a one-time event, the use of blended approaches for training and development, and the customization of services for individuals and clients being trained. Among the best *internal* companies for leaders, common themes include viewing leader development as a business strategy, constantly striving to foster a learning and development culture, and the integration of both formal (classroom) and informal (on-the-job, real-world) training on an ongoing basis.

EFFORTS BY COLLEGES AND UNIVERSITIES TO INCREASE SOFT SKILLS IN TECHNICAL FIELDS

Faculty and administrators in engineering and other technical undergraduate majors have long understood the need for expanding student skills to include the soft skills related to success in a profession. Moreover, for-profit and nonprofit organizations are the recipients of the college and university training of their employees. To the extent that colleges and universities do their job, these recipients are satisfied with today's graduates. However, as mentioned previously, many employers feel that students are not well prepared in the soft skills areas, begging the question: What are some university and college programs doing well that will lead to better prepared graduates? After reviewing some of the efforts by top colleges in the United States, specifically in the areas of engineering, medicine, and business, we discuss some of the commonalities in these programs and best practices, suggesting ways they could increase the efficacy of these programs.

Schools of Engineering

Although many schools of engineering offer a curriculum with engineering subspecialties that may include chemical, civil, mechanical, biological, ceramic, computer, architectural, construction, and others, these engineering subspecialties possess a common focus on putting ideas to work to develop or design products or process used by others. In addition, many large projects of any type require the input and coordination of many people. Engineering schools realize that today's graduates need a broad skill set to be effective. ABET, the Accreditation Board for Engineering and Technology, Inc., as part of its accreditation criteria, outlines two criteria related to interpersonal skills: (1) interpersonal skills apply as students work effectively on multidisciplinary teams, and (2) an ability to communicate effectively (ABET, 2012). At a minimum, accredited schools must provide experiences to meet these criteria for accreditation. Moreover, like many jobs today, young engineers do not plan to remain in one organization for the life of their career and therefore to remain competitive, a full portfolio of technical and leadership skills is necessary. Research on the effects of efforts for increasing these skill sets for engineers, however, is limited. Most articles describe specific programs at specific colleges, with limited information as to the program's effectiveness.

To examine the efforts of colleges and universities to develop interpersonal skills in engineering students, we searched for interpersonal or leadership skill development descriptions for the top 10 engineering schools in the United States as ranked by *US News & World Report* (2013a). These included:

1. Massachusetts Institute of Technology;
2. Stanford;
3. (tied) California Institute of Technology;
4. (tied) University of California–Berkeley;
5. (tied) Georgia Institute of Technology;
6. (tied) University of Illinois–Urbana-Champaign;
7. University of Michigan–Ann Arbor;
8. (tied) Carnegie Mellon University;
9. (tied) Cornell University;
10. Princeton.

We visited their websites and searched for leadership, interpersonal skills, or soft skills. Also, to catch any other stories about their schools' efforts, we added their name with the three search terms and searched the Web. This approach is then limited by what each school chooses to publish about their programs.

We found that a number of these schools focus skill development in the area of leadership. All of the schools reported student experiences on teams either in the classroom or within clinic and practicum teams. Often after being hired, many young engineers are asked to lead project teams of others or to move into other supervisory roles. There is also a big push across many colleges and universities for entrepreneurial leadership in engineering. Entrepreneurial ventures require one to motivate, direct, and lead others, making soft skills important (Cunningham & Lischeron, 1991). As such, schools of engineering have recognized the importance of leader soft skills in engineering entrepreneurship including effective communication, teamwork, multicultural skill, flexibility, professional ethics, creative thinking, respect and courtesy, leadership skills, compassion for others, and patience (Nichols & Armstrong, 2003).

Many of the top engineering schools recognize the importance of interpersonal/soft skills for the engineer leaders they are developing. For example, at MIT's Bernard M. Gordon Engineering Leadership Program, "*engineering leadership* is defined as the technical leadership of change: the *innovative* conception, design and *implementation* of new products, processes, projects, materials, molecules, software, systems, supported by the *invention* of enabling technologies, to meet the needs of customers and society" (Bernard M. Gordon, 2011). According to the program, engineering leaders need to have developed the *skills* of leadership, which are four main categories of "relating to others, making sense of context, creating visions and realizing the vision." Specifically relating to others is defined as "developing key relationships and networks within and across organizations, including listening to others to understand their views, and advocating for your position." For effective engineering leaders, the specific skills of relating to others include: *Inquiring and Dialoging*; *Negotiation, Compromise and Conflict Resolution*; *Advocacy*; *Diverse Connections and Grouping*; *Structured Communications* (formal communication and communicating strategy); and *Interpersonal Relations,* which the program defines as "Understanding and respecting the needs and characteristics of individuals and the group, and the resources that individuals with different backgrounds can bring to an organization. Coaching and teaching, providing and receiving evaluation and feedback, and the essential elements of gracious professionalism necessary to be an effective engineering leader." (Bernard M. Gordon, 2011, p. 4).

Stanford University's approach makes it clear that within Stanford's liberal arts focus engineers work with other people:

> We think of engineers as people who take discoveries from the sciences and use them to solve problems that change the world. Stanford Engineering aims to educate engineers who are also leaders, who understand the science of their solutions, of course, but who also understand the people, issues and systems they hope to affect. (Stanford University Engineering, 2013, para. 2)

In an effort to encourage its students to become engineering leaders, Carnegie Mellon offers a 3/2 combination engineering and MBA degree from its Tepper School of Management for specific engineering majors. To be eligible to apply, students in their junior year must have had at least one internship at a company.

Cornell University utilizes the program LeaderShape to help develop leadership skills for undergraduate engineering students. The Leader Shape Program is a nonprofit organization utilized by many colleges and universities; in fact, more than 18,000 students have participated in the program since 1988. For Cornell, LeaderShape encourages students to become involved in self-reflection and an emphasis on visioning, in addition to exploring personal characteristics, understanding leadership, working with peers, and an opportunity to work with leaders in the college, university, and community. The students in the engineering school also have an array of multidisciplinary project courses from which to choose to enhance their team leadership and technical skills to become technology leaders. Their emphasis on entrepreneurship and other electives focuses on entrepreneurial competitions as well.

At the University of Michigan Engineering school website, one immediately notices the emphasis on preparing graduates for careers with notices about upcoming career fairs and special hour-long events available to students so that they might know what to expect when meeting representatives from hiring firms. There were tips for preparing an elevator pitch (the 30-second to 60-second description of why someone should hire you or invest in your idea or company). Otherwise the program emphasizes co curricular leadership experiences to benefit students by allowing them to develop skills different from those in the classroom. The college also seems to support additional skills through its undergraduate and graduate program in engineering and entrepreneurship.

A very recently developed program at Purdue University School of Engineering allows undergraduate engineering students to enroll in a 16-credit engineering leadership minor. According to the program website, the program combines leadership theory with practice and expects students to engage in experiential leadership opportunities, faculty coaching, and technical leadership across a variety of contexts. The focus is on developing the skills required of effective engineering leaders. Specific coursework includes concentrations in "*Ethics* (which aligns closely with regulatory, legal, and policy-related aspects of engineering); *Global and Societal Impact* (the impact of leadership across diverse stakeholders and national and global communities); *Creativity and Innovation* concentration courses; and an *Entrepreneurial* and a

Communication concentration." The experiential requirements look similar to many other schools that require students to either work as a consulting team or in an internship with another organization.

According to the University of Southern California Viterbi School of Engineering website, "The curriculum has been developed to provide students with the opportunities to develop problem-solving strategies. Students learn to apply science, mathematics, and creativity to solve problems. Increasingly, engineers and computer scientists must develop the interpersonal skills to work effectively in dealing with modern enterprises. They must also understand the economic, environmental, and ethical implications of their work." As one way to fulfill these goals, the school has established the Klein Institute for Undergraduate Engineering Life (KIUEL). The mission of the institute is to provide "undergraduates a variety of personal and professional activities that will enhance undergraduate engineering student life experiences outside the classroom." To accomplish this goal, the focus is on leadership, cross-disciplinary activities, and service learning, as well as globalization. According to its website, the program both supports and enhances already existing student development programs at the School of Engineering.

At Georgia Tech, the Technology and Management Program enables undergraduate engineering students to earn a minor in engineering and management. As the website notes: "This select group of students learn one another's language through coursework in their respective fields and teamwork to solve real-world problems with the help and support of Corporate Affiliates." It also appears that students are encouraged to take co curricular courses or experiences through the LEAD program described as: "The LEAD Program at Georgia Tech complements the institution's outstanding academic programs by providing instruction to undergraduates in the kinds of knowledge and skills essential to becoming visionary and skilled leaders. The LEAD Program assumes that leadership is an observable and learnable set of practices and that provided the opportunity for proper instruction and practice, every student with persistence can substantially improve his or her leadership abilities. The students work in teams to plan, design, and research the economic and social impacts of a selected engineering problem, as well as participate in corporate visits, laboratory tours, and collegiate/skill workshops."

In summary, engineering schools realize the need to educate students in more than the technical aspects of their fields. There appears to be an understanding of the entire range of behaviors to develop the engineering professional. Our review highlights the fact that some schools appear more intentional in their focus on interpersonal and leadership skills that will make their engineering students competitive in the job market with the focus on team-work and entrepreneurship. Other schools attempt to distinguish themselves by a strong focus on this skill set by setting up co-curricular classes or programs that combine other courses or minors (and even degrees such as MBAs or entrepreneurship) that focus on management, communication, and interper-sonal skills. Some schools also partner with other offices on campus that have a focus on leadership. Other schools seem to have a more limited focus (at least given what they include on their websites), but all know the importance of stu-dent teamwork to gain skills in the areas of interpersonal communication and conflict management. Contextualizing the leadership learning through theory and application is a good way for students to explore issues of leader identity and to create leadership development plans.

Medical Schools

Medical schools have been under enormous pressure to train doctors who can simultaneously meet the health care needs of the U.S. population and work to reduce costs. The United States spends more on health care than any other developed nation and in 2011 spending reached an all-time high of 18.2% of GDP (National Coalition on Healthcare, 2011); by 2013 an estimated $800 billion will be counted as waste (National Coalition on Healthcare, 2013). To address these concerns in the medical field, many have called for scrutiny of medical school training. Reviews of this process suggest that better training could "help physicians provide better patient care, reduce medical errors, improve compliance, lessen burnout, reduce health care disparities and improve quality and outcomes" (AMA, 2012b). In addition, giving doctors an "engaged, holistic worldview" that takes into account the complexity of responses and interactions and incorporates knowledge from behavioral and social sciences to improve health behav-iors (AAMC, 2011).

In looking at how to improve patient care, some have pointed to physi-cians' lack of interpersonal skills. A recent poll published in the *Wall Street Journal* reported that patients rate doctors' interpersonal skills as more important than their medical judgment or experience (Bright, 2004). The poll also revealed that inadequate interpersonal skills led patients to switch doctors. A large percentage of the respondents said that treating a patient with dignity and respect was an extremely important quality in a doctor, and just as many mentioned listening carefully and being easy to talk to as important qualities. These problems are not new. In 2005, the Accreditation Council for Graduate Medical Education (ACGME) published a report targeting soft skills entitled *Advancing Education in Interpersonal and Communication Skills: An Education Resource of ACGME Outcome Project* (ACGME, 2005) to address the need for these competencies. The revised American Medical Association guidelines for medical school curriculum now show a broad range of competencies and include interpersonal skills and communication. Other guidelines under development include decision making, supporting emotions, and helping patients with behavior change (AMA, 2012). *These changing requirements were a response to research that showed* soft skills, such as doctor empathy, improve patient satisfaction (Roter, 1997) and can improve patient health (Adler, 2002). Later research also showed that skills such as negotiation and influence were important for the success of leaders in the medical field (Mountford & Webb, 2009). Not only do doctors who communicate and connect with patients have more satisfied patients, they also have healthier patients and experience fewer lawsuits. The problems of physician-patient communication and interpersonal skills have been highlighted in research showing the relationship between clear communication and patient outcomes (Levinson & Pizzo, 2011). One study found doctors with low patient satisfaction ratings were more likely to experience a claim of malpractice (Hickson et al., 2002). Therefore, many schools of medicine are focusing on ways to specifically increase the interpersonal skills of effective physicians (Morahan et al., 1998).

Although those in the profession acknowledge that interpersonal and soft skills must be taught and practiced, the skills are undervalued compared to either scientific knowledge or medical technology. In fact, the authors go as far as to say, "Although time to listen to patients and teach communication skills may be scarce, technology is plentiful. Academic medical centers almost worship technology" (Levinson & Pizzo, 2011, p. 1803). The authors of this research suggest that academic medical centers that value patient-doctor communication should use metrics and perhaps tie them to financial incentives. Their thinking is that physicians then would be recognized for spending more time with patients instead of less, as opposed to the current system that rewards physicians based on the number of patients seen in a given amount of time.

In addition to introducing interpersonal skills development into the curriculum, medical schools are also focusing on ways to select future physicians who already possess these skills or may be ready to further develop these skills. The Multiple Mini Interview is a series of brief situational interviews—which as one source noted are similar to speed dating—to allow medical students to show that they possess the social skills necessary for the field of medicine (Harris, 2011). Eight medical schools including Virginia Tech, Stanford, University of California, Los Angeles, and the University of Cincinnati, as well as schools in Canada use this technique. The interviews also provide ethical dilemmas as well as ask the applicants to work in teams and think on their feet. "Candidates who jump to improper conclusions, fail to listen or are overly opinionated fare poorly because such behavior undermines teams," according to the article. The article cites a follow-up study that showed that medical school students' scores on this assessment were positively related to scores on a medical licensing exam three to five years later on dimensions of decision making, patient interactions, and cultural competency. Other research has backed this approach by showing that students selected through an interpersonal skills training assessment did better later in clinical work with patients than those selected with a previous process (Lievens, 2013).

Given the research evidence tying soft skills to patient satisfaction and outcomes, we chose to look at how the top 10 schools of medicine for primary care physicians incorporate soft skills training. They are:

1. University of Washington;
2. University of North Carolina–Chapel Hill;
3. (tied). Oregon Health and Science University;
4. (tie). University of California–San Francisco;
5. University of Colorado–Denver;
6. University of Nebraska Medical Center;
7. University of Massachusetts–Worcester;
8. University of Michigan–Ann Arbor;
9. (tied). University of Minnesota;
10. University of California–Los Angeles (Geffen) (*US News and World Report*, 2012).

We used the same search techniques as we used in researching information on the schools of engineering by reviewing the school's web page and following up with web searches using the medical school's name and the terms *interpersonal skills* or *soft skills* for other articles.

The top-rated University of Washington School of Medicine is currently undertaking an extensive curriculum renewal project to identify ways to improve doctor training. Fourteen renewal committees consist of students, faculty, and staff from the surrounding region to focus on ways to renew the medical school curriculum in areas identified in a self-study. According to the website, one committee, the Interpersonal and Communications Committee is charged to "Develop recommendations for curricular approaches to developing communication skills with patients, families, other members of the health care team, and the community; Develop recommendations for curriculum approaches to fostering teamwork; Consider the composition and timing of interprofessional experiences."

Other medical schools make salient to students the need for interpersonal skill development in working with patients. For example, at the University of North Carolina–Chapel Hill, students are directed to a website with a checklist of interpersonal behaviors to be exhibited when working with patients that include behaviors such as whether the student shook the patient's hand, introduced himself or herself, or greeted the patient warmly. Other behaviors included whether they were not condescending to their patients, listened carefully to their needs, and avoided interrupting. The University of California–San Francisco also uses interpersonal and communication skills checklists as part of its assessment of student-patient relationships.

Oregon Health Sciences demonstrates its focus on communication and interpersonal skills by including these skills in student performance evaluations. The University of Minnesota's focus on interpersonal skills appears in its overall curriculum, and also appears in the description of essential and desired characteristics in potential applicants. These include: "Oral and written communication skills must be excellent, both to share knowledge and to convey empathy (essential); Teamwork skills require acknowledging other team members' expertise, accurate self-assessment, assuming leadership when appropriate, and subsuming individual interests to the work of the team (essential); Tolerance (essential); Leadership & diversity experiences (desired)." In addition to the explicit selection criteria, Minnesota allows students once they arrive at school to participate in a seven-week to ten-week simulation in patient interviewing. The process includes initial focus on the interviewing and facilitation skills that encourage a patient to tell his or her story. As the student moves through the program, he or she then begins to learn how to address the emotional aspects of patients' complaints. During the entire process, students receive feedback from the patient, the physician tutor, and their peers.

The University of California–Los Angeles Geffen School focuses on a comprehensive set of interpersonal and communication skills for the purpose of "effective information exchange and teaming with patients, their families, and other health professionals." Within this program they are looking for ways for students to learn to build rapport and engage in "empathic communication with patients of different backgrounds." The school also recognizes the need for increased teamwork among physicians and other medical staff, so its education also focuses on teamwork and ways to be more compassionate and nonjudgmental with patients. This emphasis too recognizes that doctors work with many types of patients and their guidelines ask that doctors engage in communication with patients that is "culturally-sensitive, jargon-free and appropriate to their needs."

The remaining medical schools on the top ten list also include interpersonal and communication skills within their learning objectives. Most schools, however, did not provide additional information as to the delivery method for skills development. However, taken as a whole it is apparent that medical schools recognize the importance of soft skill development, as this focus appears to be ubiquitous in the curricular learning objectives. In addition, many of the schools use interpersonal skills as admissions criteria. With the research suggesting the many outcomes tied to physician satisfaction, of course it is imperative to develop this skill set. More research on effective delivery of training and resulting patient satisfaction can focus the future of these efforts.

Business Schools

Many of the same soft skills essential for engineering and medical school students are necessary for students of business to complement the technical skills taught in finance, accounting, and management of technology. As mentioned previously, jobs today demand interpersonal understanding of diverse coworkers and customers. Business schools are looking at ways of increasing the soft skills for their undergraduate students before they graduate and are hired by organizations. Many feel that this "competitive edge" helps their students in the interview process and beyond.

There is also an increased interest in soft skills training within graduate programs of business. A recent study of 5,000 MBA recruiters showed four important soft skills they look at when hiring: Interpersonal Skills, Communication Skills, Strategic Thinking, and Leadership (Quacquarelli, 2011). Research suggests that as individuals move up within organizations, the requirements for soft skills become even more complex (Hooijberg & Schneider, 2001). To rise to higher levels of management, employees must have the soft skills to resolve conflict, negotiate, and influence others, while the technical skills for which they were hired become less important. A problem occurs, however, when only a small percentage of the curriculum in MBA programs focuses on skills such as managing decision making and human capital (Rubin & Dierdorff, 2009).

To address these curricular needs many undergraduate and graduate business schools have increased their focus on soft skills necessary to manage others. A *Wall Street Journal* article summarized some of the recent efforts by many business schools such as Columbia, Stanford, and University of California–Berkeley Haas School to teach the softer skills, or what some refer to as the "touchy feely" courses (Korn & Light, 2011). For example, Columbia University has a program on social intelligence that provides training to MBAs, and many graduates of Stanford report appreciating the skills they acquired while in the program that help them in the businesses they currently manage. Most of these more programmatic efforts though seem to be aimed at MBAs. It may be that because MBAs have a richer context for understanding the necessity for these skills they are better able to participate in the types of activities necessary to develop the skills further such as assessments, coaching, role play, or action learning. In looking at many of these business schools, it appears that there is less of an emphasis on undergraduate soft skills or leadership development than there is for the MBA programs. It appears that the undergraduate emphasis of soft skills mainly occurs when students are asked to work in teams, participate in experiential learning activities inside the classroom, or take on substantial internships outside of class (Murphy & Johnson, 2011).

One of the problems noted in the article was not that these soft skills courses are new to business school curricula, but that they are not taken as seriously as the more technical courses offered in the curriculum. In fact, a few years ago one of the most often-quoted studies by organizational behavior faculty, perhaps based on a 20-year-old *Wall Street Journal* article, was that the courses in human capital and decision making that were rated as the least important to business undergraduates were rated later as the most important courses when students were surveyed after having worked for a number of years. Today many business schools package soft skills as part of effective leadership, which may be an easier sell to students, and goes hand in hand with a reframing of the notion of leadership (Murphy & Johnson, 2011). Montgomery (2008) argued that business schools treat strategic management as making economic decisions, rather than what it really entails: leadership. Leading an organization does require economic decision making, but in addition, strategic management requires a whole host of soft skills to capture and retain talent within an organization, to motivate individuals and groups to reach organizational goals, and to innovate. To achieve management concepts such as "employee buy in," "alignment," "corporate reframing," "employee engagement," and so forth requires much more than technical skills.

In reviewing what some schools are doing with respect to interpersonal skills training, we reviewed the activities of the top ten undergraduate colleges or schools of business. These included:

1. University of Pennsylvania;
2. Massachusetts Institute of Technology;
3. University of California–Berkeley,
4. University of Michigan–Ann Arbor;
5. New York University;
6. University of Virginia;
7. Carnegie Mellon;
8. University of North Carolina–Chapel Hill;
9. University of Texas–Austin;
10. Cornell University (*US News & World Report*, 2013b).

We also reviewed other schools mentioned in articles on the topic.

It was apparent that some schools placed much effort in integrating soft skills and leadership development across the curriculum as well as within co curricular activities such as internships, assessments, and coaching opportunities. For example, the Leadership Center at MIT's Sloan School of Management is an important contributor to the overall undergraduate and MBA programs. Its philosophy of leadership development uses a hands-on, action-based model that challenges students.

One of the four competencies in its overall leadership model shows that soft skills are front and center: *Relating: Developing key relationships within and across organizations.* The Leadership Center has a comprehensive focus on research and education and is staffed with affiliated faculty from the business school and personnel who specialize in professional development.

New York University's Stern School of Business has unique undergraduate programs that incorporate a broad range of interpersonal skills. For example, in the Social Impact Program sophomores take a course entitled *Organizational Communications and Its Social Context.* According to the website, this course "reiterates themes introduced in *Business and its Publics,* as you study social processes of influence and persuasion and learn how to most effectively communicate your own verbal and written messages to different audiences." At the University of Virginia McIntire School of Commerce, students are able to complete a leadership minor in addition to a more typical concentration in finance, accounting, or marketing. This program combines some background in leadership studies across disciplines as well as experiential learning through field projects and work with a faculty advisor and a mentor outside of the university. Cornell provides a unique opportunity for MBAs through the Johnson School and the Roy H. Park Leadership Fellows program, which is a two-year, full-tuition fellowship award for up to 25 students who have demonstrated outstanding leadership potential. According to the website, the program provides "A dynamic leadership development program that is among the richest leadership development experiences in any top school in scope and impact."

Cultural intelligence as a way of working well in other cultures is an important skill set for today's managers and leaders (Alon & Higgens, 2005). As noted in their article, one study found that only one third of leaders who are working abroad are considered successful leaders (Manning, 2003). There are many difficulties for managers and leaders working abroad, so many schools are focusing on ways to improve what some call cultural competence (Johnson, Lenartowicz, & Apud, 2006). For master's-level programs, AACSB standards mention that students need a capacity for operating in a global environment.

Wharton MBAs, who are multilingual, can take part in a newly launched program where, in addition to earning an MBA, they will earn an MA in a program focusing on international economics, comparative politics, diplomacy, international law, and cross-cultural negotiations and communications through the Joseph H. Lauder Institute of Management and International Studies at the University of Pennsylvania. The focus is for students to learn cross-cultural competence and analytical skills. The first class began the program in May 2013. According to the website, "The demand for MBAs with specific training in these areas is increasing and we recognize that international organizations, multinational corporations and governments want to attract MBAs who possess the requisite skills to operate in this global environment."

For undergraduates, courses on soft skills are often found under communication or business communication course offerings. At the University of Southern California, both business undergraduates and MBA students have access to cutting-edge courses in management communication such as: Developing Your Personal Brand, Communicating in Teams and with Clients, and Understanding Gender, Work, and Communication. In the course Advanced Managerial Communication, MBA students work with their professors in an "executive coaching" model that helps with interpersonal communication as well as cultural and emotional intelligence. Another course works on the communication and interpersonal skills used in being a team player and leader. For undergraduates, the courses cover many communication areas and also cross-cultural communication.

Although one would expect that business schools would have a stronger focus on soft skills than engineering and medical schools because a large part of management involves interacting with others, the technical majors in business, such as finance, economics, or information systems, dismiss the interpersonal side of their respective majors. This is evident in the lack of curricular emphasis (Rubin & Dierdorff, 2009). However, many business schools have close relationships with recruiters who provide pressure to incorporate soft skills in the curriculum. Integration may be the key to ensuring the success of soft skills and leadership offerings. For example, Yale revised its course offerings to integrate technical and human capital foci across the curriculum (Porter, 2007). In addition, a more integrated approach is helpful when developing ways to assess learning (or Assurance of Learning) as required by the accrediting body for business schools, AACSB. Following Mintzberg's (2004) advice, soft skills should be taught through experiential and applied work. He believes that practicing managers should be taught only when they have enough experience and are encouraged to learn from their own experiences, therefore, involving undergraduates and MBAs in hands-on activities is important. As he noted, no one can create a manager in a classroom.

Summary

Colleges and universities are looking for ways to increase the interpersonal acumen of their technically trained students. Many of the top schools address deficits through co curricular offerings that range from short courses to more comprehensive multi-element programs. There is wide variation in the centrality of these efforts within these schools. Although our analysis was limited to the schools' websites and other articles written about their program content, we could glean a sense of their efforts and how they used this for competitive advantage in the education marketplace. Many schools were quite clear on the importance of interpersonal skills in this regard such as Trinity's Undergraduate Department of Engineering Science description: "Our focus on teaching and design, in addition to our special attention to developing students' communication, interpersonal, and leadership skills, differentiates us from the hundreds of other engineering programs across the country."

Although the websites searched contained a description of course content, less information was given regarding methods of training. One method that appears to come up repeatedly is the use of teams. Most students have been individual contributors throughout their academic careers, and teams are an important method for learning to work with others. Whether these are classroom-based teams or those used in response to client experiences such as consulting projects in engineering, students can gain important soft skills around conflict resolution, influence, persuasion, listening, and leadership. However, not all students will have equal team experiences to draw those learning experiences. Service learning was another useful method for allowing students to learn about a topic and then apply the individual and team soft skills to serve their communities.

In what ways can these programs improve? Curricular integration of skills training may be important and ways to enhance the ways students learn from their experiences. The assessment, challenge, support model suggested by the Center for Creative Leadership may be a way to increase the effectiveness of soft skills training for these populations (Van Velsor, McCauley, & Ruderman, 2010). This process begins with the use of tools to determine an individual's strengths and weaknesses as a basis for skill development. Challenge comes from situations that demand the practice of these soft skills and can include job transitions or "stretch" assignments where a person's skills are challenged (Day, Harrison, & Halpin, 2009). Finally, support can take the form of bosses, coaches, peers, or mentors who help the person improve his or her skills. Other methods unique to particular majors could be borrowed as new ways to develop skills. For example, in medicine, the use of simulations either with computers or with robotic-typed patients allows students to experience the range of interactions they might face. Even good old-fashioned role play, job shadowing with effective role models, or other methods of training mentioned for corporate groups can work in colleges and universities.

For many of these schools one issue with teaching soft skills is the assessment of learning. In many ways, technical skills are easier to assess than soft skills. Determining whether a training course has improved social intelligences, or the ability to connect with a client or a patient, becomes more difficult; but it is not impossible. Schools can learn from the models of assessment often used in industry. Assessment centers, 360-degree surveys of soft skills, and even attitude change measures can be used to assess the impact of soft skill training programs in education.

CONCLUSION

In this chapter we have reviewed the best practices in teaching leader soft skills from industry, higher education, and the training literature. We began this chapter by noting that the nature of business has changed with the increase in service-related jobs, highlighting the importance of soft skills in today's business environment. Hiring professionals indicated that soft skills were the biggest deficit needed for organizational success (ACICS, 2011). We found that both higher education and industry training experts have seen this need and have tried to meet it with increased educational programs aimed at enhancing leader soft skills. Engineering schools, medical schools, and business schools have ramped up their focus on teaching soft skills with programs like LeaderShape in Cornell's Engineering Program, the IERC and AHC Simulation Center at University of Minnesota's Medical School, Social Intelligence Training at Columbia's Business school, or the emotional, social, and cognitive competences developed for MBAs at Case Western Reserve University (Boyatzis, Passarelli, & Wei, this volume). Most of the top 10 engineering, medical, and business schools offer some type of training in leadership and soft skills. Similarly, it is estimated that half of organizational training budgets are used for interpersonal skills development (*US Banker,* 2000), and the number of internal and external consulting programs focused on leader soft skills continues to grow. All of the top leadership training companies that we reviewed offered some type of training in leader soft skills.

Despite recognition of the need for leader soft skills training, the efficacy of such programs often goes untested. In "The Myth of Soft-Skills Training," Georges (1996) suggests that there is often a lack of demonstrable results from soft skills training because programs focus on "education," or the imparting of knowledge, rather than "training," or practicing to increase skill proficiency. In our review of the best practices of top leadership training companies, there was a strong focus on practice, coaching, and feedback as methods to develop leader soft skills. Of course, we only reviewed the top programs. We would suggest that other programs heed this advice and ensure that the training of leader soft skills goes beyond typical classroom instruction and allows leaders to observe, practice, and receive feedback on their soft skills. This advice is particularly relevant for educational programs, where classroom learning is most often the norm.

Leader soft skills are highly relevant and highly teachable. By utilizing the best practices reviewed here, schools and companies can develop these often-deficient skills and maximize leader effectiveness. Of course, like the industry experts, we agree that leader development (and leader soft skill development) is a lifelong process rather than a one-time event, and unlike other types of training, requires self-management on the part of the leader to continue developing and demonstrating effective interpersonal skills in daily interactions. A lack of leader soft skills relates to leader derailment among upper management positions (Lombardo, Ruderman, & McCauley, 1988), suggesting that leaders must continue to work to maintain their soft skills or risk their careers. Executive coaching and continuous feedback should aid in the continued development and demonstration of leader soft skills.

REFERENCES

2012 top 20 leadership training companies. (2012). Retrieved September 3, 2012, from http://www.trainingindustry.com/leadership/top-companies-listings/2012/2012-top-20-leadership-training-companies.aspx.

AAMC (2011, November). *Behavioral and social science foundations for future physicians.* Retrieved from https://www.aamc.org/download/271020/data/behavioralandso cialsciencefoundationsforfuturephysicians.pdf.

ABET (2012). Criteria for accrediting engineering schools. Retrieved from http://www.abet .org/DisplayTemplates/DocsHandbook.aspx?id=3149.

ACGME (2005). *Advancing education in interpersonal and communication Skills: An education resource of ACGME outcome project.* American Council of Graduate Medical Education Chicaco, IL.

ACICS (2011). *Survey of hiring decision makers.* Accrediting Council for Independent Colleges and Schools (ACICS). Retrieved from http://www.acics.org/events/content .aspx?id=4718 Washington, DC.

Adler, H.M. (2002). The sociophysiology of caring in the doctor-patient relationship. *J Gen Intern Med, 17,* 883–890.

Alon, I., & Higgens, J.M. (2005). Global leadership success through emotional and cultural intelligences. *Business Horizons, 48,* 501–512.

AMA (2012). MEDed Online. New report calls for advancing the art of medicine in medical education. http://www.ama-assn.org/ama/pub/meded/2012-february/2012-february .shtml.

American Society for Training and Development (ASTD) (2000, February). Shareholders reap what you sow. *Training and Development Journal, 16.*

Arthur, Jr., W., Bennett, Jr., W., Edens, P.S., & Bell, S.T. (2003). Effectiveness of training in organizations: A meta-analysis of design and evaluation features. *Journal of Applied Psychology, 88*(2), 234.

Austen, J. (1813/1980). *Pride and prejudice.* Franklin Center, PA: The Franklin Library.

Baldwin, T.T. (1992). Effects of alternative modeling strategies on outcomes of interpersonal-skills training. *Journal of Applied Psychology, 77*(2), 147–154.

Baron, L., & Morin, L. (2010). The impact of executive coaching on self-efficacy related to management soft-skills. *Leadership & Organization Development Journal, 31*(1), 18–38.

Beard, R.L., Salas, E., & Prince, C. (1995). Enhancing transfer of training: Using role-play to foster teamwork in the cockpit. *The International Journal of Aviation Psychology, 5*(2), 131–143.

Bernard M. Gordon–MIT Engineering Leadership Program (2011, June). Capabilities of effective engineering leaders (Version 3.6). Retrieved from http://web.mit.edu/gordonelp /leadershipcapabilities.pdf.

Bright, B. (2004, September 28). Doctors' interpersonal skills are valued more than training. *The Wall Street Journal.* Retrieved from http://online.wsj.com/article /SB109630288893728881.html.

Burke, M.J., & Day, R.R. (1986). A cumulative study of the effectiveness of managerial training. *Journal of Applied Psychology, 71*(2), 232.

Bushweller, K. (1997). Teaching to the test. *American School Board Journal, 184*(9), 20–25.

Cunningham, J.B., & Lischeron, J. (1991). Defining entrepreneurship. *Journal of Small Business Management, 29*(1), 45–61.

Day, D.V., Harrison, M.M., & Halpin, S.M. (2009). *An integrative approach to leader development: Connecting adult development, identity, and expertise.* New York: Psychology Press.

Deloitte CFO Journal (2012, August 7). CFOs see growing demand for soft skills, more stress from company performance. *Wall Street Journal.* Retrieved from http://deloitte.wsj .com/cfo/2012/08/07/cfos-see-growing-demand-for-soft-skills-more-stress-from-company-performance/.

DeRue, D. S., & Wellman, N. (2009). Developing leaders via experience: The role of developmental challenge, learning orientation, and feedback availability. *Journal of Applied Psychology, 94*(4), 859.

Ferris, G. R., Witt, L. A., & Hochwarter, W. A. (2001). Interaction of social skill and general mental ability on job performance and salary. *Journal of Applied Psychology, 86*, 1075–1082.

Foxon, M. (1993). A process approach to the transfer of training. Part 1: The impact of motivation and supervisor support on transfer maintenance. *Australian Journal of Educational Technology, 9*(2), 130–143.

Georgenson, D. L. (1982). The problem of transfer calls for partnership. *Training and Development Journal, 36*(10), 75–78.

Georges, J. C. (1996). The myth of soft-skills training. *Training, 33*(1), 48–50.

Giber, D., Lam, S., Goldsmith, M., & Bourke, J. (2009). *Linkage Inc.'s best practices in leadership development handbook* (2nd ed.). San Francisco, CA: Pfeiffer.

Goldstein, A. P., & Sorcher, M. (1974). *Changing supervisor behavior.* Pergamon Oxford, UK.

Harris, G. (2011, July 10). New for aspiring doctors, the people skills test. *The New York Times.* Retrieved from http://www.nytimes.com/2011/07/11/health/policy/11docs .html?_r=2&emc=eta1&

Hartman, J. L., & McCambridge, J. (2011). Optimizing millennials' communication styles. *Business Communication Quarterly, 74*(1), 22–44.

Henderson, R. (2012). Employment outlook: 2010–2020—Industry employment and output projections to 2020. *Monthly Labor Review, 135*(1), 65–83.

Hickson, G. B., Federspiel, C. F., Pichert, J. W., Miller, C. S., Gauld-Jaeger, J., & Bost, P. (2002). *Journal of the American Medical Association, 287*(22), 2951–2957.

Holsbrink-Engels, G. A. (1997). Computer-based role-playing for interpersonal skills training. *Simulation & Gaming, 28*(2), 164–180.

Hoojiberg, R., & Schneider, M. (2001). Behavioral complexity and social intelligence: How executive leaders use stakeholders to form a systems perspective. In S. J. Zaccaro & R. Klimoski (Eds.), *The nature of organizational leadership: Understanding the performance imperatives confronting today's leaders* (pp. 104–131). San Francisco, CA: Jossey-Bass.

Johnson, J. P., Lenartowicz, T., & Apud, S. (2006). Cross-cultural competence in international business: Toward a definition and a model. *Journal of International Business Studies, 37*, 525–543.

Kahai, S. (2013). Leading in a digital age: What's different, issues raised, and what we know. In M. Bligh & R. Riggio (Eds.), *Exploring distance in leader-follower relationships: When near is far and far is near* (pp. 63–108). New York: Routledge.

Kim, K. H. (2011). The creativity crisis: The decrease in creative thinking scores on the Torrance Tests of Creative Thinking. *Creativity Research Journal, 23*, 285–295.

Kirkpatrick, D. L. (1994). *Evaluating training programs: The four levels.* San Francisco, CA: Berrett-Koehler.

Klaus, P. (2010). Communication breakdown. *California Job Journal, 28*, 1–9.

Klein, C. R. (2009). *What do we know about interpersonal skills? A meta-analytic examination of antecedents, outcomes, and the efficacy of training* (PhD dissertation). Proquest Dissertations and Theses database. (UMI No. 3357877)

Klein, C., DeRouin, R. E., & Salas, E. (2006). Uncovering workplace interpersonal skills: A review, framework, and research agenda. *International Journal of Industrial and Organizational Psychology, 21*, 79–126.

Klein, C., DiazGranados, D., Salas, E., Le, H., Burke, C.S., Lyons, R., & Goodwin, G.F. (2009). Does team building work? *Small Group Research, 40*(2), 181–222.

Knowles, M.S. (1990). *The adult learner: A neglected species.* Houston, TX: Gulf.

Knowles, M.S., Holton, E.F., III, & Swanson, R.A. (2005). *The adult learner: The definitive classic in adult education and human resource development.* Woburn, MA: Butterworth-Heineman.

Korn, M., & Light, J. (2011, June 7). On the lesson plan: Feelings. *The Wall Street Journal.* Retrieved from http://online.wsj.com/article/SB10001424052748704740604576301491797067346.html.

Kraiger, K. (2002). Decision-based evaluation. In K. Kraiger (Ed.), *Creating, implementing, and maintaining effective training and development: State-of-the-art lessons for practice* (pp. 331–375). San Francisco, CA: Jossey-Bass.

Kraiger, K., Ford, J.K., & Salas, E. (1993). Application of cognitive, skill-based, and affective theories of learning outcomes to new methods of training evaluation. *Journal of Applied Psychology, 78,* 311–328.

Kupritz, V.W. (2002). The relative impact of workplace design on training transfer. *Human Resource Development Quarterly, 13*(4), 427–447.

Laker, D.R., & Powell, J.L. (2011). The differences between hard and soft skills and their relative impact on training transfer. *Human Resource Development Quarterly, 22*(1), 111–122.

Latham, G.P., & Frayne, C.A. (1989). Self-management training for increasing job attendance: a follow-up and a replication. *Journal of Applied Psychology, 74,* 411–416.

Levinson, W., & Pizzo, P.A. (2011). Patient-physician communication: It's about time. *Journal of the American Medical Association, 305,* 1802–1803.

Lievens, F. (2013). Adjusting medical school admission: Assessing interpersonal skills using situational judgment tests. *Med Educ., 47*(2), 182–189.

Lombardo, M.M., Ruderman, M.N., & McCauley, C.D. (1988). Explanations of success and derailment in upper-level management positions. *Journal of Business and Psychology, 2*(3), 199–216.

Manning, T.T. (2003). Leadership across cultures: Attachment style influences. *Journal of Leadership & Organizational Studies, 9*(3), 20–30.

May, G.L., & Kahnweiler, W.M. (2000). The effect of a mastery practice design on learning and transfer in behavior modeling training. *Personnel Psychology, 53*(2), 353–373.

McCall, Jr., M.W., Lombardo, M.M., & Morrison, A.M. (1988). *The lessons of experience.* Lexington, MA: Lexington Press.

McCauley, C.D., Ruderman, M.N., Ohlott, P.J., & Morrow, J.E. (1994). Assessing the developmental components of managerial jobs. *Journal of Applied Psychology, 79*(4), 544.

Mintzberg, H. (2004). *Managers not MBAs: A hard look at the soft practices of managing and management development.* San Francisco, CA: Berrett Koehler.

Montgomery, C.A. (2008). Putting leadership back into strategy. *Harvard Business Review, 86*(1), 54–61.

Morahan, P.S., Kasperbauer, D., McDade, S.A., Aschenbrener, C.A., Triólo, P.K., Monteleone, P.L., Counte, M., & Meyer, M.J. (1998). Training future leaders of academic medicine: Internal programs at three academic health centers. *Academic Medicine, 73*(1), 1159–1168.

Mountford, J., & Webb, C. (2009, February). When clinicians lead. *The McKinsey Quarterly.* Retrieved from http://www.mckinseyquarterly.com/When_clinicians_lead_2293?

Munson, L.J., Phillips, G., Clark, G.C., & Mueller-Hanson, R. (2004). Everything you need to know about I-O internships: Results from the 2003 SIOP internship survey. *The Industrial-Organizational Psychologist, 42,* 117–126.

Murphy, S. E., & Johnson, S. K. (2011). Leadership research and education: How business schools approach leadership. In M. Harvey & R. Riggio (Eds.), *Leadership studies: The dialogue of discipline* (pp. 129–148). London: Edward Elgar.

Murphy, S. E., & Reichard, R. J. (Eds.) (2011). *Early development and leadership: Building the next generation of leaders.* New York: Psychology Press/Routledge.

National Coalition on Healthcare (2011, September 12). *Health Sector Economic Indicators Reports.* Retrieved from http://nchc.org/node/1171.

National Coalition on Healthcare (2013). *Homepage coalition members.* Retrieved http://nchc.org/issue-areas/cost.

Nichols, S. P., & Armstrong, N. E. (2003). Engineering entrepreneurship: Does entrepreneurship have a role in engineering education? *IEEE Antennas and Propagation Magazine, 45*(1), 134–138.

Phillips, J. J., & Phillips, P. (2007). Measuring return on investment in leadership development. In K. M. Hannum, J. W. Martineau, & C. Reinelt (Eds.), *The handbook of leadership development evaluation* (pp. 137–166). Hoboken, NJ: Wiley.

Porter, J. (2007, August 2). B-schools soft on "soft skills." *Business Week.* Retrieved from http://www.businessweek.com/stories/2007–08–02/b-schools-soft-on-soft-skills-businessweek-business-news-stock-market-and-financial-advice.

Quacquarelli, N. (2011). *QS top MBA job & salary trends 2010/11.* Retrieved from http://www.topmba.com/articles/general/soft-skills-demand-say-mba-recruiters.

Reichard, R. J., & Johnson, S. K. (2011). Leader self-development as organizational strategy. *Leadership Quarterly, 22*, 33–42.

Roter, D. (1997). Communication patterns of primary care physicians. *Journal of the American Medical Association, 277*, 350–356.

Rubin, R. S., & Dierdorff, E. C. (2009). How relevant is the MBA? Assessing the alignment of required curricula and required managerial competencies. *Academy of Management Learning and Education, 8*(2), 208–224.

Rubin, R. S., & Dierdorff, E. C. (2011). On the road to Abilene: Time to manage agreement about MBA curricular relevance. *The Academy of Management Learning and Education, 10*(1), 148–161.

Salas, E., Burke, C. S., Bowers, C. A., & Wilson, K. A. (2001). Team training in the skies: Does crew resource management (CRM) training work?. *Human Factors: The Journal of the Human Factors and Ergonomics Society, 43*(4), 641–674.

Salas, E., Burke, C. S., & Cannon-Bowers, J. A. (2001). What we know about designing and delivering team training: tips and guidelines. In K. Kraiger, *Creating, implementing, and managing effective training and development: State-of-the-art lessons for practice* (pp. 234–261). San Francisco, CA: Jossey-Bass.

Smith-Jentsch, K. A., Griffin, A., & Onyejiaka, U. U. (2006). Empirical support for a new approach to computer-based simulation. Poster presented at the 21st Annual Conference of the Society for Industrial and Organizational Psychology, Dallas, TX.

Stanford University Engineering (2013). Retrieved from http://engineering.stanford.edu/education.

Ten best companies for leaders: How focusing on leadership development creates a competitive advantage (2012). Retrieved from http://chiefexecutive.net/top-10-best-companies-for-leaders-2012-slideshow.

Thompson, L. L. (2007). *Making the team: A guide for managers* (2nd ed.). Upper Saddle River, NJ: Pearson Prentice Hall.

Tews, M.J., & Tracey, J.B. (2008). An empirical examination of posttraining on-the-job supplements for enhancing the effectiveness of interpersonal skills training. *Personnel Psychology, 61*(2), 375–401.

US Banker (2000). Hard lessons in soft skills. *US Banker, 110,* 44–47.

US News & World Report (2012). Best schools of medicine—primary care. Retrieved http://grad-schools.usnews.rankingsandreviews.com/best-graduate-schools /top-medical-schools/primary-care-rankings.

US News & World Report (2013a). Best undergraduate engineering programs ranking. http:// colleges.usnews.rankingsandreviews.com/best-colleges/rankings/engineering-doctorate.

US News & World Report (2013b). Best undergraduate business program ranking. Retrieved from http://colleges.usnews.rankingsandreviews.com/best-colleges/rankings/business -overall.

Van Velsor, E., McCauley, C., & Ruderman, M. (2010). *The Center for Creative Leadership handbook of leadership development.* New York: John Wiley & Sons.

Appendix A

TrainingIndustry.com's 2012 Top 20 Leadership Training Companies List
(not ranked, in alphabetical order)

1. AchieveGlobal
2. American Management Association International
3. BTS
4. Center for Creative Leadership
5. Dale Carnegie Training
6. DDI
7. Disney Institute
8. Duke Corporate Education
9. eCornell
10. Forum Corporation
11. FranklinCovey Co.
12. Hemsley Fraser
13. Impact International
14. InsideOut Development
15. Interaction Associates
16. Kenexa
17. Linkage
18. Skillsoft
19. The Ken Blanchard Companies
20. Wilson Learning Corporation

ChiefExecutive.net's 2012 Best Companies for Leaders (ranked)

1. Procter & Gamble
2. IBM
3. General Electric
4. 3M
5. Southwest Airlines
6. ADP
7. PepsiCo
8. Cardinal Health
9. Caterpillar
10. Discovery Communication

13

Developing Emotional, Social, and Cognitive Competencies in MBA Programs

A Twenty-Five Year Perspective

Richard E. Boyatzis, Angela Passarelli, and Hongguo Wei

The bottom line of management education is retained learning. Our mission is to develop our students so that they can enter, reenter, or continue in the workforce and be more effective as managers, leaders, or professionals. In the process, we hope they become productive citizens of the world, family, and community members. Developing as managers, leaders, and professionals includes: (1) acquiring knowledge; (2) learning to effectively use that knowledge; and (3) discovering why one is driven to use one's knowledge and competencies.

Acquiring knowledge is development of functional, declarative, procedural, and meta-cognitive knowledge needed to manage and lead. Market segmentation for a new products or international exchange rates or calculating the present value of a capital acquisition or ethical principles in international business transactions are these types of knowledge, respectively. Knowledge is necessary but not sufficient for the leader, manager, or professional to be effective (Boyatzis, 1982, 2008; Goleman, 1998; Spencer & Spencer). Although we believe knowledge can be acquired with relative ease in days, weeks, or months, it can be lost just as quickly. Specht and Sandlin (1991) showed that the half-life of accounting knowledge from the introductory accounting course in a top-ranked MBA program was six and a half weeks.

To be an effective leader, manager, or professional, a person needs to use knowledge and to make things happen. These capabilities can be called competencies, which Boyatzis (1982) defined as "the underlying characteristics of a person that lead to or cause effective and outstanding performance." Competencies are the behavioral level of emotional intelligence (Boyatzis, 2009; Cherniss & Boyatzis, this volume) and have been shown empirically to cause or predict outstanding leader, manager, or professional performance in the literature (Boyatzis, 1982, 2008; Boyatzis, Massa, & Good, 2012; Bray, Campbell, & Grant, 1974; Druskat, Mount, & Sala, 2005; Howard & Bray, 1988; Kotter, 1982; Luthans, Hodgetts, & Rosenkrantz, 1988; Thornton & Byham, 1982; also see special issue of the *Journal of Management Development* in February 2008 on "Competencies in the 21st Century" (Boyatzis, editor); special issue of the *Journal of Management Development* in April, 2009 on "Competencies in the EU" (Boyatzis, editor); special issue of the *Journal of Cross-Cultural Management*, 2012, "Emotional and Social Intelligence Competencies: Cross Cultural Implications" (Emmerling and Boyatzis, editors)). Conceptual syntheses have also shown this relationship to effectiveness (Campbell, Dunnette, Lawler, & Weick, 1970; Goleman, 1998; Spencer & Spencer, 1993).

Synthesizing this prior work, these competencies appear in three clusters: (1) cognitive intelligence (CI) competencies, such as systems thinking and pattern recognition; (2) emotional intelligence (EI) competencies, such as adaptability, emotional self-control, emotional self-awareness, positive outlook, and achievement orientation; and (3) social intelligence (SI) competencies, such as empathy, organizational awareness, inspirational leadership, influence, coaching and mentoring, conflict management, and teamwork. Several other cognitive capabilities appear to be threshold competencies from the research cited earlier. They are needed to be adequate, but more use of them does not lead to effectiveness. Given research to date, these would include knowledge (technical and functional), deductive reasoning, and quantitative reasoning.

Beyond knowledge and competencies, the desire to use one's talent seems driven by a person's values, philosophy, sense of calling or mission, unconscious motives, and traits (Boyatzis & Sala, 2004; Cherniss & Boyatzis, this volume). These motives and traits affect the way a person sees the world, especially the perception of opportunities and challenges they perceive in the environment (McClelland, 1985). But they also are persistent and generalized drivers. They arouse dispositional ways a person responds to his or her environment and create a focus for a person's behavior (McClelland, 1985).

Knowledge, competencies, and motivational drivers help us to understand *what* a person can do (i.e., knowledge), *how* a person can do it (i.e., competencies), and *why* a person feels the need to do it (i.e., values, motives, and unconscious dispositions). Our role in management education is to help people develop the what, how, and why in order to move toward greater effectiveness in their future jobs and careers.

In order to add value, educators must motivate and engage students in learning, beginning with exploring new possibilities. But the history of sustained change from graduate programs is dismal, and often appears to have less impact than corporate training (Boyatzis, 2008). One key to increase impact is the observation that most sustained behavioral change is intentional. Intentional change is a desired change in an aspect of who you are (i.e., the Real) or who you want to be (i.e., the Ideal), or both. The process of intentional change is shown in Figure 13.1 (Boyatzis, 2008; Boyatzis & McKee, 2005).

Intentional Change Theory (ICT) describes the essential components and processes that encourage sustained, desired change to occur in a person's behaviors, thoughts, feelings, and/or perceptions (Boyatzis, 2008). Drawing on the properties of complex, nonlinear processes (O'Boyle & Aguinis, 2012), the theory includes five phases or discontinuities called

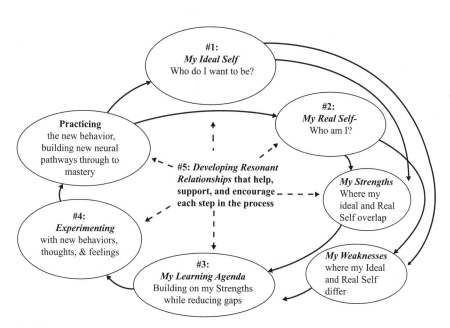

FIGURE 13.1
Boyatzis's Intentional Change Theory (Boyatzis, 2001, 2008)

"discoveries" (Boyatzis, 2008; Goleman, Boyatzis, & McKee, 2002). The five phases include: (1) the ideal self or personal vision; (2) the real self or personal balance sheet; (3) creation of a learning agenda and plan; (4) experimentation and practice with new behaviors, thoughts, or feelings outlined in the learning plan; and (5) trusting, resonant relationships that support a person's development experience.

The discovery of a person's deepest aspirations for life is his or her *ideal self*. There are three major components of the ideal self or personal vision: (1) an image of a desired future; (2) hope that one can attain it; and (3) inclusion of one's core identity, which serves as a foundation upon which to build the desired image (Boyatzis & Akrivou, 2006). The ideal self is quite different from the "ought self" in which others impose their image of what the ideal should be (Boyatzis, 2008; Higgins, 1987). Positive imaging or visioning in sports psychology, meditation, and biofeedback research and other psycho physiological research has shown that focusing one's thoughts on the desired state or condition is driven by the emotional components of the brain (Boyatzis & McKee, 2005).

The *real self* is the person that others see and with whom they interact. It includes a person's own perceptions, or self-assessment. This discovery involves a personal assessment of one's strengths and weaknesses that serves as a basis for creating a personal balance sheet. Ego-defense mechanisms serve to protect us and conspire to delude us into an image of whom we are that may become self-perpetuating, and even dysfunctional (Goleman, 1985).

The third discovery is development of a *learning agenda*, which encompasses the individual's personal vision, learning goals, and actions. It guides a person to his or her desired future. To maximize the benefits of a positive psychophysiological state and the desire to seek possibilities, a learning agenda should place greater emphasis on the development process itself and less on discrete outcomes such as improved performance or greater fulfillment at work (Boyatzis & Howard, in press). It differs from a traditional development plan by focusing on a learning orientation rather than a performance orientation. A learning orientation arouses a positive belief in one's capability and the hope of improvement. Contrary to a learning orientation, a performance orientation often evokes anxiety and doubts about whether or not change is possible or even desired (Chen, Gully, Whiteman, & Kilcullen, 2000). An agenda that is learning focused can be achieved by connecting elements of one's ideal self to broad learning goals and specific intended actions.

The fourth discovery is *experimentation and practice* with new thoughts, feelings, perceptions, and behavior. This stage involves taking risks to develop new behavioral "habits." Experimentation and practice is most effective when it occurs in conditions in which the person feels safe (Kolb & Boyatzis, 1970). This sense of psychological safety creates an atmosphere in which the person can try new behaviors, perceptions, and thoughts with relatively low risk of shame, embarrassment, or serious consequences of failure. One source of safety is the resonant relationships that form a secure foundation in attachment theory terms (Bowlby, 1988).

Learning from ongoing experiences at school or elsewhere is the key— not taking more courses. The process of translating practice into effective learning occurs by trying something new in the context of everyday school, work, and life, extracting the best of what worked from the experience through reflection and intentional planning with a commitment to further experimentation. During this part of the process, intentional change looks and feels like a "continuous improvement" process.

Our relationships are an essential part of our environment. These relationships and groups give us a sense of identity (i.e., social identity groups), guide us as to what is appropriate and good behavior, and provide feedback on our behavior. These relationships create a context within which we interpret our progress on desired changes, the utility of new learning, and even contribute significant input to formulation of the ideal self (Kram, 1996).

Social identity groups and our most salient relationships both mediate and moderate our sense of who we are and who we want to be. We develop or elaborate our ideal self in these conversations. We label and interpret our real self from others' reactions. Our relationships are sources of feedback, support, and permission for the learning we seek. They may also be the most important source of protection from relapses. Wheeler (2008) analyzed the extent to which MBA graduates worked on their goals in multiple "life spheres" (i.e., work, family, recreational groups, etc.). In a two-year follow-up study of two graduating classes of part-time MBA students, she found those who worked on their goals and plans in multiple sets of relationships improved the most and to a greater degree than those working on goals in only one setting, such as work or within one relationship.

The process of experiencing sustained desired change is an iterative, cyclical process. Using complexity theory, the process of development engages the cycle through two self-organizing properties of the human organism. Two attractors are the Positive Emotional Attractor (PEA) and the Negative

Emotional Attractor (NEA) (Boyatzis, in press). According to ICT, the dis-equilibrium occurs through tipping points between the PEA and NEA. The PEA pulls a person toward his or her Ideal Self. It includes arousal of the Para-sympathetic Nervous System (PNS) (Boyatzis, Smith, & Blaize, 2006). Once the PNS is aroused, the person is cognitively, perceptually, and emotionally open and working at his or her best. In this state, a person experiences neuro-genesis (i.e., the conversion of hippocampal stem cells into new neurons). It is even suggested that formation of learning goals or learning-oriented goals works from this attractor and results in more successful change (Boyatzis & Howard, in press).

The other attractor is the NEA. It includes arousal of the Sympathetic Nervous System (SNS), which helps the human deal with threat and protect itself. The NEA pulls a person toward defensive positions. In this state, the body shunts blood to the large muscle groups, closes down nonessential neural circuits, suspends the immune system, and produces cortisol—important for protection under threat (Boyatzis et al., 2006). But cortisol inhibits neurogenesis and overexcites older neurons, rendering them useless (Boyatzis et al., 2006).

ACTIVATING THE POSITIVE EMOTIONAL ATTRACTOR

Throughout the course and supportive work afterward, the focus for the coaches, faculty, and staff is to arouse, activate, or pull students into the PEA. Although we need the NEA to survive, we need the PEA to thrive. The PEA allows us to be more cognitively, perceptually, and emotionally open to new ideas and people. It allows us to consider new possibilities. In the already heavily stress-laden coursework and job worries inherent in any MBA pro-gram, the students need a heavy dose of PEA to keep learning. Otherwise, they go into defensive mode, shorten their time horizon, and think about passing tests and courses instead of learning and developing new talents.

Those of us helping students, including other students, can increase our effectiveness by being mindful of the differences between arousing the PEA and NEA. Differences are shown in Table 13.1.

There are themes or topics in each of the stages of ICT that encourage the PEA. Drawing on positive emotions research, it is believed that we must over-sample the PEA in a ratio from 3:1 to 6:1 to maintain a balance of openness

TABLE 13.1

Two Attractors

	Positive Emotional Attractor	**Negative Emotional Attractor**
Neuroendocrine	PNS Arousal	SNS Arousal
Affect	Positive	Negative
Ideal Self	Possibilities, dreams, optimism, hope	Problems, expectations, pessimism, fear
Real Self	Strengths	Weaknesses
Learning Agenda	Excited about trying	Should do, performance improvement plan
Experiment	Novelty, experiments	Actions expected, things you are supposed to do
Practice	Practice to mastery	Practice to comfort
Relationships	Resonant	Dissonant or annoying

Source: Adapted from Boyatzis (in press).

and the useful stresses of adapting and growing (Fredrickson & Losada, 2005; Gottman, Murray, Swanson, Tyson, & Swanson, 2002; Losada & Heaphy, 2004). Because there will be so many NEA-inducing experiences in students' lives, it is part of the responsibility of the faculty and staff to create opportunities and encounters where students will have a chance to remind themselves that they are in school to pursue and achieve their dream (not merely get a diploma or a job). We can remind them that they have strengths, not just weaknesses. We can encourage students to experiment with new behavior, attitudes, feelings, and thoughts. We can provide a secure foundation of relationships to insure that they feel we care.

USING ICT TO DEVELOP COMPETENCIES

Drawing on ICT as a theoretical framework and with careful attention to an optimal balance of PEA and NEA experiences, educators can create the conditions to support the sustained development of emotional and social competencies. At the Weatherhead School of Management, a leadership course was created and implemented in 1990 using this approach. It was based on developing the "whole person" with the underlying philosophy that adult sustainable behavioral change has to be intentional. One of the core courses in the MBA curriculum, Leadership Assessment and Development (LEAD), is designed with five benchmarks: (1) a personal vision, emerging from Discovery #1; (2) a personal balance sheet, emerging from Discovery #2; (3) coaching sessions with a specially trained professional coach, emerging from Discovery #5; (4) a learning agenda, emerging from Discovery #3; and (5) development of new social identity groups, including peer groups and a personal board of directors, emerging from Discovery #5, as shown in Figure 13.1. Short-term opportunities for practice and experimentation, Discovery #4, are embedded in course activities such as group work and discussions. However, the majority of practice and experimentation occurs within the individual's own life context.

The first component is devoted to helping the MBA develop his or her personal vision, including the search for the most meaningful and appropriate job and career for him or her situated in his or her desired life context. The specific assignment from a typical syllabus for the course is shown in Figure 13.2. As you can see, the development of personal vision requires extensive reflection, writing and rewriting, a comprehensive examination of one's dreams, and talking about the emerging vision with a specially trained coach on our staff and peers. Recent fMRI studies are revealing that the PEA conversation with a coach is an essential part of the process (Boyatzis, Jack, Cesaro, Passarelli, & Khawaja, 2010; Boyatzis et al., 2012). The discussion of a future-looking dream with someone trained to bring students into the PEA and try to keep them there activates neural circuits needed for openness to new ideas and contemplating possibilities.

Once a personal vision is created and discussed, the student is ready for the more stressful assessment and feedback. Originally, we used a wide array of assessments, including audiotaped critical incident interviews of work samples (encoded by trained coders), videotapes of group simulations, and self-assessment and informant assessment of competencies questionnaires. Since 2000, we have been using a multisource feedback instrument called the Emotional and Social Competency Inventory—University version (ESCI-U) or one of its earlier versions (Wolff, 2007). Observed data is collected to provide feedback on how others see the person's EI, SI, and CI competencies in action. Following receipt of the results, the student works alone, with other students, and then with his or her coach to develop a personal balance sheet, as described in detail in Figure 13.2.

Discovery #1: Graded Assignment: My Personal Vision

The objective of this paper is for you to present an image of your desired future. In developing the paper, you should use your responses to the exercises from chapter 4 of the *Becoming a Resonant Leader* workbook. The paper should have the following three sections plus a one-page vision statement summary. The approximate number of pages expected for a double-spaced discussion of each section are indicated in brackets following the item.

(1) My values, and philosophy [3–4 pages];
(2) My dreams and calling [3–4 pages];
(3) My career and life aspirations [3–4 pages]; and
(4) My Personal Vision Statement. [1 page]

In the "My values and philosophy" section, describe your values and your philosophy from the My Values exercise and the Philosophical Orientation Questionnaire. Articulate what is most important to you in life and explore the origins of your values. Examine the links and consistency or inconsistency between these elements.

In the "My dreams and calling" section, explore your dreams and fantasies. Look for themes or patterns among them as to what is really important to you. Also explore your purpose in life, legacy, or "calling."

In the "My career and life aspirations" section, you will be integrating the thoughts from the previous two sections into a specific image and direction for your life and career. In describing your career aspirations, please describe long-term possibilities beyond 5 to 10 years. If your desired and/or predicted image of your career over the next 7 to 10 years involves a sequence of jobs and moves, please describe them and your rationale for this being the desired or likely sequence. If you are not sure, but have identified two or more desired paths, please feel free to elaborate each one. Regarding the life aspirations, please describe your desired lifestyle, including a description of the type of person you want to be.

The "My Personal Vision Statement" page should be a concisely stated, one-page summary of your vision that brings together the most important elements from the above sections. It should be something that could conceivably be laminated and used as a motivational tool and consistent reminder of your vision for the future.

Discovery #2: Assignment due Prior to the Second Coaching Session: Developing a Personal Balance Sheet

Through diagnosis of your current competency strengths and gaps related to leadership, this assignment is part of the preparation for the one-on-one coaching session with your assigned master coach.

This analysis will follow receiving the results from the 360-degree assessment or by analyzing your other information. A crucial aspect of development is to collect observations about our behavior from others—what they see us doing and how it affects them. This need has given rise to a popular use of questionnaires in organizations these days, called a 360-degree assessment. In this process, you ask people with whom you work to complete a questionnaire about a variety of behaviors and the frequency with which you use them. In our programs at WSOM, we have extended this to include asking for information, if appropriate, from your spouse or partner, siblings, friends, classmates, and clients or customers.

To create your Personal Balance Sheet, this analysis should identify:

(1) A list of your distinctive strengths—competencies others consistently see you as using. You can include behaviors and habits that are not on our list of competencies but important to you or your life/work (Strengths or Assets);

(2) A list of the competencies that appear to be needed for effective leadership or are important for your life/work, but there are consistent views from others that you are not using sufficiently (Gaps or Liabilities);

(3) You should look for themes or patterns that explain the observed data across competencies—for Strengths as well as Gaps.

Discovery #3: Assignment due: Outline of Learning Goals

The assignment for the last residency is to draft a few (ideally three to five) major learning goals for discussion in class and in your final coaching practice activity.

Identifying and constructing learning goals should not be a simple one-to-one correspondence to developmental needs or strengths. To be effective in our lives and work, a learning goal should reflect some "contextual" integration of strengths, developmental needs, and work/life benchmarks. The learning goals should be desired end states that build on your strengths and would result in achieving your desired scenario for the next era of your life.

Discovery #3: Graded Assignment due: My Learning Plan

This final assignment is the creation of your individual learning plan. The paper should have three parts: (1) Ideal Future Work/Life Scenario, (2) Major Learning Goals, which should include subgoals and action steps, and (3) An Integrated Timeline.

Identifying and constructing learning goals and subgoals should not be a simple one-to-one correspondence to developmental needs or strengths. To be effective in our lives and work, a learning goal and/or subgoal should reflect some "contextual" integration of strengths, developmental needs, and work/life benchmarks.

The learning goals should be three, four, or five (more than five will not be feasible) desired end states that build on your strengths and would result in achieving your desired scenario for the next era of your life. For this final learning plan, each learning goal will probably have two to four subgoals, sometimes called milestones or benchmarks.

Each subgoal should have two to four action steps identified that will result in reaching or achieving the subgoal. Review the action steps and address the following issues:

1. Do the goals and actions build on your strengths?
2. Will they lead you closer to your Ideal Self, life, and work?
3. Are they consistent with your learning and planning style?
4. Do they fit into the structure of your life and work?
   – What will you say "no" to or stop doing to make time for it?
   – What are the potential obstacles to doing or fulfilling each action?

The Ideal Future Work/Life Scenario section should be written in narrative form. The Learning Goals section can be in outline form (i.e., major goals, subgoals for each major goal, and action items for each subgoal).

Last should be an integrated Timeline. You should have a time chart on which you have placed all of the action steps to which you have committed. This Timeline is an important reality check on the feasibility of your action plans.

Discovery #4: No courses offered. Students are expected to enact their learning plan, which includes using in course activities as well as activities outside of courses for competency development. But no special competency courses or workshops are offered.

Discovery #5: Development of social identity groups within class and your cohort. Also, as part of the learning plan activities, you are asked to develop your personal board of directors, the people with whom you will discuss your learning plan and progress during the coming months and years. Several sessions with the coach assigned to you in class will be supplemented with several peer coaching exercises.

FIGURE 13.2
Course assignment details from a typical Masters syllabus

Each component is accompanied by a coaching session with a specially trained, professional coach as well as peer coaching. These help to create and strengthen the relationships needed for Discovery #5. In developing the Personal Balance Sheet, the coaching sessions focus on identifying and preserving their strengths while looking at a few of their gaps close to the tipping point to make progress toward their personal vision. Close to the tipping point means that to be efficacious, a person should select targets for change that are close to the frequency of behavior or level of action that would enable the person to be effective. Working on extreme weaknesses is an exercise in futility and deflates the motivation to change.

On the basis of the personal vision and personal balance sheet, students create a learning agenda. This document highlights competencies they use frequently and wish to maintain and a few on which they would like to improve during their MBA program. A key component of this assignment is the articulation of the connection between selected growth areas and one's personal vision. The details of the assignment are shown in Figure 13.2.

An observation is that this approach to competency development emphasizes the students using their day-to-day experiences to practice and develop their competencies. We do not offer special courses or workshops on the various competencies. We believe and have shown in the longitudinal data explained in the next section that a powerful, personal vision with interpersonal supports is far more important as a motivator of learning and change than courses.

To assess the development of competencies and value added of the MBA program, an Exit Assessment is required in which students take the ESCI-U 360-degree feedback in their last semester prior to graduation. In the Exit Assessment seminar, students evaluate their development of competencies, review their learning agenda, and engage in discussions of their internship or work experiences. They use this to update what work environment they would prefer and make adjustments to their personal vision and learning agenda moving forward.

ASSESSING COMPETENCY DEVELOPMENT OUTCOMES AT A PROGRAM LEVEL

Although ICT encourages individuals to regularly assess progress toward one's personal vision, few management programs systematically measure student outcomes beyond factors necessary for rankings (e.g., graduation and job placement rates). In order to test the efficacy of ICT as a theoretical framework for development of EI and SI competencies and to document the value added to graduates of ICT-based programs, an ongoing longitudinal outcome assessment is conducted at the Weatherhead School of Management. Results from this effort are shared later in this chapter, following a short history of competency assessment.

Before the humbling Porter and McKibbin (1988) report showed that MBA graduates were not fulfilling the needs of employers, the Association to Advance Collegiate Schools of Business (AACSB) started a series of outcome assessment studies in 1978. Boyatzis and Sokol (1982) showed that students' scores had significantly increased on up to 50% of the competencies assessed in two MBA programs, while Development Dimensions International (DDI) (1985) reported that students in the two MBA programs in their sample had significantly increased on 44% of the variables assessed. They also decreased significantly on 10% of the variables in the Boyatzis and Sokol study. When the overall degree of improvement in these abilities was calculated (Goleman, Boyatzis, & McKee, 2002), these studies showed about a 2% increase in emotional and social intelligence competencies in the one to two years students were in the MBA programs.

In the early 1990s, only a few management schools had conducted student-change outcome studies, comparing their graduates to their students at entry into the program (Albanese et al., 1990). Today, many schools have conducted other types of outcome studies, namely studies of their alumni or studies with employers and prospective employers. Some schools have examined the student-change from specific courses (Bigelow, 1991; Specht & Sandlin, 1991). Student-change outcome studies have been a focus in under-graduate programs (Astin, 1993; Mentkowski & Associates, 2000; Pascarella & Terenzini, 1991; Winter, McClelland, & Stewart, 1981), but still relatively little has been documented about the effects of graduate programs.

The "honeymoon effect" starts with positive change, but atrophies within months (Campbell et al., 1970). The Consortium on Research on Emotional Intelligence in Organizations found 15 programs that had improved emo-tional intelligence (Cherniss & Adler, 2000). Five of them are still offered. They reported impact on job outcomes or life outcomes (Cherniss & Adler, 2000). Published studies reporting improvement on more than one of the EI com-petencies showed an overall improvement of about 10% in the 3–18 months after training (Hand, Richards, & Slocum, 1973; Latham & Saari, 1979; Noe & Schmidt, 1986; Wexley & Memeroff, 1975; Young & Dixon, 1996).

A series of longitudinal studies underway at the Weatherhead School of Management of Case Western Reserve University have shown that people can change on this complex set of competencies that distinguish outstand-ing leaders, managers, and professions. The pattern of improvement lasted for years (Boyatzis, Baker, Leonard, Rhee, & Thompson, 1996; Boyatzis, Cowen, & Kolb, 1995; Boyatsis, Lingham, & Passarelli, 2010; Boyatzis & Saatcioglu, 2008; Boyatzis, Stubbs, & Taylor, 2002).

Four cadres of full-time MBA students graduating in 1992, 1993, 1994, and 1995 showed 47% improvement on self-awareness competencies like self-confidence and on self-management competencies such as the drive to achieve and adaptability in the one to two years prior to graduation compared to when they first entered. When it came to social awareness and relationship management skills, improvements were even greater: 75% on competen-cies such as empathy and team leadership. Along with two additional recent cohorts, those graduating in 2011 and 2012, findings reported in Boyatzis, Stubbs and Taylor (2002), Boyatzis and Saatcioglu (2008), and Boyatzis, Pas-sarelli, and Lingham (2010) are summarized in Tables 13.2 and 13.3.

Studying two cohorts of part-time MBAs, Wheeler (2008) determined that competency improvement lasted two years after they graduated. This group of students showed similar sustained improvements: 63% on EI competencies and 45% on SI competencies. In contrast, both full-time

TABLE 13.2

Summary of Statistical Significance in Competency Improvement, 1990 to 2011 (based on self-assessments)

Cluster	Competency	Pre 90	90–96	99–01	02–04	03–05	04–06	06–08	07–09	08–10	09–11	10–12
Emotional Intelligence	Emotional Self-awareness	na	na	na	na			~		✓		✓
	Emotional Self-control	na	na	✓	✓	✓	✓	✓		✓		✓
	Achievement Orientation	~	✓	✓	✓	✓	✓	✓	✓	✓		
	Adaptability	na	na	✓	✓	✓	✓	✓		✓		✓
	Positive Outlook	na	na	na	na		~	✓		✓		
Social Intelligence	Empathy	na	~	✓	✓			~				~
	Organizational Awareness	na	na	na	na		~	~	✓	✓		~
	Inspirational Leadership	na	✓	na	na	✓	✓	✓	~	~		✓
	Conflict Management	na	na	✓	✓	✓	✓					~
	Influence	na	na	✓	✓	✓	~	~	✓	~		✓
	Coach & Mentor	na	✓		✓	✓	✓					✓
	Teamwork	na	na		✓							
Cognitive Intelligence	Systems Thinking	✓	✓		✓	✓	✓	✓	✓	✓	✓	✓
	Pattern Recognition	~	✓	✓	✓	✓	✓	✓	✓	✓		✓

Source: Boyatzis, Passarelli, & Wei (in review).

na = not assessed. ~ = some evidence of improvement (near-significant, $p < .10$). ✓ = significant improvement ($p < .05$).

TABLE 13.3

Summary of Statistical Significance in Competency Improvement, 1990 to 2011 (informant assessments)

Cluster	Competency	90–96	99–01	02–04	03–05	04–06	06–08	07–09	08–10	09–11	10–12
Emotional Intelligence	Emotional Self-awareness	na	na	na	✓		✓	~	✓	✓	~
	Emotional Self-control	✓	✓	✓	✓	✓	✓		✓	✓	✓
	Achievement Orientation	✓	✓	✓	✓	✓	✓				
	Adaptability	na	✓	✓	✓	✓	~		✓	✓	✓
	Positive Outlook	na	na	na	✓	✓	~		✓		
Social Intelligence	Empathy	✓	✓	✓	✓	✓	✓	✓			
	Organizational Awareness	na	na	na							~
	Inspirational Leadership	na	na	na			✓	~	✓	~	
	Conflict Management	~	✓	✓	✓	✓	✓	✓	✓	~	
	Influence	~	✓	✓	✓	✓	✓	✓	✓	✓	~
	Coach & Mentor	~	✓	✓							
	Teamwork	✓	✓	✓	✓		~				
Cognitive Intelligence	Systems Thinking	✓	✓	✓	✓	✓	✓	✓	✓	✓	✓
	Pattern Recognition	✓	✓	✓	✓	✓	~	✓	✓	✓	✓

Source: Boyatzis, Passarelli, & Wei (in review).

Note: Data collected between 1990 and 1996 were analyzed using both informant assessments and behavior coded from critical incident interviews and video taped simulations (these were only collected during this time period).

na = not assessed. ~ = some evidence of improvement (near-significant, $p < .10$). ✓ = significant improvement ($p < .05$).

and part-time MBA students who graduated from the WSOM in 1988 and 1989 before the LEAD course was introduced showed improvement in substantially fewer of the competencies.

WHAT IF LEARNING WERE THE PURPOSE OF EDUCATION OR TRAINING?

Borrowing from the title of chapter 10 of Boyatzis, Cowen, and Kolb's (1995) book for the title of this section of this chapter, we can offer a promising answer. An MBA education or management training *can* help people develop cognitive, emotional, and social intelligence competencies needed to be outstanding managers, leaders, and professionals. We cannot use the typical pedagogy with its focus on knowledge, theory, and analysis. We must offer a balance with a more holistic pedagogy whereby students are inspired to become the best version of themselves—and encourage others to do the same.

For practitioners or educators, the major implications of this chapter are the design of effective programs. Conducting outcome research may be humbling, but it keeps you honest. Using ICT will improve the impact of an MBA or other development program in teaching people the competencies needed to be effective.

REFERENCES

Albanese, R. (chair), Bernardin, H. J., Connor, P. E., Dobbins, G. H., Ford, R. C., Harris, M. M., Licata, B. J., . . . Ulrich, D. O. (1990). *Outcome measurement and management education: An Academy of Management Task Force Report.* Presentation at the Annual Academy of Management Meeting, San Francisco.

Astin, A. W. (1993). *What matters in college? Four critical years.* San Francisco, CA: Jossey-Bass.

Bigelow, J. D. (Ed.). (1991). *Managerial skills: Explorations in practical knowledge.* Newbury Park, CA: Sage.

Bowlby, J. (1988). *A secure base: Parent-child attachment and healthy human development.* New York: Basic Books.

Boyatzis, R. E. (1982). *The competent manager: A model for effective performance.* New York: John Wiley & Sons.

Boyatzis, R. E. (2001). How and why individuals are able to develop emotional intelligence. In C. Cherniss & D. Goleman (Eds.), *The emotionally intelligent workplace: How to select for, measure, and improve emotional intelligence in individuals, groups, and organizations* (pp. 234–253). San Francisco, CA: Jossey-Bass.

Boyatzis, R. E. (2008). Leadership development from a complexity perspective. *Consulting Psychology Journal, 60*(4), 298–313.

Boyatzis, R. E. (2009). A behavioral approach to emotional Intelligence. *Journal of Management Development, 28*(9), 749–770.

Boyatzis, R. E. (in press). When pulling to the negative emotional attractor is too much or not enough to inspire and sustain outstanding leadership. In R. Burke, C. Cooper, & G. Woods (Eds.), *The fulfilling workplace: the organization's role in achieving individual and organizational health.* London: Gower.

Boyatzis, R. E., & Akrivou, K. (2006). The ideal self as a driver of change. *Journal of Management Development, 25*(7), 624–642.

Boyatzis, R. E., Cowen, S. S., & Kolb, D. A. (1995). *Innovation in professional education: Steps on a journey from teaching to learning.* San Francisco, CA: Jossey-Bass.

Boyatzis, R. E., & Howard, A. (in press). When goal setting helps and hinders sustained, desired change. In S. David, D. Clutterbuck, & D. Megginson (Eds.). *Goal setting and goal management in coaching and mentoring* Farnham, UK: Gower Publishing.

Boyatzis, R. E., Jack, A., Cesaro, R., Passarelli, A., & Khawaja, M. (2010), *Coaching with compassion: An fMRI study of coaching to the positive or negative emotional attractor,* Presented at the Annual Meeting of the Academy of Management, Montreal.

Boyatzis, R. E., Leonard, D., Rhee, K., & Wheeler, J. V. (1996). Competencies can be developed, but not the way we thought. *Capability, 2*(2), 25–41.

Boyatzis, R. E., Lingham, A., & Passarelli, A. (2010). Inspiring the development of emotional, social, and cognitive intelligence competencies in managers. In M. Rothstein & R. Burke (Eds.), *Self-management and leadership development* (pp. 62–90). Cheltenham, UK: Edward Elgar.

Boyatzis, R. E., Massa, R., & Good, D. (2012). Emotional, social and cognitive intelligence as predictors of sales leadership performance. *Journal of Leadership and Organizational Studies, 19*(2), 191–201.

Boyatzis, R. E., & McKee, A. (2005). *Resonant leadership: renewing yourself and connecting with others through mindfulness, hope, and compassion.* Boston, MA: Harvard Business School Press.

Boyatzis, R. E., Passarelli, A. M., Koenig, K., Lowe, M., Mathew, B., Stoller, J. K., & Phillips, M. (2012). Examination of the neural substrates activated in memories of experiences with resonant and dissonant leaders. *Leadership Quarterly, 23*(2), 259–272.

Boyatzis, R. E. , Passarelli, A. & Wei, H. (in review). A Study of Developing Emotional, Social, and Cognitive Competencies in 16 Cohorts of an MBA Program, Case Western Reserve University; Cleveland.

Boyatzis, R. E., & Saatcioglu, A. (2008). A twenty year view of trying to develop emotional, social and cognitive intelligence competencies in graduate management education. *Journal of Management Development, 27*(3), 92–108.

Boyatzis, R. E., & Sala, F. (2004). Assessing emotional intelligence competencies. In G. Geher (Ed.), *The measurement of emotional intelligence* (pp. 147–180). Hauppauge, NY: Nova Science.

Boyatzis, R. E., Smith, M., & Blaize, N. (2006). Developing sustainable leaders through coaching and compassion. *Academy of Management Journal on Learning and Education, 5*(1): 8–24.

Boyatzis, R. E., & Sokol, M. (1982). *A pilot project to assess the feasibility of assessing skills and personal characteristics of students in collegiate business programs.* Report to the Association to Advance Collegiate Schools of Business (St. Louis, MO).

Boyatzis, R. E., Stubbs, E. C., & Taylor, S. N. (2002). Learning cognitive and emotional intelligence competencies through graduate management education. *Academy of Management Journal on Learning and Education, 1*(2), 150–162.

Bray, D. W., Campbell, R. J., & Grant, D. L. (1974). *Formative years in business: A long term AT&T study of managerial lives.* New York: John Wiley & Sons.

Campbell, J. P., Dunnette, M. D., Lawler, E. E., III, & Weick, K. E. (1970). *Managerial behavior, performance, and effectiveness.* New York: McGraw Hill.

Chen, G., Gully, S. M., Whiteman, J. A., & Kilcullen, R. N. (2000). Examination of relationships among trait-like individual differences, state-like individual differences, and learning performance. *Journal of Applied Psychology, 85*(6), 835–847.

Cherniss, C., & Adler, M. (2000). *Promoting emotional intelligence in organizations: Make training in emotional intelligence effective.* Washington, DC: American Society of Training and Development.

Cherniss, C., & Boyatzis, R. E. (in press). Using a multi-level theory of performance based on emotional intelligence to conceptualize and develop "soft" leader skills. In R. E. Riggio and S. J. Tan (Eds.). *Leader Interpersonal and Influence Skills: The Soft Skills of Leadership.* New York, NY: Taylor and Francis.

Development Dimensions International (DDI) (1985). *Final report: Phase III.* Report to the Association to Advance Collegiate Schools of Business (St. Louis, MO).

Druskat, V., Mount, G., & Sala, F. (Eds.) (2005). *Emotional intelligence and work performance.* Mahwah, NJ: Lawrence Erlbaum.

Fredrickson, B. L., & Losada, M. (2005). Positive affect and the complex dynamics of human flourishing. *American Psychologist, 60*(7), 678–686.

Goleman, D. (1985). *Vital lies, simple truths: The psychology of self-deception.* New York: Simon and Schuster.

Goleman, D. (1998). *Working with emotional intelligence.* New York: Bantam.

Goleman, D., Boyatzis, R. E., & McKee, A. (2002). *Primal leadership: Realizing the power of emotional intelligence.* Boston, MA: Harvard Business School Press.

Gottman, J. M., Murray, J. D., Swanson, C. C., Tyson, R., & Swanson, K. R. (2002). *The mathematics of marriage: Dynamic nonlinear models.* Cambridge, MA: MIT Press.

Hand, H. H., Richards, M. D., & Slocum, J. W., Jr. (1973). Organizational climate and the effectiveness of a human relations training program. *Academy of Management Journal, 16*(2), 185–246.

Higgins, E. T. (1987). Self-discrepancy: A theory relating self and affect. *Psychological Review, 94*(3), 319–340.

Howard, A., & Bray, D. (1988). *Managerial lives in transition: Advancing age and changing times.* New York: Guilford Press.

Kolb, D. A., & Boyatzis, R. E. (1970). Goal-setting and self-directed behavior change. *Human Relations, 23*(5), 439–457.

Kotter, J. P. (1982). *The general managers.* New York: Free Press.

Kram, K. E. (1996). A relational approach to careers. In D. T. Hall (Ed.), *The career is dead: Long live the career* (pp. 132–157). San Francisco, CA: Jossey-Bass.

Latham, G. P., & Saari, L. M. (1979). Application of social-learning theory to training supervisors through behavioral modeling. *Journal of Applied Psychology, 64*(3), 239–246.

Losada, M., & Heaphy, E. (2004). The role of positivity and connectivity in the performance of business teams. *American Behavioral Scientist, 47*(6), 740–765.

Luthans, F., Hodgetts, R. M., & Rosenkrantz, S. A. (1988). *Real managers.* Cambridge, MA: Ballinger Press.

McClelland, D.C. (1985). *Human motivation.* New York: Cambridge University Press.

McKee, A., Boyatzis, R.E., & Johnston, F. (2008). *Becoming a resonant leader and renewing yourself and others.* Boston, MA: Harvard Business School Press.

Mentkowski, M., & Associates (2000). *Learning that lasts: Integrating learning, development, and performance in college and beyond.* San Francisco, CA: Jossey-Bass.

Noe, R.A., & Schmitt, N. (1986). The influence of trainee attitudes on training effectiveness: Test of a model. *Personnel Psychology, 39,* 497–523.

O'Boyle, E., & Aguinis, H. (2012). The best and the rest: Revisiting the norm of normality of individual performance. *Personnel Psychology, 65,* 79–119.

Pascarella, E.T., & Terenzini, P.T. (1991). *How college affects students: Findings and insights from twenty years of research.* San Francisco, CA: Jossey-Bass.

Porter, L., & McKibbin, L. (1988). *Management education and development: Drift or thrust into the 21st century?* New York: McGraw-Hill.

Specht, L., & Sandlin, P. (1991). The differential effects of experiential learning activities and traditional lecture classes in accounting. *Simulations and Gaming, 22*(2), 196–210.

Spencer, L.M., Jr., & Spencer, S.M. (1993). *Competence at work: Models for superior performance.* New York: John Wiley & Sons.

Thornton, G.C., III, & Byham, W.C. (1982). *Assessment centers and managerial performance.* New York: Academic Press.

Wexley, K.N., & Memeroff, W.F. (1975). Effectiveness of positive reinforcement and goal setting as methods of management development. *Journal of Applied Psychology, 60*(4), 446–450.

Wheeler, J.V. (2008). The impact of social environments on emotional, social, and cognitive competency development. *Journal of Management Development, 27*(1), 129–145.

Winter, D.G., McClelland, D.C., & Stewart, A.J. (1981). *A new case for the liberal arts: Assessing institutional goals and student development.* San Francisco, CA: Jossey-Bass.

Wolff, S.B. (2007). *Emotional and Social Competency Inventory: Technical manual up-dated ESCI research titles and abstracts.* Boston, MA: The Hay Group.

Young, D.P., & Dixon, N.M. (1996). *Helping leaders take effective action: A program evaluation.* Greensboro, NC: Center for Creative Leadership.

Author Index

Subject Index